DATABASE SYSTEM CONCEPTS

HENRY F. KORTH
ABRAHAM SILBERSCHATZ
University of Texas at Austin

McGraw-Hill Book Company
New York   St. Louis   San Francisco   Auckland   Bogotá   Hamburg
Johannesburg   London   Madrid   Mexico   Montreal   New Delhi
Paris   Panama   São Paulo   Singapore   Sydney   Tokyo   Toronto

McGraw-Hill Advanced Computer Science Series

Davis and Lenat: Knowledge-Based Systems in Artificial Intelligence
Kogge: The Architecture of Pipelined Computers
Lindsay, Buchanan, Feigenbaum, and Lederberg: Applications of Artificial Intelligence
for Organic Chemistry: The Dendral Project
Nilsson: Problem-Solving Methods in Artificial Intelligence
Wulf, Levin, and Harbison: HYDRA / C.mmp: An Experimental Computer System

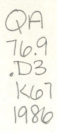

DATABASE SYSTEM CONCEPTS

2 3 4 5 6 7 8 9 0 HALHAL 8 9 8 7 6

ISBN 0-07-044752-7

The editor was Kaye Pace; the production supervisor was Joe Campanella; the
cover was designed by Anne Canevari Green. Project supervision was done by
Caliber Design Planning, Inc. Arcata Graphics/Halliday was printer and binder.

In memory of my father Joseph Silberschatz,
  and my grandparents Stepha and Aaron Rosenblum.

  Avi Silberschatz

To my parents.

  Hank Korth

McGraw-Hill Computer Science Series

Contents

Chapter 3   Relational Model

Chapter 4   Network Data Model

Chapter 5   Hierarchical Data Model

Chapter 6   Relational Database Design

Chapter 7 File and System Structure

Chapter 8 Indexing and Hashing

Chapter 9 Query Processing

Chapter 10 Crash Recovery

Chapter 11 Concurrency Control

Chapter 12 Distributed Databases

Chapter 13 Security and Integrity

Chapter 14 New Database Applications

Chapter 15 Case Studies

Bibliography

Index

Preface

Database systems have become an important part of a computer system, and as such, are an essential part of a computer science education. This book is intended as a text for an introductory course in database systems at the junior, senior, or first-year graduate level. Our purpose in this book is to provide a clear description of the *concepts* underlying database systems. This book is not centered around any particular database system or hardware. Our emphasis is on solving the problems encountered in designing and using a database system, regardless of the underlying hardware and operating system on which the system will run.

Content of this Book

The basic content and structure of the book is as follows:

1 Introduction
2 Entity-Relationship Model
3 Relational Model
4 Network Model
5 Hierarchical Model
6 Relational Database Design
7 File and System Structure
8 Indexing and Hashing
9 Query Processing
10 Crash Recovery
11 Concurrency Control
12 Distributed Databases
13 Security and Integrity
14 New Database Applications
15 Case Studies

As prerequisites, we assume the reader is familiar with general high-level language programming and has an elementary understanding of data structures and computer organization.

Chapter 1 provides a general overview of the nature and purpose of database systems. We explain how the concept of a database system has developed, the common features of database systems, what a database system does for the user, and how a database system interfaces with operating systems. We also introduce an example database application: a banking enterprise consisting of multiple bank branches. This example is used as a running example throughout the book. This chapter is motivational, historical, and explanatory in nature.

Chapters 2 through 5 describe the four major database models: the entity-relationship model, the relational model, the network model and the hierarchical model. We describe these models at a high-level without presenting the details of system-level implementation of these models. Our emphasis is on how these models assist in the design of databases and in the extraction of information from databases. Although all four major models are covered, we emphasize the entity-relationship and relational models due to their increasing importance in both academic database research and practical industrial application. These chapters are suitable for those individuals or lower-level classes who want to learn what a database system is, without getting into the details of the internal algorithms and structure.

Chapter 6 provides an introduction to the theory of relational database design. Such topics as normalization and data dependencies are covered with emphasis on the motivation for each normal form and the intuitive meaning of each type of data dependency.

Chapters 7 through 9 cover the internal structure of database systems. Chapter 7 deals with the mapping of high-level data models to a file system. A variety of data access techniques are presented in Chapter 8, including hashing, balanced-tree indices, and secondary key indices. Chapter 9 addresses optimization, both from the standpoint of physical organization and the standpoint of query modification.

Chapter 10 presents an introduction to recovery from system crashes and failed transactions. The concepts of transactions, logs, and shadow pages are presented. The material on recovery in this chapter motivates the topics in Chapters 11 and 12 (Concurrency Control and Distributed Databases).

Chapters 11 through 14 present advanced topics and current trends. A body of fundamental definitions and results exist for these topics, although research is still ongoing and the ultimate solutions to the problems are still being sought. These chapters cover techniques used by existing systems, and by systems currently in experimental stages. Anyone working with database systems over the next five years will need to be aware of the developments in these areas. Chapter 11 deals with the problems encountered when several users may access the database concurrently. The concept of *serializability* is presented, and several techniques for ensuring serializability are covered including locking, timestamping, and optimistic (validation) techniques. Chapter 12 revisits the issues discussed in the first eleven chapters in order to address the problems encountered if the database is distributed over several computers. In particular, the issues of transaction management, concurrency, and deadlock detection and recovery are addressed. Special techniques for optimizing queries in a distributed system are also presented.

Chapter 13 deals with the protection of the data from accidental and malicious abuse. Chapter 14 gives a brief introduction to new applications of database concepts in the areas of computer-aided design and artificial intelligence.

Chapter 15 concludes with case studies that briefly describe the principal features of some of the most influential database systems.

Organization

Database systems first began to appear in the 1960's, and for twenty years underwent major changes in concepts and technology. As a result, the first-generation database system textbooks that appeared during this period tried to explain a subject that changed even as the text was being written. Now, however, much of database system theory and practice appears to have matured and stabilized. The fundamental database system concepts are now well defined and well understood. While there will undoubtably be new developments, the basic approach to database management is not likely to change. Our primary goal in this book is to present well-understood, agreed-upon, classical database system material.

Concepts are presented using intuitive descriptions, many of which are based on our running example of a bank enterprise. Important theoretical results are covered, but formal proofs are omitted. The bibliographic notes contain pointers to research papers in which results were first presented and proved. In place of proofs, figures and examples are used to suggest why one should expect the result in question to be true.

The fundamental concepts and algorithms covered in the book are often based upon those used in existing commercial or experimental database systems. Our aim is to present these concepts and algorithms in a general setting not tied to one particular database system. The final chapter provides some insight into how various system implementors have incorporated these concepts in real systems.

Acknowledgments

During the time we were writing this book we clarified our organization by teaching several types of database courses including the CS 386 course at the University of Texas at Austin, the database management and file structures course at the Institute for Retraining in Computer Science of Clarkson University, and the database concepts course in the IBM technical education program. The students in these courses were a major help to us in determining the best way in which to teach database concepts.

Several of our friends and colleagues reviewed individual chapters and provided us with insightful comments. We wish especially to thank Don Batory, Haran Boral, Robert Brazile, Won Kim, Anil Nigam, and Bruce Porter. Alberto Mendelzon provided us with a most careful review of an early draft of the manuscript. Henry Korth (father of Henry F.) read the entire manuscript and made numerous suggestions and corrections.

The bugs that remain in the text are, of course, the responsibility of the authors. We would appreciate it if you, the reader, would notify us of any errors, omissions, etc. you may find. We shall be grateful for any suggestions for improvements or contributions of exercises.

The idea of using ships as part of the cover concept was originally suggested to us by Bruce Stephan. The final cover concept was formulated by the authors. Anne Green of McGraw-Hill was the cover artist. Portions of Sections 11.8. 12.8, and 12.9 are based upon *Operating System Concepts*, by Peterson and Silberschatz, 1985. This material is reprinted with permission of Addison-Wesley Publishing Company. Gio Wiederhold's on-line bibliography helped us in locating several of the bibliographic references.

This book would never have appeared without the tireless effort of Sara Strandtman who entered our text into the computer for typesetting. Carol Kroll assisted with some of the text entry and production details. Many of the typesetting tools we used in producing camera-ready copy of this text were written by Jim Peterson. The CS-Unix staff of the Computer Sciences Department of the University of Texas at Austin, especially Ron Hitchens and Fletcher Mattox, helped us with a variety of typesetting problems.

Finally, Avi Silberschatz would like to thank his wife, Haya, and his children, Aaron, Lemor, and Sivan, for their patience and support during the writing of this book.

H. F. K.
A. S.

1

Introduction

A *database management system* (DBMS) consists of a collection of interrelated data and a set of programs to access that data. The collection of data is usually referred to as the *database*. The database contains information about one particular enterprise. The primary goal of a DBMS is to provide an environment that is both *convenient* and *efficient* to use in retrieving information from and storing information into the database.

Database systems are designed to manage large bodies of information. The management of data involves both the definition of structures for the storage of information and the provision of mechanisms for the manipulation of information. In addition, the database system must provide for the safety of information stored in the database, despite system crashes or attempts at unauthorized access. If data is to be shared among several users, the system must avoid possible anomalous results.

Because of the importance of information in most organizations, the database is a valuable resource. This had led to the development of a large body of concepts and techniques for the efficient management of data. In this chapter, we present a brief introduction to the principles of database systems.

1.1 Purpose of Database Systems

Consider part of a savings bank enterprise that keeps information about all customers and savings accounts maintained at the bank. The savings account and customer records are kept in permanent system files. In addition to these files, the system has a number of application programs that allow one to manipulate the files, including:

- A program to debit or credit an account.
- A program to add a new account.
- A program to find the balance of an account.
- A program to generate monthly statements.

These application programs have been written by system programmers in response to the needs of the bank organization.

New application programs are added to the system as the need arises. For example, suppose that new government regulations allow the savings bank to offer checking accounts. As a result, new permanent files are created that contain information about all the checking accounts maintained in the bank, and new application programs may need to be written. Thus, as time goes by, more files and more application programs are added to the system. Since these files and programs have been created over a long period of time, presumably by different programmers, the files are likely to have different formats and the programs may be written in several programming languages.

The environment described above is a typical *file-processing system*, which is supported by a conventional operating system. Permanent records are stored in various files, and a number of different application programs are written to extract records from and add records to the appropriate files. This scheme has a number of major disadvantages:

- **Data redundancy and inconsistency**. Since the files and application programs are created by different programmers over a long period of time, the same piece of information may be duplicated in several places (files). For example, the address and phone number of a particular customer may appear in a file that consists of savings account records, and in a file that consists of checking account records. This redundancy leads to higher storage and access cost as well as potential data inconsistency. By data inconsistency, we mean that the various copies of the same data no longer agree. For example, if the address of a customer changes, and the change has been reflected in only savings account records, then data inconsistency results.

- **Difficulty in accessing data**. Suppose that one of the officers in the bank needs to find out the names of all the customers who live in the area of the city with zip code 78733. The officer calls the data processing department and asks them to generate such a list. As this is an unusual request that was not anticipated when the original system was designed, there is no application program on hand to generate such a list. There is, however, an application program to generate the list of *all* customers. The bank officer has now two choices. Either to get the list of customers and ask one of the secretaries to extract manually the needed information, or to ask the data-processing department to have one of the system programmers write such an application program. Both alternatives are obviously unsatisfactory. Suppose that such a program is actually written, and that several days later, the same officer needs to trim that list to include only those customers that have an account balance of $10,000 or more. As expected, a program to generate such a list does not exist. Again, the officer has the previous two options, neither of which is satisfactory.

What we are pointing out is that this environment does not allow one to retrieve needed data in a convenient and efficient manner. Better data retrieval systems must be developed for general use.

- **Data isolation**. Since data is scattered in various files, and files may be in different formats, it is difficult to write new application programs to retrieve the appropriate data.

- **Multiple users**. In order to improve the overall performance of the system and obtain a faster response time, many systems allow multiple users to update the data simultaneously. In such an environment, interaction of concurrent updates may result in inconsistent data. For example, consider bank account A with $500. If two customers withdraw funds (say $50 and $100 respectively) from account A at about the same time, the result of the concurrent executions may leave the account in an incorrect (or inconsistent) state. In particular, the account may contain either $450, or $400, rather than $350. In order to guard against this possibility, some form of supervision must be maintained in the system. Since data may be accessed by many different application programs which have not been previously coordinated, such a supervisor is very difficult to obtain.

- **Security problems**. Not every user of the database system should be able to access all the data. For example, in a banking system, a person who prepares the payroll checks can only see that part of the database that has information about the various bank employees. He or she cannot access information about customer accounts. Similarly, tellers can access only account information. They cannot access information concerning salaries of employees. Since application programs are added to the system in an ad hoc manner, it is difficult to enforce such security constraints.

- **Integrity problems**. The data values stored in the database must satisfy certain types of *consistency constraints*. For example, the balance of a bank account may never fall below a prespecified amount (for example, $25). These constraints must be enforced in the system. This enforcement can be carried out by adding appropriate code in the various application programs. However, when new constraints are added, it is difficult to change the programs to enforce them. This is compounded in the case where constraints involve several data items from different files.

These difficulties, among others, have prompted the development of database management systems.

1.2 Data Abstraction

A database management system is a collection of interrelated files and a set of programs that allow several users to access and modify these files. A major purpose of a database system is to provide users with an *abstract* view of the data. That is, the system hides certain details of how the data is stored and maintained. However, in order for the system to be usable, data must be retrieved efficiently.

The concern for efficiency leads to the design of complex data structures for the representation of data in the database. However, since database systems are often used by non-computer-trained personnel, this complexity must be hidden from database system users. This is accomplished by defining several levels of abstraction at which the database may be viewed.

- **Physical level**. This is the lowest level of abstraction, at which one describes *how* the data are actually stored. At this level, complex, low-level data structures are described in detail.

- **Conceptual level**. This is the next higher level of abstraction at which one describes *what* data are actually stored in the database, and the relationships that exist among data. This level describes the entire database in terms of a small number of relatively simple structures. Although the implementation of the simple structures of the conceptual level may involve complex physical-level structures, the user of the conceptual level need not be aware of this. The conceptual level of abstraction is used by database administrators, who must decide what information is to be kept in the database.

- **View level**. This is the highest level of abstraction at which one describes only part of the entire database. Despite the use of simpler structures at the conceptual level, there remains a form of complexity resulting from the large size of the database. Many users of the database system will not be concerned with all of this information. Instead, such users need only a part of the database. To simplify the interaction of such users with the system, the view level of abstraction is defined. There may be many views provided by the system for the same database.

The interrelationship among these three levels of abstraction is illustrated in Figure 1.1.

To illustrate the distinction among levels of abstraction, we draw an analogy to the concept of data types in programming languages. Most high-level programming languages support the notion of a record type. For example, in a Pascal-like language we may declare a record as follows:

type *customer* = **record**
>> *name* : string;
>> *street* : string;
>> *city* : string;
> **end**;

This defines a new record called *customer* with three fields. Each field has a name and a type associated with it.

In a banking enterprise, we may have several such record types, including among others:

- *account*, with fields *number* and *balance*.

- *employee*, with fields *name* and *salary*.

At the physical level, a *customer*, *account*, or *employee* record can be described as a block of consecutive storage locations (for example, words or bytes). At the conceptual level, each such record is described by a type definition, illustrated above, and the interrelation among these record types is defined. Finally, at the view level, we define several views of the database. For example, people needing to prepare the payroll checks can only see that part of the database that has information about the employees of the bank. They cannot access information about customer accounts. Similarly, tellers can access only account information. They cannot access information concerning salaries of employees.

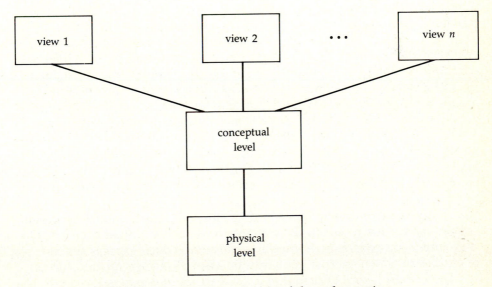

Figure 1.1   The three levels of data abstraction.

1.3 Data Models

In order to describe the structure of a database, we need to define the concept of a *data model*. A data model is a collection of conceptual tools for describing data, data relationships, data semantics, and data constraints. There are a number of different data models that have been proposed. These are partitioned into three different groups: object-based logical models, record-based logical models, and physical data models.

1.3.1 Object-Based Logical Models

Object-based logical models are used in describing data at the conceptual and view levels. They are characterized by the fact that they provide fairly flexible structuring capabilities and allow one to specify data constraints explicitly. At the last count, there are at least thirty such different models, and more are likely to come. Some of the more widely known ones are:

- The entity-relationship model.

- The binary model.

- The semantic data model.

- The infological model.

We do not cover all of these in the book. We have chosen the *entity-relationship model* as a representative of the class of the object-based logical models. This model was chosen since it has gained acceptance as an appropriate data model for database design and it is widely used in practice.

The entity-relationship (E-R) data model is based on a perception of a real world which consists of a collection of basic objects called *entities*, and *relationships* among these objects. An entity is an object that exists and is distinguishable from other objects. The distinction is accomplished by associating with each entity a set of attributes which describes the objects. For example, the attributes *number* and *balance* describe one particular account in a bank. A *relationship* is an association among several entities. For example, a *CustAcct* relationship associates a customer with each account that she or he has. The set of all entities of the same type and relationships of the same type are termed an *entity set* and *relationship set*, respectively.

In addition to entities and relationships, the E-R model represents certain constraints to which the contents of a database must conform. One such important constraint is *mapping cardinalities* which express the number of entities to which another entity can be associated via a relationship set.

The overall logical structure of a database can be expressed graphically by an *E-R diagram* which consists of the following components:

- **Rectangles**, which represent entity sets.
- **Ellipses**, which represent attributes.
- **Diamonds**, which represent relationships among entity sets.
- **Lines**, which link attributes to entity sets and entity sets to relationships.

Each component is labeled with its corresponding name.

To illustrate this, consider part of a database banking system consisting of customers and the accounts that they have. The E-R diagram corresponding to this scheme is shown in Figure 1.2. The E-R model is covered in detail in Chapter 2.

1.3.2 Record-Based Logical Models

Record-based logical models are used in describing data at the conceptual and view levels. In contrast to object-based data models, these models are used to specify both the overall logical structure of the database and a higher-level description of the implementation. They do not, however, provide facilities for specifying data constraints explicitly. In this book, we cover in detail the three most widely accepted data models:

- **Relational model**. The data and the relationships among data are represented by a collection of tables each of which has a number of columns with unique names. To illustrate this, consider a database consisting of customers and the accounts that they have. A sample relational database is shown in Figure 1.3. It shows, for example, that customer Hodges lives on Sidehill in Brooklyn, that he has two accounts, one numbered 647 with a balance of $105,366, and the other 801 with a balance of $10,533. Note that customers Shiver and Hodges share account number 647 (they may share a business venture).

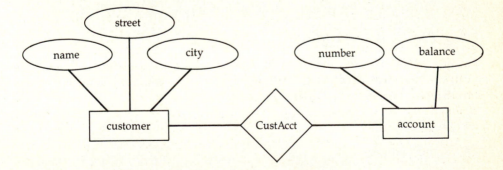

Figure 1.2   A sample E-R diagram.

name	street	city	number
Lowery	Maple	Queens	900
Shiver	North	Bronx	556
Shiver	North	Bronx	647
Hodges	Sidehill	Brooklyn	801
Hodges	Sidehill	Brooklyn	647

number	balance
900	55
556	100000
647	105366
801	10533

Figure 1.3   A sample relational database.

- **Network model**. Data in the network model are represented by collections of *records* (in the Pascal or PL/1 sense) and relationships among data are represented by *links*, which can be viewed as pointers. The records in the database are organized as collections of arbitrary graphs. A sample network database that has the same information as in Figure 1.3 is shown in Figure 1.4.

- **Hierarchical model**. The hierarchical model is similar to the network model in the sense that data and relationships among data are represented by records and links, respectively. The hierarchical model differs from the network model in that the records are organized as collections of trees rather than arbitrary graphs. A sample hierarchical database that has the same information as in Figure 1.4 is shown in Figure 1.5.

These data models are covered in detail in Chapters 3 through 5.

1.3.3 Physical Data Models

Physical data models are used to describe data at the lowest level. In contrast to logical data models, there are very few physical data models in use. Some of the widely known ones are:

- Unifying model.
- Frame memory.

The physical data models capture aspects of database system implementation that are not covered in this book.

1.4 Instances and Schemes

Databases change over time as information is inserted into the database and deleted from it. The collection of information stored in the database at a particular instant of time is called an *instance* of the database. The overall design of the database is called the *database scheme*. Schemes are changed infrequently, if at all.

To illustrate the distinction between schemes and instances, we draw an analogy with the concepts of data types, variables, and values in programming languages. Returning to the *customer* record type definition of Section 1.2, note that in declaring the type *customer*, we have *not* declared any variables. To declare such variables in a Pascal-like language, we write:

var *customer*1 : *customer*;

Variable *customer*1 now corresponds to an area of storage containing a *customer* type record.

The concept of a database *scheme* corresponds to the programming language notion of type definition. A variable of a given type has a particular value at a given instant in time. Thus, the concept of the value of a variable in programming languages corresponds to the concept of an *instance* of a database scheme.

There exist several schemes in the database, and these are partitioned following the levels of abstraction discussed in Section 1.2. At the lowest level we have the *physical scheme*; at the intermediate level we have the *conceptual scheme*; while at the highest level we have a *subscheme*. In general, database systems support one physical scheme, one conceptual scheme, and several subschemes.

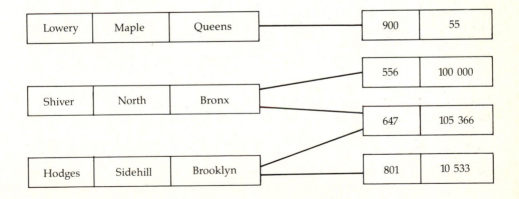

Figure 1.4   A sample network database.

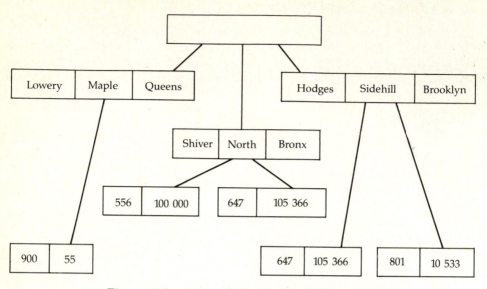

Figure 1.5   A sample hierarchical database.

1.5 Data Independence

In Section 1.2, we defined three levels of abstraction at which the database may be viewed. The ability to modify a scheme definition in óne level without affecting a scheme definition in the next higher level is called *data independence*. There are two levels of data independence:

- **Physical data independence**, the ability to modify the physical scheme without causing application programs to be rewritten. Modifications at the physical level are occasionally necessary in order to improve performance.

- **Logical data independence**, the ability to modify the conceptual scheme without causing application programs to be rewritten. Modifications at the conceptual level are necessary whenever the logical structure of the database is altered (for example, the addition of money market accounts in a banking system).

Logical data independence is more difficult to achieve than physical data independence since application programs are heavily dependent on the logical structure of the data they access.

The concept of data independence is similar in many respects to the concept of *abstract data types* in modern programming languages. Both hide implementation details from the users. This allows users to concentrate on the general structure rather than low-level implementation details.

1.6 Data Definition Language

A database scheme is specified by a set of definitions which are expressed by a special language called a *data definition language* (DDL). The result of compilation of DDL statements is a set of tables which are stored in a special file called *data dictionary* (or *directory*).

A data directory is a file that contains *metadata*; that is, "data about data." This file is consulted before actual data is read or modified in the database system.

The storage structure and access methods used by the database system are specified by a set of definitions in a special type of DDL called a *data storage and definition* language. The result of compilation of these definitions is a set of instructions to specify the implementation details of the database schemes which are usually hidden from the users.

1.7 Data Manipulation Language

The levels of abstraction we discussed in Section 1.2 apply not only to the definition or structuring of data but also to the manipulation of data. By data manipulation we mean:

- The retrieval of information stored in the database.

- The insertion of new information into the database.

- The deletion of information from the database.

At the physical level, we must define algorithms that allow for efficient access to data. At higher levels of abstraction, an emphasis is placed on ease of use. The goal is to provide for efficient human interaction with the system.

A *data manipulation language* (DML) is a language that enables users to access or manipulate data as organized by the appropriate data model. There are basically two types of DML:

- **Procedural**, which requires a user to specify *what* data is needed and *how* to get it.

- **Nonprocedural**, which requires a user to specify *what* data is needed, *without* specifying how to get it.

Nonprocedural DMLs are usually easier to learn and use than procedural DMLs. However, since a user does not have to specify how to get the data, these languages may generate code which is not as efficient as that produced by procedural languages. This difficulty can be remedied through the use of various optimization techniques.

A *query* is a statement requesting the retrieval of information. The portion of a DML that involves information retrieval is called *query language*. Although technically incorrect, it is common practice to use the terms *query language* and *data manipulation language* synonymously.

1.8 Database Manager

Databases typically require a large amount of storage space. Corporate databases are usually measured in terms of *gigabytes* of data. A gigabyte is 1000 megabytes or a billion bytes. Since the main memory of computers cannot store this information, it is stored on disks. Data is moved between disk storage and main memory as needed. Since the movement of data to and from disk is slow relative to the speed of the central processing unit of computers, it is imperative that the database system structure the data so as to minimize the need to move data between disk and main memory.

The goal of a database system is to simplify and facilitate access to data. High-level views help to achieve this. Users of the system should not be burdened unnecessarily with the physical details of the implementation of the system. Nevertheless, a major factor in a user's satisfaction or lack thereof with a database system is its performance. If the response time for a request is too long, the value of the system is diminished. The performance of a system depends on the efficiency of the data structures used to represent the data in the database and on how efficiently the system is able to operate on these data structures. As is the case elsewhere in computer systems, a tradeoff must be made not only between space and time but also between the efficiency of one kind of operation versus that of another.

A database manager is a program module which provides the interface between the low-level data stored in the database and the application programs and queries submitted to the system. The database manager is responsible for the following tasks:

- **Interaction with the file manager**. The raw data is stored on the disk using the file system which is usually provided by a conventional operating system. The database manager translates the various DML statements into low-level file system commands. Thus, the database manager is responsible for the actual storing, retrieving, and updating of data in the database.

- **Integrity enforcement**. The data values stored in the database must satisfy certain types of *consistency constraints*. For example, the balance of a bank account may never fall below a prespecified amount (for example, $25). Similarly, the number of hours an employee may be working in one week may not exceed some specific number (for example, 80 hours). These constraints must be specified explicitly by the database administrator (see Section 1.9). If such constraints are specified, then the database manager can check whether updates to the database result in the violation of any of these constraints, and if so, appropriate action must be taken.

- **Security enforcement**. As discussed above, not every user of the database needs to have access to the entire content of the database. It is the job of the database manager to enforce these security requirements.

- **Backup and recovery**. A computer system, like any other mechanical or electrical device, is subject to failure. There are a variety of causes of such failure, including disk crash, power failure, and software errors. In each of these cases, information concerning the database is lost. It is the responsibility of the database manager to detect such failures and restore the database to a state that existed prior to the occurrence of the failure. This is usually accomplished through the initiation of various backup and recovery procedures.

- **Concurrency control**. When several users update the database concurrently, the consistency of data may no longer be preserved. It is necessary for the system to control the interaction among the concurrent users, and achieving such a control is one of the responsibilities of the database manager.

Some database systems, designed for use on small personal computers, are missing several of the features noted above. This allows for a smaller data manager. A small data manager has less requirement for physical resources, especially main memory, and costs less to implement. For example, many small systems impose the restriction of only one user being allowed to access the database at a time. Others leave the tasks of backup, recovery, and security enforcement to the user. Although this low-cost, low-feature approach is sufficient for small personal databases, it is inadequate to meet the needs of a medium- to large-scale enterprise.

1.9 Database Administrator

One of the main reasons for having database management systems is to have central control of both data and programs accessing that data. The person having such central control over the system is called the *database administrator* (DBA). The functions of the database administrator include:

- **Scheme definition**, the creation of the original database scheme. This is accomplished by writing a set of definitions which are translated by the DDL compiler to a set of tables that are permanently stored in the *data dictionary*.

- **Storage structure and access method definition**, the creation of appropriate storage structures and access methods. This is accomplished by writing a set of definitions which are translated by the data storage and definition language compiler.

- **Scheme and physical organization modification**, either the modification of the database scheme or the description of the physical storage organization. These changes, although relatively rare, are accomplished by writing a set of definitions which are used by either the DDL compiler or the data storage and definition language compiler to generate modifications to the appropriate internal system tables (for example, the data dictionary).

- **Granting of authorization for data access**, the granting of different types of authorization for data access to the various users of the database. This allows the database administrator to regulate which parts of the database various users can access.

- **Integrity constraint specification**, the specification of integrity constraints. These constraints are kept in a special system structure that is consulted by the database manager whenever an update takes place in the system.

1.10 Database Users

A primary goal of a database system is to provide an environment for retrieving information from and storing new information into the database. There are three different types of users of a database system and these are differentiated by the way they expect to interact with the system.

- **Application programmers**. These are computer professionals, who interact with the system through DML calls, which are embedded in a program written in a *host* language (for example, Cobol, PL/1, Pascal, C). These programs are commonly referred to as *application programs*. Examples of application programs in a banking system include a program that generates the payroll checks, that debits an account, that credits an account, that transfers funds between accounts, and so on.
    Since the DML syntax is usually quite different from the host language syntax, DML calls are usually prefaced by a special character so that the appropriate code can be generated by a special preprocessor, called the DML *precompiler*. The DML precompiler converts the DML statements to normal procedure calls in the host language. The resulting program is then run through the host language compiler, which generates appropriate object code.

There are special types of programming languages which combine control structures of Pascal-like languages with control structures for the manipulation of a database object (for example, relations). Examples include Pascal R, Focus, and Nomad.

- **Casual users**. These are sophisticated users who interact with the system without writing programs. Instead, they form their requests by writing their queries in a database query language. Each such query is submitted to a *query processor* whose function is to take a DML statement and break it down into instructions that the database manager understands.

- **Naive users**. These are unsophisticated users who interact with the system by invoking one of the permanent application programs that have been written previously. For example, a bank teller who needs to transfer $50 from account *A* to account *B* would invoke a program called *transfer*. This program would ask the teller for the amount of money to be transferred, the account from which the money is being transferred, and the account to which the money is to be transferred.

- **Specialized users**. These are sophisticated users that write database applications that do not fit into the traditional data-processing framework. Among these applications are computer-aided design systems, knowledge-base and expert systems, systems that store data with complex datatypes (for example, graphics data and audio data), and environment-modeling systems. Some of these will be covered in Chapter 14.

1.11 Overall System Structure

A database system is partitioned into modules that deal with each of the responsibilities of the overall system. Some of the functions of the database system may be provided by the computer's operating system. In most cases, the operating system provides only the most basic services and the database system must build on that base. Thus, the design of a database system must include consideration of the interface between the database system and the operating system.

A database system consists of a number of functional components, including:

- **File manager**, which manages the allocation of space on disk storage and the data structures used to represent information stored on disk.

- **Database manager**, which provides the interface between the low-level data stored in the database and the application programs and queries submitted to the system.

- **Query processor**, which translates statements in a query language into low-level instructions that the database manager understands. In addition, the query processor attempts to transform a user's request into an equivalent but more efficient form, thus finding a good strategy for executing the query.

- **DML precompiler**, which converts DML statements embedded in an application program to normal procedure calls in the host language. The precomplier must interact with the query processor in order to generate the appropriate code.

- **DDL compiler**, which converts DDL statements to a set of tables containing metadata. These tables are then stored in the data dictionary.

In addition, several data structures are required as part of the physical system implementation, including:

- **Data files**, which store the database itself.

- **Data dictionary**, which stores information about the structure of the database. The data dictionary is used heavily. Therefore, great emphasis should be placed on developing a good design and efficient implementation of the dictionary.

- **Indices**, which provide for fast access to data items holding particular values.

Figure 1.6 shows these components and the connections among them.

1.12 Summary

A database management system (DBMS) consists of a collection of interrelated data and a collection of programs to access that data. The data contains information about one particular enterprise. The primary goal of a DBMS is to provide an environment which is both *convenient* and *efficient* to use in retrieving information from and storing information into the database.

Database systems are designed to manage large bodies of information. The management of data involves both the definition of structures for the storage of information and the provision of mechanisms for the manipulation of information. In addition, the database system must provide for the safety of information stored in the database, despite system crashes or attempts at unauthorized access. If data is to be shared among several users, the system must avoid possible anomalous results.

A major purpose of a database system is to provide users with an abstract view of the data. That is, the system hides certain details of how

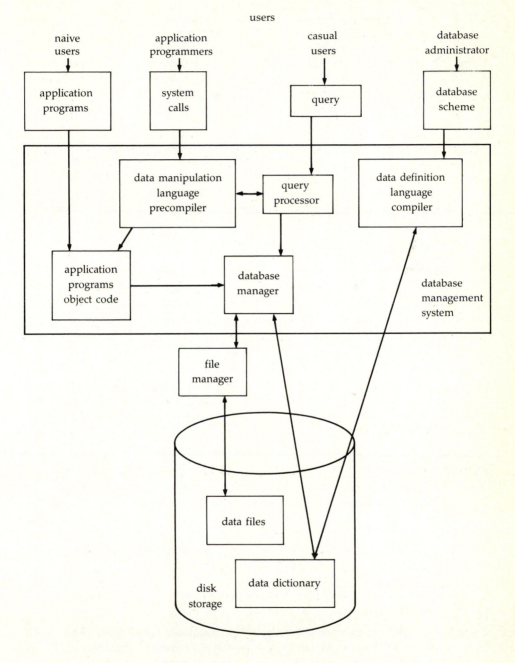

Figure 1.6   System structure.

the data is stored and maintained. This is accomplished by defining three levels of abstraction at which the database may be viewed: the *physical level*, the *conceptual level*, and the *view level*.

In order to describe the structure of a database, the concept of a *data model* is defined. A data model is a collection of conceptual tools for describing data, data relationships, data semantics, and data constraints. There are a number of different data models that have been proposed. These are partitioned into three different groups: *object-based logical* models, *record-based logical* models, and *physical data* models.

Databases change over time as information is inserted into the database and deleted from it. The collection of information stored in the database at a particular instant of time is called an *instance* of the database. The overall design of the database is called the *database scheme*. The ability to modify a scheme definition in one level without affecting a scheme definition in the next higher level is called *data independence*. There are two levels of data independence: physical data independence and logical data independence.

A database scheme is specified by a set of definitions which are expressed by a *data definition language* (DDL). The result of compilation of DDL statements is a set of tables which are stored in a special file called the *data dictionary* which contains *metadata*; that is, "data about data."

A *data manipulation language* (DML) is a language that enables users to access or manipulate data. There are basically two types of DML: procedural, which requires a user to specify what data is needed and how to get it, and nonprocedural, which requires a user to specify what data is needed, without specifying how to get it.

A database manager is a program module which provides the interface between the low-level data stored in the database and the application programs and queries submitted to the system. The database manager is responsible for interaction with the file manager, integrity enforcement, security enforcement, backup and recovery, and concurrency control.

Exercises

1.1 What are the main differences between a file-processing system and a database management system?

1.2 In this chapter we have listed some of the major advantages of a database system. Are there any disadvantages?

1.3 Explain the difference between physical and logical data independence.

1.4 List the responsibilities of the database manager. For each responsibility, explain those problems that would arise if the responsibility were not met.

1.5 What are the main functions of a database administrator?

1.6 List several different programming languages which are

a. Procedural.

b. Nonprocedural.

Which group is easier to learn and use?

1.7 List the major steps that need to be taken in setting up a database for a particular enterprise.

1.8 Consider a two-dimensional integer array of size $n \times m$ which is to be used in your favorite programming language.

a. Illustrate the difference between the three levels of data abstraction.

b. Illustrate the difference between a scheme and instances.

Bibliographic Notes

The three levels of data abstraction were introduced in the CODASYL DBTG report [CODASYL 1971]. A similar proposal was put forward in the ANSI/SPARC report, in which these levels were termed *internal*, *conceptual*, and *external* [ANSI 1975]. Additional discussions concerning the ANSI/SPARC proposal are offered by Tsichritzis and Klug [1978] and Jardine [1977].

The entity-relationship, relational, network, and hierarchical models are covered in great detail in Chapters 2 through 5, respectively. The bibliographic notes for these chapters should provide ample references. Detailed discussions of these data models can be found in Tsichritzis and Lochovsky [1982]. Surveys discussing various types of data models are offered by Kerschberg et al. [1976] and Senko [1977]. Detailed discussions of various object-based logical data models can be found in Tsichritzis and Lochovsky [1982].

The first binary data model was proposed by Abrial [1974]. Other related work is offered by Deheneffe et al. [1974], Hainant and Lecharlier [1974], Senko [1975], and Bracchi et al. [1976].

Semantic network data models were initially developed in connection with artificial intelligence. Discussion concerning the various models can be found in Quillian [1968], Raphael [1968], Roussopoulos and Mylopoulos [1975], Woods [1975], Mylopoulos et al. [1976], Bachman and Daya [1977], Hayes [1977], Hendrix [1977], Wong and Mylopoulos [1977], Brachman [1979], and Levesque and Mylopolous [1979].

The infological data model was first introduced by Langefors [1963, 1977, 1980]. Additional discussions are offered by Bubenko et al. [1971] and Sundgren [1974, 1975].

The unifying model was introduced by Batory and Gotlieb [1982]. The frame memory structure was introduced by March et al. [1981].

Discussions concerning data dictionaries can be found in [Uhrowczik 1973]. Discussions concerning the importance of data independence are offered by Stonebraker [1974], Ullman [1982a], and Date [1986]. Reis [1980] and McCracken [1980] present an overview of Nomad. Pascal/R is discussed in Schmidt et al. [1983].

Entity-Relationship Model

The entity-relationship (E-R) data model is based on a perception of a real world which consists of a set of basic objects called *entities* and *relationships* among these objects. It was developed in order to facilitate database design by allowing the specification of an *enterprise scheme*. Such a scheme represents the overall logical structure of the database.

2.1 Entities and Entity Sets

An *entity* is an object that exists and is distinguishable from other objects. For example, John Harris with social number 890-12-3456 is an entity since it uniquely identifies one particular person in the universe. Similarly, account number 115 at the Downtown branch is an entity since it uniquely identifies one particular account. An entity may be either concrete, such as a person or a book, or it may be abstract, such as a holiday or a concept.

An *entity set* is a set of entities of the same type. The set of all persons having an account at a bank, for example, can be defined as the entity set *customer*. Similarly, the entity set *account* might represent the set of all accounts in a particular bank.

Entity sets need not be disjoint. For example, it is possible to define the entity set of all employees of a bank (*employee*) and the entity set of all customers of the bank (*customer*). A *person* entity may be an *employee* entity, a *customer* entity, both, or neither.

An entity is represented by a set of *attributes*. Possible attributes of the *customer* entity set are *name*, *social-security*, *street*, and *city*. Possible attributes of the *account* entity set are *number* and *balance*. For each attribute there is a set of permitted values, called the *domain* of that attribute. The domain of attribute *name* might be the set of all text strings of a certain length. Similarly, the domain of attribute *number* might be the set of all positive integers.

Formally, an attribute is a function which maps an entity set into a domain. Thus, every entity is described by a set of (attribute, data value) pairs, one pair for each attribute of the entity set. Thus, a particular *customer* entity is described by the set {(*name*, Harris), (*social-security*, 890-12-3456), (*street*, North), (*city*, Georgetown)}, which means the entity describes a person named Harris with social security number 890-12-3456, residing at North Street in Georgetown.

To illustrate the difference between an entity set and a particular entity of the set, we refer to the analogy we drew with programming languages in Chapter 1.

The concept of an entity set corresponds to the programming language notion of type definition. A variable of a given type has a particular value at a given instant in time. Thus, a variable in programming languages corresponds to the concept of an *entity* in the E-R model.

A database thus includes a collection of entity sets each of which contains any number of entities of the same type. Figure 2.1 shows part of a bank database which consists of two entity sets: *customer* and *account*.

In this chapter, we shall be dealing with five entity sets. To avoid confusion unique attribute names are used.

- *branch*, the set of all branches of a particular bank. Each branch is described by the attributes *branch-name*, *branch-city*, and *assets*.

- *customer*, the set of all people who have an account at the bank. Each customer is described by the attributes *customer-name*, *social-security*, *street*, and *customer-city*.

- *employee*, the set of all people who work at the bank. Each employee is described by the attributes *employee-name* and *phone-number*.

- *account*, the set of all accounts maintained in the bank. Each account is described by the attributes *account-number* and *balance*.

- *transaction*, the set of all account transactions executed in the bank. Each transaction is described by the attributes *transaction-number*, *date*, and *amount*.

2.2 Relationships and Relationship Sets

A *relationship* is an association among several entities. For example, we may define a relationship which associates customer "Harris" with account 401. This specifies that Harris is a customer with bank account number 401.

A *relationship set* is a set of relationships of the same type. Formally, it is a mathematical relation on $n \geq 2$ (possibly nondistinct) entity sets. If $E_1, E_2, ..., E_n$ are entity sets, then a relationship set R is a subset of

$$\{(e_1, e_2, ..., e_n) \mid e_1 \in E_1, e_2 \in E_2, ..., e_n \in E_n \}$$

where $(e_1, e_2, ..., e_n)$ is a relationship.

To illustrate this, consider the two entity sets *customer* and *account* of Figure 2.1. We define the relationship set *CustAcct* to denote the association between customers and the bank accounts that they have. This association is depicted in Figure 2.2.

The relationship *CustAcct* is an example of a binary relationship set, that is, one which involves two entity sets. Most of the relationship sets in a database system are binary. Occasionally, however, there are relationship sets which involve more than two entity sets. As an example, consider the ternary relationship (Harris, 401, Redwood) which specifies

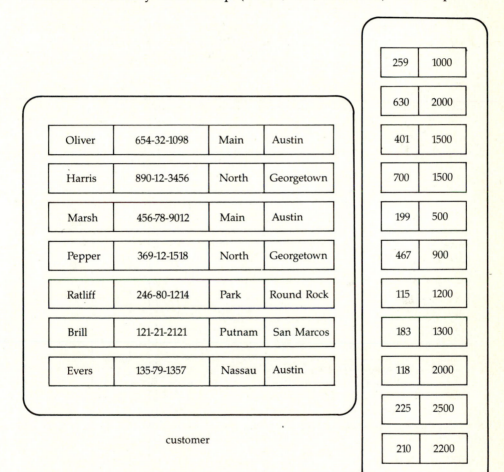

Figure 2.1   Entity sets *customer* and *account*.

that customer Harris has account 401 in the Redwood branch. This relationship is an instance of a relationship *CAB* which involves entity sets *customer*, *account*, and *branch*.

The function that an entity plays in a relationship is called its *role*. Roles are normally implicit and are not usually specified. However, they are useful when the meaning of a relationship needs clarification. Such is the case when the entity sets of a relationship set are not distinct. For instance, the relationship set *works-for* might be modeled by ordered pairs of *employee* entities. The first employee of a pair takes the role of manager,

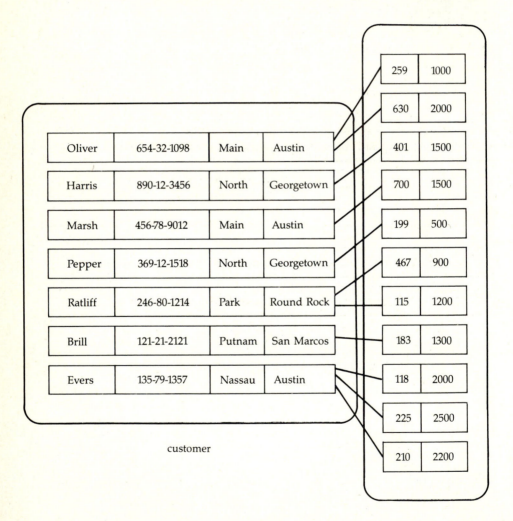

Figure 2.2   Relationship set involving *customer* and *account* entity sets.

while the second takes the role of worker. In this way, all relationships of *works-for* are characterized by (manager, worker) pairs. Thus, (worker, manager) pairs are excluded.

A relationship may also have descriptive attributes. For example, *date* could be an attribute of the *CustAcct* relationship set. This specifies the last date on which a customer has accessed the account. The *CustAcct* relationship of (Harris, 401) is described by {(*date*, 23 May 1985)}, which means that the last time Harris accessed account 401 was on 23 May 1985.

2.3 Mapping Constraints

An E-R enterprise scheme may define certain constraints to which the contents of a database must conform. One important constraint is *mapping cardinalities* which express the number of entities to which another entity can be associated via a relationship.

Mapping cardinalities are most useful in describing binary relationship sets, although occasionally they contribute to the description of relationship sets that involve more than two entity sets. In this section, we shall be concentrating only on binary relationship sets. We shall deal with n-ary ($n > 2$) relationship sets later.

For a binary relationship set R between entity sets A and B, the mapping cardinality must be one of the following:

- **One-to-one**. An entity in A is associated with at most one entity in B, and an entity in B is associated with at most one entity in A. (See Figure 2.3.)

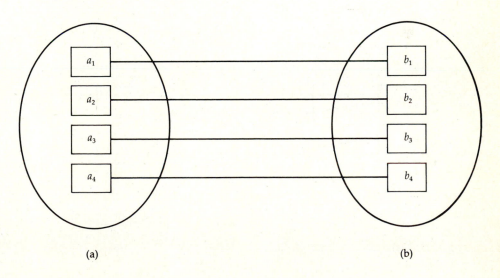

(a)   (b)

Figure 2.3   One-to-one relationship.

- **One-to-many**. An entity in *A* is associated with any number of entities in *B*. An entity in *B*, however, can be associated with at most one entity in *A*. (See Figure 2.4.)

- **Many-to-one**. An entity in *A* is associated with at most one entity in *B*. An entity in *B*, however, can be associated with any number of entities in *A*. (See Figure 2.5.)

- **Many-to-many**. An entity in *A* is associated with any number of entities in *B* and an entity in *B* is associated with any number of entities in *A*. (See Figure 2.6.)

The appropriate mapping cardinality for a particular relationship set is obviously dependent on the real world that is being modeled by the relationship set.

To illustrate this, consider the *CustAcct* relationship set. If in a particular bank an account can belong to only one customer, and a customer can have several accounts, then the relationship set is one-to-many from *customer* to *account*. If an account can belong to several customers (as in joint accounts held by several family members), the relationship set is many-to-many.

Existence dependencies form another important class of constraints. Specifically, if the existence of entity *x* depends on the existence of entity *y*, then *x* is said to be *existence dependent* on *y*. Operationally, this means

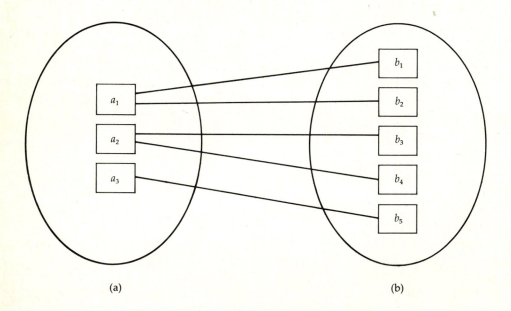

(a)   (b)

Figure 2.4   One-to-many relationship.

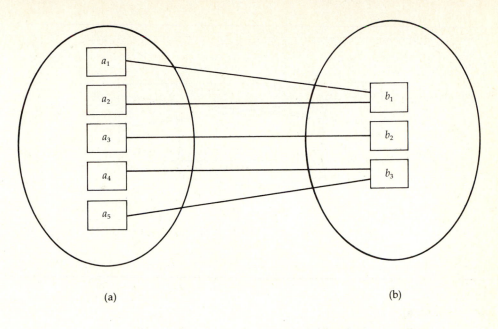

Figure 2.5   Many-to-one relationship.

that if y is deleted, so is x. Entity y is said to be a *dominant entity* and x is said to be a *subordinate entity*.

To illustrate this, consider the entity sets *account* and *transaction*. We form a relationship *log* between these two sets which specifies that for a particular account there may be several transactions. This relationship is one-to-many from *account* to *transaction*. Every *transaction* entity must be associated with an *account* entity. If an *account* entity is deleted, then all of its associated *transaction* entities must be deleted also. In contrast, *transaction* entities can be deleted from the database without affecting any *account*. The entity set *account*, therefore, is dominant and *transaction* is subordinate in the *log* relationship.

2.4 Primary Keys

An important task in database modeling is to specify how entities and relationships are distinguished. Conceptually, individual entities and relationships are distinct, but from a database perspective the difference among them must be expressed in terms of their attributes. To make such distinctions, a *superkey* is assigned to each entity set. The superkey is a set of one or more attributes, which, taken collectively, allow us to identify uniquely an entity in the entity set. For example, the *social-security* attribute of the entity set *customer* is sufficient to distinguish one *customer* entity from another. Thus, *social-security* is a superkey. Similarly, the combination

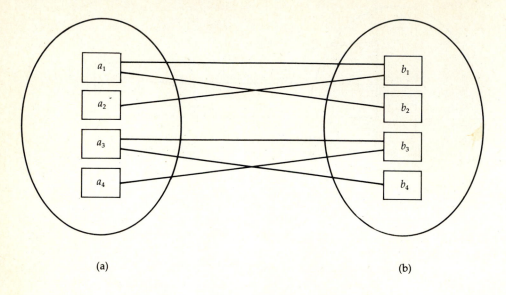

(a)   (b)

Figure 2.6   Many-to-many relationship.

of *customer-name* and *social-security* is a superkey for the entity set *customer*. The *customer-name* attribute of *customer* is not a superkey, as several people might have the same name.

The concept of a superkey is not sufficient for our purposes, since, as we saw above, a superkey may contain extraneous attributes. If K is a superkey, then so is any superset of K. We are often interested in the *smallest* possible superkeys. That is, we are interested in superkeys for which no proper subset is a superkey. Such minimal superkeys are called *candidate keys*.

It is possible that there are several distinct sets of attributes which could serve as a candidate key. A combination of *customer-name* and *street*, for example, might be sufficient to distinguish among members of the *customer* entity set. Thus both {*social-security*} and {*customer-name, street*} are candidate keys. Although the attributes *social-security* and *customer-name* together can distinguish *customer* entities, their combination does not form a candidate key, since the attribute *social-security* alone is a candidate key.

We shall use the term *primary key* to denote a candidate key that is chosen by the database designer as the principal means of identifying entities within an entity set.

It is possible that an entity set does not have sufficient attributes to form a primary key. For example, consider the entity set *transaction* which has the three attributes: *transaction-number*, *date*, and *amount*. Although each *transaction* entity is distinct, transactions on different accounts may share the same transaction number. Thus, this entity set does not have a primary key. Such an entity set is termed a *weak entity*. An entity which has a primary key is termed a *strong entity*.

The concept of strong and weak entities is related to the "existence dependency" concept introduced in Section 2.3. A strong entity is by definition a dominant entity, while a weak entity is a subordinate entity.

A weak entity set does not have a primary key. However, we need a means of distinguishing among all those entities in the entity set that depend on one particular strong entity. The *discriminator* of a weak entity set is a set of attributes that allows this distinction to be made. For example, the discriminator of the weak entity set *transaction* is the attribute *transaction-number*, since for each account these transaction numbers uniquely identify one single transaction.

The primary key of a weak entity set is formed by the primary key of the strong entity on which it is existence dependent, plus its discriminator. In the case of the entity set *transaction*, its primary key is (*account-number*, *transaction-number*), where *account-number* identifies the dominant entity of a *transaction*, and *transaction-number* distinguishes *transaction* entities within the same account.

Relationship sets also have primary keys. Their primary keys are formed by taking all the attributes that comprise the primary keys of the entity sets that define the relationship set. For example, *social-security* is the primary key of *customer* and *account-number* is the primary key of *account*. Thus, the primary key of the relationship set *CustAcct* is (*social-security*, *account-number*). Similarly, the primary key of the *log* relationship set is (*account-number*, *transaction-number*).

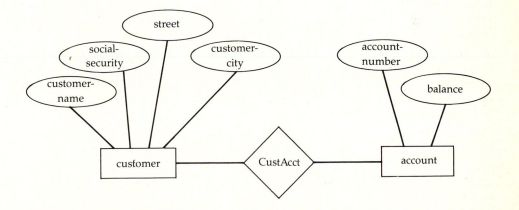

Figure 2.7   E-R diagram.

2.5 Entity-Relationship Diagram

The overall logical structure of a database can be expressed graphically by an *E-R diagram* which consists of the following components:

- **Rectangles**, which represent entity sets.
- **Ellipses**, which represent attributes.
- **Diamonds**, which represent relationship sets.
- **Lines**, which link attributes to entity sets and entity sets to relationship sets.

Each component is labeled with its corresponding name.

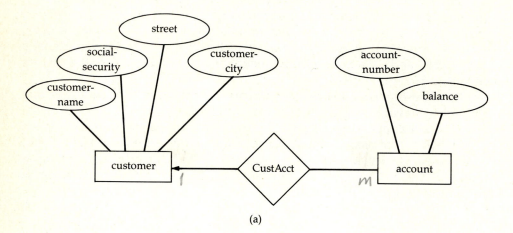

(a)

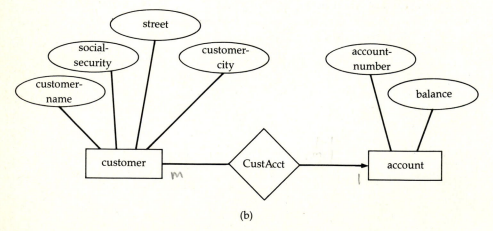

(b)

Figure 2.8   One-to-many and many-to-one relationships.

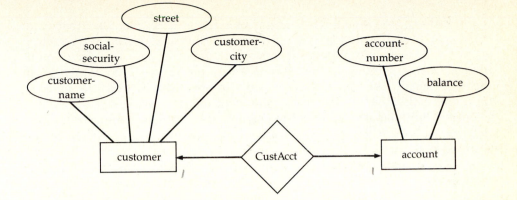

Figure 2.9   One-to-one relationship.

To illustrate this, consider the entity-relationship diagram of Figure 2.7, which consists of two entity sets, *customer* and *account*, related through a binary relationship set *CustAcct*. The attributes associated with *customer* are *customer-name*, *social-security*, *street*, and *customer-city*. The attributes associated with *account* are *account-number* and *balance*.

The relationship set *CustAcct* may be many-to-many, one-to-many, many-to-one, or one-to-one. To distinguish among these, we shall draw either a directed line or an undirected line between the relationship set and the entity set in question. A directed line from the relationship set *CustAcct* to the entity set *account* specifies that the *account* entity set participates in either a one-to-one or a many-to-one relationship with the *customer* entity set. It cannot participate in either a many-to-many or a one-to-many relationship with the *customer* entity set. An undirected line from the relationship set *CustAcct* to the entity set *account* specifies that the *account* entity set participates in either a many-to-many or many-to-one relationship with the *customer* entity set.

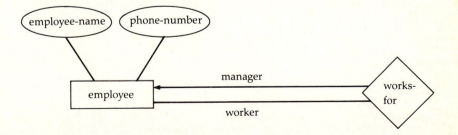

Figure 2.10   E-R diagram with role indicators.

Returning to the E-R diagram of Figure 2.7, we see that the relationship set *CustAcct* is many-to-many. If the relationship set *CustAcct* were one-to-many, from *customer* to *account*, then the link *CustAcct* would have an arrow pointing to the *customer* entity set (Figure 2.8a). Similarly, if the relationship set *CustAcct* were many-to-one from *customer* to *account*, then the link *CustAcct* has an arrow pointing to the *account* entity set (Figure 2.8b). Finally, if the relationship set *CustAcct* were one-to-one, then the link *CustAcct* has two arrows, one pointing to *account* entity set and one pointing to *customer* entity set (Figure 2.9).

Roles are indicated in E-R diagrams by labeling the lines that connect rectangles to diamonds. Figure 2.10 shows the *employee* entity set and the *works-for* relationship set.

A weak entity set is indicated in E-R diagrams by a doubly outlined box. The relationship which connects it to the strong entity set on which its primary key is formed is indicated by darkened lines. Figure 2.11 shows an example where a weak entity set *transaction* is dependent on a strong entity set *account* via the relationship set *log*.

Nonbinary relationship sets can be specified easily in an E-R diagram. Figure 2.12 consists of three entity sets *customer*, *account*, and *branch*, related through the relationship set *CAB*. This diagram specifies that a customer may have several accounts each located in a specific bank branch, and that an account may belong to several different customers.

2.6 Reducing E-R Diagrams to Tables

A database which conforms to an E-R diagram can be represented by a collection of tables. For each entity set and for each relationship set in the database, there is a unique table which is assigned the name of the

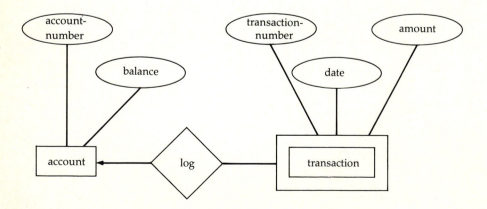

Figure 2.11   E-R diagram with a weak entity set.

corresponding entity set, or relationship set. Each table has a number of columns which, again, have unique names. We shall present our concepts by considering a tabular representation of the E-R diagram of Figure 2.13.

2.6.1 Representation of Strong Entity Sets

Let E be a strong entity set with descriptive attributes $a_1, a_2, ..., a_n$. We represent this entity by a table called E with n distinct columns each of which corresponds to one of the attributes of E. Each row in this table corresponds to one entity of the entity set E.

To illustrate this, consider the entity set *account* of the E-R diagram of Figure 2.13. This entity set has two attributes: *account-number* and *balance*. We represent this entity set by a table called *account*, with two columns as shown in Figure 2.14. The row

$$(259, 1000)$$

in the *account* table means that account number 259 has a balance of $1000. We may add a new entity to the database by inserting a row into a table. We may also delete or modify rows.

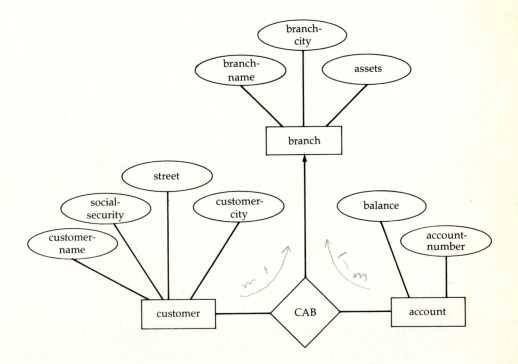

Figure 2.12   E-R diagram with a ternary relationship.

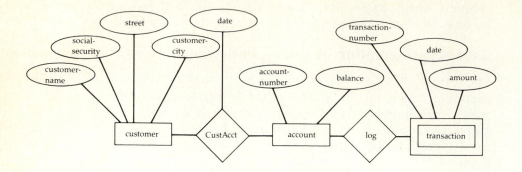

Figure 2.13   E-R diagram.

Let D_1 denote the set of all account numbers and let D_2 denote the set of all balances. Any row of the *account* table must consist of a 2-tuple (v_1, v_2) where v_1 is an account number (that is, v_1 is in set D_1) and v_2 is a balance (that is, v_2 is in set D_2). In general, the *account* table will contain only a subset of the set of all possible rows. We refer to the set of all possible rows of *account* as the *cartesian product* of D_1 and D_2, which we denote by

$$D_1 \times D_2$$

or, alternatively, as

$$\overset{2}{\underset{i = 1}{\times}} D_i$$

In general, if we have a table of n columns, we denote the cartesian product of $D_1, D_2, ..., D_n$ by

$$\overset{n}{\underset{i = 1}{\times}} D_i$$

As another example, consider the entity set *customer* with the four descriptive attributes *customer-name*, *social-security*, *street*, and *customer-city*. The table corresponding to *customer* has four columns as shown in Figure 2.15.

2.6.2 Representation of Weak Entity Sets

Let A be a weak entity set with descriptive attributes $a_1, a_2, ..., a_r$. Let B be the strong entity set on which A is dependent. Let the primary key of B

account-number	balance
259	1000
630	2000
401	1500
700	1500
199	500
467	900
115	1200
183	1300
118	2000
225	2500
210	2200

Figure 2.14   The *account* table.

consist of attributes $b_1, b_2, ..., b_s$. We represent the entity set A by a table called A with one column for each attribute of the set

$$\{a_1, a_2, ..., a_r\} \cup \{b_1, b_2, ..., b_s\}$$

To illustrate this, consider the entity set *transaction* of the E-R diagram of Figure 2.13. This entity set has three attributes: *transaction-number*, *date*, and *amount*. The primary key of the *account* entity set, on which *transaction* is dependent, is *account-number*. Thus, *transaction* is represented by a table with four columns labeled *account-number*, *transaction-number*, *date*, and *amount* as depicted in Figure 2.16.

customer-name	social-security	street	customer-city
Oliver	654-32-1098	Main	Austin
Harris	890-12-3456	North	Georgetown
Marsh	456-78-9012	Main	Austin
Pepper	369-12-1518	North	Georgetown
Ratliff	246-80-1214	Park	Round Rock
Brill	121-21-2121	Putnam	San Marcos
Evers	135-79-1357	Nassau	Austin

Figure 2.15   The *customer* table.

account-number	transaction-number	date	amount
259	5	11 May 1985	+50
630	11	17 May 1985	+70
401	22	23 May 1985	−300
700	69	28 May 1985	−500
199	103	3 June 1985	+900
259	6	7 June 1985	−44
115	53	7 June 1985	+120
199	104	13 June 1985	−200
259	7	17 June 1985	−79

Figure 2.16   The *transaction* table.

2.6.3 Representation of Relationship Sets

Let R be a relationship set involving entity sets $E_1, E_2, ..., E_n$. Let primary-key(E_i) denote the set of attributes which form the primary key for entity set E_i. Suppose that R has no descriptive attributes. Then the table corresponding to relationship set R has the following set of attributes

$$\bigcup_{i=1}^{n} \text{primary-key}(E_i)$$

In the case that R has descriptive attributes, say $\{a_1, a_2, ..., a_m\}$, then the table corresponding to it has the following set of attributes

$$\bigcup_{i=1}^{n} \text{primary-key}(E_i) \cup \{a_1, a_2, ..., a_m\}$$

To illustrate this, consider the relationship set *CustAcct* in the E-R diagram of Figure 2.13. This relationship set involves the following two entity sets:

- *customer*, with the primary key being *social-security*.
- *account*, with the primary key being *account-number*.

Since the relationship set has a descriptive attribute *date*, the table *CustAcct* has three columns labeled *social-security*, *account-number*, and *date*, as shown in Figure 2.17.

As a final example, consider the ternary relationship set *CAB* of Figure 2.12. This relationship involves the following three entity sets:

social-security	account-number	date
654-32-1098	259	17 June 1985
654-32-1098	630	17 May 1985
890-12-3456	401	23 May 1985
456-78-9012	700	28 May 1985
369-12-1518	199	13 June 1985
246-80-1214	467	7 June 1985
246-80-1214	115	7 June 1985
121-21-2121	183	13 June 1985
135-79-1357	118	17 June 1985
135-79-1357	225	19 June 1985
135-79-1357	210	27 June 1985

Figure 2.17   The *CustAcct* table.

- *customer*, with the primary key being *social-security*.

- *account*, with the primary key being *account-number*.

- *branch*, with the primary key being *branch-name*.

Thus, the table *CAB* has three columns as shown in Figure 2.18.

2.7 Generalization and Specialization

Consider the entity set *account* with attributes *account-number* and *balance*. We extend our previous example by classifying each account as being one of the following:

- *savings-account*.

- *checking-account*.

Each of these is described by a set of attributes which include all the attributes of entity set *account* plus additional attributes. For example, *savings-account* entities are described further by the attribute *interest-rate* while *checking-accounts* are described further by the attribute *overdraft-amount*. There are similarities between the *checking-account* entity set and the *savings-account* entity set in the sense that they have several attributes in common. This commonality can be expressed by *generalization* and *specialization* which are containment relationships that exist between a *higher-level* entity set and one or more *lower-level* entity sets.

- **Generalization** is the result of taking the union of two or more (lower level) entity sets to produce a higher-level entity set.

- **Specialization** is the result of taking a subset of a higher-level entity set to form a lower-level entity set.

In the above example, *account* is the higher-level entity set and *savings-account* and *checking-account* are lower-level entity sets.

There are only slight differences between generalization and specialization. In generalization, every higher-level entity must also be a lower-level entity. Specialization does not have this constraint. For example, generalization would require that every *account* entity be either a *savings-account* entity or a *checking-account* entity. Specialization allows for the possibility of an *account* entity being neither a *savings-account* entity nor a *checking-account* entity (for example, it might be a money market account).

In terms of an E-R diagram, both generalization and specialization are depicted through a *triangle* component labeled "ISA," as shown in Figure 2.19. The label "ISA" stands for "is a" and represents, for example, that a savings account "is a" account. Generalization is distinguished from specialization in an E-R diagram by the user of thick lines between the ISA triangle and each entity. Generalization is shown in Figure 2.19a, while specialization is shown in Figure 2.19b.

It is possible for both generalization and specialization to be used together. Suppose that each *employee* is either a *secretary* or a *loan-officer*. Furthermore, each *secretary* and *loan-officer* has a *manager*, who is an *employee*. Figure 2.20 shows how these relationships can be expressed.

Generalization is used to emphasize the similarities among lower-level entity types and to hide their differences. Specialization is the inverse. It emphasizes the distinction between higher-level and lower-level entity sets. Attributes are used as the means for distinction. This is accomplished through attribute inheritance. The attributes of the higher-level entity sets

social-security	account-number	branch-name
654-32-1098	259	Downtown
654-32-1098	630	Redwood
890-12-3456	401	Perryridge
456-78-9012	700	Downtown
369-12-1518	199	Mianus
246-80-1214	467	Round Hill
246-80-1214	115	Pownal
121-21-2121	183	North Town
135-79-1357	118	Downtown
135-79-1357	225	Perryridge
135-79-1357	210	Brighton

Figure 2.18   The *CAB* table.

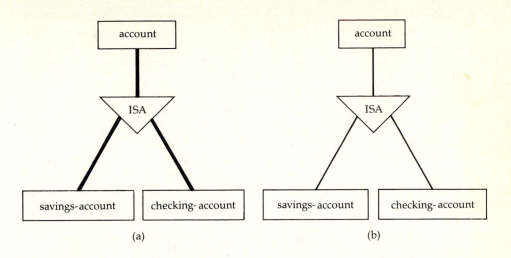

Figure 2.19   (a) Generalization and (b) specialization relationships.

are said to be *inherited* by lower-level entity sets. For example, *savings-account* and *checking-account* inherit the attributes of *account*. Thus, *savings-account* is described by its *account-number*, *balance*, and *interest-rate* attributes, while *checking-account* is described by its *account-number*, *balance*, and *overdraft-amount* attributes.

There are two different methods for transforming an E-R diagram which includes generalization and specialization to a tabular form.

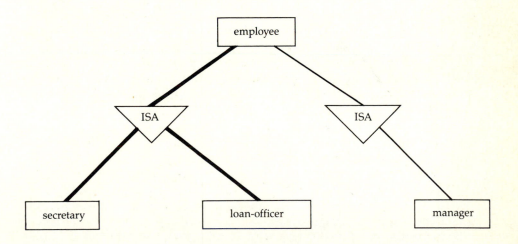

Figure 2.20   Generalization and specialization combined.

- Create a table for the higher-level entity as described in Section 2.6. For each lower-level entity, create a table which includes a column for each of the descriptive attributes of that entity plus a column for each attribute of the primary key of the high-level entity. Thus, for the E-R diagram of Figure 2.19a, we have three tables:

  account, with attributes *account-number* and *balance*.

  savings-account, with attributes *account-number* and *interest-rate*.

  checking-account, with attributes *account-number* and *overdraft-amount*.

- Do not create a table for the higher-level entity. Instead, for each lower-level entity, create a table which includes a column for each of the descriptive attributes of that entity plus a column for *each* attribute of the higher-level entity. Then for the E-R diagram of Figure 2.19a, we have two tables.

  savings-account, with attributes *account-number*, *balance*, and *interest-rate*.

  checking-account, with attributes *account-number*, *balance*, and *overdraft-amount*.

2.8 Aggregation

One limitation of the E-R model is that it is not possible to express relationships among relationships. To illustrate the need for such a construct, consider a database describing information about employees who work on a particular project and use a number of different machines doing that work. Using our basic E-R modeling constructs, we obtain the E-R diagram of Figure 2.21. The relationship sets *work* and *uses* can be combined into one single relationship set. Nevertheless, they should not be combined since otherwise the logical structure of this scheme is obscured.

The solution is to use *aggregation*. Aggregation is an abstraction through which relationships are treated as higher-level entities. Thus, for our example, we treat the relationship set *work* and the entity sets *employee* and *project* as a higher-level entity set called *work*. Such an entity set is treated in the same manner as any other entity set. A common notation for aggregation is shown in Figure 2.22.

Transforming an E-R diagram which includes aggregation to a tabular form is straightforward. For our diagram of Figure 2.22, we create the following tables:

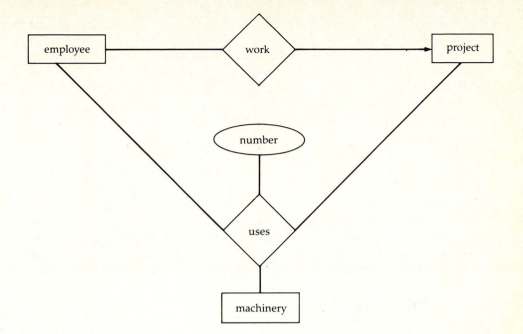

Figure 2.21   E-R diagram with redundant relationships.

- *employee.*
- *department.*
- *work.*
- *machinery.*
- *uses.*

in the same manner as we have done before. The table for the relationship set *uses* includes a column for each attribute in the primary key of the entity set *machinery* and the relationship *work*. It also includes a column for the descriptive attribute of the relationship *uses*.

2.9 Summary

The entity-relationship (E-R) data model is based on a perception of a real world which consists of a set of basic objects called *entities* and *relationships* among these objects. The model is intended primarily for the database design process. It was developed in order to facilitate database design by allowing the specification of an *enterprise scheme*. Such a scheme represents the overall logical structure of the database.

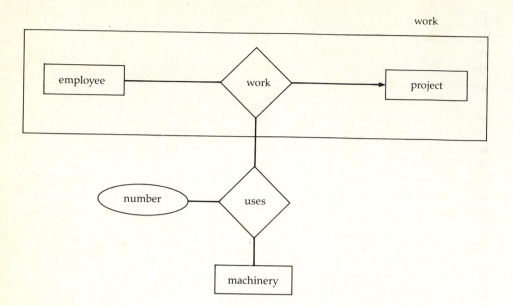

Figure 2.22   E-R diagram with aggregation.

An *entity* is an object that exists and is distinguishable from other objects. The distinction is accomplished by a associating with each entity a set of attributes which describe the object. A *relationship* is an association among several entities. The collection of all entities of the same type and all relationships of the same type are termed an *entity set* and a *relationship set*, respectively.

Mapping cardinalities express the number of entities to which another entity can be associated via a relationship set. Another form of constraint is the *existence dependency*, which specifies that the existence of entity x depends on the existence of entity y.

An important task in database modeling is to specify how entities and relationships are distinguished. Conceptually, individual entities and relationships are distinct, but from a database perspective, their difference must be expressed in terms of their attributes. To make such distinctions, a *primary key* is assigned to each entity set. The primary key is a set of one or more attributes, which, taken collectively, allows us to identify uniquely an entity in the entity set and a relationship in a relationship set. It is possible that an entity set does not have sufficient attributes to form a primary key. Such an entity set is termed a *weak entity*. An entity which has a primary key is termed a *strong entity*.

The overall logical structure of a database can be expressed graphically by an *E-R diagram*. A database which conforms to an E-R diagram can be represented by a collection of tables. For each entity set and for each relationship set in the database, there is a unique table which is assigned the name of the corresponding entity set or relationship set. Each table has a number of columns which, again, have unique names.

Relationship sets among closely related entity sets can be expressed by *generalization* and *specialization* which are containment relationships that exist between a higher-level entity set and one or more lower-level entity sets. Generalization is the result of taking the union of two or more disjoint (lower-level) entity sets to produce a higher-level entity set, while specialization is the result of taking a subset of a higher-level entity set to form a lower-level entity set. There are only slight differences between generalization and specialization. In generalization, every higher-level entity must also be a lower-level entity, while specialization does not have this constraint.

One limitation of the E-R model is that one cannot express relationships among relationships. The solution is to use *aggregation* which is an abstraction where relationship sets are treated as higher-level entity sets. Thus one can view a relationship set and its associated entity sets as a higher-level entity which is treated in the same manner as any other entity.

Exercises

2.1 Construct an E-R diagram for a university registrar's office. The office maintains data about each class, including the instructor, the enrollment, and the time and place of the class meetings. For each student-class pair, a grade is recorded.

2.2 Construct an E-R diagram for a car insurance company with a set of customers each of which owns a number of cars. Each car has a number of recorded accidents associated with it.

2.3 Construct an E-R diagram for a hospital with a set of patients and a set of medical doctors. With each patient a log of the various conducted tests is also associated.

2.4 Construct the appropriate tables for each of the E-R diagrams of problems 2.1 to 2.3.

2.5 Define the concept of aggregation. Show several examples where this concept is useful.

2.6 Explain the difference between a weak and a strong entity set.

2.7 Every weak entity set can be converted to a strong entity set by simply adding appropriate attributes. Why, then, do we have weak entities?

2.8 Suppose that you design an E-R diagram in which the same entity set appears several times. Why is this a bad practice that should be avoided whenever possible?

2.9 When designing an E-R diagram for a particular enterprise, there exists several alternative designs.

   a. What criteria should you consider in deciding on the appropriate choice?

   b. Come up with several alternative E-R diagrams to represent an enterprise. List the merits of each alternative and argue in favor of one of the alternatives.

2.10 Explain the difference between generalization and specialization.

Bibliographic Notes

The entity relationship data model was introduced by Chen [1976]. Discussions concerning the applicability of the E-R approach to database design are offered by Chen [1977], Sakai [1980], and Ng [1981]. Modeling techniques based on the E-R approach are covered by Schiffner and Scheuermann [1979], Lusk et al. [1980], Casanova [1984], and Wang [1984].

Various data manipulation languages for the E-R model have been proposed. These include CABLE [Shoshani 1978], GERM [Benneworth 1981], and GORDAS [ElMasri and Wiederhold 1983]. A graphical query language for the E-R database was proposed by Zhang and Mendelzon [1983].

The concepts of generalization, specialization, and aggregation were introduced by Smith and Smith [1977]. Lenzerini and Santucci [1983] have used these concepts in defining cardinality constraints in the E-R model.

Basic textbook discussions are offered by Tsichritzis and Lochovsky [1982] and by Chen [1983].

Relational Model

From a historical perspective, the relational data model is relatively new. The first database systems were based on either the hierarchical model (see Chapter 5) or the network model (see Chapter 4). Those two older models are tied more closely to the underlying implementation of the database than is the relational model.

The relational data model represents the database as a collection of tables. Although tables are a simple, intuitive notion, there is a direct correspondence between the concept of a table and the mathematical concept of a relation.

In the years following the introduction of the relational model, a substantial theory has developed for relational databases. This theory assists in the design of relational databases and in the efficient processing of user requests for information from the database. We shall study this theory in Chapter 6, after we have introduced all the major data models.

3.1 Structure of Relational Databases

A relational database consists of a collection of *tables*, each of which is assigned a unique name. Each table has a structure similar to that presented in Chapter 2, where we represented E-R databases by tables. A row in a table represents a *relationship* among a set of values. Since a table is a collection of such relationships, there is a close correspondence between the concept of *table* and the mathematical concept of *relation*, from which the relational data model takes its name. In what follows, we introduce the concept of relation.

In this chapter, we shall be using a number of different relations to illustrate the various concepts underlying the relational data model. These relations represent part of a banking enterprise. They differ slightly from the tables that were used in Chapter 2 in order to simplify our presentation. We shall discuss appropriate relational structures in great detail in Chapter 6.

Consider the *deposit* table of Figure 3.1. It has four attributes: *branch-name, account-number, customer-name, balance*. For each attribute, there is a set of permitted values, called the *domain* of that attribute. For the

branch-name	account-number	customer-name	balance
Downtown	101	Johnson	500
Mianus	215	Smith	700
Perryridge	102	Hayes	400
Round Hill	305	Turner	350
Perryridge	201	Williams	900
Redwood	222	Lindsay	700
Brighton	217	Green	750

Figure 3.1   The *deposit* relation.

attribute *branch-name*, for example, the domain would be the set of all branch names. Let D_1 denote this set and let D_2 denote the set of all account-numbers, D_3 the set of all customer names, and D_4 the set of all balances. As we saw in Chapter 2, any row of *deposit* must consist of a 4-tuple (v_1, v_2, v_3, v_4) where v_1 is a branch name (that is, v_1 is in domain D_1), v_2 is an account number (that is, v_2 is in domain D_2), v_3 is a customer name (that is, v_3 is in domain D_3), and v_4 is a balance (that is, v_4 is in domain D_4). In general, *deposit* will contain only a subset of the set of all possible rows. Therefore *deposit* is a subset of:

$$\underset{i=1}{\overset{4}{\times}} D_i$$

In general, a table of n columns must be a subset of

$$\underset{i=1}{\overset{n}{\times}} D_i$$

Mathematicians define a *relation* to be a subset of a cartesian product of a list of domains. This corresponds almost exactly with our definition of table. The only difference is that we have assigned names to attributes, while mathematicians rely on numeric "names," using the integer 1 to denote the attribute whose domain appears first in the list of domains, 2 for the attribute whose domain appears second, etc. Because tables are essentially relations, we shall use the mathematical terms *relation* and *tuple* in place of the terms *table* and *row*.

In the *deposit* relation of Figure 3.1, there are seven tuples. Let the *tuple variable* t refer to the first tuple of the relation. We use the notation $t[branch\text{-}name]$ to denote the value of t on the *branch-name* attribute. Thus, $t[branch\text{-}name]$ = "Downtown". Similarly, $t[account\text{-}number]$ denotes the value of t on the *account-number* attribute, etc. Alternatively, we may write *t*[1] to denote the value of tuple *t* on the first attribute (*branch-name*), *t*[2] for *account-number*, etc. Since a relation is a set of tuples, we use the mathematical notation of *t* ε *r* to denote that tuple *t* is in relation *r*.

When we talk about a database, we must differentiate between the *database schema*, that is, the logical design of the database, and a *database instance*, which is the data in the database at a given instant in time.

The concept of a relation *scheme* corresponds to the programming language notion of type definition. A variable of a given type has a particular value at a given instant in time. Thus, a variable in programming languages corresponds to the concept of an *instance* of a relation.

It is convenient to give a name to a relation scheme, just as we give names to type definitions in programming languages. We adopt the convention of using lowercase names for relations and names beginning with an uppercase letter for relation schemes. Following this notation, we use *Deposit-scheme* to denote the relation scheme for relation *deposit*. Thus,

Deposit-scheme = (*branch-name*, *account-number*, *customer-name*, *balance*)

In general, a relation scheme is a list of attributes and their corresponding domains. We denote the fact that *deposit* is a relation on scheme *Deposit* by

deposit (*Deposit-scheme*)

We shall not, in general, be concerned about the precise definition of the domain of each attribute until we discuss file systems in Chapter 7. However, when we do wish to define our domains, we use the notation

(*branch-name* : string, *account-number* : integer,
customer-name : string, *balance* : integer)

to define the relation scheme for the relation *deposit*.

As another example, consider the *customer* relation of Figure 3.2. The scheme for that relation is

Customer-scheme = (*customer-name*, *street*, *customer-city*)

Note that the attribute *customer-name* appears in both relation schemes. This is not a coincidence. Rather, the use of common attributes in relation schemes is one way of relating tuples of distinct relations. For example, suppose we wish to find the cities where depositors of the Perryridge branch live. We would look first at the *deposit* relation to find all depositors of the Perryridge branch. Then, for each such customer, we look in the *customer* relation to find the city he or she lives in. Using the terminology

customer-name	street	customer-city
Jones	Main	Harrison
Smith	North	Rye
Hayes	Main	Harrison
Curry	North	Rye
Lindsay	Park	Pittsfield
Turner	Putnam	Stamford
Williams	Nassau	Princeton
Adams	Spring	Pittsfield
Johnson	Alma	Palo Alto
Glenn	Sand Hill	Woodside
Brooks	Senator	Brooklyn
Green	Walnut	Stamford

Figure 3.2   The *customer* relation.

of the entity-relationship model, we would say that the attribute *customer-name* represents the same entity set in both relations.

It would appear that, for our banking example, we could have just one relation scheme rather than several. That is, it may be easier for a user to think in terms of one relation scheme rather than several. Suppose we used only one relation for our example, with scheme

Account-info-scheme = (branch-name, account-number, customer-name,
*   balance, street, customer-city)*

Observe that if a customer has several accounts, we must list her or his address once for each account. That is, we must repeat certain information several times. This repetition is wasteful and was avoided by our use of two relations. If a customer has one or more accounts, but has not provided an address, we cannot construct a tuple on *Account-info-scheme,* since the values for the *street* and *customer-city* are not known. To represent incomplete tuples, we must use *null values.* Thus, in the above example, the values for *street* and *customer-city* must be null. By using two relations, one on *Customer-scheme* and one on *Deposit-scheme,* we can represent customers whose address is unknown, without using null values. We simply use a tuple on *Deposit-scheme* to represent the information about the account, and create no tuple on *Customer-scheme* until the address information becomes available. In Chapter 6, we shall study criteria to help us decide when one set of relation schemes is better than another. For now, we shall assume the relation schemes are given.

For the purpose of this chapter, we assume that the relation schemes for our banking enterprise are as follows:

Branch-scheme = (*branch-name, assets, branch-city*)
Customer-scheme = (*customer-name, street, customer-city*)
Deposit-scheme = (*branch-name, account-number, customer-name, balance*)
Borrow-scheme = (*branch-name, loan-number, customer-name, amount*)

We have already seen an example of a *deposit* relation and a *customer* relation. Figure 3.3 shows a sample *borrow* (*Borrow-scheme*) relation.

The notion of a *superkey*, *candidate key*, and *primary key*, as discussed in Chapter 2, is applicable also to the relational model. For example, in *Branch-scheme*, {*branch-name*} and {*branch-name, branch-city*} are both superkeys. {*branch-name, branch-city*} is not a candidate key because {*branch-name*} ⊆ {*branch-name, branch-city*} and {*branch-name*} itself is a superkey. {*branch-name*}, however, *is* a candidate key, which for our purpose will also serve as a primary key. The attribute *branch-city* is not a superkey since two branches in the same city may have different names (and different asset figures). The primary key for the *customer-scheme* is *customer-name*. We are not using the *social-security* number, as was done in Chapter 2, in order to have smaller relation schemes in our running example of a bank database. We expect that in a real world database the *social-security* attribute would serve as a primary key.

Let R be a relation scheme. If we say that a subset K of R is a *superkey* for R, we are restricting consideration to relations $r(R)$ in which no two distinct tuples have the same values on all attributes in K. That is, if t_1 and t_2 are in r and $t_1 \neq t_2$, then $t_1[K] \neq t_2[K]$.

branch-name	loan-number	customer-name	amount
Downtown	17	Jones	1000
Redwood	23	Smith	2000
Perryridge	15	Hayes	1500
Downtown	14	Jackson	1500
Mianus	93	Curry	500
Round Hill	11	Turner	900
Pownal	29	Williams	1200
North Town	16	Adams	1300
Downtown	18	Johnson	2000
Perryridge	25	Glenn	2500
Brighton	10	Brooks	2200

Figure 3.3   The *borrow* relation.

3.2 Formal Query Languages

A *query language* is a language in which a user requests information from the database. These languages are typically higher-level languages than standard programming languages. Query languages can be categorized as being either *procedural* or *nonprocedural*. In a procedural language, the user instructs the system to perform a sequence of operations on the database to compute the desired result. In a nonprocedural language, the user describes the information desired without giving a specific procedure for obtaining that information.

Most commercial relational database systems offer a query language that includes elements of both the procedural and the nonprocedural approaches. We shall study several commercial languages later in this chapter. First, we look at two "pure" languages: one procedural and one nonprocedural. These "pure" languages lack the "syntactic sugar" of commercial languages, but they illustrate the fundamental techniques for extracting data from the database.

3.2.1 The Relational Algebra

The relational algebra is a procedural query language. There are five fundamental operations in the relational algebra. These operations are: *select*, *project*, *cartesian-product*, *union*, and *set-difference*. All of these operations produce a new relation as their result.

In addition to the five fundamental operations, we shall introduce several other operations, namely, *set intersection*, *theta join*, *natural join*, and *division*. These operations will be defined in terms of the fundamental operations.

Fundamental operations

The select and project operations are called *unary* operations, since they operate on one relation. The other three relations operate on pairs of relations and are, therefore, called *binary* operations.

The *select* operation selects tuples that satisfy a given predicate. We use the lowercase Greek letter sigma (σ) to denote selection. The predicate appears as a subscript to σ. The argument relation is given in parentheses

branch-name	loan-number	customer-name	amount
Perryridge	15	Hayes	1500
Perryridge	25	Glenn	2500

Figure 3.4   Result of $\sigma_{branch\text{-}name\ =\ \text{"Perryridge"}}$ (*borrow*).

following the σ. Thus, to select those tuples of the *borrow* relation where the branch is "Perryridge," we write

$$\sigma_{branch\text{-}name\ =\ \text{"Perryridge"}}\ (borrow)$$

If the borrow relation is as shown in Figure 3.3, then the relation that results from the above query is as shown in Figure 3.4. We may find all tuples in which the amount borrowed is more than $1200 by writing

$$\sigma_{amount\ >\ 1200}\ (borrow)$$

In general, we allow comparisons using =, ≠, <, ≤, >, ≥ in the selection predicate. Furthermore, several predicates may be combined into a larger predicate using the connectives *and* (∧) and *or* (∨). Thus, to find those tuples pertaining to loans of more than $1200 made by the Perryridge branch, we write

$$\sigma_{branch\text{-}name\ =\ \text{"Perryridge"}\ \wedge\ amount\ >\ 1200}\ (borrow)$$

The selection predicate may include comparisons between two attributes. To illustrate this, we consider the relation scheme

$$Client\text{-}scheme = (customer\text{-}name,\ employee\text{-}name)$$

indicating that the employee is the "personal banker" of the customer. The relation *client* (*Client-scheme*) is shown in Figure 3.5. We may find all those customers who have the same name as their personal banker by writing

$$\sigma_{customer\text{-}name\ =\ employee\text{-}name}\ (client)$$

If the *client* relation is as given in Figure 3.5, the answer is the relation shown in Figure 3.6.

In the above example, we obtained a relation (Figure 3.6) on (*customer-name*, *employee-name*) in which $t[customer\text{-}name] = t[employee\text{-}name]$ for all tuples t. It seems redundant to list the person's name twice. We would

customer-name	employee-name
Turner	Johnson
Hayes	Jones
Johnson	Johnson

Figure 3.5   The *client* relation.

prefer a one attribute relation on (*customer-name*) which lists all those who have the same name as their personal banker. The *project* operation allows us to produce this relation. The project operation is a unary operation that copies its argument relation, with certain columns left out. Projection is denoted by the Greek letter pi (Π). We list those attributes that we wish to appear in the result as a subscript to Π. The argument relation follows Π in parentheses.

Suppose we want a relation showing customers and the branches from which they borrow, but do not care about the amount of the loan, nor the loan number. We may write

$$\Pi_{branch\text{-}name,\ customer\text{-}name}\ (borrow)$$

Let us revisit the query "Find those customers who have the same name as their personal banker." We write

$$\Pi_{customer\text{-}name}\ (\sigma_{customer\text{-}name\ =\ employee\text{-}name}\ (client))$$

Notice that instead of giving the name of a relation as the argument of the projection operation, we give an expression that evaluates to a relation.

The operations we have discussed up to this point allow us to extract information from only one relation at at time. We have not yet been able to combine information from several relations. One operation that allows us to do that is the *cartesian product* operation, denoted by a cross (×). This operation is a binary operation. We shall use infix notation for binary operations and, thus, write the cartesian product of relations r_1 and r_2 as $r_1 \times r_2$. We saw the definition of cartesian product earlier in this chapter (recall that a relation is defined to be a subset of a cartesian product of a set of domains). From that definition we should already have some intuition about the definition of the relational algebra operation ×. However, we face the problem of choosing the attribute names for the relation that results from a cartesian product.

Suppose we want to find all clients of bank employee Johnson, as well as the cities in which the clients live. We need the information in both the *client* relation and the *customer* relation in order to do so. Figure 3.7 shows the relation r = *client* × *customer*. The relation scheme for r is

customer-name	employee-name
Johnson	Johnson

Figure 3.6   Result of $\sigma_{customer\text{-}name\ =\ employee\text{-}name}\ (client)$.

client. customer-name	client. employee-name	customer. customer-name	customer. street	customer. customer-city
Turner	Johnson	Jones	Main	Harrison
Turner	Johnson	Smith	North	Rye
Turner	Johnson	Hayes	Main	Harrison
Turner	Johnson	Curry	North	Rye
Turner	Johnson	Lindsay	Park	Pittsfield
Turner	Johnson	Turner	Putnam	Stamford
Turner	Johnson	Williams	Nassau	Princeton
Turner	Johnson	Adams	Spring	Pittsfield
Turner	Johnson	Johnson	Alma	Palo Alto
Turner	Johnson	Glenn	Sand Hill	Woodside
Turner	Johnson	Brooks	Senator	Brooklyn
Turner	Johnson	Green	Walnut	Stamford
Hayes	Jones	Jones	Main	Harrison
Hayes	Jones	Smith	North	Rye
Hayes	Jones	Hayes	Main	Harrison
Hayes	Jones	Curry	North	Rye
Hayes	Jones	Lindsay	Park	Pittsfield
Hayes	Jones	Turner	Putnam	Stamford
Hayes	Jones	Williams	Nassau	Princeton
Hayes	Jones	Adams	Spring	Pittsfield
Hayes	Jones	Johnson	Alma	Palo Alto
Hayes	Jones	Glenn	Sand Hill	Woodside
Hayes	Jones	Brooks	Senator	Brooklyn
Hayes	Jones	Green	Walnut	Stamford
Johnson	Johnson	Jones	Main	Harrison
Johnson	Johnson	Smith	North	Rye
Johnson	Johnson	Hayes	Main	Harrison
Johnson	Johnson	Curry	North	Rye
Johnson	Johnson	Lindsay	Park	Pittsfield
Johnson	Johnson	Turner	Putnam	Stamford
Johnson	Johnson	Williams	Nassau	Princeton
Johnson	Johnson	Adams	Spring	Pittsfield
Johnson	Johnson	Johnson	Alma	Palo Alto
Johnson	Johnson	Glenn	Sand Hill	Woodside
Johnson	Johnson	Brooks	Senator	Brooklyn
Johnson	Johnson	Green	Walnut	Stamford

Figure 3.7   Result of *client* × *customer*.

(*client.customer-name, client.employee-name, customer.customer-name,
customer.street, customer.customer-city*)

That is, we simply list all the attributes of both relations, and attach the name of the relation from which the attribute originally came. We need to attach the relation name to distinguish *client.customer-name* from *customer.customer-name*.

Now that we know the relation scheme for $r = client \times customer$, what tuples appear in r? As you may have suspected, we construct a tuple of r out of each possible pair of tuples: one from the *client* relation and one from the *customer* relation. Thus r is a large relation, as can be seen from Figure 3.7.

Assume we have n_1 tuples in *client* and n_2 tuples in *customer*. Then there are $n_1 n_2$ ways of choosing a pair of tuples: one tuple from each relation, so there are $n_1 n_2$ tuples in r. In particular, note that it may be the case for some tuples t in r that $t[client.customer-name] \neq t[customer.customer-name]$.

In general, if we have relations $r_1(R_1)$ and $r_2(R_2)$, then $r_1 \times r_2$ is a relation whose scheme is the concatenation of R_1 and R_2. Relation R contains all tuples t for which there is a tuple t_1 in r_1, and t_2 in r_2 for which $t[R_1] = t_1[R_1]$ and $t[R_2] = t_2[R_2]$.

Returning to the query "Find all clients of Johnson and the city in which they live," we consider the relation $r = client \times customer$. If we write

$$\sigma_{client.employee-name \,=\, \text{``Johnson''}} (client \times customer)$$

then the result relation is as shown in Figure 3.8. We have a relation pertaining only to employee Johnson. However, the *client.customer-name* column may contain customers of employees other than Johnson (if you don't see why, look at the definition of cartesian product again). Note that the *client.customer-name* column contains only customers of Johnson. Since the cartesian product operation associates *every* tuple of *customer* with every tuple of *client*, we know that some tuple in $client \times customer$ has the address of the employee's customer. This occurs in those cases where it happens that *client.customer-name* = *customer.customer-name*. So if we write

$$\sigma_{client.customer-name \,=\, customer.customer-name}$$
$$(\sigma_{client.employee-name \,=\, \text{``Johnson''}} (client \times customer))$$

we get only those tuples of $client \times customer$ that:

- Pertain to Johnson.
- Have the street and city of the customer of Johnson.

client. *customer-name*	*client.* *employee-name*	*customer.* *customer-name*	*customer.* *street*	*customer.* *customer-city*
Turner	Johnson	Jones	Main	Harrison
Turner	Johnson	Smith	North	Rye
Turner	Johnson	Hayes	Main	Harrison
Turner	Johnson	Curry	North	Rye
Turner	Johnson	Lindsay	Park	Pittsfield
Turner	Johnson	Turner	Putnam	Stamford
Turner	Johnson	Williams	Nassau	Princeton
Turner	Johnson	Adams	Spring	Pittsfield
Turner	Johnson	Johnson	Alma	Palo Alto
Turner	Johnson	Glenn	Sand Hill	Woodside
Turner	Johnson	Brooks	Senator	Brooklyn
Turner	Johnson	Green	Walnut	Stamford
Johnson	Johnson	Jones	Main	Harrison
Johnson	Johnson	Smith	North	Rye
Johnson	Johnson	Hayes	Main	Harrison
Johnson	Johnson	Curry	North	Rye
Johnson	Johnson	Lindsay	Park	Pittsfield
Johnson	Johnson	Turner	Putnam	Stamford
Johnson	Johnson	Williams	Nassau	Princeton
Johnson	Johnson	Adams	Spring	Pittsfield
Johnson	Johnson	Johnson	Alma	Palo Alto
Johnson	Johnson	Glenn	Sand Hill	Woodside
Johnson	Johnson	Brooks	Senator	Brooklyn
Johnson	Johnson	Green	Walnut	Stamford

Figure 3.8   Result of $\sigma_{client.employee\text{-}name\,=\,\text{"Johnson"}}$ (*client* × *customer*).

Finally, since we want only *customer-name* and *customer-city*, we do a projection

$$\Pi_{client.customername,\ customer.customer\text{-}city}$$

$$(\sigma_{client.customer\text{-}name\,=\,customer.customer\text{-}name}$$

$$(\sigma_{client.employee\text{-}name\,=\,\text{"Johnson"}}$$

$$(client\ \times\ customer)))$$

The result of this expression is the correct answer to our query.

Let us now consider a query that might be posed by a bank's advertising department: "Find all customers of the Perryridge branch." That is, find everyone who has a loan, an account, or both. To answer this query, we need the information in the *borrow* relation (Figure 3.3) and the *deposit* relation (Figure 3.1). We know how to find all customers with a loan at the Perryridge branch:

$$\Pi_{customer\text{-}name} \ (\sigma_{branch\text{-}name} = \text{``Perryridge''} \ (borrow))$$

We know also how to find all customers with an account at the Perryridge branch:

$$\Pi_{customer\text{-}name} \ (\sigma_{branch\text{-}name} = \text{``Perryridge''} \ (deposit))$$

To answer the query, we need the *union* of these two sets, that is, all customers appearing in either or both of the two relations. This is accomplished by the binary operation union, denoted, as in set theory, by $\cup$. So the expression the advertising department needs in our example is

$$(\Pi_{customer\text{-}name} \ (\sigma_{branch\text{-}name} = \text{``Perryridge''} \ (borrow)))$$
$$\cup \ (\Pi_{customer\text{-}name} \ (\sigma_{branch\text{-}name} = \text{``Perryridge''} \ (deposit)))$$

The result relation for this query appears in Figure 3.9. Notice that there are three tuples in the result even though the Perryridge branch has two borrowers and two depositors. This is due to the fact that Hayes is both a borrower and a depositor of the Perryridge branch. Since relations are sets, duplicate values are eliminated.

Observe that, in our example, we took the union of two sets, both of which consisted of *customer-name* values. In general, we must ensure that unions are taken between *compatible* relations. For example, it would not make sense to take the union of the *borrow* relation and the *customer* relation. The former is a relation of four attributes and the latter of three. Furthermore, consider a union of a set of customer names and a set of cities. Such a union would not make sense in most situations. Therefore, for a union operation $r \cup s$ to be legal, we require that two conditions hold:

1. The relations r and s must be of the same arity. That is, they must have the same number of attributes.

customer-name
Hayes
Glenn
Williams

Figure 3.9   Names of all customers of the Perryridge branch.

2. The domains of the *i*th attribute of *r* and the *i*th attribute of *s* must be the same. *same meaning w r t domain*

The *set-difference* operator, denoted by −, allows us to find tuples that are in one relation, but not in another. The expression *r* − *s* results in a relation containing those tuples in *r* but not in *s* .

We can find all customers of the Perryridge branch who have an account there but do not have a loan there by writing:

$$(\Pi_{customer\text{-}name} \ (\sigma_{branch\text{-}name \ = \ \text{``Perryridge''}} \ (deposit)))$$
$$- \ (\Pi_{customer\text{-}name} \ (\sigma_{branch\text{-}name \ = \ \text{``Perryridge''}} \ (borrow)))$$

The result relation for this query appears in Figure 3.10.

Formal definition of the relational algebra

The five operators we have just seen allow us to give a complete definition of an expression in the relational algebra. A basic expression in the relational algebra consists of either one of the following:

- A relation in the database.
- A constant relation.

A general expression in the relational algebra is constructed out of smaller subexpressions. Let E_1 and E_2 be relational algebra expressions. Then,

- $E_1 \cup E_2$
- $E_1 - E_2$
- $E_1 \times E_2$
- $\sigma_P (E_1)$, where P is a predicate on attributes on E_1
- $\Pi_S (E_1)$, where S is a list consisting of some of the attributes appearing in E_1

are all relational algebra expressions.

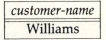

customer-name
Williams

Figure 3.10   Customers with only an account at the Perryridge branch.

Additional operators

We have now seen the five fundamental operations of the relational algebra: σ, Π, $\times$, $\cup$, $-$. These five operators are sufficient to express any relational algebra query. However, if we restrict ourselves to just the five fundamental operators, some common queries are lengthy to express. Therefore, we define additional operators. These new operators do not add any power to the algebra, but they do simplify common queries.

For each new operator we define, we give an equivalent expression using only the five fundamental operators.

The first additional relational algebra operation we shall define is *set intersection* ($\cap$). Suppose we wish to find all customers that have *both* a loan and an account at the Perryridge branch. Using set intersection, we could write:

$$(\Pi_{customer\text{-}name} (\sigma_{branch\text{-}name\, =\, \text{“Perryridge”}} (borrow)))$$
$$\cap\, (\Pi_{customer\text{-}name} (\sigma_{branch\text{-}name\, =\, \text{“Perryridge”}} (deposit)))$$

The result relation for this query appears in Figure 3.11.

Note, however, that we do not include set intersection as a fundamental operation. We do not do so because we can rewrite any relational algebra expression using set intersection by replacing the intersection operation with a pair of set difference operations as follows:

$$r \cap s = r - (r - s)$$

Thus, set intersection does not add any power to the relational algebra. It is simply more convenient to write $r \cap s$ than $r - (r - s)$.

The next operations we add to the algebra are used to simplify many queries that require a cartesian product. Typically, a query that involves a cartesian product includes a selection operation on the result of the cartesian product. Consider the query "Find all customers of the Perryridge branch and the cities in which they live." We first form the cartesian product of the *borrow* and *customer* relations, then we select those tuples that pertain to Perryridge and pertain to only one *customer-name*. Thus we write

$$\Pi_{borrow.customer\text{-}name,\ customer.customer\text{-}city} (\sigma_P(borrow \times customer))$$

Where:

$$P = borrow.branch\text{-}name = \text{“Perryridge”}$$
$$\wedge\ borrow.customer\text{-}name = customer.customer\text{-}name$$

customer-name
Hayes

Figure 3.11   Customers with an account and a loan at the Perryridge branch.

The *theta join* is a binary operation that allows us to combine the selection and cartesian product into one operation. The theta join is denoted by $\bowtie_{\Theta}$, where $\bowtie$ is the "join" symbol and the subscript Θ (the Greek letter theta) is replaced by the selection predicate. The theta join operator forms the cartesian product of its two arguments and then performs a selection using the predicate Θ.

We rewrite our relational algebra expression for "Find all customers having a loan at the Perryridge branch and the cities in which they live," using the theta join as follows:

$$\Pi_{borrow.customer\text{-}name,\ customer.customer\text{-}city}\ (borrow \bowtie_{\Theta} customer)$$

In this example, Θ is the predicate:

$$borrow.branch\text{-}name = \text{"Perryridge"}$$
$$\wedge\ borrow.customer\text{-}name = customer.customer\text{-}name$$

In general, Θ can be an arbitrary predicate. Given two relations, r and s, and a predicate Θ,

$$r \bowtie_{\Theta} s = \sigma_{\Theta} (r \times s)$$

The *natural-join* operation is a further notational simplification of the relational algebra. Let us consider a simpler version of the above example, "Find all customers having a loan *at some branch* and their cities." If we write this query as a theta join we obtain

$$\Pi_{borrow.customer\text{-}name,\ customer.customer\text{-}city}$$
$$(borrow \bowtie_{borrow.customer\text{-}name\ =\ customer.customer\text{-}name} customer)$$

Observe that this particular theta join forces equality on those attributes that appear in both relation schemes. This sort of predicate occurs frequently in practice. Indeed, if we are printing out pairs of (*customer-name, customer-city*), we would normally want the city to be the city in which customer lives, and not some arbitrary city. The *natural-join* operation is designed precisely for this sort of query.

Although the definition of natural-join is a bit complicated, it is applied easily. We can use the natural join to write the query "Find all customers having a loan at some branch and their cities" as follows:

$$\Pi_{customer\text{-}name,\ customer\text{-}city}\ (borrow \bowtie customer)$$

Since the schemes for *borrow* and *customer* (that is, *Borrow-scheme* and *Customer-scheme*) have the attribute *customer-name* in common, the natural-join operation considers only pairs of tuples that have the same value on *customer-name*. It combines each such pair of tuples into a single tuple on the union of the two schemes (that is, *branch-name, loan-number, customer-name, amount, street, customer-city*). After performing the projection, we obtain the relation shown in Figure 3.12. The earlier example, "Find all customers having a loan at the Perryridge branch and their cities," can be written as

$$\Pi_{customer\text{-}name,\ customer\text{-}city}$$
$$(\sigma_{branch\text{-}name\ =\ \text{``Perryridge''}}\ (borrow \bowtie customer))$$

We are now ready for a formal definition of the natural join. Consider two relation schemes R and S which are, of course, lists of attribute names. Let us consider the schemes to be *sets* rather than lists. This allows us to denote those attributes in both R and S by $R \cap S$, and to denote those attributes that appear in R, in S, or in both by $R \cup S$. Note that we are talking, here, about union and intersection on sets of attributes, not relations.

Consider two relations $r(R)$ and $s(S)$. The natural join of r and s, denoted by $r \bowtie s$ is a relation on scheme $R \cup S$. It is the projection onto

customer-name	customer-city
Jones	Harrison
Smith	Rye
Hayes	Harrison
Curry	Rye
Turner	Stamford
Williams	Princeton
Adams	Pittsfield
Johnson	Palo Alto
Glenn	Woodside
Brooks	Brooklyn

Figure 3.12   Result of $\Pi_{customer\text{-}name,\ customer\text{-}city}\ (borrow \bowtie customer)$.

$R \cup S$ of a theta join where the predicate requires $r.A = s.A$ for each attribute A in $R \cap S$. Formally,

$$r \bowtie s = \Pi_{R \cup S} (r \bowtie_{r.A_1 = s.A_1 \wedge \dots, \wedge r.A_n = s.A_n} s)$$

where $R \cap S = \{A_1, \dots, A_n\}$.

Now that we have introduced the natural join, we adopt the following convention for attribute names in cartesian products of relations: We shall use the notation *relation-name.attribute-name* only when necessary to avoid ambiguity. When no ambiguity results, we shall drop the *relation-name* prefix.

Because the natural join is central to much of relational database theory and practice, we give several examples of its use:

- Find the assets and name of all branches which have depositors (that is, customers with an account) living in Port Chester.

$$\Pi_{branch\text{-}name,\ assets}$$
$$(\sigma_{customer\text{-}city\ =\ \text{``Port Chester''}} (customer \bowtie deposit \bowtie branch))$$

Notice that we wrote customer $\bowtie$ deposit $\bowtie$ branch without inserting parentheses to specify

$$(customer \bowtie deposit) \bowtie branch$$
$$\text{or} \quad customer \bowtie (deposit \bowtie branch)$$

We did not specify which expression we intended because they are equivalent. That is, the natural join is associative.

- Find all customers who have *both* an account and a loan at the Perryridge branch.

$$\Pi_{customer\text{-}name} (\sigma_{branch\text{-}name\ =\ \text{``Perryridge''}} (borrow \bowtie deposit))$$

Note that we could have written an expression for this query using set intersection:

$$(\Pi_{customer\text{-}name} (\sigma_{branch\text{-}name\ =\ \text{``Perryridge''}} (deposit)))$$
$$\cap (\Pi_{customer\text{-}name} (\sigma_{branch\text{-}name\ =\ \text{``Perryridge''}} (borrow)))$$

This example illustrates a general fact about the relational algebra: It is possible to write several equivalent relational algebra expressions that are quite different from each other.

- Let $r(R)$ and $s(S)$ be relations without any attributes in common, that is, $R \cap S = \emptyset$. ($\emptyset$ denotes the empty set.) Then $r \bowtie s = r \times s$.

We now introduce one final relational algebra operation, called *division* ($\div$). The division operation is suited to queries that include the phrase "for all." Suppose we wish to find all customers who have an account at all branches located in Brooklyn. We can obtain all branches in Brooklyn by the expression:

$$r_1 = \Pi_{branch\text{-}name} \; (\sigma_{branch\text{-}city = \text{"Brooklyn"}} \; (branch))$$

We can find all *customer-name, branch-name* pairs for which the customer has an account at the branch by writing

$$r_2 = \Pi_{customer\text{-}name, \; branch\text{-}name} \; (deposit)$$

Now we need to find customers who appear in r_2 with *every* branch name in r_1. The operation that provides exactly those customers is the divide operation. The query can be answered by writing

$$\Pi_{customer\text{-}name, \; branch\text{-}name} \; (deposit)$$
$$\div \; \Pi_{branch\text{-}name} \; (\sigma_{branch\text{-}city = \text{"Brooklyn"}} \; (branch))$$

Formally, let $r(R)$ and $s(S)$ be relations, and let $S \subseteq R$. The relation $r \div s$ is a relation on scheme $R - S$. A tuple t is in $r \div s$ if for every tuple t_s in s there is a tuple t_r in r satisfying both of the following:

$$t_r [S] = t_s [S]$$
$$t_r [R - S] = t[R - S]$$

It may be surprising to discover that the division operation can, in fact, be defined in terms of the five fundamental operations. Let $r(R)$ and $s(S)$ be given, with $S \subseteq R$.

$$r \div s = \Pi_{R - S} \; (r) - \Pi_{R - S} \; (\; (\Pi_{R - S} \; (r) \times s) - r)$$

To see that this is true, observe that $\Pi_{R - S} \; (r)$ gives us all tuples t that satisfy the second condition of the definition of division. The expression on the right side of the set difference operator,

$$\Pi_{R - S} \; (\; (\Pi_{R - S} \; (r) \times s) - r)$$

serves to eliminate those tuples that fail to satisfy the first condition of the definition of division. Let us see how it does this. Consider $\Pi_{R - S}(r) \times s$. This is a relation on scheme R which pairs every tuple in $\Pi_{R - S}(r)$ with every tuple in s. Thus $(\Pi_{R - S}(r) \times s) - r$ gives us those pairs of tuples from $\Pi_{R - S}(r)$ and s which do not appear in r. If a tuple t is in

$$\Pi_{R - S}((\Pi_{R - S}(r) \times s) - r)$$

then there is some tuple t_s in s that does not combine with tuple t to form a tuple in r. Thus t holds a value for attributes $R - S$ which does not appear in $r \div s$. It is these values that we eliminate from $\Pi_{R - S}(r)$.

3.2.2 The Relational Calculus

The relational algebra is a procedural language because, when we write a relational algebra expression, we provide a sequence of operations that generates the answer to our query. The relational calculus, on the other hand, is a nonprocedural language. In the relational calculus, we give a formal description of the information desired without specifying how to obtain that information.

There are two forms of the relational calculus, one in which the variables represent tuples, and one in which the variables represent values of domains. These variants are called the *tuple relational calculus* and the *domain relational calculus*. The two forms are very similar. As a result, we shall emphasize the tuple relational calculus.

A query in the tuple relational calculus is expressed as

$$\{t \mid P(t)\}$$

that is, the set of all tuples t such that predicate P is true for t. Following our earlier notation, we use $t[A]$ to denote the value of tuple t on attribute A, and we use $t \in r$ to denote that tuple t is in relation r.

Before we give a formal definition of the tuple relational calculus, we return to some of the queries for which we wrote relational algebra expressions in the last section.

Find the *branch-name*, *loan-number*, *customer-name*, and *amount* for loans of over $1200:

$$\{t \mid t \in borrow \wedge t[amount] > 1200\}$$

Suppose we want only the *customer-name* attribute, rather than all attributes of the *borrow* relation. To write this query in the tuple relational calculus, we need to write an expression for a relation on scheme (*customer-name*).

We need those tuples on (*customer-name*) such that there is a tuple in *borrow* pertaining to that *customer-name* with the *amount* attribute > 1200. In order to express this, we need the construct "there exists" from the predicate calculus in mathematical logic. The notation

$$\exists\ t\ (Q(t))$$

means "there exists a tuple t such that predicate $Q(t)$ is true."

Using this notation, we may write the query "Find all customers who have a loan for an amount greater than \$1200" as:

$$\{t\ |\ \exists\ s\ (s \in borrow \land t[customer\text{-}name] = s[customer\text{-}name]$$
$$\land\ s[amount] > 1200)\}$$

In English, we read the above expression as "the set of all tuples t such that there exists a tuple s in relation *borrow* for which the values of t and s for the *customer-name* attribute are equal, and the value of s for the *amount* attribute is greater than \$1200."

Consider the query "Find all customers having a loan from the Perryridge branch and the cities in which they live." This query is slightly more complex than we have seen so far since it involves two relations, namely, *customer* and *borrow*. But as we shall see, all this requires is that we have two "there exists" clauses in our tuple relational calculus expression. We write the query as follows:

$$\{t\ |\ \exists\ s\ (s \in borrow \land t[customer\text{-}name] = s[customer\text{-}name]$$
$$\land\ s[branch\text{-}name] = \text{"Perryridge"}$$
$$\land\ \exists\ u\ (u \in customer \land u[customer\text{-}name] = s[customer\text{-}name]$$
$$\land\ t[customer\text{-}city] = u[customer\text{-}city]))\}$$

In English, this is "the set of all (*customer-name, customer-city*) tuples for which *customer-name* is a borrower at Perryridge branch and *customer-city* is the city of *customer-name*." Tuple variable s ensures that the customer is a borrower at the Perryridge branch. Tuple variable u is restricted to pertain to the same customer as s, and u ensures that the *customer-city* is the city of the customer.

To find all customers having a loan, an account, or both at the Perryridge branch, we used the union operation in the relational algebra. In the tuple relational calculus, we shall need two "there exists" clauses, connected by "or" ($\lor$).

$$\{t\ |\ \exists\ s\ (s \in borrow \land t[customer\text{-}name] = s[customer\text{-}name]$$
$$\land\ s[branch\text{-}name] = \text{"Perryridge"})$$
$$\lor\ \exists\ u\ (u \in deposit \land t[customer\text{-}name] = u[customer\text{-}name]$$
$$\land\ u[branch\text{-}name] = \text{"Perryridge"})\}$$

The above expression gives us the set of all *customer-name* tuples such that at least one of the following holds:

- The *customer-name* appears in some tuple of the *borrow* relation as a borrower from Perryridge branch.

- The *customer-name* appears in some tuple of the *deposit* relation as a depositor of Perryridge branch.

If some customer has both a loan and an account at the Perryridge branch, that customer appears only once in the result because the mathematical definition of a set does not allow duplicate members of a set.

If we now want *only* those customers that have *both* an account and a loan at Perryridge branch, all we need to do is change the "or" ($\lor$) to "and" ($\land$) in the above expression.

$$\{t \mid \exists\, s\, (s \in borrow \land t[customer\text{-}name] = s[customer\text{-}name]$$
$$\land\ s[branch\text{-}name] = \text{``Perryridge''})$$
$$\land\ \exists\, u\, (u \in deposit \land t[customer\text{-}name] = u[customer\text{-}name]$$
$$\land\ u[branch\text{-}name] = \text{``Perryridge''})\}$$

Now consider the query, "Find all customers who have an account at the Perryridge branch but do not have a loan from the Perryridge branch." The tuple relational calculus expression for this query is similar to those we have just seen, except for the use of the "not" ($\neg$) symbol.

$$\{t \mid \exists\, u\, (u \in deposit \land t[customer\text{-}name] = u[customer\text{-}name]$$
$$\land\ u[branch\text{-}name] = \text{``Perryridge''})$$
$$\land\ \neg\, \exists\, s\, (s \in borrow \land t[customer\text{-}name] = s[customer\text{-}name]$$
$$\land\ s[branch\text{-}name] = \text{``Perryridge''})\}$$

The above tuple relational calculus expression uses the $\exists\, u\, (\dots)$ clause to require that the customer have an account at Perryridge branch, and it uses the $\neg\, \exists\, s\, (\dots)$ clause to eliminate those customers who appear in some tuple of the *borrow* relation as having a loan from the Perryridge branch.

Finally, let us consider the query we used in Section 3.2.1 to illustrate the division operation, "Find all customers who have an account at all branches located in Brooklyn." To write this query in the tuple relational calculus, we introduce the "for all" construct, denoted $\forall$. The notation

$$\forall\, t(Q(t))$$

means "*Q* is true for all tuples *t*." We write the expression for our query as follows:

$$\{t \mid \forall u \ (u \notin branch \lor u[branch\text{-}city] \neq \text{``Brooklyn''}$$
$$\lor \exists s \ (s \in deposit \land t[customer\text{-}name] = s[customer\text{-}name]$$
$$\land u[branch\text{-}name] = s[branch\text{-}name]))\}$$

In English, we interpret the above expression as "the set of all (*customer-name*) tuples *t* such that for *all* (*branch-name, branch-city*) tuples at least one of the following is true:

- *u* is not a tuple of the *branch* relation (and therefore, does not pertain to a branch in Brooklyn).

- The value of *u* on attribute *branch-city* is not Brooklyn.

- The customer has an account at the branch whose name appears in the *branch-name* attribute of *u*.

We are now ready to give a formal definition of the tuple relational calculus. A tuple relational calculus expression is of the form:

$$\{t \mid P(t)\}$$

where *P* is a *formula*. Several tuple variables may appear in a formula. A tuple variable is said to be a *free variable* unless it is quantified by a "∃" or "∀". Thus in:

$$t \in borrow \land \exists s \ (t[customer\text{-}name] = s[customer\text{-}name])$$

t is a free variable. Tuple variable *s* is said to be a *bound* variable.

A tuple relational calculus formula is built up out of *atoms*. An atom is of one of the following forms:

- $s \in r$, where *s* is a tuple variable and *r* is a relation.

- $s[x] \ \Theta \ u[y]$, where *s* and *u* are tuple variables, *x* is an attribute on which *s* is defined, *y* is an attribute on which *y* is defined, and Θ is a comparison operation ($<, \leq, =, \neq, >, \geq$). We require that attributes *x* and *y* have domains whose members can be compared by Θ.

- $s[x] \ \Theta \ c$, where *s* is a tuple variable, *x* is an attribute on which *s* is defined, Θ is a comparison operator, and *c* is a constant in the domain of attribute *x*.

Formulae are built up from atoms using the following rules:

- An atom is a formula.
- If P_1 is a formula, then so are $\neg P_1$ and (P_1).
- If P_1 and P_2 are formulae, then so are $P_1 \vee P_2$ and $P_1 \wedge P_2$.
- If $P_1(s)$ is a formula containing a free tuple variable s, then:

$$\exists\, s\, (P_1(s)) \quad \text{and} \quad \forall\, s\, (P_1(s))$$

are also formulae.

As was the case for the relational algebra, it is possible to write equivalent expressions that are not identical in appearance. In the tuple relational calculus, these equivalences include two rules:

1. $P_1 \wedge P_2$ is equivalent to $\neg\,(\neg P_1 \vee \neg P_2)$.
2. $\forall\, t\, (P_1(t))$ is equivalent to $\neg\, \exists\, t\, (\neg P_1(t))$.

There is one final issue we must address in the tuple relational calculus. A tuple relational calculus may generate an infinite relation. Suppose we wrote the expression:

$$\{t \mid t \notin borrow \}$$

There are infinitely many tuples that are not in *borrow*. Most of these tuples contain values that do not even appear in the database! Clearly, we do not wish to allow such expressions. Another type of expression we wish to disallow is:

$$\{t \mid \exists\, s\, (s[x] \neq c \wedge t[y] = s[y])\}$$

where x and y are attributes and c is a constant. It is possible that the only tuples that satisfy $s[x] \neq c$ are tuples whose values do not appear in the database. Finding such a tuple requires a search among the potentially infinite number of tuples that do not appear in the database.

To assist us in defining a restriction of the tuple relational calculus, we introduce the concept of the *domain* of a tuple relational calculus formula. Let P be a formula. Intuitively, the domain of P, denoted $dom(P)$, is the set of all values referenced in P. These include values mentioned in P itself as well as values that appear in a tuple of a relation mentioned in P. Thus, the domain of P is the set of all values that appear explicitly in P or that appear in one or more of the relations whose names appear in P.

These considerations motivate the concept of *safe* tuple relational calculus expressions. We say an expression $\{t \mid P(t)\}$ is safe if all of the following hold:

1. All values that appear in tuples of the expression are values from *dom(P)*.

2. For every "there exists" subformula of the form $\exists s \, (P_1(s))$, the subformula is true if and only if there is a tuple s with values from $dom(P_1)$ such that $P_1(s)$ is true.

3. For every "for all" subformula of the form $\forall s \, (P_1(s))$, the subformula is true if and only if $P_1(s)$ is true for all tuples s with values from $dom(P_1)$.

The purpose of the notion of safety is to ensure that only values from *dom(P)* appear in the result and to ensure that we can test "for all" and "there exists" subformulae without having to test infinitely many possibilities.

Consider the second rule in the definition of safety. For $\exists s \, (P_1(s))$ to be true, we need to find only one s for which $P_1(s)$ is true. In general, there would be infinitely many tuples to test. However, if the expression is safe, we know that we may restrict our attention to tuples with values from $dom(P_1)$. This reduces the number of tuples we must consider to a finite number. The situation for subformulae of the form $\forall s \, (P_1(s))$ is similar. To assert that $\forall s \, (P_1(s))$ is true, we must, in general, test all possible tuples. This requires us to examine infinitely many tuples. As above, if we know the expression is safe, it is sufficient for us to test $P_1(s)$ for those tuples s whose values are taken from $dom(P_1)$.

All the tuple relational calculus expressions we have written in the examples of this section are safe.

The tuple relational calculus, restricted to safe expressions, is equivalent in expressive power to the relational algebra. This means that for every relational algebra expression, there is an equivalent safe expression in the tuple relational calculus, and for every safe tuple relational calculus expression there is an equivalent relational algebra expression. We will not prove this fact here, but the bibliographic notes contain references to the proof. Some parts of the proof are included in the exercises.

There is a second form of the relational calculus called the *domain relational calculus*. In this form of the relational calculus, we use *domain* variables that take on values from an attribute's domain, rather than values for an entire tuple. The domain relational calculus, however, is closely related to the tuple relational calculus.

An expression in the domain relational calculus is of the form $\{<x_1, x_2, ..., x_n> \mid P(x_1, x_2, ..., x_n)\}$ where the $x_i, 1 \le i \le n$, represent domain variables. P represents a formula. As was the case for the tuple relational calculus, a formula is composed of atoms. An atom in the domain relational calculus is of the following forms:

- $<x_i, ..., x_n> \in r$, where r is a relation on n attributes and $x_i, 1 \le i \le n$ are domain variables or domain constants.

- $x \Theta y$, where x and y are domain variables and Θ is a comparison operator ($<, \le, =, \ne, >, \ge$). We require that attributes x and y have domains that can be compared by Θ.

- $x \Theta c$, where x is a domain variable, Θ is a comparison operator, and c is a constant in the domain of the attribute for which x is a domain variable.

Formulae are built up from atoms using the following rules:

- An atom is a formula.
- If P_1 is a formula, then so are $\neg P_1$ and (P_1).
- If P_1 and P_2 are formulae, then so are $P_1 \vee P_2$ and $P_1 \wedge P_2$.
- If $P_1(x)$ is a formula in x, where x is a domain variable, then

$$\exists x (P_1(x)) \text{ and } \forall (P_1(x))$$

are also formulae.

As a notational shorthand, we write

$$\exists a,b,c (P(a,b,c))$$

for:

$$\exists a (\exists b (\exists c (P(a,b,c))))$$

The notion of safety applies to the domain calculus as well. The domain relational calculus, restricted to safe expressions, is equivalent to the tuple relational calculus, restricted to safe expressions. Since we noted earlier that the tuple relational calculus, restricted to safe expressions, is equivalent to the relational algebra, all three of the following are equivalent:

- The relational algebra.
- The tuple relational calculus restricted to safe expressions.
- The domain relational calculus restricted to safe expressions.

We now give domain relational calculus queries we considered earlier. Note the similarity of these expressions with the corresponding tuple relational calculus expressions:

Find the branch name, loan number, customer name, and amount for loans of over $1200:

$$\{<b,l,c,a> \mid <b,l,c,a> \epsilon \; borrow \wedge a > 1200\}$$

Find all customers who have a loan for an amount greater than $1200:

$$\{<c> \mid \exists \; b,l,a \; (<b,l,c,a> \epsilon \; borrow \wedge a > 1200)\}$$

Find all customers having a loan from the Perryridge branch and the city in which they live:

$$\{<c,x> \mid \exists \; b,l,a \; (<b,l,c,a> \epsilon \; borrow \wedge b = \text{``Perryridge''}$$
$$\wedge \; \exists \; y \; (<c,y,x> \epsilon \; customer))\}$$

Find all customers having a loan, an account, or both at the Perryridge branch:

$$\{<c> \mid \exists \; b,l,a \; (<b,l,c,a> \epsilon \; borrow \wedge b = \text{``Perryridge''})$$
$$\vee \; \exists \; b,a,n \; (<b,a,c,n> \epsilon \; deposit \wedge b = \text{``Perryridge''})\}$$

Find all customers who have an account at all branches located in Brooklyn:

$$\{<c> \mid \forall \; x,y,z \; (<x,y,z> \notin branch \vee z \neq \text{``Brooklyn''}$$
$$\vee \; (\exists \; a,n \; (<x,a,c,n> \epsilon \; deposit)))\}$$

3.3 Commercial Query Languages

The formal languages we have just seen provide a concise language for representing queries. However, database system products require a more "user-friendly" query language. In this section, we study three of these product languages: SQL, Quel, and QBE. We have chosen these languages because they represent a variety of styles. QBE is based on the domain relational calculus; Quel is based on the tuple relational calculus; and SQL uses a combination of relational algebra and relational calculus constructs. All three of these languages have been influential not only in research database systems but also in commercially marketed systems.

Although we refer to these languages as "query languages," this is actually incorrect. SQL, Quel, and QBE contain many other capabilities besides querying a database. These include features for defining the structure of the data, features for modifying data in the database, and features for specifying security constraints. We shall defer discussion of these features to subsequent chapters and sections.

Our goal is not to provide a complete users' guide for these languages. Rather, we present the fundamental constructs and concepts of these languages. Individual implementations of these languages may differ in details, or support only a subset of the full language. We discuss some of these details in Chapter 15.

3.3.1 SQL

SQL was introduced as the query language for System R. SQL is an acronym for Structured Query Language. It is still referred to frequently by its former name, Sequel.

The basic structure of an SQL expression consists of three clauses: **select**, **from**, and **where**.

- The **select** clause corresponds to the projection operation of the relational algebra. It is used to list the attributes desired in the result of a query.

- The **from** clause is a list of relations to be scanned in the execution of the expression.

- The **where** clause corresponds to the selection predicate of the relational algebra. It consists of a predicate involving attributes of the relations that appear in the **from** clause.

The different meaning of the term "select" in SQL and the relational algebra is an unfortunate historical fact. We emphasize the different interpretations here to minimize potential confusion.

A typical SQL query has the form:

$$\textbf{select } A_1, A_2, ..., A_n$$
$$\textbf{from } r_1, r_2, ..., r_m$$
$$\textbf{where } P$$

The A_is represent attributes, the r_is, represent relations, and P is a predicate. This query is equivalent to the relational algebra expression:

$$\Pi_{A_1, A_2, ..., A_n} (\sigma_P (r_1 \times r_2 \times \cdots \times r_m))$$

If the **where** clause is omitted, the predicate P is **true**. The list $A_1, A_2, ..., A_n$ of attributes may be replaced with a star (*) to select all attributes of all relations appearing in the **from** clause.

SQL forms the cartesian product of the relations named in the **from** clause, performs a relational algebra selection using the **where** clause predicate, and projects the result onto the attributes of the **select** clause. In practice, SQL may convert the expression into an equivalent form that can be processed more efficiently. However, we shall defer concerns about efficiency to Chapter 9.

The result of an SQL query is, of course, a relation. Let us consider a very simple query using our banking example, "Find the names of all branches in *deposit* relation":

> **select** *branch-name*
> **from** *deposit*

In the formal query languages, the mathematical notion of a relation being a set was used. Thus, duplicate tuples did not ever appear in relations. In practice, duplicate elimination is relatively time-consuming. Therefore, SQL (and most other commercial query languages) allow duplicates in relations. The above query will, thus, list each *branch-name* once for every tuple in which it appears in the *deposit* relation.

In those cases where we want to force the elimination of duplicates, we insert the keyword **distinct** after **select**. We can rewrite the above query as

> **select distinct** *branch-name*
> **from** *deposit*

if we want duplicates removed. We note for historical accuracy that early implementations of SQL used the keyword **unique** in place of **distinct**.

SQL includes the operations **union**, **intersect**, and **minus**, which operate on relations, and correspond directly to the relational algebra operations $\cup$, $\cap$, and $-$.

Let us see how the example queries that we considered earlier are written in SQL. First, we find all customers having an account at Perryridge branch:

> **select** *customer-name*
> **from** *deposit*
> **where** *branch-name* = "Perryridge"

Next, let us find all customers having a loan from the Perryridge branch:

> **select** *customer-name*
> **from** *borrow*
> **where** *branch-name* = "Perryridge"

To find all customers having a loan, an account, or both at Perryridge branch we write

> (**select** *customer-name*
> **from** *deposit*
> **where** *branch-name* = "Perryridge")
> **union**
> (**select** *customer-name*
> **from** *borrow*
> **where** *branch-name* = "Perryridge")

Similarly, to find all customers who have both a loan and an account at Perryridge branch, we write

> (**select** *customer-name*
> **from** *deposit*
> **where** *branch-name* = "Perryridge")
> **intersect**
> (**select** *customer-name*
> **from** *borrow*
> **where** *branch-name* = "Perryridge")

To find all customers of the Perryridge branch who have an account there but no loan there, we write

> (**select** *customer-name*
> **from** *deposit*
> **where** *branch-name* = "Perryridge")
> **minus**
> (**select** *customer-name*
> **from** *borrow*
> **where** *branch-name* = "Perryridge")

SQL does not have a direct representation of the natural-join operation. However, since the natural join is defined in terms of a cartesian product, a selection, and projection, it is a relatively simple matter to write a SQL expression for the natural join.

Recall that we wrote the relational algebra expression:

$$\Pi_{customer\text{-}name,\ customer\text{-}city}\ (borrow \bowtie customer)$$

for the query "Find all customers having a loan at some branch and their city." In SQL, we write

> **select** *customer.customer-name, customer-city*
> **from** *borrow, customer*
> **where** *borrow.customer-name = customer.customer-name*

Notice that SQL uses the notation *relation-name.attribute-name,* as did the relational algebra, to avoid ambiguity in cases where an attribute appears in the scheme of more than one relation. We could have written *customer.customer-city* instead of *customer-city* in the **select** clause. However, since the attribute *customer-city* appears in only one of the relations named in the **from** clause, there is no ambiguity when we write *customer-city.*

Let us consider a somewhat more complicated query in which we require that the customers have a loan from Perryridge branch: "Find the names of all customers having a loan at Perryridge branch and their respective city." In order to state this query, we shall need to state two constraints in the **where** clause, connected by "and."

> **select** *customer.customer-name, customer-city*
> **from** *borrow, customer*
> **where** *borrow.customer-name = customer.customer-name* **and**
>   *branch-name* = "Perryridge"

SQL uses the logical connectives "**and**," "**or**," and "**not**" rather than the mathematical symbols "∧," "∨" and "¬."

SQL draws on the relational calculus for operations that allow testing tuples for membership in a relation. To illustrate this, reconsider the query "Find all customers who have both a loan and an account at the Perryridge branch." Earlier, we took the approach of intersecting two sets: the set of account holders at Perryridge branch and the set of borrowers from Perryridge branch. We can take the alternative approach of finding all account holders at Perryridge branch who are members of the set of borrowers from Perryridge branch. Clearly, this is an equivalent approach, but it leads us to write our query using the **in** connective of SQL.

The **in** connective tests for set membership, where the set is a collection of values produced by a **select** clause. The **not in** connective tests for the absence of set membership.

Let us use **in** to write the query "Find all customers who have both a loan and account at the Perryridge branch." We begin by finding all account holders, and write the subquery:

> (**select** *customer-name*
> **from** *deposit*
> **where** *branch-name* = "Perryridge")

We then need to find those customers who are borrowers from the Perryridge branch and who appear in the list of account holders obtained in the above subquery. We do this by embedding the above subquery in an outer **select**. The resulting query is

> **select** *customer-name*
> **from** *borrow*
> **where** *branch-name* = "Perryridge" **and**
>   *customer-name* **in** (**select** *customer-name*
>   **from** *deposit*
>   **where** *branch-name* = "Perryridge")

These last two examples show that it is possible to write the same query several ways in SQL. This is beneficial since it allows a user to think about the query in the way that appears most natural. We shall see that there is a substantial amount of redundancy in SQL.

In the above example, we tested membership in a one-attribute relation. It is possible to test for membership in an arbitrary relation. SQL uses the notation $<v_1, v_2, ..., v_n>$ to denote a tuple of arity n containing values $v_1, v_2 ..., v_n$. Using this notation, we can write the query "Find all customers who have both an account and a loan at Perryridge branch" in a third way:

> **select** *customer-name*
> **from** *borrow*
> **where** *branch-name* = "Perryridge" **and**
>   *<branch-name, customer-name>* **in**
>   (**select** *branch-name, customer-name*
>   **from** *deposit*)

We now illustrate the use of the "**not in**" construct. To find all customers who have an account at the Perryridge branch but do not have a loan at Perryridge branch, we can write

> **select** *customer-name*
> **from** *deposit*
> **where** *branch-name* = "Perryridge" **and**
>   *customer-name* **not in** (**select** *customer-name*
>   **from** *borrow*
>   **where** *branch-name* = "Perryridge")

SQL borrows the notion of tuple variables from the tuple relational calculus. A tuple variable in SQL must be associated with a particular relation. Tuple variables are defined in the **from** clause. We illustrate the use of tuple variables by rewriting the query "Find all customers having a loan at some bank and their city":

> **select** *T.customer-name, customer-city*
> **from** *borrow S, customer T*
> **where** *S.customer-name* = *T.customer-name*

Note that a tuple variable is defined in the **from** clause by placing it after the name of the relation it is associated with.

Tuple variables are most useful when we need to compare two tuples in the same relation. Suppose we want to find all customers who have an account at some bank at which Jones has an account. We write this query as follows:

> **select** *T.customer-name*
> **from** *deposit S, deposit T*
> **where** *S.customer-name* = "Jones" **and**
>   *S.branch-name* = *T.branch-name*

Observe that we could not use the notation *deposit.branch-name* since it would not be clear which reference to *deposit* is intended.

We note that an alternative way to express this query is

> **select** *customer-name*
> **from** *deposit*
> **where** *branch-name* **in**
>   (**select** *branch-name*
>   **from** *deposit*
>   **where** *customer-name* = "Jones")

We were able to use the **in** construct in the above query because we were testing for equality between two branch names. Consider the query "Find all branches that have greater assets than some branch located in Brooklyn." We can write the SQL expression:

> **select** *T.branch-name*
> **from** *branch T, branch S*
> **where** *T.assets > S.assets* **and**
>   *S.branch-city* = "Brooklyn"

Since the comparison is a "greater than" comparison, we cannot write this expression using the **in** construct.

SQL does, however, offer an alternative style for writing the above query. The phrase "greater than some" is represented in SQL by > **any**. This construct allows us to rewrite the query in a form that resembles closely our formulation of the query in English.

> **select** *branch-name*
> **from** *branch*
> **where** *assets* > **any**
>   (**select** *assets*
>   **from** *branch*
>   **where** *branch-city* = "Brooklyn")

The subquery

>   (**select** *assets*
>   **from** *branch*
>   **where** *branch-city* = "Brooklyn")

generates the set of all asset values for branches in Brooklyn. The "> **any**" comparison in the where clause of the outer select is true if the *assets* value of the tuple is greater than at least one member of the set of all asset values for branches in Brooklyn.

SQL also allows "< **any**," "≤ **any**," "≥ **any**," "= **any**," and "≠ **any**" comparisons. As an exercise, verify that "= **any**" is identical to "**in**."

Now let us modify our query slightly. Let us find all branches that have greater assets than all branches in Brooklyn. We write this query using the "> **all**" construct:

> **select** *branch-name*
> **from** *branch*
> **where** *assets* > **all**
>   (**select** *assets*
>   **from** *branch*
>   **where** *branch-city* = "Brooklyn")

The constructs **in**, > **any**, > **all**, etc. allow us to test a single value against members of an entire set. Since a **select** generates a set of tuples, we may, at times, want to compare sets to determine if one set contains all the members of some other set. Such comparisons are made in SQL using the **contains** and **not contains** constructs.

Consider the query "Find all customers who have an account at all branches located in Brooklyn." For each customer, we need to see if the set of all branches at which that customer has an account contains the set of all branches in Brooklyn.

> **select** *customer-name*
> **from** *deposit S*
> **where** (**select** *branch-name*
>   **from** *deposit T*
>   **where** *S.customer-name* = *T.customer-name*)
>   **contains**
>   (**select** *branch-name*
>   **from** *branch*
>   **where** *branch-city* = "Brooklyn")

The subquery

> (**select** *branch-name*
> **from** *branch*
> **where** *branch-city* = "Brooklyn")

finds all the branches in Brooklyn. The subquery

> (**select** *branch-name*
> **from** *deposit T*
> **where** *S.customer-name* = *T.customer-name*)

finds all the branches at which customer *S.customer-name* has an account. Thus, the outer **select** takes each customer and tests whether the set of all branches at which that customer has an account contains the set of all branches in Brooklyn.

SQL offers the user some control over the order in which tuples in a relation are displayed. The **order by** clause causes the tuples in the result of a query to appear in sorted order. To list in alphabetic order all customers having a loan at Perryridge branch, we can write

> **select** *customer-name*
> **from** *borrow*
> **where** *branch-name* = "Perryridge"
> **order by** *customer-name*

In order to fulfill an **order by** request, SQL must perform a sort. Since sorting a large number of tuples may be costly, it is desirable to sort only when necessary.

SQL offers the ability to compute functions of groups of tuples using the **group by** clause. The attribute given in the **group by** clause is used to form groups. Tuples with the same value on this attribute are placed in one group. SQL includes functions to compute:

- average: **avg**

- minimum: **min**

- maximum: **max**

- total: **sum**

- count: **count**

To find the average account balance at all branches, we write

> **select** *branch-name*, **avg** (*balance*)
> **from** *deposit*
> **group by** *branch-name*

Operations like **avg** are called *aggregate operations* because they operate on aggregates of tuples.

At times it is useful to state a condition that applies to groups rather than to tuples. For example, we might be interested only in branches where the average account balance is more than \$1,200. To express such a query, we use the **having** clause of SQL. Predicates in the **having** clause are applied after the formation of groups, so aggregate operators may be used in the **having** clause. We express this query in SQL by

> **select** *branch-name*, **avg** (*balance*)
> **from** *deposit*
> **group by** *branch-name*
> **having avg** (*balance*) > 1200.

The aggregate operator **count** is used frequently to count the number of tuples in a relation. The notation used for this in SQL is **count** (*). Thus, to find the number of tuples in the *customer* relation, we write

> **select count** (*)
> **from** *customer*.

Counting can be used to check for negative information. Suppose we wish to find all customers who have a deposit at the Perryridge branch, but for whom no address is on file. Our approach is to count the number of *customer* tuples pertaining to each depositor of the Perryridge branch. If the count is 0 for a depositor, we know we have no address for that person.

>   **select** *customer-name*
>   **from** *deposit*
>   **where** *branch-name* = "Perryridge"
>   **and** 0 =
>   **select count** (*)
>   **from** *customer*
>   **where** *deposit.customer-name* = *customer.customer-name*

As an alternative, SQL includes a special construct for the application of **count** used in the above example. The predicate **exists** takes a select statement as its argument and returns true unless the select results in an empty relation. We rewrite the example as follows:

>   **select** *customer-name*
>   **from** *deposit*
>   **where** *branch-name* = "Perryridge"
>   **and** not **exists**
>   **select** *
>   **from** *customer*
>   **where** *deposit.customer-name* = *customer.customer-name*

SQL is as powerful in expressiveness as the relational algebra (which, as we said earlier, is equivalent in power to the relational calculus). SQL includes the five basic relational algebra operators. Cartesian product is represented by the **from** clause of SQL. Projection is performed in the **select** clause. Algebra selection predicates are represented in SQL's **where** clause. Set union and difference appear in both the relational algebra and SQL. SQL allows intermediate results to be stored in temporary relations; thus we may encode any relational algebra expression in SQL.

SQL offers features that do not appear in the relational algebra. Most notable among these features are the aggregate operators. Thus, SQL is strictly more powerful than the algebra.

In this section, we have seen that SQL offers a rich collection of features, including capabilities not included in the formal query languages: aggregate operations, ordering of tuples, etc. Many SQL implementations allow SQL queries to be submitted from a program written in a general purpose language such as Pascal, PL/1, Fortran, C, or Cobol. This extends the programmer's ability to manipulate the database even further. We show how PL/1 and SQL are combined in an actual system in Chapter 15.

3.3.2 Quel

Quel was introduced as the query language for the Ingres database system. The basic structure of the language closely parallels that of the tuple relational calculus. Most Quel queries are expressed using three types of clauses: **range of, retrieve,** and **where**.

- Each tuple variable is declared in a **range of** clause. We say **range of** t **is** r to declare t to be a tuple variable restricted to take on values of tuples in r.

- The **retrieve** clause is similar in function to the **select** clause of SQL.

- The **where** clause contains the selection predicate.

A typical Quel query is of the form:

> **range of** t_1 **is** r_1
> **range of** t_2 **is** r_2
> **range of** t_m **is** r_m
> **retrieve** $(t_{i_1}.A_{j_1}, t_{i_2}.A_{j_2}, ..., t_{i_n}.A_{j_n})$
> **where** P

The t_i, are the tuple variables. The r_i, are relations, and the A_{j_k}, are attributes. Quel uses the notation

$$t.A$$

to denote the value of tuple variable t on attribute A. This means the same as $t[A]$ in the tuple relational calculus.

Quel does not include relational algebra operations like **intersect, union,** or **minus**. Furthermore, Quel does not allow nested subqueries (unlike SQL). That is, we *cannot* have a nested **retrieve-where** clause inside a **where** clause.

Let us return to our bank example, and write some of our earlier queries using Quel. First, we find all customers having an account at Perryridge branch:

> **range of** t **is** *deposit*
> **retrieve** (t.*customer-name*)
> **where** t.*branch-name* = "Perryridge"

To show a Quel query involving more than one relation, let us consider the query "Find all customers having a loan at Perryridge branch and their city."

> **range of** *t* **is** *borrow*
> **range of** *s* **is** *customer*
> **retrieve** (*t.customer-name, s.customer-city*)
> **where** *t.branch-name* = "Perryridge" **and**
>   *t.customer-name* = *s.customer-name*

Note that Quel, like SQL, uses the logical connectives **and**, **or**, and **not**, rather than the mathematical symbols "∧," "∨," and "¬" as used in the tuple relational calculus.

As another example of a query involving two relations, consider the query "Find all customers who have both a loan and an account at the Perryridge branch."

> **range of** *s* **is** *borrow*
> **range of** *t* **is** *deposit*
> **retrieve** (*s.customer-name*)
> **where** *t.branch-name* = "Perryridge" **and** *s.branch-name* = "Perryridge"
>   **and** *t.customer-name* = *s.customer-name*

In SQL, we had the option of writing a query such as the above one using the relational algebra operation **intersect**. As we noted above, Quel does not include this operation.

Let us consider a query for which we used the **union** operation in SQL: "Find all customers who have an account, a loan, or both at Perryridge branch." Since we do not have a **union** operation in Quel, and we know that Quel is based on the tuple relational calculus, we might be guided by our tuple relational calculus expression for this query:

$$\{t \mid \exists \, s \, (s \in borrow \land t[customer\text{-}name] = s[customer\text{-}name]$$
$$\land \, s[branch\text{-}name] = \text{``Perryridge''})$$
$$\lor \exists \, u \, (u \in deposit \land t[customer\text{-}name] = u[customer\text{-}name]$$
$$\land \, u[branch\text{-}name] = \text{``Perryridge''})\}$$

Unfortunately, the above expression does not lead us to a Quel query. The problem is that in the tuple relational calculus query, we obtain customers from *both* tuple variable *s* (whose range is *borrow*) and tuple variable *u* (whose range is *deposit*). In Quel, our **retrieve** clause must be either

> **retrieve** *s.customer-name*
> or   **retrieve** *u.customer-name*

If we choose the former, we exclude those depositors who are not borrowers. If we choose the latter, we exclude those borrowers who are not depositors.

In order to write this query in Quel, we must create a new relation and insert tuples into this new relation. Let us call this new relation *temp*. We obtain all depositors of Perryridge branch by writing

>**range of** *u* **is** *deposit*
>**retrieve into** *temp* (*u.customer-name*)
>**where** *u.branch-name* = "Perryridge"

The **into** *temp* clause causes a new relation, *temp*, to be created to hold the result of this query. Now we can find all borrowers of Perryridge branch and insert them in the newly created relation *temp*. We do this using the **append** command.

>**range of** *s* **is** *borrow*
>**append to** *temp* (*s.customer-name*)
>**where** *s.branch-name* = "Perryridge"

The **append** command operates similarly to the **retrieve** command except that the tuples retrieved are added to the relation appearing after the keyword **to**.

We now have a relation *temp* containing all customers who have an account, a loan, or both, at Perryridge branch. This relation may, of course, have the same customer appearing more than once. Quel, like SQL, eliminates duplicates only if specifically requested to do so. If we write

>**range of** *t* **is** *temp*
>**retrieve unique** (*t.customer-name*)

Quel sorts *temp* and eliminates duplicates.

The strategy of using **append** allows us to perform unions in Quel. To perform a set difference *r* − *s* (**minus** in SQL), we create a temporary relation representing *r* and delete tuples of this temporary relation that are also in *s*. To find all customers who have an account at the Perryridge branch but do not have a loan from the Perryridge branch, we write the following

>**range of** *u* **is** *deposit*
>**retrieve into** *temp* (*u.customer-name*)
>**where** *u.branch-name* = "Perryridge"

At this point *temp* has all customers who have an account at the Perryridge branch, including those with a loan from that branch. We now delete those customers who have a loan.

>   **range of** s **is** *borrow*
>   **range of** t **is** *temp*
>   **delete** (t)
>   **where** s.*branch-name* = "Perryridge" **and**
>   t.*customer-name* = s.*customer-name*

The relation *temp* contains the desired list of customers. We write

>   **range of** t **is** *temp*
>   **retrieve** (t.*customer-name*)

to complete our query.

Fortunately, there is a more natural way to express this query in Quel. First, however, we must introduce the Quel aggregate expressions, which take the form

$$\text{<aggregate-operation>} \ (t.A \ \textbf{where} \ P)$$

where <aggregate-operation> is one of **count**, **sum**, **avg**, **max**, **min**, or **any**, t is a tuple variable, A is an attribute, and P is a predicate similar to the **where** clause in a **retrieve**. An aggregate expression may appear anywhere a constant may appear.

Thus, to find the average account balance for all accounts at the Perryridge branch, we write

>   **range of** t **is** *deposit*
>   **retrieve avg** (*balance* **where** *branch-name* = "Perryridge")

Aggregates may appear in the **where** clause. Suppose we wish to find all accounts whose balance is higher than the average balance at the branch where the account is held. We write:

>   **range of** u **is** *deposit*
>   **range of** t **is** *deposit*
>   **retrieve** t.*account-number*
>   **where** t.*balance* > **avg** (u.*balance* **where**
>   u.*branch-name* = t.*branch-name*)

The above **avg** (...) expression computes the average balance of all accounts at the branch represented by t. Because expressions of this sort are frequent, Quel allows the syntax:

>   **range of** t **is** *deposit*
>   **retrieve** t.*account-number*
>   **where** t.*balance* > **avg** (t.*balance* **by** t.*branch-name*)

The **avg** (...) expression performs the same computation as above. For a given t, the average balance is computed of the set of all tuples having the same value on the *branch-name* attribute as *t.branch-name*.

Let us return to the query "Find all customers who have an account at the Perryridge branch but do not have a loan from the Perryridge branch." We can write this query using the **count** aggregate operation if we think of the query as "Find all customers who have an account at the Perryridge branch and for whom the count of the number of loans from the Perryridge branch is zero."

> **range of** t **is** *deposit*
> **range of** u **is** *borrow*
> **retrieve** *t.customer-name*
> **where** *t.branch-name* = "Perryridge" **and**
>   **count** (*u.loan-number* **where** *u.branch-name* = "Perryridge"
>   **and** *u.customer-name* = *t.customer-name*) = 0

This is a more natural way to express this query than our earlier example.

Quel offers another aggregate operation that is applicable to this example, called **any**. If we replace **count** in the above query with **any**, we obtain 1 if the count is greater than 0; otherwise we obtain 0. The advantage in using **any** is that processing can stop as soon as one tuple is found. This allows faster execution of the query.

As a more complicated example, consider the query "Find all customers who have an account at all branches located in Brooklyn." Our strategy for expressing this query in Quel is as follows: First find out how many branches there are in Brooklyn. Then compare this number with the number of distinct branches in Brooklyn at which each customer has an account. The **count** aggregate operation we used earlier counts duplicates. Therefore, we use the **countu** operation, which counts unique values.

> **range of** t **is** *deposit*
> **range of** u **is** *branch*
> **range of** s **is** *branch*
> **retrieve** *t.customer-name*
> **where countu** (*s.branch-name* **where** *s.branch-city* = "Brooklyn"
>   **and** *s.branch-name* = *t.branch-name*) =
>   **countu** (*u.branch-name* **where** *u.branch-city* = "Brooklyn")

We have observed that Quel is related closely to the tuple relational calculus. The **range of** clause corresponds to the "there exists." However, there is no analog in Quel to "for all." That is why we needed to use insertion and deletion to state in Quel some of the queries that we could write in the tuple relational calculus. To see more clearly the relationship between Quel and the tuple relational calculus, consider the following Quel query

> **range of** t_1 **is** r_1
> **range of** t_2 **is** r_2
> **range of** t_m **is** r_m
> **retrieve** $(t_{i_1}.A_{j_1}, t_{i_2}.A_{j_2}, ..., t_{i_n}.A_{j_n})$
> **where** P

The above Quel query would be expressed in the tuple relational calculus as:

$$\{t \mid \exists \, t_1, t_2, ..., t_m \, (t_1 \in r_1 \wedge t_2 \in r_2 \wedge t_m \in r_m \, \wedge$$
$$t[r_{i_1}.A_{j_1}] = t_{i_1}[A_{j_1}] \wedge t[r_{i_1}.A_{j_1}] = t_{i_2}[A_{j_2}] \wedge ... \wedge$$
$$t[r_{i_n}.A_{j_n}] = t_{i_n}[A_{j_n}] \wedge P \, (t_1, t_2, ..., t_m))\}$$

This expression can be understood by looking at the formula within the "there exists" formula in three parts:

- $t_1 \in r_1 \wedge t_2 \in r_2 \wedge ... \wedge t_m \in r_m$. This part constrains each tuple in $t_1, t_2, ..., t_m$ to take on values of tuples in the relation it ranges over.

- $t[r_{i_1}.A_{j_1}] = t_{i_1}[A_{j_1}] \wedge t_{i_2}[A_{j_2}] = t[r_{i_2}.A_{j_2}] \wedge ... \wedge t[r_{i_n}.A_{j_n}] = t_{i_n}[A_{j_n}]$. This part corresponds to the **retrieve** clause of the Quel query. We need to ensure that the kth attribute in tuple t corresponds to the kth entry in the **retrieve** clause. Consider the first entry: $t_{i_1}.A_{j_1}$. This is the value of some tuple of r_{i_1} (since range of t_{i_1} is r_{i_1}) on attribute A_{j_1}. Thus, we need $t[A_{j_1}] = t_{i_1}[A_{j_1}]$. We used the more cumbersome notation $t[r_{i_1}.A_{j_1}] = t_{i_1}[A_{j_1}]$ to be able to deal with the possibility that the same attribute name appears in more than one relation.

- $P(t_1, t_2, ..., t_m)$. This part is the constraint on acceptable values for $t_1, t_2, ..., t_m$ imposed by the **where** clause in the Quel query.

3.3.3 Query-by-Example

Query-by-Example (QBE) is the name of both a query language and the database system which includes this language. There are two distinctive features of QBE. Unlike most query languages and programming languages, QBE has a *two-dimensional* syntax. A query in a one-dimensional

branch	branch-name	assets	branch-city

customer	customer-name	street	customer-city

borrow	branch-name	loan-number	customer-name	amount

deposit	branch-name	account-number	customer-name	balance

Figure 3.13   QBE skeleton tables for the bank example.

language (for example, SQL or Quel) *can* be written in one (possibly very long) line. A two-dimensional language *requires* two dimensions for its expression. (There does exist a one-dimensional version of QBE. We shall not consider this version in our discussion of QBE.) The second distinctive feature of QBE is that queries are expressed *"by example."* Instead of giving a procedure for obtaining the desired answer, the user gives an example of what is desired. The system generalizes this example to compute the answer to the query. Despite these unusual features, there is a close correspondence between QBE and the domain relational calculus.

Queries in QBE are expressed using *skeleton tables*. These tables show the relation scheme, and appear as in Figure 3.13. Rather than clutter the display with all skeletons, the user selects those skeletons needed for a given query. The user fills in these skeletons with "*example rows.*" An example row consists of constants and "*example elements.*" An example element is really a domain variable. To distinguish domain variables from constants, domain variables are preceded by an underscore character (" _ ") as in _ x. Constants appear without any qualification. This is in contrast to most other languages in which constants are quoted and variables appear without any qualification.

To find all customers having an account at the Perryridge branch, we bring up the skeleton for the *deposit* relation and fill it in as follows:

deposit	branch-name	account-number	customer-name	balance
	Perryridge		P. _ x	

The above query causes the system to look for tuples in *deposit* that have "Perryridge" as the value for the *branch-name* attribute. For each such tuple, the value of the *customer-name* attribute is assigned to the variable x. The value of the variable x is "printed" (actually displayed) because the command "P." appears in the *customer-name* column next to the variable x.

Unlike Quel and SQL, QBE performs duplicate elimination automatically. To suppress duplicate elimination, the command "ALL." is inserted after the "P." command.

deposit	branch-name	account-number	customer-name	balance
	Perryridge		P.ALL. _ x	

The primary purpose of variables in QBE is to force values of certain tuples to have the same value on certain attributes. Suppose we wish to find all customers having a loan from the Perryridge branch, and their cities. We write:

borrow	branch-name	loan-number	customer-name	amount
	Perryridge		_ x	

customer	customer-name	street	customer-city
	P. _ x		P. _ y

To execute the above query, the system finds tuples in *borrow* with "Perryridge" as the value for the *branch-name* attribute. For each such tuple, the system finds tuples in *customer* with the same value for the *customer-name* attribute as the *borrow* tuple. The values for the *customer-name* and *customer-city* attributes are displayed. Observe that this is similar to what would be done to answer the domain relational calculus query:

$$\{<x,y> \mid \exists\, s\, (<x,s,y> \in customer)\}$$

A technique similar to the one above can be used to write the query "Find all customers who have both an account and a loan at the Perryridge branch":

deposit	branch-name	account-number	customer-name	balance
	Perryridge		P. _ x	

borrow	branch-name	loan-number	customer-name	amount
	Perryridge		_ x	

Suppose our query involves a less than or greater than comparison, rather than an equality comparison, as in "Find all account numbers with a balance of more than $1200":

deposit	branch-name	account-number	customer-name	balance
		P. _ x		>1200

Until now, all the conditions we have imposed were connected by "*and*." To express an "*or*" in QBE, we give a separate example row for the two conditions being "*or*"-ed, using distinct domain variables. Consider the query "Find all customers having an account at the Perryridge branch, the Redwood branch, or both":

deposit	branch-name	account-number	customer-name	balance
	Perryridge		P. _ x	
	Redwood		P. _ y	

Contrast the above query with "Find all customers having an account at *both* the Perryridge branch and the Redwood branch":

deposit	branch-name	account-number	customer-name	balance
	Perryridge		P. _ x	
	Redwood		_ x	

The critical distinction between these two queries is the use of the same domain variable (x) for both rows in the latter query, while, in the former query, we used distinct domain variables (x and y). To illustrate this, note that in the domain relational calculus, the former query would be written as

$$\{<x> \mid \exists\, b,a,n\, (<b,a,x,n> \in deposit \wedge b = \text{``Perryridge''})$$
$$\vee\, \exists\, b,a,n\, (<b,a,x,n> \in deposit \wedge b = \text{``Redwood''})\}$$

while the latter query would be written as

$$\{<x> \mid \exists\, b,a,n\, (<b,a,x,n> \in deposit \wedge b = \text{``Perryridge''})$$
$$\wedge\, \exists\, b,a,n\, (<b,a,x,n> \in deposit \wedge b = \text{``Redwood''})\}$$

Queries that involve negation are expressed in QBE by placing a not sign ($\neg$) in a table skeleton under the relation name and next to an example row.

Let us now consider the query "Find all customers who have an account at the Perryridge branch but do not have a loan from that branch":

deposit	branch-name	account-number	customer-name	balance
	Perryridge		P. _ x	

borrow	branch-name	loan-number	customer-name	amount
$\neg$	Perryridge		_ x	

Compare the above query with our earlier query "Find all customers who have both an account and a loan at the Perryridge branch." The only difference is the "$\neg$" appearing next to the example row in the borrow skeleton. This difference, however, has a major effect on the processing of the query. QBE finds all x values for which

1. There is a tuple in the *deposit* relation in which *branch-name* is "Perryridge" and *customer-name* is the domain variable x.

2. There is no tuple in the *borrow* relation in which *branch-name* is "Perryridge" and *customer-name* is the same as in the domain variable x.

The "$\neg$" can be read as "there does not exist."

The fact that we placed the "$\neg$" under the relation name rather than under an attribute name is important. Use of a "$\neg$" under an attribute name is a shorthand for "$\neq$." To find all customers who have accounts at two different branches, we write

deposit	branch-name	account-number	customer-name	balance
	_ y		P. _ x	
	$\neg$ _ y		_ x	

In English, the above query reads "display all *customer-name* values that appear in at least two tuples, with the second tuple having a *branch-name* different from the first."

It is inconvenient at times to express all the constraints on the domain variables within the table skeletons. QBE includes a *condition box* feature that allows the expression of such constraints. Suppose we modify the above query to "Find all customers not named "Jones" who have accounts at two different branches." We want to include an "$x \neq$ Jones" constraint in the above query. We do that by bringing up the condition box and entering the constraint "$x \neq$ Jones":

conditions
$x \neq$ Jones

QBE includes aggregate operations similar to those of SQL and Quel. To find the average balance at all branches, we may write:

deposit	branch-name	account-number	customer-name	balance
	P.G			P.**avg**.ALL

Besides **avg**, the aggregate operators **max**, **min**, **count**, and **sum** are included in QBE. The "G" in the "P.G" entry in the *branch-name* column is analogous to SQL's "**group by** *branch-name*" construct. The average balance is computed on a branch-by-branch basis. The "ALL" in the "P.**avg**.ALL" entry in the balance column ensures that all balances are considered (recall that QBE eliminates duplicates by default).

3.4 Modifying the Database

We have restricted our attention until now to the extraction of information from the database. We have not, however, shown how to add new information, remove information, or change information. While we did do some **insert** and **delete** operations in our Quel examples, we never altered the database. Instead, we dealt with temporary relations constructed for the sole purpose of helping us to express the query.

The formal query languages (the relational algebra and the relational calculi) do not include any provision for modifying the database. All commercial languages do include such features, but we shall restrict our attention to examples in SQL.

3.4.1 Deletion

Deletion of tuples from a relation is simple. A delete request is expressed in much the same way as a query. However, instead of displaying tuples to the user, the selected tuples are removed from the database. We may delete only whole tuples; we cannot delete values on only particular attributes. In SQL, a deletion is expressed by

delete *r*
where *P*

P represents a predicate and *r* represents a relation. Those tuples *t* in *r* for which *P* (*t*) is true are deleted from *r*.

We note that a **delete** command operates on only one relation. If we want to delete tuples from several relations, we must use one **delete** command for each relation. The predicate in the **where** clause may be as complex as a **select** command's **where** clause. At the other extreme, we can have an empty **where** clause. The request:

delete *borrow*

deletes all tuples from the borrow relation. (Well-designed systems will seek confirmation from the user before executing such a devastating request.)

We give some examples of SQL delete requests:

- Delete all of Smith's account records.

delete *deposit*
where *customer-name* = "Smith"

- Delete all loans with loan numbers between 1300 and 1500.

delete *borrow*
where *loan-number* > 1300 **and** *loan-number* < 1500

- Delete all accounts at branches located in Needham

delete *deposit*
where *branch-name* **in** (**select** *branch-name*
           from *branch*
           where *branch-city* = "Needham")

The above **delete** request first finds all branches in Needham, and then deletes all *deposit* tuples pertaining to those branches.

Note that although we may delete tuples from only one relation at a time, we may reference any number of relations in a **select-from-where** embedded in the **where** clause of a **delete**.

If the **delete** request contains an embedded **select** that references the relation from which tuples are to be deleted, we face potential anomalies. Suppose we want to delete the records of all accounts with balances below the average. We might write

> **delete** *deposit*
> **where** *balance* < (**select avg** (*balance*)
>   **from** *deposit*)

However, as we delete tuples from deposit, the average balance changes! If we reevaluate the **select** for each tuple in deposit, the final result will depend upon the order in which we process tuples of *deposit*!

Such ambiguities are avoided by the following simple rule: During the execution of a **delete** request, we only mark tuples to be deleted; we do not actually delete them. Once we have finished processing the request, that is, once we are done marking tuples, then we delete all marked tuples. This rule guarantees a consistent interpretation of deletion. Thus, our delete request above does, in fact, work the way we would hope and expect. (Some implementations of SQL simply disallow delete requests like the above one.)

3.4.2 Insertion

To insert data into a relation, we either specify a tuple to be inserted or write a query whose result is a set of tuples to be inserted. Obviously, the attribute values for inserted tuples must be members of the attribute's domain. Similarly, tuples inserted must be of the correct arity.

The simplest **insert** is a request to insert one tuple. Suppose we wish to insert the fact that Smith has $1200 in account 9732 at the Needham branch. We write

> **insert into** *deposit*
>   **values** ("Needham", 9732, "Smith", 1200)

More generally, we might want to insert tuples based on the result of a query. Suppose that we want to provide all loan customers in the Needham branch with a $200 savings account. Let the loan number serve as the account number for the new savings account. We write

> **insert into** *deposit*
>   **select** *branch-name*, *loan-number*, *customer-name*, 200
>   **from** *borrow*
>   **where** *branch-name* = "Needham"

Instead of specifying a tuple as we did earlier, we use a **select** to specify a set of tuples. Each tuple has the *branch-name* (Needham), a *loan-number* (which serves as the account number for the new account), the name of the loan customer who is being given the new account, and the initial balance of the new account, $200.

3.4.3 Updating

There are situations in which we wish to change a value in a tuple without changing *all* values in the tuple. If we make these changes using **delete** and **insert**, we may not be able to retain those values that we do not wish to change. Instead, we use the **update** statement. As was the case for **insert** and **delete**, we may choose the tuples to be updated using a query.

Suppose interest payments are being made, and all balances are to be increased by 5 percent. We write

> **update** *deposit*
> **set** *balance* = *balance* * 1.05

The above statement is applied once to each tuple in *borrow*.

Let us now suppose that accounts with balances over $10,000 receive 6 percent interest, while all others receive 5 percent. We write two **update** statements:

> **update** *deposit*
> **set** *balance* = *balance* * 1.06
> **where** *balance* > 10000

> **update** *deposit*
> **set** *balance* = *balance* * 1.05
> **where** *balance* ≤ 10000

In general, the **where** clause of the **update** statement may contain any construct legal in the **where** clause of the **select** statement (including nested **select**s). Note that in the above example the order in which we wrote the two **update** statements is important. If we changed the order of the two statements, an account whose balance is just under $10,000 would receive 11.3 percent interest!

3.5 Views

In our examples up to this point, we have operated at the conceptual model level. That is, we have assumed that the collection of relations we are given are the actual relations stored in the database.

It is not desirable for all users to see the entire conceptual model. Security considerations may require that we "hide" certain data from certain users. Consider, for example, a clerk who needs to know a customer's loan number but has no need to see the loan amount. This clerk should see a relation described, in the relational algebra, by

$$\Pi_{branch\text{-}name,\ loan\text{-}number,\ customer\text{-}name}\ (borrow)$$

Aside from security concerns, we may wish to create a personalized collection of relations that is better matched to a certain user's intuition than is the conceptual model. An employee in the advertising department, for example, might like to see a relation consisting of the customers of each branch; that is, for each branch we would like to list those people who have either an account or a loan at that branch. The relation we would like to create for the employee is

$$\Pi_{branch\text{-}name,\ customer\text{-}name}\ (deposit)$$
$$\cup\ \Pi_{branch\text{-}name,\ customer\text{-}name}\ (borrow)$$

We use the term *view* to refer to any relation not part of the conceptual model that is made visible to a user as a "virtual relation." It is possible to support a large number of views on top of any given set of actual relations.

Since the actual relations in the conceptual model may be modified by **insert**, **update**, or **delete** operations, it is not generally possible to store views. Instead, a view must be recomputed for each query that refers to it. In Chapter 9 we shall consider techniques for reducing the overhead of this recomputation. For now, we restrict our attention to the definition and use of views in SQL.

A view is defined in SQL using the **create view** command. To define a view, we must give the view a name and state the query that computes the view. The form of the **create view** command is

create view *v* **as** <query expression>

where <query expression> is any legal query expression. The view name is represented by *v*.

As an example, consider the view consisting of branches and their customers. Assume we wish this view to be called *all-customer*. We define this view as follows:

create view *all-customer* **as**
    (**select** *branch-name, customer-name*
    from *deposit*)
  union
    (**select** *branch-name, customer-name*
    from *borrow*)

Once we have defined a view, the view name can be used to refer to the virtual relation the view generates. View names may appear in any place that a relation name may appear. Using the view *all-customer*, we can find all customers of the Perryridge branch by writing

> **select** *customer-name*
> **from** *all-customer*
> **where** *branch-name* = "Perryridge"

Recall that we wrote the same query in Section 3.3 without using views.

Although views are a useful tool for queries, they present significant problems if updates, insertions, or deletions are expressed using views. The difficulty is that a modification to the database expressed in terms of a view must be translated to a modification to the actual relations in the conceptual model of the database. We illustrate the problem of database modification through views with a simple example.

Consider the clerk we discussed earlier who needs to see all loan data in the *borrow* relation except *loan-amount*. Let *loan-info* be the view given to the clerk. We define this view as

> **create view** *loan-info* **as**
>   **select** *branch-name, loan-number, customer-name*
>   **from** *borrow*

Since SQL allows a view name to appear wherever a relation name is allowed, the clerk may write

> **insert into** *loan-info*
>   **values** ("Perryridge", 3, "Ruth")

This insertion must be represented by an insertion into the relation *borrow*, since *borrow* is the actual relation from which the view *loan-info* is constructed. However, to insert a tuple into *borrow*, we must have some value for *amount*. There are two reasonable approaches to dealing with this insertion:

- Reject the insertion and return an error message to the user.
- Insert a tuple ("Perryridge", 3, "Ruth", *null*) into the *borrow* relation.

The symbol *null* represents a *null-value*, or *place-holder value*. It signifies that the value is unknown or does not exist.

Most systems take the latter approach and create null values. However, the presence of null values adds complexity to database queries.

Assume we have inserted the above tuple, producing the relation shown in Figure 3.14. Consider the following query to total all loan balances:

> **select sum** (*balance*)
> **from** *borrow*

It is not possible to perform addition using *null*. Similar problems arise using other aggregate operators. As a result, all aggregate operations except *count* ignore tuples with null values on the argument attributes.

All comparisons involving *null* are **false** by definition. However, a special keyword, **null** may be used in a predicate to test for a null value. To find all customers who appear in the *borrow* relation with null values for *balance*, we write

> **select** *customer-name*
> **from** *borrow*
> **where** *balance* **is null**

The predicate **is not null** tests for the absence of a null value.

We illustrate another problem resulting from modification of the database through views with an example involving the following view:

> **create view** *branch-city* **as**
>   **select** *branch-name, customer-city*
>   **from** *borrow, customer*
>   **where** *borrow.customer-name = customer.customer-name*

branch-name	loan-number	customer-name	amount
Downtown	17	Jones	1000
Redwood	23	Smith	2000
Perryridge	15	Hayes	1500
Downtown	14	Jackson	1500
Mianus	93	Curry	500
Round Hill	11	Turner	900
Pownal	29	Williams	1200
North Town	16	Adams	1300
Downtown	18	Johnson	2000
Perryridge	25	Glenn	2500
Brighton	10	Brooks	2200
Perryridge	3	Ruth	*null*

Figure 3.14   A *borrow* relation containing null values.

This view lists the cities in which borrowers of each branch live. Consider the following insertion through this view:

insert into *branch-city*
values ("Brighton", "Woodside")

The only possible method of inserting tuples into the *borrow* and *customer* relations is to insert ("Brighton", *null, null, null*) into *borrow* and (*null, null,* "Woodside") into *customer*. Suppose the system did that. Then we obtain the relations shown in Figure 3.15. This turns out to be unsatisfactory since

select *
from *branch-city*

does *not* include the tuple ("Brighton", "Woodside"). To see why this is so, recall that all comparisons involving **null** are defined to be **false**. Thus, the **where** clause in the view definition (*borrow.customer-name* = *customer.customer-name*) is never satisfied for the tuples added to the *borrow* and *customer* relations.

As a result of the anomaly we have just discussed, many database systems impose the following constraint on modifications allowed through views:

- A modification is permitted through a view only if the view in question is defined in terms of one relation of the actual relational database.

Under this constraint, **update**, **insert**, and **delete** operations would be forbidden on the example views *branch-city*, *loan-info*, and *all-customer* that we defined above.

The general problem of database modification through views is a subject of current research. The bibliographic notes mention recent works on this subject.

Another view-related research area of interest is the *universal relation* model. In this model, the user is given a view consisting of one relation. This one relation is the natural join of all relations in the actual relational database. The major advantage of this model is that users need not be concerned with remembering what attributes are in which relation. Thus, most queries are easier to formulate in a universal-relation database system than in a standard relational database system. For example, a universal-relation version of SQL would not need a **from** clause.

There remain unresolved questions regarding modifications to universal relation databases. Furthermore, a consensus has not yet developed on the best definition of the meaning of certain complex types of universal-relation queries.

branch-name	loan-number	customer-name	amount
Downtown	17	Jones	1000
Redwood	23	Smith	2000
Perryridge	15	Hayes	1500
Downtown	14	Jackson	1500
Mianus	93	Curry	500
Round Hill	11	Turner	900
Pownal	29	Williams	1200
North Town	16	Adams	1300
Downtown	18	Johnson	2000
Perryridge	25	Glenn	2500
Brighton	10	Brooks	2200
Brighton	null	null	null

customer-name	street	customer-city
Jones	Main	Harrison
Smith	North	Rye
Hayes	Main	Harrison
Curry	North	Rye
Lindsay	Park	Pittsfield
Turner	Putnam	Stamford
Williams	Nassau	Princeton
Adams	Spring	Pittsfield
Johnson	Alma	Palo Alto
Glenn	Sand Hill	Woodside
Brooks	Senator	Brooklyn
Green	Walnut	Stamford
null	null	Woodside

Figure 3.15 Tuples inserted into *borrow* and *customer*.

We can summarize our discussion of views briefly as follows. Views are a useful mechanism for simplifying database queries, but modification of the database through views has potentially disadvantageous consequences. A strong case can be made for requiring all database modifications to refer to actual relations in the database.

3.6 Summary

The relational data model is based on a collection of tables. The user of the database system may query these tables, insert new tuples, delete tuples, and update (modify) tuples. There are several languages for expressing these operations. The tuple relational calculus and the domain relational calculus are nonprocedural languages that represent the basic power required in a relational query language. The relational algebra in a procedural language that is equivalent in power to both forms of the relational calculus. The algebra defines the basic operations used within relational query languages.

The relational algebra and the relational calculi are terse, formal languages that are inappropriate for casual users of a database system. Commercial database system have, therefore, used languages with more "syntactic sugar." These languages include constructs for update, insertion, and deletion of information as well for querying the database. We have considered the three most influential of the commercial languages: SQL, Quel, and QBE.

Different users of a shared database may benefit from individualized views of the database. We used SQL as an example to show how such views can be defined and used.

Exercises

3.1 Design a relational database for a university registrar's office. The office maintains data about each class, including the instructor, the enrollment, and the time and place of the class meetings. For each student-class pair, a grade is recorded.

3.2 Describe the differences between the terms *relation* and *relation scheme*. Illustrate your answer be referring to your solution to Exercise 3.1.

3.3 Design a relational database corresponding to the E-R diagram of Figure 3.16.

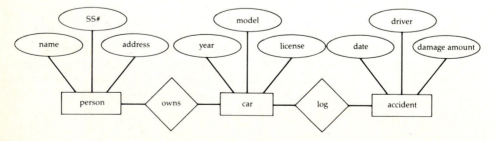

Figure 3.16   E-R diagram.

3.4 Construct the following SQL queries for the relational database of Exercise 3.3.

    a. Find the total number of users that have had an accident in 1983.

    b. Find the number of accidents the cars belonging to "John Smith" were involved in during the term of the policy.

    c. Add a new customer to the database.

    d. Delete the car "Mazda" belonging to "John Smith."

    e. Add a new accident record for the Toyota belonging to "Jones."

3.5 Consider the relational database of Figure 3.17. Give an expression in:

- The relational algebra
- The tuple relational calculus
- The domain relational calculus
- SQL
- Quel
- QBE

for each of the queries below:

    a. Find the name of all people who work for First Bank Corporation.

    b. Find the name and city of all people who work for First Bank Corporation.

    c. Find the name, street, and city of all people who work for First Bank Corporation and earn more than $10,000.

> *lives (person-name, street, city)*
> *works (person-name, company-name, salary)*
> *located-in (company-name, city)*
> *manages (person-name, manager-name)*

Figure 3.17   Relational database.

d. Find all people who live in the same city as the company they work for.

e. Find all people who live in the same city and on the same street as their manager.

f. Find all people who do not work for First Bank Corporation.

g. Find all people who earn more than every employee of Small Bank Corporation.

h. Assume the companies may be located in several cities. Find all companies located in every city in which Small Bank Corporation is located.

3.6 Consider the relational database of Figure 3.17. Give an expression in:

- SQL
- Quel
- QBE

for each of the queries below:

a. Find all people who earn more than the average salary of people working in their company.

b. Find the company employing the most people.

c. Find the company with the smallest payroll.

d. Find those companies that pay more, on average, than the average salary at First Bank Corporation.

3.7 Consider the relational database of Figure 3.17. Give an expression in SQL for each query below:

a. Modify the database so that Jones now lives in Newtown.

b. Give all employees of First Bank Corporation a 10 percent raise.

c. Give all managers a 10 percent raise.

d. Give all managers a 10 percent raise unless the salary becomes greater than $10,0000. In such cases, give only a 3 percent raise.

e. Delete all tuples in the *works* relation for employees of Small Bank Corporation.

3.8 In Chapter 2, we showed how to represent many-to-many, many-to-one, one-to-many, and one-to-one relationship sets. Explain how primary keys help us to represent such relationship sets in the relational model.

3.9 Let the following relation schemes be given:

$$R = (A,B,C)$$
$$S = (D,E,F)$$

Let relations $r(R)$ and $s(S)$ be given. Give an expression in the tuple relational calculus that is equivalent to each of the following:

a. $\Pi_A(r)$

b. $\sigma_{B = 17}(r)$

c. $r \times s$

d. $\Pi_{A,F}(\sigma_{C = D}(r \times s))$

3.10 Let $R = (A,B,C)$ and let r_1 and r_2 both be relations on scheme R. Give an expression in the domain relational calculus that is equivalent to:

a. $\Pi_A(r_1)$

b. $\sigma_{B = 17}(r_1)$

c. $r_1 \cup r_2$

d. $r_1 \cap r_2$

e. $r_1 - r_2$

f. $\Pi_{AB}(r_1) \bowtie \Pi_{BC}(r_2)$

3.11 Let $R = (A,B)$ and $S = (A,C)$, and let $r(R)$ and $s(S)$ be relations. Write relational algebra expressions equivalent to the following domain relational calculus expressions.

a. $\{<a> \mid \exists\, b\, (<a,b> \in r \wedge b = 17)\}$

b. $\{<a,b,c> \mid <a,b> \in r \wedge <a,c> \in s)\}$

c. $\{<b> \mid \forall\, a\, (<a,b> \notin r \vee \exists\, c\, (<a,c> \in s)\}$

d. $\{<a> \mid \exists\, c\, (<a,c> \in s \wedge \exists\, b_1,b_2\, (<a,b_1> \in r$
$\wedge <c, b_2> \in r \wedge b_1 > b_2))\}$

3.12 Write expressions for the queries of Exercise 3.11 in

    a. QBE

    b. QUEL

    c. SQL

3.13 Consider the relational database of Figure 3.17. Using SQL define a view consisting of *manager-name* and the average salary of employees working for that manager. Explain why the database system should not allow updates to be expressed in terms of this view.

3.14 List reasons why null values may be introduced into the database.

3.15 Some systems allow *marked* nulls. A marked null $\perp_i$ is equal to itself, but if $i \neq j$, then $\perp_i \neq \perp_j$. One application of marked nulls is to allow certain updates through views. Consider the view *branch-city* (Section 3.5). Show how marked nulls can be used to allow the insertion of the tuple (Brighton, Woodside) through *branch-city*.

Bibliographic Notes

The relational model was proposed by E. F. Codd of the IBM San Jose Research Laboratory in the late 1960s [Codd 1970]. Following Codd's original paper, several research projects were formed with the goal of constructing practical relational database systems, including System R at the IBM San Jose Research Laboratory, Ingres at the University of California at Berkeley, Query-by-Example at the IBM T. J. Watson Research Center, and PRTV (Peterlee Relational Test Vehicle) at the IBM Scientific Center in Peterlee, United Kingdom. System R and Ingres are discussed in Chapter 15. The bibliographic notes of that chapter provide references to those systems. Query-by-Example is described in Zloof [1977] and IBM [1978b]. PRTV is described in Todd [1976]. The original definition of the relational algebra is in Codd [1970] and that of the relational calculi is in Codd [1972b]. A formal proof of the equivalence of the relational calculus and relational algebra can be found in Codd [1972b] and Ullman [1982a].

    The query language SQL was first defined by Chamberlin et al. [1976]. Current versions of SQL available in commercial systems include those described by IBM [1982] and Oracle [1983]. There is a proposal in progress under the auspices of the American National Standards Institute (ANSI) for a standard SQL language. The SQL language served as the basis for a proposal for a more general relational database language being developed by ANSI Committee X3H2 (Committee on Computer and Information Processing).

Quel is defined by Stonebraker et al. [1976], Wong and Youssefi [1976], and Zook et al. [1977]. A commercial version of Quel is described in RTI [1983].

The problem of updating relational databases through views is addressed by Cosmadakis and Papadimitriou [1984], Dayal and Bernstein [1978, 1982], and Keller [1982, 1985]. The universal relation view is discussed by Sciore [1980], Fagin et al. [1982] and Ullman [1982a, 1982b]. Several experimental database systems have been built to test the claim that a universal relation view is simpler to use. In such systems, the user views the entire database as one relation and the system translates operations on the universal relation view into operations on the set of relations forming the conceptual scheme. One such system is System/U, which was developed at Stanford University in 1980-1982. System/U is described by Ullman[1982a, 1982b] and Korth et al. [1984]. The System/U query language is similar to that of Quel. However, since the user sees only one relation, the **from** clause is eliminated. Another universal relation system, PITS, is discussed by Maier et al. [1981] and Maier [1983].

General discussion of the relation data model appears in most database texts, including Ullman [1982a] and Date [1986]. Maier [1983] is a text devoted exclusively to the relational data model.

— SQL lacks orthogonality is redundant
— Union not in view.
— select cannot use DISTINCT more than once
— No explicit lock.
— other types

4

Network Data Model

In the relational model, the data and the relationships among data are represented by a collection of tables. The network model differs from the relational model in that data is represented by collections of *records* and relationships among data are represented by *links*.

4.1 Basic Concepts

A network database consists of a collection of records which are connected with each other through links. A record is in many respects similar to an entity in the entity-relationship model. Each record is a collection of fields (attributes), each of which contains only one data value. A link is an association between precisely two records. Thus, a link can be viewed as a restricted (binary) form of relationship in the sense of the E-R model.

To illustrate this, consider a database representing a *customer-account* relationship in a banking system. There are two record types, *customer* and *account*. As we saw earlier, the *customer* record type can be defined, using Pascal-like notation, as follows:

```
type customer = record
                    name: string;
                    street: string;
                    city: string;
                end
```

The *account* record type can be defined as follows:

```
type account = record
                    number: integer;
                    balance: integer;
                end
```

A sample database is shown in Figure 4.1. It shows that Lowman has account 305, Camp has accounts 226 and 177, and Kahn has account 155.

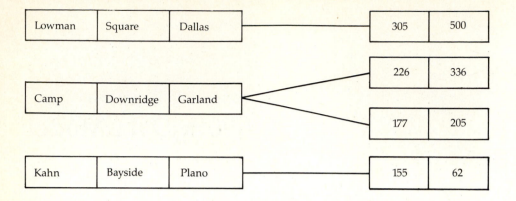

Figure 4.1   Sample database.

4.2 Data-Structure Diagrams

A *data-structure diagram* is a scheme representing the design of a network database. Such a diagram consists of two basic components:

- **Boxes**, which correspond to record types.
- **Lines**, which correspond to links.

A data-structure diagram serves the same purpose as an entity-relationship diagram; namely, it specifies the overall logical structure of the database. To understand how such diagrams are structured, we shall show how to transform entity-relationship diagrams to their corresponding data-structure diagrams.

4.2.1 Binary Relationship

Consider the entity-relationship diagram of Figure 4.2a, consisting of two entity sets *customer* and *account* related through a binary, many-to-many relationship *CustAcct*, with no descriptive attributes. This diagram specifies that a customer may have several accounts and that an account may belong to several different customers. The corresponding data-structure diagram is illustrated in Figure 4.2b. The record type *customer* corresponds to the entity set *customer*. It includes three fields: *name*, *street*, and *city*, as defined in Section 4.1. Similarly, *account* is the record type corresponding to the entity set *account*. It includes the two fields *number* and *balance*. Finally, the relationship *CustAcct* has been replaced with the link *CustAcct*.

The relationship *CustAcct* is many-to-many. If the relationship *CustAcct* were one-to-many, from *customer* to *account* then the link *CustAcct* has an arrow pointing to *customer* record type (Figure 4.3a). Similarly, if the relationship *CustAcct* were one-to-one, then the link *CustAcct* has two arrows, one pointing to *account* record type and one pointing to *customer*

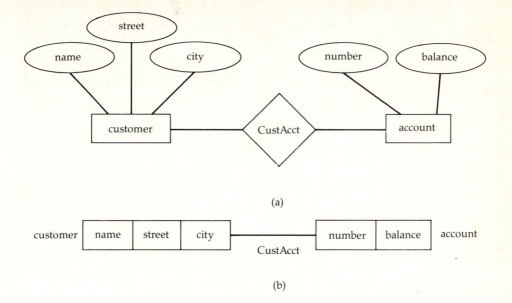

(a)

customer | name | street | city |———| number | balance | account

CustAcct

(b)

Figure 4.2   E-R diagram and its corresponding data-structure diagram.

record type (Figure 4.3b). Since, in the E-R diagram of Figure 4.2a, the *CustAcct* relationship is many-to-many, we draw no arrows on the link *CustAcct* in Figure 4.2b.

An instance of a database corresponding to the above-described scheme may thus contain a number of *customer* records linked to a number of *account* records as depicted in Figure 4.1.

A sample database corresponding to the data-structure diagram of Figure 4.2 is shown in Figure 4.4. Since the relationship is many-to-many, we show that Katz has accounts 256 and 347 and that account 347 is owned by both Katz and Doner. A sample database corresponding to the

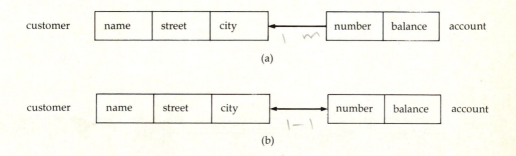

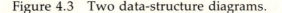

Figure 4.3   Two data-structure diagrams.

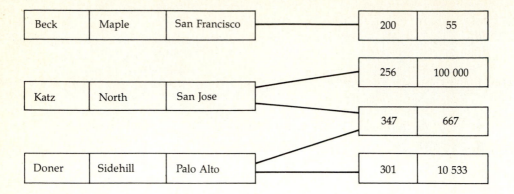

Figure 4.4   Sample database corresponding to diagram of Figure 4.2b.

data-structure diagram of Figure 4.3a is depicted in Figure 4.1. Since the relationship is one-to-many from *customer* to *account*, a customer may have more than one account, as is the case with Camp who owns both 226 and 177. An *account*, however, cannot belong to more than one customer, as is indeed observed in the sample database. Finally, a sample database corresponding to the data-structure diagram of Figure 4.3b is shown in Figure 4.5. Since the relationship is one-to-one, an account can be owned by precisely one customer, and a customer can have only one account, as is indeed the case in the sample database.

If a relationship includes descriptive attributes, the transformation from an E-R diagram to a data-structure diagram is somewhat more complicated. This is due to the fact that a link cannot contain any data value. In this case, a new record type needs to be created and links need to be established as described below.

Consider the E-R diagram of Figure 4.2a. Suppose that we add the attribute *date* to the relationship *CustAcct*, to denote the last time the

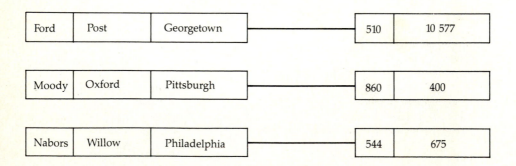

Figure 4.5   Sample database corresponding to diagram of Figure 4.3b.

customer has accessed the account. This newly derived E-R diagram is depicted in Figure 4.6a. To transform this diagram to a data-structure diagram we need to:

1. Replace entities *customer* and *account* with record types *customer* and *account*, respectively.

2. Create a new record type *date* with a single field to represent the date.

3. Create the following many-to-one links:

   - *CustDate* from the *date* record type to the *customer* record type.

   - *AcctDate* from the *date* record type to the *account* record type.

The resulting data-structure diagram is depicted in Figure 4.6b.

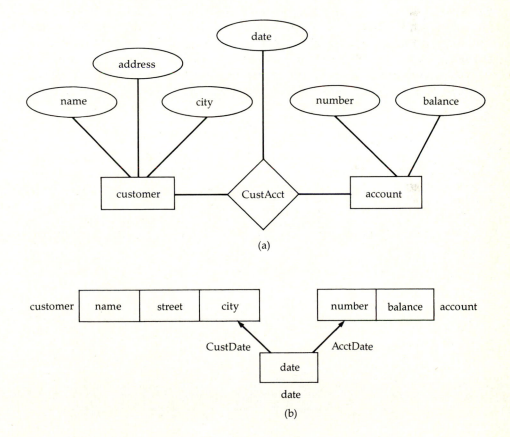

Figure 4.6   E-R diagram and its corresponding network diagram.

An instance of a database corresponding to the above described scheme appears in Figure 4.7. It shows the following:

- Lowman has account 305 which was last accessed on 15 September 1980.

- Camp has two accounts: 226 which was last accessed on 1 October 1983, and 177 which was last accessed on 23 November 1984.

- Kahn has account 155 which was last accessed on 15 September 1980.

4.2.2 General Relationships

Consider the entity-relationship diagram of Figure 4.8a consisting of three entity sets *account*, *customer*, and *branch*, related through the general relationship *CAB* with no descriptive attribute. This diagram specifies that a customer may have several accounts each located in a specific bank branch, and that an account may belong to several different customers.

Since a link can connect precisely two different record types, we need to connect these three record types through a new record type that is linked to each of these three records directly, as described below.

To transform the E-R diagram of Figure 4.8 to a network data-structure diagram we need to do the following:

1. Replace entity sets *account*, *customer*, and *branch* with record types *account*, *customer*, and *branch*, respectively.

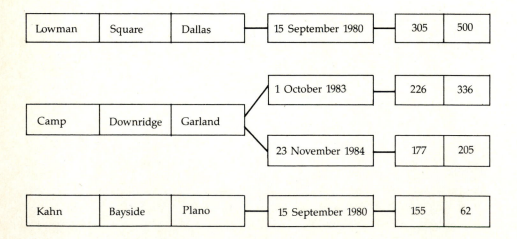

Figure 4.7   Sample database corresponding to diagram of Figure 4.6b.

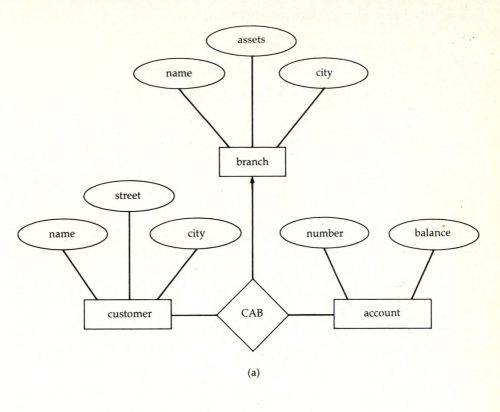

(a)

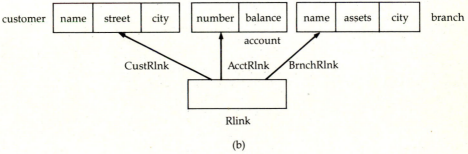

(b)

Figure 4.8   E-R diagram and its corresponding data-structure diagram.

2. Create a new record type *Rlink* that may either have no fields, or have a single field containing a unique identifier. This identifier is supplied by the system and is not used directly by the application program. This new type of record is sometimes referred to as a *dummy* (or *link* or *junction*) record type.

3. Create the following many-to-one links:

- *CustRlnk* from *Rlink* record type to *customer* record type.
- *AcctRlnk* from *Rlink* record type to *account* record type.
- *BrncRlnk* from *Rlink* record type to *branch* record type.

The resulting data-structure diagram is depicted in Figure 4.8b.

An instance of the database corresponding to the above-described scheme appears in Figure 4.9. It shows that Lowman has account 305 in the Hillside branch, Camp has accounts 226 and 177 in the Hillside and Valleyview branches, respectively, and Kahn has account 155 in the Valleyview branch.

We note that this technique can be extended in a straightforward manner to deal with relationships that span more than three entity sets. We create a many-to-one link from the *Rlink* record to the record types corresponding to each entity set involved in the relationship. This technique can also be extended to deal with a general relationship that has some descriptive attributes. We need to add one field to the dummy record type for each descriptive attribute.

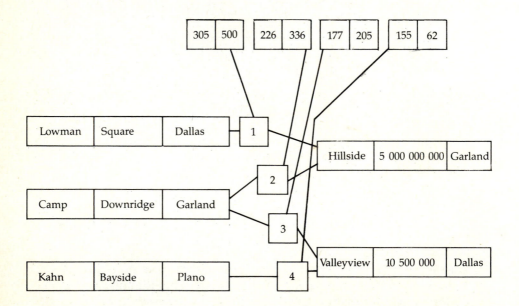

Figure 4.9   Sample database corresponding to diagram of Figure 4.8b.

4.3 The DBTG CODASYL Model

The first database standard specification, called the CODASYL DBTG 1971 report, was written in the late 1960s by the Database Task Group. Since then, a number of changes have been suggested to that report, the last official one in 1978. In 1981, a new draft proposal was published which has not yet been officially adopted. We have chosen this draft as the primary source for our discussion concerning the DBTG model.

4.3.1 Link Restriction

In the DBTG model, only one-to-one and many-to-one links can be used. Many-to-many links are disallowed in order to simplify the implementation. This restriction implies that our algorithm for transforming a entity-relationship diagram to a data-structure diagram must be revised.

Consider a binary relationship that is either one-to-many or one-to-one. In this case, the transformation algorithm defined in Section 4.2.1 can be applied directly. Thus, for our customer-account database, if the *CustAcct* relationship is one-to-many with no descriptive attributes, then the appropriate data-structure diagram is as shown in Figure 4.10a. If the relationship has a descriptive attribute, for example, *date*, then the appropriate data-structure diagram is as shown in Figure 4.10b.

If the *CustAcct* relationship, however, is many-to-many, then our transformation algorithm must be refined as follows. If the relationship has

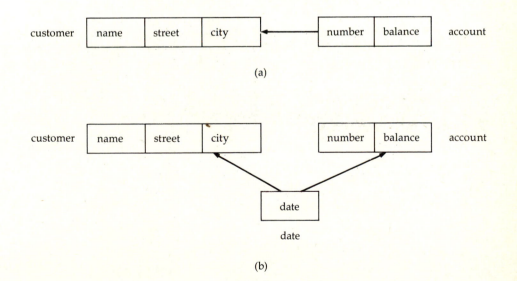

Figure 4.10   Two data-structure diagrams.

no descriptive attributes (Figure 4.11a), then the following algorithm must be employed:

- Replace the entity sets *customer* and *account* with record types *customer* and *account*, respectively.
- Create a new dummy record type, *Rlink*, that may either have no fields or have a single field containing an externally defined unique identifier.
- Create the following two many-to-one links:

    CustRlnk from *Rlink* record type to *customer* record type.

    AcctRlnk from *Rlink* record type to *account* record type.

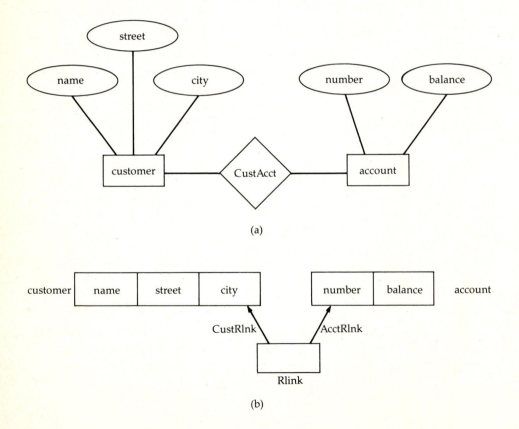

(a)

(b)

Figure 4.11   E-R diagram and its corresponding data-structure diagram.

The corresponding data-structure diagram is as shown in Figure 4.11b. An instance of a database corresponding the above-described scheme is depicted in Figure 4.12. We encourage the reader to compare this sample database to the one described in Figure 4.4.

If the relationship *CustAcct* is many-to-many with a descriptive attribute, for example, *date*, then the transformation algorithm is similar to the one described above. The only difference is that the new record type *R* now contains the field *date*.

In the case of general relationships (that is, nonbinary), the transformation algorithm is the same as the one described in Section 4.2.2. Thus the E-R diagram of Figure 4.8a is transformed to the data-structure diagram of Figure 4.8b.

4.3.2 DBTG Sets

Given that only one-to-one and many-to-one links can be used, a data-structure diagram consisting of two record types that are linked together has the general form of Figure 4.13. This structure is referred to in the DBTG model as a *DBTG-set*. The name of the set is usually chosen to be the same as the name of the link connecting the two record types.

In each such DBTG-set, the record type *A* is designated as the *owner* (or *parent*) of the set, and the record type *B* is designated as the *member* (or *child*) of the set. Each DBTG-set can have any number of *set occurrences*, that is, actual instances of linked records. For example, in Figure 4.14, we have three set occurrences corresponding to the DBTG-set of Figure 4.13.

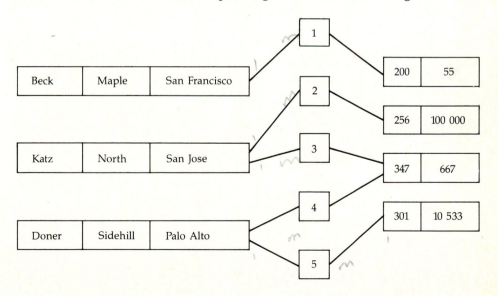

Figure 4.12   Sample database corresponding to the diagram of Figure 4.11.

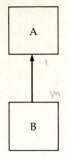

Figure 4.13   DBTG-set.

*because 1-1,
1-m
restriction*

Since many-to-many links are disallowed, each set occurrence has precisely one owner and zero or more member records. In addition, no member record of a set can participate in more than one occurrence of the set at any point. A member record, however, can participate simultaneously in several set occurrences of *different* DBTG-sets.

To illustrate this, consider the data-structure diagram of Figure 4.15. There are two DBTG-sets:

● *CustAcct*, having *customer* as the owner of the DBTG-set, and *account* as the member of the DBTG-set.

● *BrncAcct*, having *branch* as the owner of the DBTG-set, and *account* as the member of the DBTG-set.

The set *CustAcct* may be defined as follows:

> **set name is** *CustAcct*
> **owner is** *customer*
> **member is** *account*

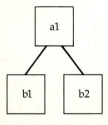
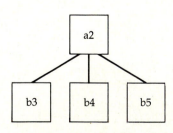
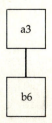

Figure 4.14   Three set occurrences.

The set *BrncAcct* may be defined similarly as:

> **set name is** *BrncAcct*
> **owner is** *branch*
> **member is** *account*

An instance of the database is depicted in Figure 4.16. There are five set occurrences listed below, three of set *CustAcct* (sets 1, 2, and 3), and two of set *BrncAcct* (sets 4 and 5).

1. Owner is *customer* record Lowman with a single member *account* record 305.

2. Owner is *customer* record Camp with two member *account* records 177 and 226.

3. Owner is *customer* record Kahn with three member *account* records 155, 402, and 408.

4. Owner is *branch* record Hillside with three member *account* records 305, 226, and 155.

5. Owner is *branch* record Valleyview with three member *account* records 177, 402, and 408.

Note that an *account* record (which is, in this case, a member of both DBTG-sets) cannot appear in more than one set occurrence of one individual set type. This is because an account can belong to exactly one customer, and can be associated with only one bank branch. An account, however, can appear in two set occurrences of different set types. For example, account 305 is a member of set occurrence (1) of type *CustAcct* and is also a member of set occurrence (4) of type *BrncAcct*.

The member records of a set occurrence may be ordered in a variety of ways. We shall discuss this issue in greater detail in Section 4.6.6, after we describe the mechanism for inserting and deleting records into a set occurrence.

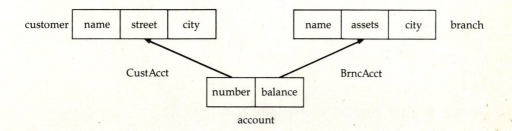

Figure 4.15   Data-structure diagram.

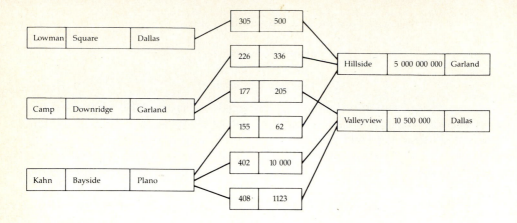

Figure 4.16   Five set occurrences.

The DBTG model allows more complicated set structures in which there exists one single owner type and several different member types. For example, suppose that we have two types of bank accounts: checking and saving. Then the data-structure diagram for the customer-account scheme is as depicted in Figure 4.17a. Such a scheme is similar in nature to the E-R diagram of Figure 4.17b.

The DBTG model also provides for the definition of a special set, referred to as a *singular set* (or *system set*). In such a set, the owner is a system-defined, unique record type, called *system*, with no fields. Such a set has *one single* set occurrence. This scheme is useful in searching records of one particular type, as will be discussed in Section 4.4.4.

4.3.3 Repeating Groups

The DBTG model provides a mechanism for a field (or collection of fields) to have a set of values, rather than one single value. For example, suppose that a customer has several addresses. In this case, the *customer* record type will have the (*street, city*) pair of fields defined as a repeating group. Thus, the *customer* record for Kahn may be as shown in Figure 4.18.

The repeating-groups construct is another way of representing the notion of weak entities in the E-R model. To illustrate this, suppose that we partition the entity set *customer* into two sets:

- *customer*, with descriptive attribute *name*.

- *address*, with descriptive attributes *street* and *city*.

The *address* entity is a weak entity since it depends on the strong entity *customer*.

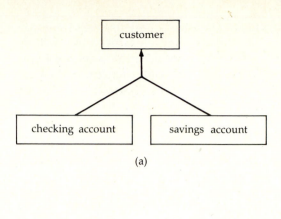

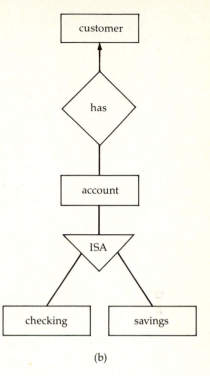

Figure 4.17 Data-structure and E-R diagram.

The E-R diagram describing this scheme is depicted in Figure 4.19a. If we do not use the repeating-group construct in the scheme, then the corresponding data-structure diagram is the one in Figure 4.19b. If, on the other hand, the repeating-group construct is used, then the data structure diagram simply consists of one single record type *customer*.

4.4 DBTG Data Retrieval Facility

The data manipulation language of the DBTG proposal consists of a number of commands that are embedded in a host language. In this

Kahn	Bayside	Plano
	Main	Garland

Figure 4.18 A *customer* record.

section, we shall present some of these commands and use the language Pascal as the host language. We shall use one simple example to illustrate the various concepts. The example is the customer-account-branch scheme discussed in Section 4.3.2. In particular, the data-structure diagram corresponding to our scheme is the one depicted in Figure 4.15, and the database sample is the one shown in Figure 4.16.

4.4.1 Program Workarea

Each application program executing in the system consists of a sequence of statements; some are Pascal statements while others are DBTG command statements. Each such program is called a *run unit*. These statements access and manipulate database items as well as locally declared variables. For each such application program, the system maintains a *program workarea* (referred to in the DBTG model as a *user work area*), a buffer storage area which contains the following variables:

- **Record templates**, a record (in the Pascal sense) for each record type accessed by the application program.

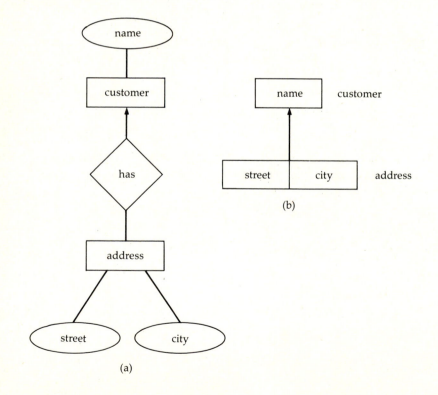

(a)

(b)

Figure 4.19   E-R and data-structure diagram.

- **Currency pointers**, a set of pointers to various database records most recently accessed by the application program. Currency pointers are of the following types:

  Current of record type, one currency pointer for each record type T referenced by the application program. Each pointer contains the *address* (location on disk) of the most recently accessed record of type T.

  Current of set type, one currency pointer for each set type S referenced by the application program. Each pointer contains the *address* of the most recently accessed record of that set type. Note that this pointer may point to a record of either the owner or member type, depending on whether an owner or a member was most recently accessed.

  Current of run unit, one single currency pointer, containing the *address* of the record (regardless of type) most recently accessed by the application program.

- **Status flags**, a set of variables used by the system to communicate to the application program the outcome of the last operation applied to the database. The most frequently used one is:

  db-status, set to 0 if the most recent operation succeeded; otherwise, it is set to an error-code.

  There are additional status variables, including **db-set-name**, **db-record-name**, and **db-data-name**. These variables are set when the last operation fails, to help in identifying the source of the difficulty encountered.

We emphasize again that a particular program workarea is associated with precisely one application program.

For our customer-account-branch database example, a particular program workarea contains the following:

- **Templates**, three record types:

  customer record.

  account record.

  branch record.

- **Currency pointers**, six pointers:

  Three currency pointers for record types, one to the most recently accessed *customer* record, one to the most recently accessed *account* record, and one to the most recently accessed *branch* record.

  Two currency pointers for set types, one to the most recently accessed record in an occurrence of the set *CustAcct*, and one to the most recently accessed record in an occurrence of the set *BrncAcct*.

  One current of run-unit pointer.

- **Status**, the four status variables we defined above.

4.4.2 The Find and Get Commands

The two most frequently used DBTG commands are the **find** and **get** commands:

- **find** locates a record in the database and sets the appropriate currency pointers.
- **get** copies the record to which the current of run-unit points from the database to the appropriate program workarea template.

There are a number of different forms of the **find** command. We shall present only some of these in the examples that follow. Before doing so, however, let us illustrate the general effect that the **find** and **get** statements have on the program workarea.

Consider the sample database of Figure 4.16. Suppose that the current state of the program workarea of a particular application program is as shown in Figure 4.20. Further suppose that a **find** command is issued to locate the customer record belonging to Camp. This command causes the following changes to occur in the state of the program workarea:

- The current of record type *customer* now points to the record of "Camp."
- The current of set type *CustAcct* now points to the set owned by Camp.
- The current of run unit now points to *customer* record "Camp."

If the **get** command is executed, the result is to load the information pertaining to Camp into the *customer* record template.

4.4.3 Access of Individual Records

There are two different **find** commands for locating individual records in the database. The simplest command has the form:

find any <record type> **using** <record-field>

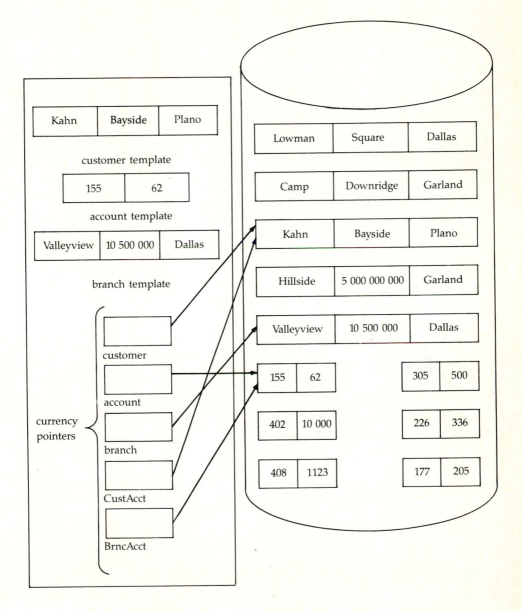

Figure 4.20　Program workarea.

This command locates a record of type <record type> whose <record-field> value is the same as the value of <record-field> in the <record type> template in the program workarea. Once such a record is found, the following currency pointers are set to point to that record:

- The current of run unit pointer.

- The record-type currency pointer for <record type>.

- For each set in which that record belongs, the appropriate set currency pointer.

To illustrate this, let us construct the DBTG query that prints the street address of Lowman.

> *customer.name* := "Lowman";
> **find any** *customer* **using** *name*;
> **get** *customer*;
> **print** (*customer.street*);

There may be several records with the specified value. The **find** command locates the first of these in some prespecified ordering (see Section 4.6.6). In order to locate other database records which match the <record-field>, we use the command:

find duplicate <record type> **using** <record-field>

which locates the next (according to a system dependent ordering) record which matches the <record-field>. The currency pointers noted above are affected.

To illustrate this, let us construct the DBTG query that prints the names of all the customers who live in Dallas:

> *customer.city* := "Dallas";
> **find any** *customer* **using** *city*;
> **while** *DB-status* = 0 **do**
> **begin**
>   **get** *customer*;
>   **print** (*customer.name*);
>   **find duplicate** *customer* **using** *city*;
> **end**;

We have enclosed part of the query in a **while** loop since we do not know in advance how many such customers exist. We exit from the loop when DB-status ≠ 0. This indicates that the last **find duplicate** operation failed, implying that we have exhausted all customers residing in Dallas.

4.4.4 Access of Records within a Set

The previous **find** commands located *any* database record of type <record type>. In this subsection, we concentrate on **find** commands that locate records in a particular DBTG-set. The set in question is the one that is pointed to by the <set-type> currency pointer. There are three different types of commands. The basic **find** command is

find first <record type> **within** <set-type>

which locates the first database record of type <record type> belonging to the current <set-type>. The various ways in which a set may be ordered are discussed in Section 4.6.6.

In order to locate the other members of a set, the following format can be used:

find next <record type> **within** <set-type>

This command finds the next element in the set <set-type>.

To illustrate how these commands execute, let us construct the DBTG query that prints the total balance of all accounts belonging to Lowman.

```
sum := 0;
customer.name := "Lowman";
find any customer using name;
find first account within CustAcct;
while DB-status = 0 do
    begin
        get account;
        sum := sum + account.balance;
        find next account within CustAcct;
    end
print (sum);
```

Note that we exit from the **while** loop and print out the value of *sum* only when the DB-status is set to a value not equal 0. This occurs after the **find next** operation fails indicating that we have exhausted all the members of a set occurrence of type *CustAcct*, whose owner is the record of customer Lowman.

In addition to the previous **find** commands, which locate records within a particular set, it may be necessary also to be able to locate the owner of a particular set. This can be accomplished through the following command:

find owner within <set-type>

The set in question is <set-type>. Note that for each set occurrence, there exists precisely one single owner.

To illustrate this, consider the DBTG query that prints all the customers of the Hillside branch:

> *branch.name* := "Hillside";
> **find any** *branch* **using** *name*;
> **find first** *account* **within** *BrncAcct*;
> **while** *DB-status* = 0 **do**
>   **begin**
>   **find owner within** *CustAcct*;
>   **get** *customer*;
>   **print** (*customer.name*);
>   **find next** *account* **within** *BrncAcct*;
>   **end**

Note that if a customer has several accounts in the Hillside branch, then his name will be printed several times.

As a final example, consider the DBTG query that prints the names of all the customers of the bank. Such a query cannot be formed easily with the mechanism we have described thus far. This is due to the fact that there exists no one single set that has all the customer records as its members. The remedy is to define a singular set (Section 4.3.2) consisting of members of type *customer*. This set is defined as follows:

> **set name is** *AllCust*
> **owner is** *system*
> **member is** *customer*

Once such a set has been defined, we can form our query as follows:

> **find first** *customer* **within** *AllCust*;
> **while** *DB-status* = 0 **do**
>   **begin**
>   **get** *customer*;
>   **print** (*customer.name*);
>   **find next** *customer* **within** *AllCust*;
>   **end**

4.4.5 Predicates

The **find** statements described above allow one to match the value of a field in one of the record templates with the corresponding field in the appropriate database records. Although with this technique we can formulate a variety of DBTG queries in a convenient and concise way, there are many queries in which one needs to match a field value with a specified range of values, not only one. To accomplish this, we need to **get** the appropriate records into memory and examine each separately for a match in order to determine whether they are the target of our **find** statement.

To illustrate this, consider the DBTG query to print the total number of accounts in the Hillside branch with a balance greater than $10,000:

```
count := 0;
branch.name := "Hillside";
find any branch using name;
find first account within BrncAcct;
while DB-status = 0 do
    begin
        get account;
        if account.balance > 10000 then count := count + 1;
        find next account within BrncAcct;
    end
print (count);
```

4.5 DBTG Update Facility

In Section 4.4, we described the various DBTG commands for querying the database. In this section, we describe the mechanisms available for updating information in the database. These include the creation and deletion of new records as well as the modification of the content of existing records.

4.5.1 Creating New Records

In order to create a new record of type <record type>, we insert the appropriate values in the corresponding <record type> template. Once this is done, we add this new record to the database by executing:

store <record type>

Note that this technique allows us to create and add new records only one at a time.

To illustrate this, consider the DBTG program for adding a new customer, Jackson, to the database:

> *customer.name* := "Jackson";
> *customer.street* := "Old Road";
> *customer.city* := "Richardson";
> **store** *customer*;

We note that if a new record is created that must belong to a particular DBTG set (for example, a new *account*), then in addition to the **store** operation we must have a mechanism for inserting records into sets. This mechanism is described in Section 4.6.

4.5.2 Modifying an Existing Record

In order to modify an existing record of type <record type>, we must find that record in the database, get that record into memory, and then change the desired fields in the template of <record type>. Once this is accomplished, we reflect the changes in the database by executing:

> **modify** <record type>

The DBTG model requires that when we find a record prior to modifying it, the **find** command must have the additional clause **for update** so that the system is aware of the fact that a record is to be modified. Note that we are not required to update a record that we "find for update." However, we cannot update a record unless it is found for update.

To illustrate this, consider the DBTG program to change the street address of Kahn to North Loop.

> *customer.name* := "Kahn";
> **find for update any** *customer* **using** *name*;
> **get** *customer*;
> *customer.city* := "North Loop";
> **modify** *customer*;

4.5.3 Deleting a Record

In order to delete an existing record of type <record type>, the currency pointer of that type must point to the record in the database to be deleted. Following this, we can delete that record by executing:

> **erase** <record type>

Note that as in the case of record modification, the **find** command must have the attribute **for update** attached to it.

To illustrate this, consider the DBTG program to delete account 402 belonging to Kahn:

> *finish* := false;
> *customer.name* := "Kahn";
> **find any** *customer* **using** *name*;
> **find for update first** *account* **within** *CustAcct*;
> **while** *DB-status* = 0 **and not** finish **do**
>   **begin**
>   **get** *account*;
>   **if** *account.number* = 402 **then**
>   **begin**
>   **erase** *account*;
>   *finish* := true;
>   **end**
>   **else find for update next** *account* **within** *CustAcct*;
>   **end**

It is possible to delete an entire set occurrence by finding the owner of the set, say a record of type <record type>, and executing:

erase all <record type>

This will delete the owner of the set as well as all of its members. If a member of the set is an owner of another set, the members of that set are also deleted. Thus the **erase all** operation is recursive.

To illustrate this, consider the DBTG program to delete customer "Camp" and all of her accounts:

> *customer.name* := "Camp";
> **find for update any** *customer* **using** *name*;
> **erase all** *customer*;

A natural question arises as to what needs to be done in the case where we wish to delete a record which is an owner of a set, but we do not specify **all** in the erase statement. In this case several possibilities exist, including:

- Delete only that record.
- Delete the record and all its members.
- Do not delete any records.

It turns out that each of these options may be specified in the DBTG model. We discuss this in Section 4.6.

4.6 DBTG Set-Processing Facility

We saw in Section 4.5 that the **store** and **erase** statements are closely tied to the set-processing facility. In particular, we noted the need for providing a mechanism for inserting records into and removing records from a particular set occurrence. We also noted that, in case of deletion, we have a number of different options to consider if the record to be deleted is the owner of a set. These issues are the subject of this section.

4.6.1 The Connect Statement

In order to insert a new record of type <record type> into a particular occurrence of <set-type>, we must first insert the record into the database (if it is not already there). Then, we need to set the currency pointers of <record type> and <set-type> to point to the appropriate record and set occurrence. Once this is accomplished, the new record can be inserted into the set by executing:

$$\textbf{connect} \text{ <record type> } \textbf{to} \text{ <set-type>}$$

A new record insertion can be done as follows:

1. Create a new record of type <record type> (see Section 4.5.1). This sets the appropriate <record type> currency pointer.

2. Find the appropriate owner of the set <set-type>. This automatically sets the appropriate currency pointer of <set-type>.

3. Insert the new record into the set by executing the **connect** statement.

To illustrate this, consider the DBTG query for creating new account 267 which belongs to Jackson:

> *account.number* := 267;
> *account.balance* := 0;
> **store** *account*;
> *customer.name* := "Jackson";
> **find any** *customer* **using** *name*;
> **connect** *account* **to** *CustAcct*;

4.6.2 The Disconnect Statement

In order to remove a record of type <record type> from a set occurrence of type <set-type>, we need to set the currency pointer of <record type> and <set-type> to point to the appropriate record and set occurrence. Once this is accomplished, the record can be removed from the set by executing:

$$\textbf{disconnect} \text{ <record type> } \textbf{from} \text{ <set-type>}$$

Note that this operation only removes a record from a set; it does not delete that record from the database. If deletion is desired, the record can be deleted by executing **erase** <record type>.

To illustrate this, assume we wish to close account 177. To do so, we need to delete the relationship between account 177 and its customer. However, we shall need to keep the record of account 177 in the database for the bank's internal archives. The program below shows how we would do this within the DBTG model. This program will remove account 177 from the set occurrence of type *CustAcct*. The account will still be accessible in the database for record-keeping purposes.

> *account.number* := 177;
> **find for update any** *account* **using** *name*;
> **get** *account*;
> **find** *owner* **within** *CustAcct*;
> **disconnect** *account* **from** *CustAcct*;

4.6.3 The Reconnect Statement

In order to move a record of type <record type> from one set occurrence to another set occurrence of type <set-type>, we need to find the appropriate record and the owner of the set occurrences to which that record is to be moved. Once this is done, we can move the record by executing:

> **reconnect** <record type> **to** <set-type>

To illustrate this, consider the DBTG program to move all accounts of Lowman that are currently at the Hillside branch to the Valleyview branch.

> *customer.name* := "Lowman";
> **find any** *customer* **using** *name*;
> **find first** *account* **within** *CustAcct*;
> **while** *DB-status* = 0 **do**
> **begin**
>   **find** *owner* **within** *BrncAcct*;
>   **get** *branch*;
>   **if** *branch.name* = "Hillside" **then**
>   **begin**
>   *branch.name* := "Valleyview";
>   **find any** *branch* **using** *name*;
>   **reconnect** *account* **to** *BrncAcct*;
>   **end**
>   **find next** *account* **within** *CustAcct*;
> **end**

4.6.4 Set Insertion and Retention

When a new set is defined, we must specify how member records are to be inserted. In addition, we must specify the conditions under which a record must be retained in the set occurrence in which it was initially inserted.

Set insertion

A newly created member record of type <record type> of a set type <set-type> can be added to a set occurrence either explicitly (manually) or implicitly (automatically). This distinction is specified at set definition time via:

insertion is <insert mode>

where <insert mode> can be:

- **Manual**. The new record can be inserted into the set manually (explicitly) by executing:

connect <record type> **to** <set-type>

- **Automatic**. The new record is inserted into the set automatically (implicitly) when it is created, that is, when we execute:

store <record type>

In either case, just prior to insertion, the <set-type> currency pointer must point to the set occurrence into which the insertion is to be made.

To illustrate this, consider the creation of account 535 that belongs to Lowman and is at the Valleyview branch. Suppose that set insertion is **manual** for set type *CustAcct* and is **automatic** for set type *BrncAcct*. The appropriate DBTG program is:

```
branch.name := "Valleyview";
find any branch using name;
account.number := 535;
account.balance := 0;
store account;
customer.name := "Lowman";
find any customer using name;
connect account to CustAcct;
```

Set retention

There are various restrictions on how and when a member record can be removed from a set occurrence into which it has been inserted previously. These restrictions are specified at set definition time via:

retention is <retention-mode>

where <retention-mode> can be:

- **Fixed**. Once a member record has been inserted into a particular set occurrence, it cannot be removed from that set. If retention is fixed, then to reconnect a record to another set, we must first erase that record, recreate it, and then insert it into the new set occurrence.

- **Mandatory**. Once a member record has been inserted into a particular set occurrence, it can be reconnected only to another set occurrence of type <set-type>. It can neither be disconnected, nor be reconnected to a set of another type.

- **Optional**. No restrictions are placed on how and when a member record can be removed from a set occurrence. A member record can be reconnected, disconnected, and connected at will.

The decision as to which options to choose is dependent on the application. For example, in our banking database, the **optional** retention mode seems to be appropriate for the *CustAcct* set, while the **mandatory** retention mode seems to be appropriate for the *BrncAcct* set.

4.6.5 Deletion

When a record is deleted (erased) and that record is the owner of set occurrence of type <set-type>, then there are a number of different ways of handling this deletion. These depend on the specification of the set retention of <set-type>.

- If the retention status is **optional**, then the record will be deleted and every member of the set it owns will be disconnected. These records, however, are kept in the database.

- If the retention status is **fixed**, then the record and all of its owned members will be deleted. This follows from the fact that the fixed status indicates that a member record cannot be removed from the set occurrence without being deleted.

- If the retention status is **mandatory**, then the record cannot be erased. This is because the mandatory status indicates that a member record must belong to a set occurrence; it cannot be disconnected from that set.

4.6.6 Set Ordering

The members of a set occurrence of type <set-type> may be ordered in a variety of ways. These orders are specified by a programmer when the set is defined via:

order is <order-mode>

where <order-mode> can be:

- **first**. When a new record is added to a set, it is inserted in the first position. Thus, the set is ordered in reverse chronological ordering.

- **last**. When a new record is added to a set, it is inserted in the last position. Thus, the set is ordered in chronological ordering.

- **next**. Suppose that the currency pointer of <set-type> points to record X. If X is a member type, then when a new record is added to the set, it is inserted in the next position following X. If X is an owner type, then when a new record is added, it is inserted in the first position.

- **prior**. Suppose that the currency pointer of <set-type> points to record X. If X is a member type, then when a new record is added to the set, it is inserted in the position just prior to X. If X is an owner type, then when a new record is added, it is inserted in the last position.

- **system default**. When a new record is added to a set, it is inserted in an arbitrary position determined by the system.

- **sorted**. When a new record is added to a set, it is inserted in a position that ensures that the set will remain sorted. The sorting order is specified by a particular key value when a programmer defines the set. The programmer must specify whether members are ordered in ascending or descending order relative to that key.

To illustrate this, consider Figure 4.16, where the set occurrence of type *CustAcct* with the owner record customer Kahn and member records accounts 155, 402, and 408 are ordered as indicated. Suppose that we add a new account 125 into that set. For each <order-mode> option, the new set ordering is as follows:

- first: {125,155,402,408}.
- last: {155,402,408,125}.

- next: Suppose that the currency pointer points to record "Kahn." Then the new set order is {125,155,402,408}.

- prior: Suppose that the currency pointer points to record 402. Then the new set order is {155,125,402,408}.

- system default: Any arbitrary order is acceptable. Thus {155,402,125,408} is a valid set ordering.

- sorted: The set must be ordered in ascending order with account number being the key. Thus, the ordering must be {125,155,402,408}.

4.7 Summary

A network database consists of a collection of *records* which are connected with each other through *links*. A link is an association between precisely two records. Records are organized in the form of an arbitrary graph.

A *data-structure diagram* is a scheme for a network database. Such a diagram consists of two basic components: boxes, which correspond to record types, and lines, which correspond to links. A data-structure diagram serves the same purpose as an entity-relationship diagram; namely, it specifies the overall logical structure of the database. For every entity-relationship diagram, there is a corresponding data-structure diagram.

In the late 1960s, several commercial database systems based on the network model emerged. These systems were studied extensively by the Database Task Group (DBTG) within the CODASYL group. In the DBTG model, only one-to-one and one-to-many links can be used; many-to-many links are disallowed in order to simplify the implementation. A data-structure diagram consisting of two record types that are linked together is referred to in the DBTG model as a *DBTG-set*. Each DBTG-set has one record type designated as the *owner* of the set, and the other record type designated as the *member* of the set. A DBTG-set can have any number of *set occurrences*.

The data manipulation language of the DBTG model consists of a number of commands that are embedded in a host language. These commands access and manipulate database variables as well as locally declared variables. For each such application program the system maintains a *program workarea* which contains *record templates*, *currency pointers*, and *status flags*.

The two most frequently used DBTG commands are the **find** and **get** commands. There are a number of different formats for the **find** command. The main distinction among them is whether individual records are to be located or whether records within a particular set occurrence are to be located.

There are various mechanisms available in the DBTG model for updating information in the database. These include the creation and deletion of new records (via the **store** and **erase** operations) as well as the modification (via the **modify** operation) of the content of existing records. In order to insert records into and remove records from a particular set occurrence, the **connect**, **disconnect**, and **reconnect** operations are provided.

When a new set is defined, we must specify how member records are to be inserted and under what conditions they can be moved from one set occurrence to another. A newly created member record can be added to a set occurrence either explicitly or implicitly. This distinction is specified at set-definition time via the **insertion is** statement with the **manual** and **automatic** insert mode options.

There are various restrictions on how and when a member record can be removed from a set occurrence it has been previously inserted in. These restrictions are specified at set-definition time via the **retention is** statement with the **fixed**, **mandatory**, and **optional** retention mode options.

Exercises

4.1 Transform the E-R diagram of Figure 4.21 to a data-structure diagram assuming that the data model is:

   a. Network.

   b. DBTG.

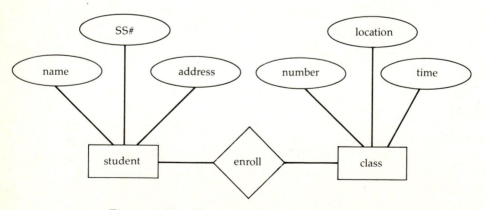

Figure 4.21   Class enrollment E-R diagram.

4.2 Construct a sample database for the data-structure diagram of Exercise 4.1, with ten students and three different classes.

4.3 Show the set of variables which exist in a program workarea for the data-structure diagram corresponding to the E-R diagram of Figure 4.21.

4.4 Suppose that we add the attribute *grade* to the relationship *enrollment* of Figure 4.21. Show the corresponding data-structure diagram assuming the network and DBTG model.

4.5 Transform the E-R diagram of Figure 4.22 to a data-structure diagram.

4.6 Define the following terms:

    a. DBTG-set.

    b. Owner of a set.

    c. Member of a set.

    d. Set occurrence.

4.7 Explain why a member record of a set occurrence cannot participate in more than one occurrence of the set at any point?

4.8 Suppose that the **find owner** statement is not provided as part of the DBTG query language. Would it be still possible to answer the set of queries as before?

4.9 The DBTG **find** statement does not allow one to specify predicates.

    a. Discuss the drawbacks of this limitation.

    b. Can you suggest a modification to the language to overcome this difficulty?

4.10 Transform the E-R diagram of Figure 4.23 to a data-structure diagram assuming the DBTG model.

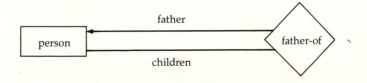

Figure 4.22   Parent-child E-R diagram.

4.11 For the data-structure diagram corresponding to the E-R diagram of Figure 4.23, construct the following DBTG queries:

   a. Find the total number of users that have had an accident in 1983.

   b. Find the number of accidents the cars belonging to "John Smith" were involved in during the term of the policy.

   c. Add a new customer to the database.

   d. Delete the car "Mazda" belonging to "John Smith."

   e. Add a new accident record for the Toyota belonging to "Jones."

4.12 What is a *system set* and why was it introduced in the DBTG model?

4.13 Explain the concept of "repeating groups." Is it necessary to have this construct available in the network model?

4.14 Explain the difference between the **connect**, **disconnect**, and **reconnect** statements.

4.15 Explain the difference between the **manual** and **automatic** option in set insertion.

4.16 Explain the difference between the **find**, **mandatory**, and **optional** options in set retention.

4.17 What are the appropriate set insertion and set retention options for the data-structure diagram corresponding to Figure 4.23.

4.18 Consider the relation scheme of Figure 4.24. Generate an appropriate data-structure diagram corresponding to this scheme.

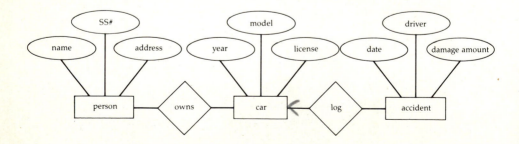

Figure 4.23 Car insurance E-R diagram.

lives (person-name, street, city)
works (person-name, company-name, salary)
located-in (company-name, city)
manages (person-name, manager-name)

Figure 4.24   Relational database.

4.19 Construct the following DBTG queries for the data-structure diagram obtained as a solution to Exercise 4.18.

a. Find the name of all people who work for First Bank Corporation.

b. Find the name and city of all people who work for First Bank Corporation.

c. Find the name, street, and city of all people who work for First Bank Corporation and earn more than $10,000.

d. Find all people who live in the same city as the company they work for.

e. Find all people who live in the same city and on the same street as their manager.

f. Find all people who do not work for First Bank Corporation.

g. Find all people who earn more than every employee of Small Bank Corporation.

h. Assume the companies may be located in several cities. Find all companies located in every city in which Small Bank Corporation is located.

i. Find all people who earn more than the average salary of people working in their company.

j. Find the company employing the most people.

k. Find the company with the smallest payroll.

l. Find those companies that pay more, on average, than the average salary at First Bank Corporation.

m. Modify the database so that Jones now lives in Newtown.

n. Give all employees of First Bank Corporation a 10 percent raise.

o. Give all managers a 10 percent raise.

p. Give all managers a 10 percent raise unless the salary becomes greater than $100,000. In such cases, give only a 3 percent raise.

q. Delete all tuples for employees of Small Bank Corporation.

Bibliographic Notes

In the late 1960s, several commercial database systems based on the network model emerged. The most influential of these were the Integrated Data Store (IDS) system which was developed in General Electric under the guidance of Charles Bachman [Bachman and Williams 1964] and Associate PL/1 (APL), [Dodd 1966]. These and other systems were studied extensively by the Database Task Group (DBTG) within the CODASYL (Conference on Data Systems Languages) group that earlier set the standard for COBOL. This study has resulted in the first database standard specification, called the CODASYL DBTG 1971 report [CODASYL 1971]. Since then, a number of changes have been suggested to that report, the last official one in 1978 [CODASYL 1978]. In 1981, a new draft proposal was published which has not yet been officially adopted.

The concept of data-structure diagrams was introduced by Bachman [1969]. The original presentation of data-structure diagrams used arrows to point from owner to member record types. This corresponds to the physical pointer implementation. We have used the arrows pointing from member to owner record types to be consistent with our presentation of the E-R model. The same convention is used by Ullman [1982a].

Implementation issues concerning the DBTG model are discussed by Schenk [1974] and Gerritsen [1975]. Discussions concerning the view level of DBTG (the external level) are offered by Zaniolo [1979a, 1979b] and Clemons [1978, 1979].

Many commercial database management systems exist which are based on the network model, including DMS 1100 [Sperry Univac 1973], Total [Cincom 1974, 1978, Tsichritzis and Lochovsky 1977, Cardenas 1985], IDMS [Cullinane 1975, Tsichritzis and Lochovsky 1977], IDS II [Honeywell 1975], and ADABAS [Software AG 1978, Tsichritzis and Lochovsky 1977].

A survey paper on the DBTG model is presented by Taylor and Frank [1976]. Basic textbook discussions are offered by Tsichritzis and Lochovsky [1977], Cardenas [1985], Date [1986], Ullman [1982a], Tsichritzis and Lochovsky [1982], and Kroenke [1983].

Hierarchical Data Model

In the network model, the data is represented by collections of *records* and relationships among data are represented by *links*. The hierarchical model is similar to the network model in the sense that data and relationships among data are also represented by records and links, respectively. The hierarchical model differs from the network model in that the records are organized as collections of trees rather than arbitrary graphs.

5.1 Basic Concepts

A hierarchical database consists of a collection of *records* which are connected with each other through *links*. A record is similar to a record in the network model. Each record is a collection of fields (attributes), each of which contains only one data value. A link is an association between precisely two records. Thus, a link is similar to the link concept in the network model.

To illustrate this, consider a database representing a *customer-account* relationship in a banking system. There are two record types, *customer* and *account*. The *customer* record type can be defined in the same manner as in Chapter 4. It consists of three fields: *name*, *street*, and *city*. Similarly, the *account* record consists of two fields: *number* and *balance*.

A sample database appears in Figure 5.1. It shows that customer Lowman has account 305, customer Camp has accounts 226 and 177, and customer Kahn has account 155.

Note that the set of all customer and account records are organized in the form of a rooted tree where the root of the tree is a dummy node. As we shall see, a hierarchical database is a collection of such rooted trees, and hence forms a forest. We shall refer to each such rooted tree as a *database tree*.

The content of a particular record may have to be replicated in several different locations. For example, in our customer-account banking system, an account may belong to several customers. The information pertaining to that account, or the information pertaining to the various customers to which it may belong, will have to be replicated. This replication may occur

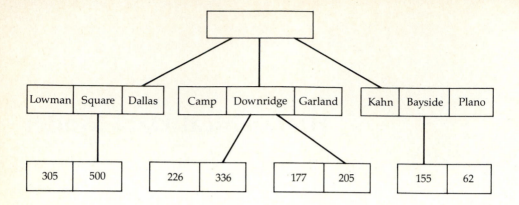

Figure 5.1   Sample database.

either in the same database tree or in several different trees. Record replication has two major drawbacks:

- Data inconsistency may result when updating takes place.
- Waste of space is unavoidable.

We shall deal with this issue in Section 5.5 by introducing the concept of a *virtual record*.

5.2 Tree-Structure Diagrams

A *tree-structure diagram* is the scheme for a hierarchical database. Such a diagram consists of two basic components:

- **Boxes**, which correspond to record types.
- **Lines**, which correspond to links.

A tree-structure diagram serves the same purpose as an entity-relationship diagram (or a data-structure diagram in the network model); namely, it specifies the overall logical structure of the database. A tree-structure diagram is similar to a data-structure diagram. The main difference is that, in the latter, record types are organized in the form of an arbitrary graph, while in the former, record types are organized in the form of a *rooted tree*.

We have to be more precise about what is meant by a rooted tree. First, there can be no cycles in the underlying graph. Second, the relationships formed in the graph must be such that only one-to-many or one-to-one relationships exist between a parent and a child. The general form of a tree structure diagram is illustrated in Figure 5.2. Note that the

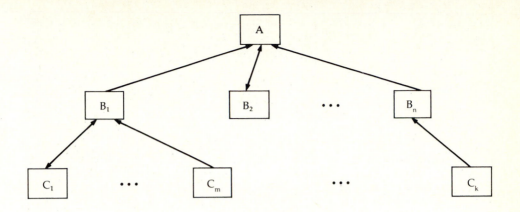

Figure 5.2   General structure of a tree-structure diagram.

arrows are pointing from children to parents. A parent may have an arrow pointing to a child, but a child must have an arrow pointing to its parent.

The database scheme is represented as a collection of tree-structure diagrams. For each such diagram, there exists one *single* instance of a database tree. The root of this tree is a dummy node. The children of that node are instances of the appropriate record type. Each such child instance may, in turn, have several instances of various record types, as specified in the corresponding tree-structure diagram.

To understand how tree-structure diagrams are structured, we shall show how to transform entity-relationship diagrams to their corresponding tree-structure diagrams. We first show how such transformations can be applied to single relationships. We shall then address the issue of how one ensures that the resulting diagrams are in the form of rooted trees.

5.2.1 Single Relationships

Consider the entity-relationship diagram of Figure 5.3a, consisting of two entity sets *customer* and *account* related through a binary, one-to-many relationship *CustAcct*, with no descriptive attributes. This diagram specifies that a customer may have several accounts but an account may belong to only one customer. The corresponding tree-structure diagram is depicted in Figure 5.3b. The record type *customer* corresponds to the entity set *customer*. It includes three fields: *name*, *street*, and *city*. Similarly, *account* is the record type corresponding to the entity set *account*. It includes the two fields: *number* and *balance*. Finally, the relationship *CustAcct* has been replaced with the link *CustAcct*, with an arrow pointing to *customer* record type.

An instance of a database corresponding to the above-described scheme may thus contain a number of *customer* records linked to a number

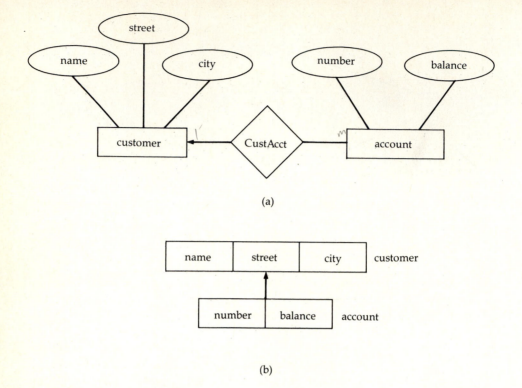

(a)

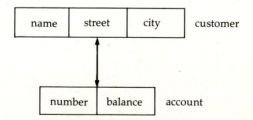

(b)

Figure 5.3   E-R diagram and its corresponding tree-structure diagram.

of *account* records as shown in Figure 5.1. Since the relationship is one-to-many from *customer* to *account*, a customer may have more than one account, as is the case with Camp who has both accounts 226 and 177. An account, however, cannot belong to more than one customer, as is indeed observed in the sample database.

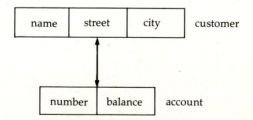

Figure 5.4   Tree-structure diagram with one-to-one relationship.

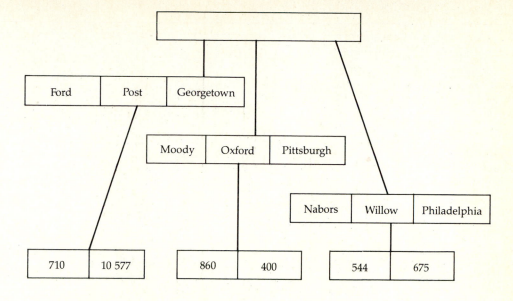

Figure 5.5   Sample database corresponding to diagram of Figure 5.4.

If the relationship *CustAcct* were one-to-one, then the link *CustAcct* has two arrows, one pointing to *account* record type, and one pointing to *customer* record type (Figure 5.4). A sample database corresponding to this scheme appears in Figure 5.5. Since the relationship is one-to-one, an account can be owned by precisely one customer, and a customer can have only one account, as is indeed the case in the sample database.

If the relationship *CustAcct* were many-to-many (see Figure 5.6a), then the transformation from an E-R diagram to a tree-structure diagram is more complicated. This is due to the fact that only one-to-many and one-to-one relationships can be directly represented in the hierarchical model.

There are a number of different ways to transform this E-R diagram to a tree-structure diagram. All these diagrams, however, share the common property that the underlying database tree (or trees) will have replicated records.

The decision as to which transformation should be used depends on many factors, including:

- The type of queries expected on the database.

- The degree to which the overall database scheme being modeled fits the given E-R diagram.

We shall present a transformation which is as general as possible. That is, all other possible transformations are a special case of our transformation.

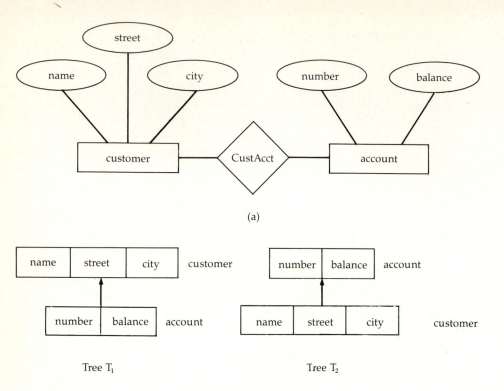

Figure 5.6   E-R diagram and its corresponding tree-structure diagram.

In order to transform the E-R diagram of Figure 5.6a to a tree-structure diagram, we need to do the following:

- Create two separate tree-structure diagrams T_1 and T_2, each having the *customer* and *account* record types. In tree T_1, *customer* is the root, while in tree T_2, *account* is the root.

- Create the following two links:

    CustAcct, a many-to-one link from *account* record type to *customer* record type, in T_1.

    AcctCust, a many-to-one link from *customer* record type to *account* record type, in T_2.

The resulting tree-structure diagram is depicted in Figure 5.6b.

A sample database corresponding to the tree-structure diagram of Figure 5.6 is shown in Figure 5.7b. There are two database trees. The first tree (Figure 5.7a) corresponds to the tree-structure diagram T_1, while the second tree (Figure 5.7b) corresponds to the tree-structure diagram T_2. As can be seen, all *customer* and *account* records are replicated in both database trees. In addition, *account* record 347 appears twice in the first tree, while *customer* records Katz and Doner appear twice in the second tree.

If a relationship also includes a descriptive attribute, the transformation from an E-R diagram to a tree-structure diagram is more complicated. This is due to the fact that a link cannot contain any data value. In this case, a new record type needs to be created and the appropriate links need to be established. The manner in which links are formed depends on the way the relationship *CustAcct* is defined, as is discussed below.

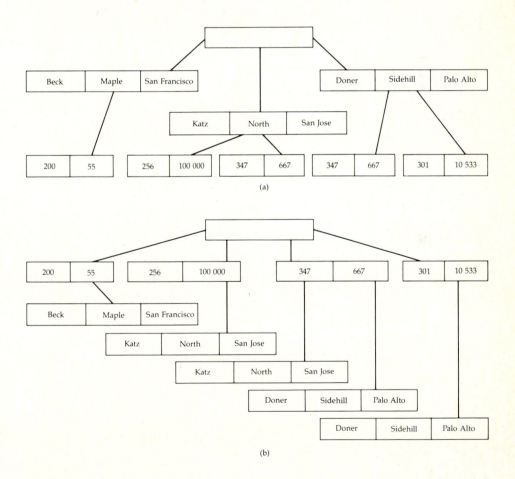

(a)

(b)

Figure 5.7   Sample database corresponding to diagram of Figure 5.6.

Consider the E-R diagram of Figure 5.3a. Suppose that we add the attribute *date* to the relationship *CustAcct*, to denote the last date on which a customer has accessed the account. This newly derived E-R diagram is depicted in Figure 5.8a. To transform this diagram to a tree-structure diagram we need to:

- Create a new record type *date* with a single field.
- Create the following two links:

> *CustDate*, a many-to-one link from *date* record type to *customer* record type.
>
> *DateAcct*, a many-to-one link from *account* record type to *date* record type.

The resulting tree-structure diagram is illustrated in Figure 5.8b.

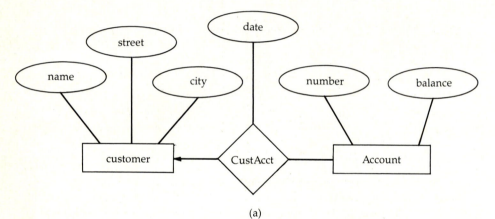

(a)

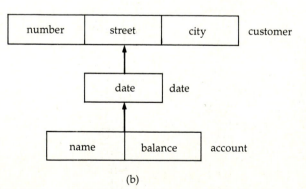

(b)

Figure 5.8   E-R diagram and its corresponding tree-structure diagram.

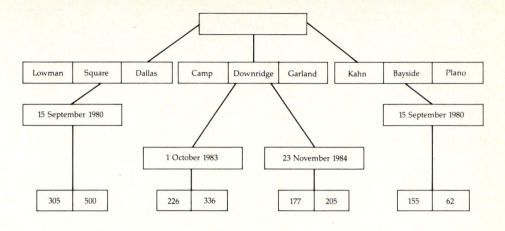

Figure 5.9   Sample database corresponding to diagram of Figure 5.8b.

An instance corresponding to the above-described scheme appears in Figure 5.9. It shows the following:

- Lowman has account 305 which was last accessed on 15 September 1980.

- Camp has two accounts: 226 which was last accessed on 1 October 1983, and 177 which was last accessed on 23 November 1984.

- Kahn has account 155 which was last accessed on 15 September 1980.

Note that two different accounts can be opened on the same date, as is the case with accounts 155 and 305. Since these accounts belong to two different customers, the *date* record must be replicated to preserve the hierarchy.

If the relationship *CustAcct* were one-to-one with the attribute *date*, then the transformation algorithm would be similar to the one described above. The only difference is that the two links *CustDate* and *DateAcct* would be one-to-one links.

If the relationship *CustAcct* were many-to-many with the attribute *date*, then there are again a number of alternative transformations. We shall use the most general transformation, similar to the one applied to the case where the relationship *CustAcct* has no descriptive attribute. The record types *customer*, *account*, and *date* need to be replicated, and two separate tree-structure diagrams must be created as depicted in Figure 5.10. A sample database corresponding to this scheme is depicted in Figure 5.11.

Until now, we have considered only binary relationships. We shift our attention now to general relationships. To transform E-R diagrams corresponding to general relationships to tree-structure diagrams is quite

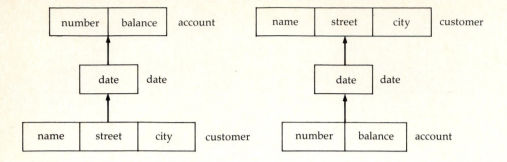

Figure 5.10   Tree-structure diagram with many-to-many relationships.

complicated. Rather than presenting a general transformation algorithm, we present a single example to illustrate the overall strategy that can be applied in dealing with such a transformation.

Consider the entity-relationship diagram of Figure 5.12a consisting of three entity sets *customer*, *account*, and *branch*, related through the general relationship *CAB* with no descriptive attribute. This diagram specifies that a customer may have several accounts each located in a specific bank branch, and that an account may belong to several different customers.

There are a number of different ways to transform this E-R diagram to a tree-structure diagram. Again, all these share the common property that the underlying database tree (or trees) will have replicated records. The most straightforward transformation is to create two tree-structure diagrams as shown in Figure 5.12b.

An instance of the database corresponding to the above-described scheme is illustrated in Figure 5.13. It shows that Beck has account 200 in the Northcross branch, Katz has accounts 256 and 347 in the Northcross and Highland branches, respectively, and that Doner has accounts 347 and 301 in the Highland branch.

We note that the above transformation algorithm can be extended in a straightforward manner to deal with relationships that span more than three entity sets. We simply replicate the various record types and generate as many tree-structure diagrams as necessary. This approach can be extended to deal with a general relationship that has some descriptive attributes. All that is needed is to create a new record type with one field for each descriptive attribute, and insert that record type in the appropriate location in the tree-structure diagram.

5.2.2 Several Relationships

The scheme described above to transform an E-R diagram to a tree-structure diagram ensures that for each single relationship, the

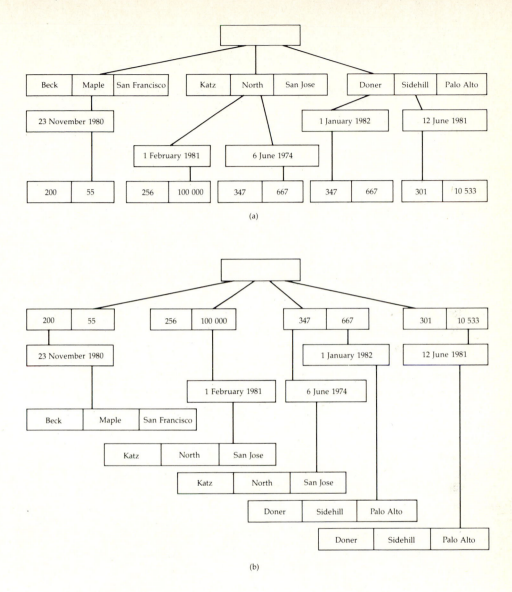

Figure 5.11   Sample database corresponding to diagram of Figure 5.10.

transformation will result in diagrams which are of the form of rooted trees. Unfortunately, applying such a transformation individually to each relationship in an E-R diagram does not necessarily result in diagrams that are rooted trees.

Below, we discuss means for resolving the problem. The technique is to split the diagrams in question into several diagrams each of which is a

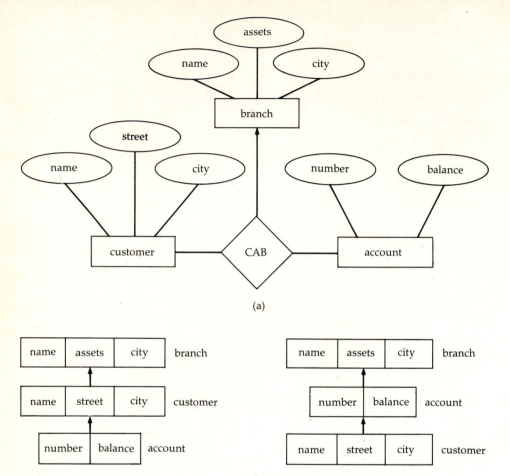

(a)

(b)

Figure 5.12   E-R diagram and its corresponding data-structure diagram.

rooted tree. Due to the number of different possibilities, rather than presenting a general transformation algorithm, we present two examples to illustrate the overall strategy that can be applied in dealing with such transformations.

Consider the E-R diagram of Figure 5.14a. By applying the transformation algorithm described in Section 5.2.1 separately to the relationships *BrncAcct* and *CustAcct*, we obtain the diagram of Figure 5.14b. This diagram is not a rooted tree, since the only possible root can be the record type *account*, but this record type has many-to-one relationships with both its children, which violates our definition of a rooted tree (see Section 5.2). To transform this diagram into one which is in the form of a

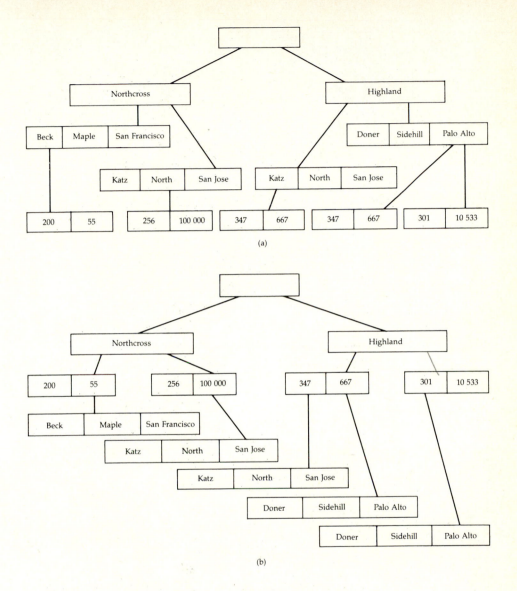

Figure 5.13   Sample database corresponding to diagram of Figure 5.12b.

rooted tree, we replicate the *account* record type, and create two separate trees as shown in Figure 5.15. Note that each such tree is indeed a rooted tree. Thus, in general, we can split such a diagram into several diagrams, each of which is a rooted tree.

Consider the E-R diagram of Figure 5.16a. By applying the transformation algorithm described in Section 5.2.1, we obtain the diagram

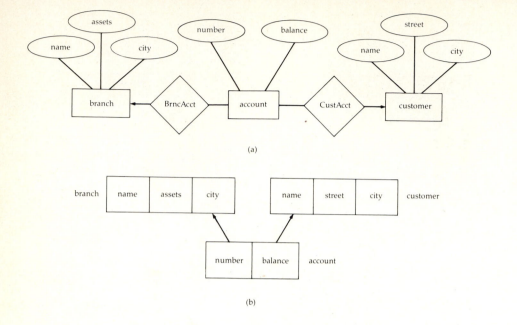

(a)

(b)

Figure 5.14   E-R diagram and its corresponding tree-structure diagram.

depicted in Figure 5.16b. This diagram is not in the form of a rooted tree, since it contains a cycle. To transform the diagram to a tree-structure diagram, we replicate all three record types and create two separate diagrams as illustrated in Figure 5.17. Note that each such diagram is indeed a rooted tree. Thus, in general, we can split such a diagram into several diagrams, each of which is a rooted tree.

5.3 Data Retrieval Facility

In this section, we present a query language for hierarchical databases which is based on DL/1, the data manipulation language of IMS. In order

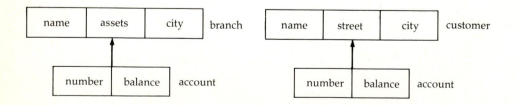

Figure 5.15   Tree-structure diagram corresponding to Figure 5.14a.

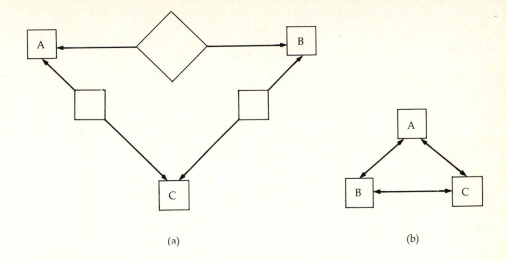

(a)   (b)

Figure 5.16   E-R diagram and its corresponding tree-structure diagram.

to simplify the presentation, we shall deviate from the DL/1 syntax and use a simplified notation. Our language consists of a number of commands that are embedded in a host language, Pascal. We shall use a simple example, of a *customer-account-branch* scheme. The tree-structure diagram corresponding to our scheme appears in Figure 5.18. It specifies that a branch may have several customers each of which may have several accounts. An account, however, may belong to only one customer, and a customer can belong to only one branch. An instance corresponding to this scheme is shown in Figure 5.19.

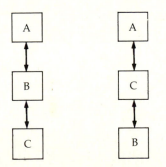

Figure 5.17   Tree-structure diagram corresponding to Figure 5.16a.

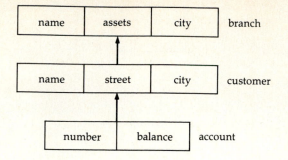

Figure 5.18   Tree-structure diagram.

5.3.1 Program Workarea

Each application program executing in the system consists of a sequence of statements, some of which are Pascal statements, while others are data manipulation language command statements. These statements access and manipulate database items as well as locally declared variables. For each such application program, the system maintains a *program workarea*, a buffer storage area which contains the following variables:

- **Record templates**, a record (in the Pascal sense) for each record type accessed by the application program.

- **Currency pointers**, a set of pointers, one for each database tree, containing the *address* of the record in that particular tree (regardless of type) most recently accessed by the application program.

- **Status flag**, a variable set by the system to indicate to the application program the outcome of the last database operation. We call this flag

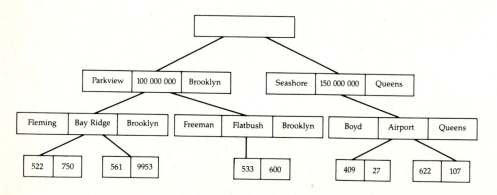

Figure 5.19   Sample database corresponding to Figure 5.18.

DB-status and use the same convention as in the DBTG model to denote failure; namely, if *DB-status* = 0, then the last operation succeeded.

We emphasize again that a particular program workarea is associated with precisely one application program.

For our branch-customer-account example, a particular program workarea contains the following:

- **Templates**, one record for each of three record types:

    branch record.

    customer record.

    account record.

- **Currency pointer**, a pointer to the last accessed record of either *branch*, *customer*, or *account* type.

- **Status**, one status variable.

5.3.2 The Get Command

Data retrieval is accomplished through the **get** command. The actions taken in response to a **get** are as follows:

- Locate a record in the database and set the currency pointer to it.

- Copy that record from the database to the appropriate program area template.

The **get** command must specify which of the database trees is to be searched. For our example, we assume that the only database tree to be searched is the sample database of Figure 5.19, and thus we omit this specification in our queries.

There are a number of different forms of the **get** command. Before presenting these, however, let us first illustrate the general effect that the **get** command has on the program workarea.

Consider the sample database of Figure 5.19. Suppose that a **get** command was issued to locate the *customer* record belonging to Freeman. Once this command successfully executed, the changes that occur in the state of the program workarea are:

- The currency pointer points now to the record of Freeman.

- The information pertaining to Freeman is copied into the *customer* record workarea template.

- *DB-status* is set to the value 0.

In order to scan all records in a consistent manner, we must impose an ordering on the records. The order commonly used is *preorder*. A preorder search starts at the root and searches the subtrees of the root from left to right, recursively. Thus, we start at the root, visit the leftmost child, visit its leftmost child, etc., until we reach a leaf (childless) node. We then move back to the parent of the leaf and visit the leftmost unvisited child. We proceed in this manner until the entire tree is visited. For example, the preordered listing of the records in the database tree of Figure 5.19 is as follows:

> Parkview, Fleming, 522, 561, Freeman, 533,
> Seashore, Boyd, 409, 622

5.3.3 Access within a Database Tree

There are two different **get** commands for locating records in a database tree. The simplest command has the form:

> **get first** \<record type\>
> **where** \<condition\>

The **where** clause is optional. The attached \<condition\> is a predicate that may involve any record type which is either an ancestor of \<record type\> or the \<record type\> itself.

The **get** command locates the first record (in preorder) of type \<record type\> in the database that satisfies the \<condition\> of the **where** clause. If the **where** clause is omitted, then the first record of type \<record-type\> is located. Once such a record is found, the currency pointer is set to point to that record, and the content of the record is copied into the appropriate workarea template. If no such record exists in the database tree, then the search fails and the variable *DB-status* is set to an appropriate error message.

To illustrate this, let us construct the database query that prints the address of customer Fleming.

> **get first** *customer*
> **where** *customer.name* = "Fleming";
> **print** (*customer.address*);

As another example, consider the query that prints an account belonging to Fleming with balance greater than $10,000 (if one such exists).

> **get first** *account*
>   **where** *customer.name* = "Fleming" **and** *account.balance* > 10000;
> **if** *DB-status* = 0 **then print** (*account.number*);

There may be several similar records in the database that we wish to retrieve. The **get first** command locates one of these. In order to locate the other database records, the following command can be used:

get next <record type>
where <condition>

This command locates the next record (in preorder) that satisfies <condition>. If the **where** clause is omitted, then the next record of type <record type> is located. Note that the currency pointer is used by the system to determine from where to resume the search. As before, the currency pointer, the workarea template of type <record-type>, and *DB-status* are affected.

To illustrate this, let us construct the database query that prints the account number of all the accounts with balance greater than $500.

> **get first** *account*
>   **where** *account.balance* > 500;
> **while** *DB-status* = 0 **do**
>   **begin**
>   **print** (*account.number*);
>   **get next** *account*
>   **where** *account.balance* > 500;
>   **end**

We have enclosed part of the query in a **while** loop since we do not know in advance how many such accounts exist. We exit from the loop when *DB-status* ≠ 0. This indicates that the last **get next** operation failed, implying that we have exhausted all account records with *account.balance* > 500.

The two previous get commands locate a database record of type <record type> within a particular database tree. There are, however, many circumstances where one wishes to locate such a record within a particular subtree. That is, we want to limit the search to one specific subtree rather than the entire database tree. The root of the subtree in question is the *last* record which was located with either **get first** or **get next** command. The **get** command to locate a record within that subtree has the following form:

> **get next within parent** <record type>
>   **where** <condition>

which locates the next record (in preorder) which satisfies <condition> in the subtree whose root is the parent of current of <record type>. If the **where** clause is omitted, then the next record of type <record type> within the designated subtree is located. Note that the currency pointer is used by the system to determine from where to resume the search. As before, the currency pointer and the workarea template of type <record type> are affected. In this case, however, the *DB-status* is set to a nonzero value if there exists no such record in the designated subtree, not the entire tree.

To illustrate how this **get** command executes, let us construct the query that prints the total balance of all accounts belonging to "Boyd":

> *sum* := 0;
> **get first** *customer*
>   **where** *customer.name* = "Boyd";
> **get next within parent** *account*;
> **while** *DB-status* = 0 **do**
>   **begin**
>   *sum* := *sum* + *account.balance*;
>   **get next within parent** *account*;
>   **end**
> **print** (*sum*);

Note that we exit from the **while** loop and print out the value of *sum* only when the *DB-status* is set to a value not equal to 0. This occurs after the **get next within parent** operation fails, indicating that we have exhausted all the accounts whose owner is customer "Boyd."

5.4 Update Facility

In Section 5.3, we described commands for querying the database. In this section, we describe the mechanisms available for updating information in the database. These include the insertion and deletion of records as well as the modification of the content of existing records.

5.4.1 Creating New Records

In order to insert a record of type <record type> into the database, we must first set the appropriate values in the corresponding <record type> workarea template. Once this is done, we add this new record to the database tree by executing:

> **insert** <record type>
> **where** <condition>

If the **where** clause is included, the system searches the database tree (in preorder) for a record that satisfies the <condition> in the **where** clause. Once such a record, say X, is found, the newly created record is inserted in the tree as the leftmost child of X. If the **where** clause is omitted, the record is inserted in the first position (in preorder) in the database tree where a record type <record type> can be inserted in accordance with the scheme specified by the corresponding tree-structure diagram.

To illustrate this, consider the program for adding a new customer "Jackson" to the Seashore branch:

> *customer.name* := "Jackson";
> *customer.street* := "Old Road";
> *customer.city* := "Queens";
> **insert** *customer*
> **where** *branch.name* = "Seashore";

The result of executing this program is the database tree of Figure 5.20.

As another example, consider the program for creating a new account numbered 655 which belongs to customer "Jackson":

> *account.name* := 655;
> *account.balance* := 100;
> **insert** *account*
> **where** *customer.name* = "Jackson";

The result of executing this program is the database tree of Figure 5.21.

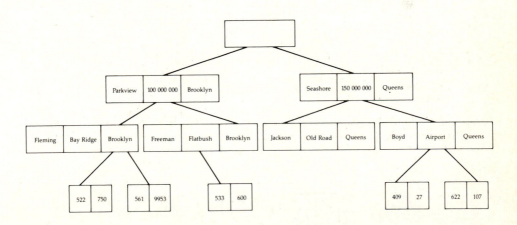

Figure 5.20   New database tree.

5.4.2 Modifying an Existing Record

In order to modify an existing record of type <record type>, we must get that record into the workarea template for <record type> and change the desired fields in that template. Once this is accomplished, we reflect the changes in the database by executing:

replace

Note that the **replace** command does not have <record type> as an argument. The record that is affected is the one to which the currency pointer points to, which must point to the desired record.

The DL/1 language requires that when we get a record prior to modifying it, the **get** command must have the additional clause **hold** so that the system is aware of the fact that a record is to be modified in the system.

To illustrate this, consider the program to change the street address of "Boyd" to Northview:

> **get hold first** *customer*
> **where** *customer.name* = "Boyd";
> *customer.street* := "Northview";
> **replace**;

Note that in our example, we have only one record containing the address of Boyd. If that was not the case, our program would have included a loop to search all Boyd records.

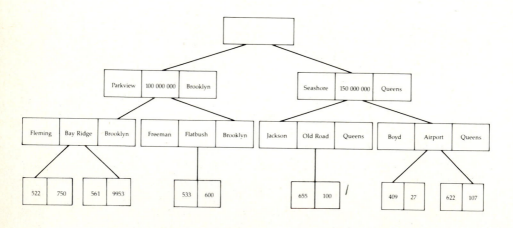

Figure 5.21   New database tree

5.4.3 Deleting a Record

In order to delete a record of type <record type>, the currency pointer must be set to point to that record. Following this, we can delete that record by executing:

delete

Note that, as in the case of record modification, the **get** command must have the attribute **hold** attached to it.

To illustrate this, consider the program to delete account 561:

> **get hold first** *account*
>   **where** *account.number* = 561;
> **delete**;

A delete operation not only deletes the record in question, but the entire subtree rooted by that record. Thus to delete customer Boyd and all of his accounts, we write:

> **get hold first** *customer*
>   **where** *customer.name* = "Boyd";
> **delete**;

5.5 Virtual Records

We have seen that in the case of many-to-many relationships, record replication is necessary if one wishes to preserve the tree-structure organization of the database. Record replication has two major drawbacks:

- Data inconsistency may result when updating takes place.

- Waste of space is unavoidable.

In the following, we discuss ways to eliminate these drawbacks.

In order to eliminate record replication, we need to relax our requirement that the logical organization of data be constrained to a tree structure. This, however, needs to be done cautiously, since otherwise we will end up with the network model.

The solution is to introduce the concept of a *virtual record*. Such a record contains no data value; it contains, however, a logical pointer to a particular physical record. When a record is to be replicated in several database trees, we keep a single copy of that record in one of the trees and replace each other record with a virtual record containing a pointer to that physical record.

To be more specific, let R be a record type that is replicated in several tree-structure diagrams, say T_1, T_2, ..., T_n. To eliminate replication, we create a new virtual record type *virtual-R*, and replace R in each of the $n - 1$ trees with a record of type *virtual-R*.

To illustrate this, consider the E-R diagram of Figure 5.6a and its corresponding tree-structure diagram which consists of two separate trees, each consisting of both *customer* and *account* record types (Figure 5.6b).

To eliminate data replication, we create two virtual record types: *customer* and *virtual-account*. We then replace record type *account* with record type *virtual-account* in the first tree, and replace record type *customer* with the record type *virtual-customer* in the second tree. We also add a dashed line from *virtual-customer* record to *customer* record, and a dashed line from *virtual-account* record to *account* record, to specify the association between a virtual record and its corresponding physical record. The resulting tree-structure diagram is depicted in Figure 5.22.

An instance of the database corresponding to the diagram of Figure 5.22 is depicted in Figure 5.23. Note that there exists only a single copy of the information for each customer and each account. Contrast this with the same information depicted in Figure 5.7, where replication is allowed.

The data manipulation language for this new configuration remains the same as in the case where record replication is allowed. Thus, a user need not be aware of these changes. Only the internal implementation is affected.

5.6 Summary

A hierarchical database consists of a collection of *records* which are connected with each other through *links*. Each record is a collection of fields, each of which contains only one data value. A link is an association between precisely two records. The hierarchical model is thus similar to the network model in the sense that data and relationships among data are also represented by records and links, respectively. The hierarchical model differs from the network model in that the records are organized as collections of trees rather than arbitrary graphs.

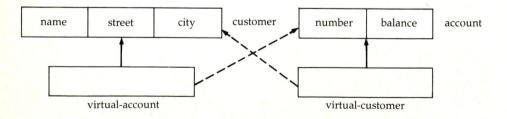

Figure 5.22   Tree-structure diagram with virtual records.

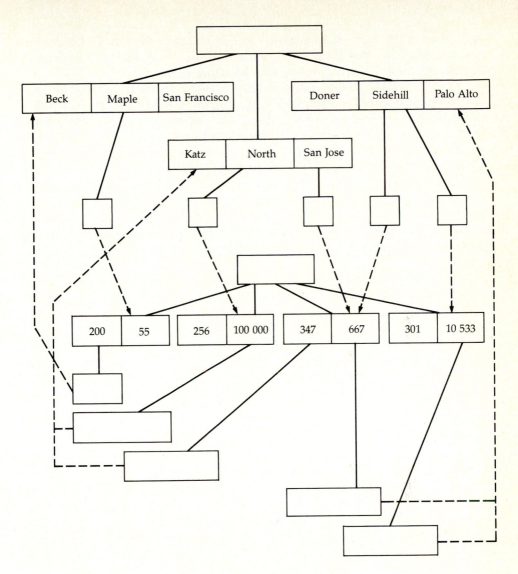

Figure 5.23   Sample database corresponding to diagram of Figure 5.22.

A *tree-structure diagram* is a scheme for a hierarchical database. Such a diagram consists of two basic components: boxes, which correspond to record types, and lines, which correspond to links. A tree-structure diagram serves the same purpose as an entity-relationship diagram; namely, it specifies the overall logical structure of the database. A tree-structure diagram is similar to a data-structure diagram in the network model. The main difference is that in the former record types are organized in the form of an arbitrary graph, while in the latter record types are organized in the form of a *rooted tree*. For every entity-relationship diagram there is a corresponding tree-structure diagram.

The database scheme is thus represented as a collection of tree-structure diagrams. For each such diagram, there exists a *single* instance of a database tree. The root of this tree is a dummy node. The children of that node are actual instances of the appropriate record type. Each such instance may, in turn, have several instances of various record types, as specified in the corresponding tree-structure diagram.

The data manipulation language discussed in this chapter consists of a number of commands that are embedded in a host language. These commands access and manipulate database items as well as locally declared variables. For each application program the system maintains a *program workarea* which contains *record templates*, *currency pointers*, and a *status flag*.

Data retrieval from the database is accomplished through the **get** command, which locates a record in the database and sets the currency pointer to point to it, and then copies that record from the database to the appropriate program workarea template. There are a number of different forms for the **get** command. The main distinction among them is whether a record is to be located in an entire database tree or within a subtree.

There are various mechanisms available for updating information in the database. These include the creation and deletion of records (via the **insert** and **delete** operations) as well as the modification (via the **replace** operation) of the content of existing records.

In the case of many-to-many relationships, record replication is necessary if one wishes to preserve the tree-structure organization of the database. Record replication has two major drawbacks: data inconsistency may result when updating takes place, and waste of space is unavoidable. The solution is to introduce the concept of a *virtual record*. Such a record contains no data value; it contains, however, logical pointer to a particular physical record. When a record is to be replicated in several database trees, we keep a single copy of that record in one of the trees and replace all other records with a virtual record containing a pointer to that physical record. The data manipulation language for this new configuration remains the same as in the case where record replication is allowed. Thus, a user need not be aware of these changes. Only the internal implementation is affected.

Exercises

5.1 Transform the E-R diagram of Figure 5.24 to a tree-structure diagram.

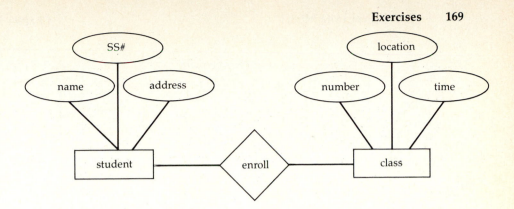

Figure 5.24   Class enrollment E-R diagram.

5.2 Construct a sample database for the tree-structure diagram of Exercise 5.1, with ten students and three different classes.

5.3 Show the preorder order of the sample database of Exercise 5.2.

5.4 Show the set of variables which exist in a program workarea for the tree-structure diagram corresponding to the E-R diagram of Figure 5.24.

5.5 Suppose that we add the attribute "grade" to the relationship *enrollment* of Figure 5.24. Show the corresponding tree-structure diagram.

5.6 Transform the E-R diagram of Figure 5.25 to a tree-structure diagram.

5.7 Compare the hierarchical model with the relational model in terms of ease of learning and ease of use.

5.8 Are there applications that are easier to code in the hierarchical model than in the relational model?

5.9 Transform the E-R diagram of Figure 5.26 to a tree-structure diagram.

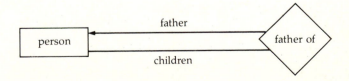

Figure 5.25   Parent-child E-R diagram.

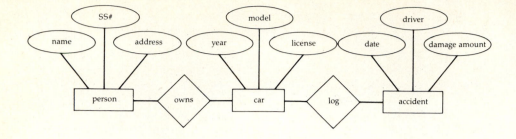

Figure 5.26   Car insurance E-R diagram.

5.10 For the tree-structure diagram corresponding to the E-R diagram of Figure 5.26, construct the following queries:

   a. Find the total number of users that have had an accident in 1983.

   b. Find the number of accidents the cars belonging to "John Smith" were involved in during the term of the policy.

   c. Add a new customer to the database.

   d. Delete the car "Mazda" belonging to "John Smith."

   e. Add a new accident record for the Toyota belonging to "Jones."

5.11 The addition of virtual records to the hierarchical model results in a structure which is no longer treelike. In effect, the underlying structure is quite similar to the network model. What are the differences between the hierarchical model with virtual records and the network model?

> lives (person-name, street, city)
> works (person-name, company-name, salary)
> located-in (company-name, city)
> manages (person-name, manager-name)

Figure 5.27   Relational database.

5.12 Consider the relation scheme of Figure 5.27. Generate an appropriate tree-structure diagram corresponding to this scheme.

5.13 Consider the database scheme corresponding to the tree-structure diagram obtained as a solution to Exercise 5.12. For each of the queries below construct the appropriate program:

    a. Find the name of all people who work for First Bank Corporation.

    b. Find the name and city of all people who work for First Bank Corporation.

    c. Find the name, street, and city of all people who work for First Bank Corporation and earn more than $10,000.

    d. Find all people who live in the same city as the company they work for.

    e. Find all people who live in the same city and on the same street as their manager.

    f. Find all people who do not work for First Bank Corporation.

    g. Find all people who earn more than every employee of Small Bank Corporation.

    h. Assume the companies may be located in several cities. Find all companies located in every city in which Small Bank Corporation is located.

    i. Find all people who earn more than the average salary of people working in their company.

    j. Find the company employing the most people.

    k. Find the company with the smallest payroll.

    l. Find those companies that pay more, on average, than the average salary at First Bank Corporation.

    m. Modify the database so that Jones now lives in Newtown.

    n. Give all employees of First Bank Corporation a 10 percent raise.

    o. Give all managers a 10 percent raise.

    p. Give all managers a 10 percent raise unless the salary becomes greater than $100,000. In such cases, give only a 3 percent raise.

    q. Delete all employees of Small Bank Corporation.

Bibliographic Notes

Two influential database systems based on the hierarchical model are IBM's Information Management System (IMS) [IBM 1978a, McGee 1977], and MRI's system 2000 [MRI 1974]. The first IMS version was developed in the late 1960s by IBM and North American Aviation (Rockwell International) for the Apollo moon landing program. System 2000 is an outgrowth of TDMS which was developed at System Development Corporation [Vorhaus and Mills 1967], and RFMS which was developed at the University of Texas at Austin [Everett et al. 1971].

A survey paper on the hierarchical data model is presented by Tsichritzis and Lochovsky [1976]. Textbook discussions covering IMS are offered by Tsichritzis and Lochovsky [1977, 1982], Cardenas [1985], Date [1986], and Ullman [1982a]. A description of DL/1, the query language of IMS can be found in Kroenke [1983]. The simplified version of DL/1 used in this chapter is similar to the one used by Ullman [1982a]. System 2000 is discussed in the textbooks by Tsichritzis and Lochovsky [1977] and Cardenas [1985].

Relational Database Design

In preceding chapters, we have emphasized the *use* of databases rather than the *design* of databases. In this chapter, we consider design issues regarding relational databases. In general, the goal of a relational database design is to generate a set of relation schemes that allow us to store information without unnecessary redundancy, yet allow us to retrieve information easily. One approach is to design schemes that are in an appropriate *normal form*. In order to determine whether a relation scheme is in one of the normal forms, we shall need additional information about the "real-world" enterprise that we are modeling with the database. This additional information is given by a collection of constraints called *data dependencies*.

6.1 Pitfalls in Relational Database Design

Before we begin our discussion of normal forms and data dependencies, let us look at what can go wrong in a bad database design. Among the undesirable properties that a bad design may have are:

- Repetition of information.

- Inability to represent certain information.

- Loss of information.

Below, we discuss these in greater detail using our banking example from Chapter 3, with the following two relation schemes:

> *Branch-scheme* = (*branch-name, assets, branch-city*)
> *Borrow-scheme* = (*branch-name, loan-number, customer-name, amount*)

Figures 6.1 and 6.2 show an instance of the relations *branch* (*Branch-scheme*) and *borrow* (*Borrow-scheme*).

branch-name	assets	branch-city
Downtown	9000000	Brooklyn
Redwood	2100000	Palo Alto
Perryridge	1700000	Horseneck
Mianus	400000	Horseneck
Round Hill	8000000	Horseneck
Pownal	300000	Bennington
North Town	3700000	Rye
Brighton	7100000	Brooklyn

Figure 6.1   Sample *branch* relation.

6.1.1 Repetition of Information

Consider an alternative design for the bank database in which we replace *Branch-scheme* and *Borrow-scheme* with the single scheme:

$$Lending\text{-}scheme = (branch\text{-}name, \ assets, \ branch\text{-}city, \ loan\text{-}number,$$
$$customer\text{-}name, \ amount).$$

Figure 6.3 shows an instance of the relation *lending* (*Lending-scheme*) produced by taking the natural join of the *branch* and *borrow* instances of Figures 6.1 and 6.2. A tuple *t* in the *lending* relation has the following intuitive meaning:

branch-name	loan-number	customer-name	amount
Downtown	17	Jones	1000
Redwood	23	Smith	2000
Perryridge	15	Hayes	1500
Downtown	14	Jackson	1500
Mianus	93	Curry	500
Round Hill	11	Turner	900
Pownal	29	Williams	1200
North Town	16	Adams	1300
Downtown	18	Johnson	2000
Perryridge	25	Glenn	2500
Brighton	10	Brooks	2200

Figure 6.2   Sample *borrow* relation.

- $t[assets]$ is the asset figure for the branch named $t[branch\text{-}name]$.
- $t[branch\text{-}city]$ is the city in which the branch named $t[branch\text{-}name]$ is located.
- $t[loan\text{-}number]$ is the number assigned to a loan made by the branch named $t[branch\text{-}name]$ to the customer named $t[customer\text{-}name]$.
- $t[amount]$ is the amount of the loan whose number is $t[loan\text{-}number]$.

Suppose we wish to add a new loan to our database. Assume the loan is made by the Perryridge branch to Turner in the amount of \$1,500. Let the number of the loan be 31. In our original design, we would add the tuple:

$$(Perryridge, 31, Turner, 1500)$$

to the *borrow* relation. Under the alternative design, we need a tuple with values on all the attributes of *Lending-scheme*. Thus, we must repeat the asset and city data for the Perryridge branch and add a tuple:

$$(Perryridge, 1700000, Horseneck, 31, Turner, 1500)$$

to the *lending* relation. In general, the asset and city data for a branch must appear once for each loan made by that branch.

The repetition of information required by the use of our alternative design is undesirable. Repeating information wastes space. Furthermore, the repetition of information complicates updating the database. Suppose,

branch-name	assets	branch-city	loan-number	customer-name	amount
Downtown	9000000	Brooklyn	17	Jones	1000
Redwood	2100000	Palo Alto	23	Smith	2000
Perryridge	1700000	Horseneck	15	Hayes	1500
Downtown	9000000	Brooklyn	14	Jackson	1500
Mianus	400000	Horseneck	93	Curry	500
Round Hill	8000000	Horseneck	11	Turner	900
Pownal	300000	Bennington	29	Williams	1200
North Town	3700000	Rye	16	Adams	1300
Downtown	9000000	Brooklyn	18	Johnson	2000
Perryridge	1700000	Horseneck	25	Glenn	2500
Brighton	7100000	Brooklyn	10	Brooks	2200

Figure 6.3   *branch* ⋈ *borrow*

for example, that the Perryridge branch moves from Horseneck to Newtown. Under our original design, one tuple of the *branch* relation needs to be changed. Under our alternative design, many tuples of the *lending* relation need to be changed. Thus, updates are more costly under the alternative design than under the original design. When we perform the update in the alternative database, we must ensure that *every* tuple pertaining to the Perryridge branch is updated, lest our database show two cities for the Perryridge branch.

The above observation is central to understanding *why* the alternative design is bad. We know that a bank branch is located in exactly one city. On the other hand, we know that a branch may make many loans. These are independent facts and, as we have seen, these facts are best represented in separate relations. We shall see that the fact that for every branch there is exactly one city can be stated formally, and this fact can be used to improve our database design.

6.1.2 Representation of Information

Let us consider a second alternative to our original design. This time, we attempt to combine the following two schemes:

> *Borrow-scheme* = (branch-name, loan-number, customer-name, amount)
> *Deposit-scheme* = (branch-name, account-number, customer-name, balance)

to create a new scheme:

> *BD-scheme* = (branch-name, loan-number, amount,
>   account-number, balance, customer-name)

Let *bd* be a relation on scheme *BD-scheme*. A tuple *t* in this relation has the following intuitive meaning:

- *t*[*loan-number*] is the number assigned to a loan made by the branch named *t*[*branch-name*] to the customer named *t*[*customer-name*].

- *t*[*amount*] is the amount of the loan whose number is *t*[*loan-number*].

- *t*[*account-number*] is the number assigned to an account at the branch named *t*[*branch-name*] and belonging to the customer named *t*[*customer-name*].

- *t*[*balance*] is the balance in the account whose number is *t*[*account-number*].

Consider a customer who has an account at the Perryridge branch but does not have a loan from that branch. We cannot represent this information directly by a tuple in the *bd* relation since tuples in the *bd* relation require values for *loan-number* and *amount*.

One solution to this problem is to introduce *null values*, as we did in Section 3.6 to handle updates through views. Recall, however, that null values are difficult to deal with. If we are not willing to deal with null values, each branch must force every depositor to take out a loan at that branch and every borrower to open an account at that branch. Presumably, the teller would inform the customer of this by saying, "We're sorry, but the computer forces us to do this." Clearly this excuse is untrue, since under our original database design, we could have depositors with no loan and borrowers with no account, and we could do so without resorting to the use of null values.

6.1.3 Loss of Information

The above examples of bad designs suggest that we should *decompose* relation schemes with many attributes into several schemes with fewer attributes. Careless decomposition, however, may lead to another form of bad design.

Consider yet another alternative design in which *Borrow-scheme* is decomposed into two schemes, *Amt-scheme* and *Loan-scheme*, as follows:

$$Amt\text{-}scheme = (amount, customer\text{-}name)$$
$$Loan\text{-}scheme = (branch\text{-}name, loan\text{-}number, amount)$$

Using the *borrow* relation of Figure 6.2, we construct our new relations *amt*(*Amt-scheme*) and *loan*(*Loan-scheme*) as follows:

$$amt = \Pi_{amount,\ customer\text{-}name}\ (borrow)$$
$$loan = \Pi_{branch\text{-}name,\ loan\text{-}number, amount}\ (borrow)$$

We show the resulting *amt* and *loan* relations in Figure 6.4.

Of course, there are cases in which we need to reconstruct the *borrow* relation. For example, suppose that we wish to find those branches from which Jones has a loan. None of the relations in our alternative database contains this data. We need to reconstruct the *borrow* relation. It appears that we can do this by writing:

$$amt \bowtie loan$$

Figure 6.5 shows the result of computing *amt* $\bowtie$ *loan* . When we compare this relation and the *borrow* relation with which we started (Figure 6.2), we notice some differences. Although every tuple that appears in *borrow*

branch-name	loan-number	amount
Downtown	17	1000
Redwood	23	2000
Perryridge	15	1500
Downtown	14	1500
Mianus	93	500
Round Hill	11	900
Pownal	29	1200
North Town	16	1300
Downtown	18	2000
Perryridge	25	2500
Brighton	10	2200

amount	customer-name
1000	Jones
2000	Smith
1500	Hayes
1500	Jackson
500	Curry
900	Turner
1200	Williams
1300	Adams
2000	Johnson
2500	Glenn
2200	Brooks

Figure 6.4   The relations *amt* and *loan*.

appears in *amt* ⋈ *loan* , there are tuples in *amt* ⋈ *loan* that are not in *borrow*. In our example, *amt* ⋈ *loan* has the following additional tuples:

(Downtown, 14, Hayes, 1500)
(Perryridge, 15, Jackson, 1500)
(Redwood, 23, Johnson, 2000)
(Downtown, 18, Smith, 2000)

Consider the query, "Find those branches from which Hayes has a loan." If we look back at Figure 6.2, we see that Hayes has only one loan, and that loan is from the Perryridge branch. However, when we apply the expression

$$\Pi_{branch\text{-}name} \ (\sigma_{customer\text{-}name \ = \ \text{"Hayes"}} \ (amt \ \bowtie \ loan))$$

we obtain *two* branch names: Perryridge and Downtown.

Let us examine this example more closely. If several loans happen to be in the same amount, we cannot tell which customer has which loan. Thus, when we join *amt* and *loan*, we obtain not only the tuples we had originally in *borrow*, but also several additional tuples. Although we have *more* tuples in *amt* ⋈ *loan* , we actually have *less* information. We are no longer able, in general, to represent in the database which customers are borrowers from which branch. Because of this loss of information, we call the decomposition of *Borrow-scheme* into *Amt-scheme* and *Loan-scheme* a *lossy decomposition*, or a *lossy-join decomposition*. A decomposition that is not a lossy-join decomposition is referred to as a *lossless-join decomposition*. It should be clear from our example that a lossy-join decomposition is, in general, a bad database design.

branch-name	loan-number	customer-name	amount
Downtown	17	Jones	1000
Redwood	23	Smith	2000
Perryridge	15	Hayes	1500
Downtown	14	Jackson	1500
Mianus	93	Curry	500
Round Hill	11	Turner	900
Pownal	29	Williams	1200
North Town	16	Adams	1300
Downtown	18	Johnson	2000
Perryridge	25	Glenn	2500
Brighton	10	Brooks	2200
Downtown	14	Hayes	1500
Perryridge	15	Jackson	1500
Redwood	23	Johnson	2000
Downtown	18	Smith	2000

Figure 6.5   The relation *amt* ⋈ *loan*

Let us examine the decomposition more closely to see why it is lossy. There is one attribute in common between *Loan-scheme* and *Amt-scheme*:

$$Loan\text{-}scheme \cap Amt\text{-}scheme = \{amount\}$$

The only way we can represent a relationship between *branch-name* and *customer-name* is through *amount*. This is not adequate because many customers may happen to have loans in the same amount, yet they do not necessarily have these loans from the same branches. Similarly, many customers may happen to have loans from the same branch, yet the amounts of their loans may be unrelated to each other.

Contrast this with *Lending-scheme*, which we discussed earlier. We argued that a better design would result if we decompose *Lending-scheme* into *Borrow-scheme* and *Branch-scheme*:

$$Branch\text{-}scheme \cap Borrow\text{-}scheme = \{branch\text{-}name\}$$

Thus, the only way we can represent a relationship between, for example, *customer-name* and *assets* is through *branch-name*. The difference between this example and the example above is that the assets of a branch are the same regardless of the customer to which we are referring, while the lending branch associated with a certain loan amount *does* depend on the customer to which we are referring. For a given *branch-name* there is exactly one *assets* value and exactly one *branch-city*, while a similar statement cannot be made for *amount*. Note that we have never stated formally in our design that a branch has a unique *assets* value and *branch-city* value. We know this from our intuition of the banking enterprise. We represented this earlier by the notion of *keys*. In Section 6.2, we shall see how to express these facts formally.

The notion of lossless joins is central to much of relational database design. Therefore, we restate the above examples below more concisely and more formally: Let U be a relation scheme. A set of relation schemes $\{R_1, R_2, ..., R_n\}$ is a *decomposition* of U if:

$$\bigcup_{i=1}^{n} R_i = U$$

That is, $\{R_1, R_2, ..., R_n\}$ is a decomposition of U if every attribute in U appears in at least one R_i, for $1 \le i \le n$. Let u be a relation on scheme U, and let $r_i = \Pi_{R_i}(u)$ for $1 \le i \le n$. That is, $\{r_1, r_2, ..., r_n\}$ is the database that results from decomposing U into $\{R_1, R_2, ..., R_n\}$. It is always the case that:

$$u \subseteq \bowtie_{i=1}^{n} r_i$$

To see this, consider a tuple t in relation u. When we compute $r_1, r_2, ..., r_n$, the tuple t gives rise to one tuple t_i in each r_i, $1 \le i \le n$. These n tuples combine to regenerate t when we compute $\bowtie_{i=1}^{n} r_i$. The details are left as an exercise to the reader. Therefore, every tuple in u appears in $\bowtie_{i=1}^{n} r_i$.

In general, $u \ne \bowtie_{i=1}^{n} r_i$. To illustrate this, consider our earlier example in which:

- $n = 2$.
- $U = $ *Borrow-scheme*.
- $R_1 = $ *Amt-scheme*.
- $R_2 = $ *Loan-scheme*.
- $u = $ the relation shown in Figure 6.2.
- r_1 and $r_2 = $ the relations shown in Figure 6.4.
- $r_1 \bowtie r_2 = $ the relation shown in Figure 6.5.

Note that the relations in Figures 6.2 and 6.5 are not the same.

In order to have a lossless-join decomposition, we need to impose some constraints on the set of possible relations. We found that decomposing *Lending-scheme* into *Borrow-scheme* and *Branch-scheme* is lossless because of the rule that "for every *branch-name* there is a unique *asset* value and a unique *branch-city* value." We say that a relation is *legal* if it satisfies all rules, or constraints, that we impose on our database.

Let *C* represent a set of constraints on the database. A decomposition $\{R_1, R_2, \ldots, R_n\}$ of a relation scheme *U* is a *lossless-join decomposition* for *U* if for all relations *u* on scheme *U* that are legal under *C*:

$$u = \overset{n}{\underset{i=1}{\bowtie}} \ \Pi_{R_i}(u)$$

We shall show how to test whether a decomposition is a lossless-join decomposition in the next section. A major part of this chapter is concerned with the question of how to specify constraints on the database and how to obtain lossless-join decompositions that avoid the pitfalls represented by the examples of bad database designs that we have seen in this section.

6.2 Normalization Using Functional Dependencies

In this section, we focus on a particular kind of constraint called a *functional dependency*. Functional dependencies are important because they lead to several highly desirable normal forms for relational databases. The notion of functional dependency is a generalization of the notion of *key*, as discussed in Chapters 2 and 3.

In general, it may not be a simple manner to determine keys from a given set of functional dependencies. In order to find keys, we need to study the properties of functional dependencies. First, we need to determine *all* the functional dependencies that hold. Second, once we have chosen a particular decomposition of a relation scheme, we need to determine those functional dependencies that hold on the decomposed schemes. We need general techniques if we are to deal with large, real-world databases. Furthermore, we need to guard against decompositions that have anomalous behavior similar to those discussed in Section 6.1.

6.2.1 Functional Dependencies

Functional dependencies are a constraint of the set of legal relations. They allow us to express facts about the enterprise that we are modeling with our database.

In Chapter 2, we defined the notion of a *superkey* as follows. Let *R* be a relation scheme. A subset *K* of *R* is a *superkey* of *R* if, in any legal relation $r(R)$, for all pairs t_1 and t_2 of tuples in *r* such that $t_1 \neq t_2$, $t_1[K] \neq t_2[K]$.

That is, no two tuples in any legal relation $r(R)$ may have the same value on attribute set K.

The notion of functional dependency generalizes the notion of superkey. Let $X \subseteq R$ and $Y \subseteq R$. The *functional dependency*

$$X \rightarrow Y$$

holds on R if in any legal relation $r(R)$, for all pairs of tuples t_1 and t_2 in r such that $t_1[X] = t_2[X]$, it is also the case that $t_1[Y] = t_2[Y]$.

Using the functional dependency notation, we say that K is a superkey of R if $K \rightarrow R$. That is, K is a superkey if whenever $t_1[K] = t_2[K]$, $t_1[R] = t_2[R]$ (that is, $t_1 = t_2$).

Functional dependencies allow us to express constraints that cannot be expressed using superkeys. Consider the scheme *Lending-scheme* that we used in one of our alternative designs in Section 6.1. We would not expect the attribute *branch-name* to be a superkey because we know that a branch may have many loans to many customers. However, we do expect the functional dependency:

$$branch\text{-}name \rightarrow branch\text{-}city$$

to hold, since we know that a branch may be located in exactly one city.

We shall use functional dependencies in two ways:

1. To test relations to see if they are legal under a given set of functional dependencies. If a relation r is legal under a set F of functional dependencies, we say that r satisfies F.

2. To specify constraints on the set of legal relations. We shall thus concern ourselves *only* with relations that satisfy a given set of functional dependencies.

Let us consider the relation r of Figure 6.6 and see which functional dependencies are satisfied. Observe that $A \rightarrow C$ is satisfied. There are two tuples that have an A value of a_1. These tuples have the same C value, namely, c_1. Similarly, the two tuples with an A value of a_2 have the same C value, c_2. There are no other pairs of distinct tuples that have the same A value. The functional dependency $C \rightarrow A$ is not satisfied, however. To see this, consider the tuples $t_1 = (a_2, b_3, c_2, d_3)$ and $t_2 = (a_3, b_3, c_2, d_3)$. These two tuples have the same C value c_2 but they have different A values, a_2 and a_3, respectively. Thus, we have found a pair of tuples t_1 and t_2 such that $t_1[C] = t_2[C]$ but $t_1[A] \neq t_2[A]$.

A	B	C	D
a_1	b_1	c_1	d_1
a_1	b_2	c_1	d_2
a_2	b_2	c_2	d_2
a_2	b_3	c_2	d_3
a_3	b_3	c_2	d_4

Figure 6.6   Sample relation r.

Many other functional dependencies are satisfied by r, including, for example, the functional dependency $AB \rightarrow D$. Note that we use "AB" as a shorthand for $\{A,B\}$, to conform with standard practice. The verification that $AB \rightarrow D$ is satisfied is left as an exercise.

Some functional dependencies are said to be *trivial*, because they are satisfied by all relations. For example, $A \rightarrow A$ is satisfied by all relations involving attribute A. Reading the definition of functional dependency literally, we see that for all tuples t_1 and t_2 such that $t_1[A] = t_2[A]$, it is also the case that $t_1[A] = t_2[A]$. In general, a functional dependency of the form $X \rightarrow Y$ is trivial if $Y \subseteq X$.

Let us return to the banking example. If we consider the *customer* relation as shown in Figure 6.7, we see that *street* $\rightarrow$ *customer-city* is satisfied. However, we do believe that, in the real world, two cities can have streets with the same name. Thus, it is possible at some time to have

customer-name	street	customer-city
Jones	Main	Harrison
Smith	North	Rye
Hayes	Main	Harrison
Curry	North	Rye
Lindsay	Park	Pittsfield
Turner	Putnam	Stamford
Williams	Nassau	Princeton
Adams	Spring	Pittsfield
Johnson	Alma	Palo Alto
Glenn	Sand Hill	Woodside
Brooks	Senator	Brooklyn
Green	Walnut	Stamford

Figure 6.7   Customer relation.

an instance of the *customer* relation in which *street* → *customer-city* is not satisfied. Thus, we would not include *street* → *customer-city* in the set of functional dependencies that hold on *Customer-scheme*.

In the *borrow* relation of Figure 6.2, we see that *loan-number* → *balance* is satisfied. Unlike the case of *customer-city* and *street*, we do not believe that the real-world enterprise that we are modeling allows loans to have several balances. Therefore, we want to require that *loan-number* → *balance* be satisfied by the *borrow* relation at all times. In other words, we impose the constraint that *loan-number* → *balance* hold on *Borrow-scheme*.

In what follows, we assume that when we design a relational database, we first list those functional dependencies that must always hold. In the banking example, our list of dependencies includes the following:

- On *Branch-scheme*:

$$branch\text{-}name \rightarrow branch\text{-}city$$
$$branch\text{-}name \rightarrow assets$$

- On *Customer-scheme*:

$$customer\text{-}name \rightarrow customer\text{-}city$$
$$customer\text{-}name \rightarrow street$$

- On *Borrow-scheme*:

$$loan\text{-}number \rightarrow amount$$
$$loan\text{-}number \rightarrow branch\text{-}name$$

- On *Deposit-scheme*:

$$account\text{-}number \rightarrow balance$$
$$account\text{-}number \rightarrow branch\text{-}name$$

6.2.2 Theory of Functional Dependencies

A large body of formal theory has been developed for functional dependencies. The bibliographic notes provide a history of this work. We shall focus on those algorithms that are most useful in applying this theory to the design of BCNF (Section 6.2.4) and 3NF (Section 6.2.5) relational databases.

In general, if we are given a set of functional dependencies, these functional dependencies may imply that other functional dependencies hold also. For example, suppose we are given a relation scheme $R = (A,B,C,G,H,I)$ and a set of functional dependencies:

$$A \rightarrow B$$
$$A \rightarrow C$$
$$CG \rightarrow H$$
$$CG \rightarrow I$$
$$B \rightarrow H$$

It is not sufficient to consider the given set of functional dependencies. Rather, we need to consider *all* functional dependencies that hold. We shall see that, given a set F of functional dependencies, we can prove that certain other functional dependencies hold. We say that such functional dependencies are *logically implied* by F.

If we are given the set of functional dependencies that appear above, the functional dependency

$$A \rightarrow H$$

is logically implied. That is, we can show that whenever our given set of functional dependencies hold, $A \rightarrow H$ must hold also. Suppose that t_1 and t_2 are tuples such that

$$t_1[A] = t_2[A]$$

Then, since we are given that $A \rightarrow B$, it follows from the definition of functional dependency that

$$t_1[B] = t_2[B]$$

Then, since we are given that $B \rightarrow H$, it follows from the definition of functional dependency that

$$t_1[H] = t_2[H]$$

Therefore, we have shown that whenever t_1 and t_2 are tuples such that $t_1[A] = t_2[A]$, it must be that $t_1[H] = t_2[H]$. But that is exactly the definition of $A \rightarrow H$.

Let F be a set of functional dependencies. We denote the *closure* of F by F^+. The closure of F is the set of all functional dependencies logically implied by F. Given F, we can compute F^+ directly from the formal definition of functional dependency. If F is large, this process would be lengthy and difficult. Such a computation of F^+ requires arguments of the type given above to show that $A \rightarrow H$ is in the closure of our example set of dependencies. We now present simpler techniques for reasoning about functional dependencies.

The first technique we present is based on three *axioms* or rules of inference for functional dependencies. By applying these rules repeatedly, we can find all of F^+ given F.

1. *Reflexivity rule.* If X is a set of attributes and $Y \subseteq X$, then $X \rightarrow Y$ holds.

2. *Augmentation rule.* If $X \rightarrow Y$ holds and W is a set of attributes, then $WX \rightarrow WY$ holds.

3. *Transitivity rule.* If $X \rightarrow Y$ holds, and $Y \rightarrow Z$ holds, then $X \rightarrow Z$ holds.

These rules are said to be *sound* because they do not generate any incorrect functional dependencies. The rules are *complete* because given a set F of functional dependencies, they allow us to find all of F^+. This collection of rules is called *Armstrong's axioms* in honor of the person who first proposed them.

Although Armstrong's axioms are complete, it is tiresome to use them directly for the computation of F^+. To simplify matters further, we list some additional rules. It is possible to use Armstrong's axioms to prove that these rules are correct (see the exercises).

4. *Union rule.* If $X \rightarrow Y$ holds and $X \rightarrow Z$ holds, then $X \rightarrow YZ$ holds.

5. *Decomposition rule.* If $X \rightarrow YZ$ holds, then $X \rightarrow Y$ holds and $X \rightarrow Z$ holds.

6. *Pseudotransitivity rule.* If $X \rightarrow Y$ holds and $WY \rightarrow Z$ holds, then $XW \rightarrow Z$ holds.

Let us apply our rules to the example we presented earlier of scheme $R = (A,B,C,G,H,I)$ and the set F of functional dependencies $\{A \rightarrow B, A \rightarrow C, CG \rightarrow H, CG \rightarrow I, B \rightarrow H\}$. We list some members of F^+ below:

- $A \rightarrow H$. Since $A \rightarrow B$ and $B \rightarrow H$ holds, we apply rule 3 (transitivity). Observe that it was much easier to use Armstrong's axioms to show that $A \rightarrow H$ holds than it was to argue directly from the definitions as we did earlier.

- $CG \rightarrow HI$. Since $CG \rightarrow H$ and $CG \rightarrow I$, the union rule (rule 4) implies that $CG \rightarrow HI$.

- $AG \rightarrow I$. We need several steps to show $AG \rightarrow I$. First, observe that $A \rightarrow C$ holds. Using the augmentation rule (rule 2), we see that $AG \rightarrow CG$. We are given that $CG \rightarrow I$, so by the transitivity rule (rule 3) $AG \rightarrow I$ holds.

Frequently, we are interested in finding those attributes functionally determined by a given set of attributes. One way to find this set is to compute the closure of the given set of functional dependencies by an exhaustive application of our inference rules. Fortunately, there is a more efficient approach.

Let X be a set of attributes. We call the set of all attributes functionally determined by X under a set F of functional dependencies the *closure* of X under F and denote it by X^+. Figure 6.8 shows an algorithm, written in pseudo Pascal, to compute X^+. The input is a set F of functional dependencies and the set X of attributes. The output is stored in the variable *result*.

To illustrate how the algorithm of Figure 6.8 works, let us use the algorithm to compute $(AG)^+$ with the functional dependencies defined above. We start with *result* = AG. The first time we execute the **while** loop to test each functional dependency we find that:

- $A \to B$ causes us to include B in *result*. To see this, observe that $A \to B$ is in F, $A \subseteq result$ (which is AG), so *result* := *result* $\cup$ B.

- $A \to C$ causes *result* to become $ABCG$.

- $CG \to H$ causes *result* to become $ABCGH$.

- $CG \to I$ causes *result* to become $ABCGHI$.

The second time we execute the **while** loop, no new attributes are added to *result* and the algorithm terminates.

Let us see why the algorithm of Figure 6.8 is correct. The first step is correct since $X \to X$ always holds (by the reflexivity rule). We claim that for any subset Y of *result*, it is the case that $X \to Y$. Since we start the **while** loop with $X \to result$ being true, the only way we can add Z to result is if $Y \subseteq result$ and $Y \to Z$. But then *result* $\to Y$ by the reflexivity rule, so $X \to Y$ by transitivity. Another application of transitivity shows

```
result := X;
while (changes to result) do
    for each functional dependency Y → Z in F do
        begin
            if Y ⊆ result then result := result ∪ Z;
        end
```

Figure 6.8 An algorithm to compute X^+, the closure of X under F.

that $X \rightarrow Z$ (using $X \rightarrow Y$ and $Y \rightarrow Z$). The union rule implies that $X \rightarrow result \cup Z$, so X functionally determines any new result generated in the **while** loop. Thus, any attribute returned by the algorithm is in X^+.

It is easy to see that the algorithm finds all of X^+. If there is an attribute in X^+ not yet in *result*, then there must be a functional dependency $Y \rightarrow Z$ for which $Y \subseteq result$ and at least one attribute in F is not in *result*. It turns out that in the worst case this algorithm may take exponential time in the size of F. There is a faster (though slightly more complex) algorithm that runs in time linear in the size of F. The algorithm is presented as part of Exercise 6.11.

6.2.3 Desirable Properties of Decomposition

A given set of functional dependencies can be used in designing a relational database in which most of the undesirable properties discussed in Section 6.1 do not occur. In designing such systems, it may become necessary to decompose a relation to a number of smaller relations.

In this subsection, we shall illustrate our concepts by considering the *Lending-scheme* scheme of Section 6.1.1:

$$Lending\text{-}scheme = (branch\text{-}name, \ assets, \ branch\text{-}city, \ loan\text{-}number,$$
$$customer\text{-}name, \ amount)$$

The set F of functional dependencies that we require to hold on *Lending-scheme* are:

$$branch\text{-}name \rightarrow assets$$
$$branch\text{-}name \rightarrow branch\text{-}city$$
$$loan\text{-}number \rightarrow amount$$
$$loan\text{-}number \rightarrow branch\text{-}name$$

As discussed in Section 6.1.1, the *Lending-scheme* is an example of a bad database design. Assume that we decompose it to the following five relations:

$$R_1 = (branch\text{-}name, \ assets)$$
$$R_2 = (branch\text{-}name, \ branch\text{-}city)$$
$$R_3 = (loan\text{-}number, \ amount)$$
$$R_4 = (loan\text{-}number, \ branch\text{-}name)$$
$$R_5 = (loan\text{-}number, \ customer\text{-}name)$$

We claim that this decomposition has several desirable properties, which we discuss below.

Lossless-join decomposition

In Section 6.1.3, we have argued that it is crucial when decomposing a relation into a number of smaller relations that the decomposition be lossless. We claim that the above decomposition is indeed lossless. To demonstrate this, we must first present a criterion for determining whether a decomposition is lossy.

Let R be a relation scheme and F a set of functional dependencies on R. Let R_1 and R_2 form a decomposition of R. This decomposition is a lossless-join decomposition of R if at least one of the following functional dependencies are in F^+.

- $R_1 \cap R_2 \to R_1$
- $R_1 \cap R_2 \to R_2$

We now show that our decomposition is a lossless-join decomposition by showing a sequence of steps that generate the decomposition. We begin by decomposing *Lending-scheme* into two schemes:

$$R_1 = (branch\text{-}name,\ assets)$$
$$R_1' = (branch\text{-}name,\ branch\text{-}city,\ loan\text{-}number,\ customer\text{-}name,\ amount)$$

Since $R_1 \cap R_1' = \{branch\text{-}name\}$ and *branch-name* $\to$ *assets*, it follows (by augmentation) that

- $R_1 \cap R_1' = branch\text{-}name$.
- *branch-name* $\to$ *branch-name assets* .
- *branch-name assets* $= R_1$.

So our initial decomposition is a lossless-join decomposition.
Next, we decompose R_1' into:

$$R_2 = (branch\text{-}name,\ branch\text{-}city)$$
$$R_2' = (branch\text{-}name,\ loan\text{-}number,\ customer\text{-}name,\ amount)$$

This step results in a lossless-join decomposition since *branch-name* $\to$ *branch-city*. We then decompose R_2' into:

$$R_3 = (loan\text{-}number,\ amount)$$
$$R_3' = (loan\text{-}number,\ branch\text{-}name,\ customer\text{-}name).$$

Then R_3' is decomposed into:

$$R_4 = (\textit{loan-number, branch-name})$$
$$R_5 = (\textit{loan-number, customer-name}).$$

It is simple, using the set F of functional dependencies on *Lending-scheme*, to verify that both of these final steps generate a lossless-join decomposition.

Dependency Preservation

There is another goal in relational database design to be considered: *dependency preservation*. When an update is made to the database, the system should be able to check that the update will not create an illegal relation; that is, one that does not satisfy all of the given functional dependencies. In order to check updates efficiently, it is desirable to design relational database schemes that allow update validation without the computation of joins.

In order to determine whether we need to compute joins, we need to determine what functional dependencies may be tested by checking only one relation. Let F be a set of functional dependencies on a scheme R and let R_1, R_2, ..., R_n be a decomposition of R. The *restriction* of F to R_i is the set F_i of all functional dependencies in F^+ that include *only* attributes of R_i. Since all functional dependencies in a restriction involve attributes of only one relation scheme, it is possible to test satisfaction of such a dependency by checking only one relation.

The set of restrictions F_1, F_2, ..., F_n is the set of dependencies that can be checked efficiently. We now must ask whether testing only the restrictions is sufficient. Let F' be the union of all the restrictions, $\cup_{i=1}^{n} F_i$. F' is a set of functional dependencies on scheme R, but, in general, $F' \neq F$. However, even if $F' \neq F$, it may be that $F'^+ = F^+$. If this is true, then every dependency in F is logically implied by F' and if we verify that F' is satisfied, we have verified that F is satisfied. We say that a decomposition having this property is a *dependency-preserving* decomposition. Figure 6.9 shows an algorithm for testing dependency preservation. The input is a set $D = \{S_1, S_2, ..., S_m\}$ of decomposed relation schemes, and a set F of functional dependencies.

We can now show that our decomposition *Lending-scheme* is dependency preserving. To see this, we consider each member of the set F of functional dependencies that we require to hold on *Lending-scheme* and show that each one can be tested in at least one relation in the decomposition.

- *branch-name* → *assets* can be tested using R_1 = (*branch-name, assets*).

- *branch-name* → *branch-city* can be tested using R_3 = (*branch-name, branch-city*).

- *loan-number* → *amount* can be tested using R_5 = (*loan-number* → *amount*).

- *loan-number* → *branch-name* can be tested using R_7 = (*loan-number, branch-name*).

As the above example shows, it is often easier not to apply the algorithm of Figure 6.9 to test dependency preservation, since the first step, computation of F^+, takes exponential time.

Repetition of information

The decomposition of *Lending-scheme* does not suffer from the problem of repetition of information that we discussed in Section 6.1.1. In *Lending-scheme*, it was necessary to repeat the city and assets of a branch for each loan. The decomposition separates branch and loan data into distinct relations, thereby eliminating this redundancy. Similarly, observe that if a single loan is made to several customers, we must repeat the amount of the loan once for each customer (as well as the city and assets of the branch). In the decomposition, the relation on scheme R_5 contains the *loan-number, customer-name* relationship, and no other scheme does. Therefore, we have one tuple for each customer for a loan only in the relation on R_5. In the other relations involving *loan-number* (those on schemes R_3 and R_4), only one tuple per loan need appear.

> compute F^+;
> **for each** scheme S_i in D **do**
>   **begin**
> F_i : = the restriction of F^+ to S_i;
>   **end**
> $F' := \cup_i F_i$;
> compute F'^+;
> **if** ($F'^+ = F^+$) **then** return (true)
>   **else** return (false);

Figure 6.9   Testing dependency preservation.

Clearly, the lack of redundancy exhibited by our decomposition is desirable. The degrees to which we can achieve this lack of redundancy is represented by several *normal forms*, which we shall discuss in the remainder of this chapter.

6.2.4 Boyce-Codd Normal Form

We now examine how we can use a given set of functional dependencies to design a relational database. Using functional dependencies, we can define several *normal forms* which represent "good" database designs. There are a large number of normal forms. Of these, one of the more desirable normal forms we can obtain is *Boyce-Codd normal form* (BCNF).

A relation scheme R is in BCNF if for all functional dependencies that hold on R of the form $X \rightarrow A$, where $X \subseteq R$ and $A \in R$, at least one of the following holds:

- $X \rightarrow A$ is a trivial functional dependency (that is, $A \in X$).

- X is a superkey for scheme R.

A database design is in BCNF if each member of the set of relation schemes comprising the design is in BCNF.

In our banking example, the relation scheme *Customer-scheme* is in BCNF. To see this, note that a candidate key for the relation is *customer-name*. The only nontrivial functional dependencies that hold on all legal instances of the *customer* relation have *customer-name* on the left side of the arrow. Since *customer-name* is a candidate key, functional dependencies with *customer-name* on the left side do not violate the definition of BCNF.

The scheme, *Borrow-scheme*, however, is *not* in BCNF. First, note that *loan-number* is not a superkey for *Borrow-scheme*. Although

$$loan\text{-}number \rightarrow customer\text{-}name$$

happens to hold on the *borrow* relation of Figure 6.2, we *could* have a pair of tuples representing a single loan made to two people:

(Downtown, 44, Mr. Bill, 1000)
(Downtown, 44, Mrs. Bill, 1000)

Because we did not list functional dependencies that rule out the above case, *loan-number* is not a candidate key. However, the functional dependency *loan-number* → *amount* is nontrivial. Therefore, *Borrow-scheme* does not satisfy the definition of BCNF.

We claim that *Borrow-scheme* is not in a desirable form since it suffers from the *repetition of information* problem described in Section 6.1.1. To illustrate this, observe that if there are several customer names associated with a loan, in a relation on *Borrow-scheme*, then we are forced to repeat the branch name and the amount once for each customer. We can eliminate this redundancy by redesigning our database so that all schemes are in BCNF. One approach to this problem is to take the existing non-BCNF design as a starting point and decompose those schemes that are not in BCNF. Consider the decomposition of *Borrow-scheme* into two schemes:

$$Loan\text{-}info\text{-}scheme = (branch\text{-}name, loan\text{-}number, amount)$$
$$Loan\text{-}customer\text{-}scheme = (loan\text{-}number, customer\text{-}name)$$

To determine whether these schemes are in BCNF, we need to determine what functional dependencies apply to the schemes. In this example, it is easy to see that

$$loan\text{-}number \rightarrow amount$$
$$loan\text{-}number \rightarrow branch\text{-}name$$

apply to *Loan-info-scheme*, and that only trivial functional dependencies apply to *Loan-customer-scheme*. Although *loan-number* is not a superkey for *Borrow-scheme*, it is a candidate key for *Loan-info-scheme*. Thus, both schemes of our decomposition are in BCNF.

It is now possible to avoid redundancy in the case where there are several customers associated with a loan. There is exactly one tuple for each loan in the relation on *Loan-info-scheme*, and one tuple for each customer of each loan in the relation on *Loan-customer-scheme*. Thus, we do not have to repeat the branch name and the amount once for each customer associated with a loan. The decomposition is a lossless-join decomposition. We shall see how to determine this in the next section.

In order for the entire design for the bank example to be in BCNF, we must decompose *Deposit-scheme* in a manner similar to our decomposition of *Borrow-scheme*. When we do this, we obtain two schemes:

$$Account\text{-}info\text{-}scheme = (branch\text{-}name, account\text{-}number, balance),$$
$$Account\text{-}customer\text{-}scheme = (account\text{-}number, customer)$$

We are now able to state a general method to generate a collection of BCNF schemes. Let R be a given relation scheme and let F be the given set of functional dependencies on R. Recall that R is in BCNF if for all functional dependencies $X \rightarrow A$ in F^+ either $X \rightarrow A$ is trivial or X is a superkey for R (that is, $X \rightarrow R$ is in F^+).

If R is not in BCNF, we can decompose R into a collection of BCNF schemes $R_1, R_2, \ldots, R_n$ using the algorithm of Figure 6.10 which generates not only a BCNF decomposition but also a lossless-join decomposition. To see why our algorithm generates only lossless-join decompositions, notice

result := {*R*};
done := false;
compute F^+;
while (**not** *done*) **do**
   if (there is a scheme R_i in *result* that is not in BCNF)
     then begin
          let $X \rightarrow Y$ be a nontrivial functional dependency that holds
          on R_i such that $X \rightarrow R_i$ is not in F^+;
          result := (*result* − R_i) ∪ (R_i − X) ∪ (X,Y);
       end
    else *done* := true;

Figure 6.10   BCNF decomposition algorithm.

that when we replace a scheme R_i with $R_i − Y$ and (X,Y), the dependency $X \rightarrow Y$ holds, and $(R_i − Y) \cup (XY) = R_i$.

Let us apply the BCNF decomposition algorithm to the *Lending-scheme* scheme that we used earlier as an example of a bad database design.

$$Lending\text{-}scheme = (branch\text{-}name, assets, branch\text{-}city, loan\text{-}number,$$
$$customer\text{-}name, amount)$$

The set F of functional dependencies that we require to hold on *Lending-scheme* are:

$$branch\text{-}name \rightarrow assets$$
$$branch\text{-}name \rightarrow branch\text{-}city$$
$$loan\text{-}number \rightarrow amount$$
$$loan\text{-}number \rightarrow branch\text{-}name$$

We can apply the algorithm of Figure 6.10 as follows:

- The functional dependency:

$$branch\text{-}name \rightarrow assets$$

holds on *Lending-scheme*, but *branch-name* is not a superkey. Thus, *Lending-scheme* is not in BCNF. We replace *Lending-scheme* by

$$R_1 = (branch\text{-}name, assets)$$
$$R_2 = (branch\text{-}name, branch\text{-}city, loan\text{-}number,$$
$$customer\text{-}name, amount)$$

- R_1 is in BCNF since *branch-name* is a key for R_1.

- The functional dependency:

$$branch\text{-}name \rightarrow branch\text{-}city$$

holds on R_2, but *branch-name* is not a key for R_2. We replace R_2 by

$$R_3 = (branch\text{-}name, branch\text{-}city)$$
$$R_4 = (branch\text{-}name, loan\text{-}number, customer\text{-}name, amount)$$

- R_3 is in BCNF.

- The functional dependency:

$$loan\text{-}number \rightarrow amount$$

causes us to decompose R_4 into

$$R_5 = (loan\text{-}number, amount)$$
$$R_6 = (branch\text{-}name, loan\text{-}number, customer\text{-}name)$$

- R_5 is in BCNF.

- The functional dependency:

$$loan\text{-}number \rightarrow branch\text{-}name$$

causes us to decompose R_6 into

$$R_7 = (loan\text{-}number, branch\text{-}name)$$
$$R_8 = (loan\text{-}number, customer\text{-}name)$$

- R_7 and R_8 are in BCNF.

Thus, the decomposition of *Lending-scheme* results in the five relation schemes R_1, R_3, R_5, R_7, and R_8, each of which is in BCNF. These relation schemes are the same as those used in Section 6.2.3 (except for naming of the schemes). We have demonstrated in that section that the resulting decomposition is both a lossless-join decomposition and a dependency-preserving decomposition.

Not every BCNF decomposition is dependency-preserving. To illustrate this, consider the *BD-scheme* defined in Section 6.1.2 that we used as an example of a bad database design.

$$BD\text{-}scheme = (branch\text{-}name, loan\text{-}number, amount, account\text{-}number,$$
$$balance, customer\text{-}name)$$

The set F of functional dependencies that we require to hold on the *BD-scheme* is:

$$loan\text{-}number \rightarrow amount$$
$$loan\text{-}number \rightarrow branch\text{-}name$$
$$account\text{-}number \rightarrow balance$$
$$account\text{-}number \rightarrow branch\text{-}name$$

If we apply the algorithm of Figure 6.10, we may obtain the following BCNF decomposition:

$$R_1 = (loan\text{-}number, amount)$$
$$R_2 = (loan\text{-}number, branch\text{-}name)$$
$$R_3 = (account\text{-}number, balance)$$
$$R_4 = (loan\text{-}number, account\text{-}number, customer\text{-}name)$$

Using our relation in scheme R_1, we can ensure that the functional dependency *loan* $\rightarrow$ *amount* is not violated by an update. Similarly, scheme R_2 allows us to ensure that *loan-number* $\rightarrow$ *branch* is satisfied, and R_3 serves this purpose for *account-number* $\rightarrow$ *balance*. However, the dependency:

$$account\text{-}number \rightarrow branch\text{-}name$$

is not preserved. That is, it is possible to insert two branch names for the same account number (violating *account-number* $\rightarrow$ *branch-name*). The violation of this dependency cannot be detected unless a join is computed.

To see why the decomposition of BD-scheme into R_1, R_2, R_3 and R_4 is not dependency-preserving, apply the algorithm of Figure 6.9. We find that the restriction of F to each scheme is as follows (trivial dependencies are omitted):

$$R_1: loan\text{-}number \rightarrow amount$$
$$R_2: loan\text{-}number \rightarrow branch\text{-}name$$
$$R_3: account\text{-}number \rightarrow balance$$
$$R_4: \text{only trivial dependencies hold}$$

Thus the set F' is

$$loan\text{-}number \rightarrow amount,$$
$$loan\text{-}number \rightarrow branch\text{-}name,$$
$$account\text{-}number \rightarrow balance$$

It is easy to see that the functional dependency

$$account\text{-}number \rightarrow branch\text{-}name$$

is not in F'^+ even though it *is* in F^+. Therefore, $F'^+ \neq F^+$ and the decomposition is not dependency-preserving.

The above example demonstrates that not every BCNF decomposition is dependency-preserving. We shall now show that it is not always possible to satisfy all three design goals:

- BCNF.

- Lossless join.

- Dependency preservation.

Consider the scheme $S = (J,K,L)$ with a given set of functional dependencies:

$$JK \rightarrow L$$
$$L \rightarrow K$$

Clearly, S is not in BCNF since $L \rightarrow K$ and L is not a superkey. However, every BCNF decomposition of S must fail to preserve $JK \rightarrow L$. The algorithm of Figure 6.10 generates the decomposition $\{(K,L) (J,L)\}$. The decomposed schemes preserve only $L \rightarrow K$ (and trivial dependencies) but the closure of $\{L \rightarrow K\}$ does not include $JK \rightarrow L$.

6.2.5 Third Normal Form

In those cases where we cannot meet all three design criteria, we abandon BCNF and accept a weaker normal form called *third normal form* (3NF). We shall see that it is always possible to find a lossless-join, dependency-preserving decomposition that is in 3NF.

BCNF requires that all nontrivial dependencies be of the form $X \rightarrow A$ where X is a superkey. 3NF relaxes this constraint slightly by allowing nontrivial functional dependencies whose left side is not a superkey.

A relation scheme R is in 3NF if for all functional dependencies that hold on R of the form $X \rightarrow A$, where $X \subseteq R$ and $A \in R$, at least one of the following holds:

- $X \rightarrow Y$ is a trivial functional dependency.
- X is a superkey for R.
- Y is contained in a candidate key for R.

The definition of 3NF allows certain functional dependencies that are not allowed in BCNF. A dependency $X \rightarrow Y$ that satisfies only the third condition of the 3NF definition is not allowed in BCNF though it is allowed in 3NF. These dependencies are called *transitive dependencies* (see Exercise 6.40).

Observe that if a relation scheme is in BCNF, then all functional dependencies are of the form "superkey determines a set of attributes" (or the dependency is trivial). Thus, a BCNF scheme cannot have *any* transitive dependencies at all. As a result, every BCNF scheme is also in 3NF, and BCNF is therefore a more restrictive constraint than 3NF.

Let us return to our simple example of a scheme that did not have a dependency-preserving, lossless-join decomposition into BCNF. Let $S = (J,K,L)$ with $F = \{JK \rightarrow L, L \rightarrow K\}$. Although scheme S is not in BCNF, it is in 3NF. To see that this is so, note that JK is a candidate key for S, so the only attribute not contained in a candidate key for R is L. The only nontrivial functional dependency of the form $X \rightarrow L$ is $JK \rightarrow L$. Since JK is a candidate key, this dependency does not violate the definition of 3NF.

Figure 6.11 shows an algorithm for finding a dependency-preserving, lossless-join decomposition into 3NF. It ensures preservation of dependencies by building explicitly a scheme for each given dependency. It ensures that the decomposition is a lossless-join decomposition by ensuring that at least one scheme contains a candidate key for the scheme being decomposed. The exercises provide some insight into the proof that this suffices to guarantee a lossless join.

We illustrate the algorithm of Figure 6.11 by using it to generate a 3NF decomposition of *BD-scheme*. The **for** loop causes us to include the following schemes in our decomposition:

> *(loan-number, account)*
> *(loan-number, branch-name)*
> *(account-number, balance)*
> *(account-number, branch-name)*

Since none of the above schemes contains a candidate key for *BD-scheme*, we add a scheme consisting of a candidate key

> *(customer-name, loan-number, account-number)*

The final **if** statement does not cause us to add any more schemes to our decomposition since all attributes of *BD-scheme* already appear in some attribute of the decomposition.

$i := 0$
for each functional dependency $X \rightarrow Y$ in F **do**
   begin
      $i := i + 1;$
      $R_i := XY;$
   end
if none of the schemes R_j, $1 \le j \le i$ contains a candidate key for R
   then begin
         $i := i + 1;$
         $R_i := $ any candidate key for R;
     end
if $\cup_{j=1}^{i} R_j \ne R$
   then begin
           $R_{i+1} := R - \cup_{j=1}^{i} R_j;$
         $i := i + 1;$
     end
return $(R_1, R_2, ..., R_i)$

Figure 6.11   Dependency-preserving, lossless-join decomposition into 3NF.

6.2.6 Comparison of BCNF and 3NF

We have seen two normal forms for relational database schemes: 3NF and BCNF. There is an advantage to 3NF in that we know that it is always possible to obtain a 3NF design without sacrificing a lossless join or dependency preservation. Nevertheless, there is a disadvantage to 3NF. If we do not eliminate all transitive dependencies, it may be necessary to use null values to represent some of the possible meaningful relationships among data items. To illustrate this, consider the scheme $S = (J, K, L)$ with $F = \{JK \rightarrow L, L \rightarrow K\}$. Since $L \rightarrow K$, we may want to represent relationships between values for L and values for K in our database. However, in order to do so, either there must be a corresponding value for J, or we must use a null value for the attribute J.

If we are forced to choose between BCNF and dependency preservation with 3NF, it is generally preferable to opt for 3NF. If we cannot test for dependency preservation efficiently, we either pay a high penalty in system performance or risk the integrity of the data in our database. Neither of these alternatives is attractive. With such alternatives, the limited amount of redundancy imposed by transitive dependencies allowed under 3NF is the lesser evil. Thus we normally choose to retain dependency preservation and sacrifice BCNF.

To summarize the above discussion, we note that our goal for a relational database design is:

- BCNF.
- Lossless join.
- Dependency preservation.

If we cannot achieve this, we accept:

- 3NF.
- Lossless join.
- Dependency preservation.

6.3 Normalization Using Multivalued Dependencies

Until now, the only form of constraint we have allowed on the set of legal relations is the functional dependency. We now define another form of constraint, called a *multivalued dependency*. As we did for functional dependencies, we shall use multivalued dependencies to define a normal form for relation schemes. This normal form, called *fourth normal form* (4NF), is more restrictive than BCNF. We shall see that every 4NF scheme is also in BCNF, but there are BCNF schemes that are not in 4NF.

6.3.1 Multivalued Dependencies

Functional dependencies rule out certain tuples from being in a relation. If $A \to B$, then we cannot have two tuples with the same A value but different B values. Multivalued dependencies do not rule out the existence of certain tuples. Instead, they *require* that other tuples of a certain form be present in the relation. For this reason, functional dependencies sometimes are referred to as "equality-generating" dependencies and multivalued dependencies are referred to as "tuple-generating" dependencies.

Let R be a relation scheme and let $X \subseteq R$ and $Y \subseteq R$. The *multivalued dependency*:

$$X \twoheadrightarrow Y$$

holds on R if in any legal relation $r(R)$, for all pairs of tuples t_1 and t_2 in r such that $t_1[X] = t_2[X]$, there exist tuples t_3 and t_4 in r such that:

X	Y	$R - X - Y$
t_1 $a_1 \cdots a_i$	$a_{i+1} \cdots a_j$	$a_{j+1} \cdots a_n$
t_2 $a_1 \cdots a_i$	$b_{i+1} \cdots b_j$	$b_{j+1} \cdots b_n$
t_3 $a_1 \cdots a_i$	$a_{i+1} \cdots a_j$	$b_{j+1} \cdots b_n$
t_4 $a_1 \cdots a_i$	$b_{i+1} \cdots b_j$	$a_{j+1} \cdots a_n$

Figure 6.12   Tabular representation of $X \twoheadrightarrow Y$.

$$t_1[X] = t_2[X] = t_3[X] = t_4[X]$$

$$t_3[Y] = t_1[Y]$$

$$t_3[R - Y] = t_2[R - Y]$$

$$t_4[Y] = t_2[Y]$$

$$t_4[R - Y] = t_1[R - Y]$$

This definition is less complicated than it appears. In Figure 6.12, we give a tabular picture of t_1, t_2, t_3, and t_4. Intuitively, the multivalued dependency $X \twoheadrightarrow Y$ says that the relationship between X and Y is independent of the relationship between X and $R - Y$. If the multivalued dependency $X \twoheadrightarrow Y$ is satisfied by all relations on scheme R, then $X \twoheadrightarrow Y$ is a *trivial* multivalued dependency on scheme R. Thus $X \twoheadrightarrow Y$ is trivial if $Y \subseteq X$ or $Y \cup X = R$.

To illustrate the difference between functional and multivalued dependencies, consider again our banking example. Let us assume that instead of the schemes *Borrow-scheme* and *Customer-scheme*, we have the single scheme:

BC-scheme = (*loan-number, customer-name, street, customer-city*)

The astute reader will recognize this as a non-BCNF scheme because of the functional dependency *customer-name → street customer-city* that we asserted earlier, and the fact that *customer-name* is not a key for *BC-scheme*. However, let us assume that our bank is attracting wealthy customers who have several addresses (say, a winter home and a summer home). Then, we no longer wish to enforce the functional dependency *customer-name → street customer-city*. If we remove this functional dependency, we find *BC-scheme* to be in BCNF with respect to our modified set of functional dependencies. Despite the fact that *BC-scheme* is now in BCNF, we still have the problem of repetition of information that we had earlier.

Consider the relation *bc* (*BC-scheme*) of Figure 6.13. We must repeat the loan number once for each address a customer has, and we must repeat the address for each loan a customer has. This repetition is unnecessary

loan-number	customer-name	street	customer-city
23	Smith	North	Rye
23	Smith	Main	Manchester
93	Curry	North	Rye
93	Curry	Main	Manchester

Figure 6.13   Relation *bc*, an example of redundancy in a BCNF relation.

since the relationship between a customer and his address is independent of the relationship between that customer and a loan. If a customer, say Smith, has a loan, say loan number 23, we want that loan to be associated with all of Smith's addresses. Thus, the relation of Figure 6.14 is illegal. To make this relation legal, we need to add the tuples (23, Smith, Main, Manchester) and (27, Smith, North, Rye) to the *bc* relation of Figure 6.14.

Comparing the above example with our definition of multivalued dependency, we see that we want the multivalued dependency:

$$customer\text{-}name \twoheadrightarrow street\ customer\text{-}city$$

to hold. (The multivalued dependency *customer-name* $\twoheadrightarrow$ *loan-number* will do as well. We shall soon see that they are equivalent.)

As was the case for functional dependencies, we shall use multivalued dependencies in two ways:

1. To test relations to determine whether they are legal under a given set of functional and multivalued dependencies.

2. To specify constraints on the set of legal relations. We shall thus concern ourselves *only* with relations that satisfy a given set of functional and multivalued dependencies.

Note that if a relation *r* fails to satisfy a given multivalued dependency, we can construct a relation *r'* that does satisfy the multivalued dependency by adding tuples to *r*.

loan-number	customer-name	street	customer-city
23	Smith	North	Rye
27	Smith	Main	Manchester

Figure 6.14   An illegal *bc* relation.

6.3.2 Theory of Multivalued Dependencies

As was the case for functional dependencies and 3NF and BCNF, we shall need to determine all the multivalued dependencies that are logically implied by a given set of multivalued dependencies.

We take the same approach here that we did earlier for functional dependencies. Let D denote a set of functional and multivalued dependencies. The closure, D^+, of D is the set of all functional and multivalued dependencies logically implied by D. As was the case for functional dependencies, we can compute D^+ from D using the formal definitions of functional dependencies and multivalued dependencies. However, it is usually easier to reason about sets of dependencies using a system of inference rules.

The following list of inference rules for functional and multivalued dependencies is *sound* and *complete*. Recall that *soundness* means that the rules do not generate any dependencies that are not logically implied by D. *Completeness* means that the rules allow us to generate all dependencies in D^+. The first three rules are Armstrong's axioms, which we saw earlier in Section 6.2.2.

1. *Reflexivity rule.* If X is a set of attributes and $Y \subseteq X$, then $X \to Y$ holds.

2. *Augmentation rule.* If $X \to Y$ holds and W is a set of attributes, then $WX \to WY$ holds.

3. *Transitivity rule.* If $X \to Y$ holds and $Y \to Z$ holds, then $X \to Z$ holds.

4. *Complementation rule.* If $X \twoheadrightarrow Y$ holds, then $X \twoheadrightarrow R - Y - X$ holds.

5. *Multivalued augmentation rule.* If $X \twoheadrightarrow Y$ holds and $W \subseteq R$ and $V \subseteq W$, then $WX \twoheadrightarrow VY$ holds.

6. *Multivalued transitivity rule.* If $X \twoheadrightarrow Y$ holds and $Y \twoheadrightarrow Z$ holds, then $X \twoheadrightarrow Z - Y$ holds.

7. *Replication rule.* If $X \to Y$ holds, then $X \twoheadrightarrow Y$.

8. *Coalescence rule.* If $X \twoheadrightarrow Y$ holds and $Z \subseteq Y$ and there is a W such that $W \subseteq R$ and $W \cap Y = \emptyset$ and $W \to Z$, then $X \to Z$ holds.

The bibliographic notes provide references to proofs that the above rules are sound and complete. The following examples provide some insight into how the formal proofs proceed.

Let $R = (A,B,C,G,H,I)$ be a relation scheme. Suppose $A \twoheadrightarrow BC$ holds. The definition of multivalued dependencies implies that if $t_1[A] = t_2[A]$ then there exist tuples t_3 and t_4 such that:

$$t_1[A] = t_2[A] = t_3[A] = t_4[A]$$
$$t_3[BC] = t_1[BC]$$
$$t_3[GHI] = t_2[GHI]$$
$$t_4[GHI] = t_1[GHI]$$
$$t_4[BC] = t_2[BC]$$

The complementation rule states that if $A \twoheadrightarrow BC$, then $A \twoheadrightarrow GHI$. Observe that t_3 and t_4 satisfy the definition of $A \twoheadrightarrow GHI$ if we simply change the subscripts.

We can provide similar justification for rules 5 and 6 (see the exercises) using the definition of multivalued dependencies.

Rule 7, the replication rule, involves functional and multivalued dependencies. Suppose that $A \rightarrow BC$ holds on R. Then if $t_1[A] = t_2[A]$, $t_1[BC] = t_2[BC]$, and t_1 and t_2 themselves serve as the tuples t_3 and t_4 required by the definition of the multivalued dependency $A \twoheadrightarrow BC$.

Rule 8, the coalescence rule, is the most difficult of the eight rules to verify (see Exercise 6.43).

We can simplify the computation of the closure of D by using the following rules which can be proved using rules 1 to 8 (see the exercises).

- *Multivalued union rule.* If $X \twoheadrightarrow Y$ holds and $X \twoheadrightarrow Z$ holds, then $X \twoheadrightarrow YZ$ holds.

- *Intersection rule.* If $X \twoheadrightarrow Y$ holds and $X \twoheadrightarrow Z$ holds, then $X \twoheadrightarrow Y \cap Z$ holds.

- *Difference rule.* If $X \twoheadrightarrow Y$ holds and $X \twoheadrightarrow Z$ holds, then $X \twoheadrightarrow Y - Z$ holds and $X \twoheadrightarrow Z - Y$ holds.

Let us apply our rules to the following example. Let $R = (A,B,C,G,H,I)$ with the following set of dependencies D given:

$$A \twoheadrightarrow B$$
$$B \twoheadrightarrow HI$$
$$CG \rightarrow H$$

We list some members of D^+ below:

- $A \twoheadrightarrow CGHI$: Since $A \twoheadrightarrow B$, the complementation rule (rule 4) implies that $A \twoheadrightarrow R - B - A$. $R - B - A = CGHI$, so $A \twoheadrightarrow CGHI$.

- $A \twoheadrightarrow HI$: Since $A \twoheadrightarrow B$ and $B \twoheadrightarrow HI$, the multivalued transitivity rule (rule 6) implies that $A \twoheadrightarrow HI - B$. Since $HI - B = HI$, $A \twoheadrightarrow HI$.

- $B \rightarrow H$: To show this fact, we need to apply the coalescence rule (rule 8). $B \twoheadrightarrow HI$ holds. Since $H \subseteq HI$ and $CG \rightarrow H$ and $CG \cap HI = \emptyset$, we satisfy the statement of the coalescence rule with X being B, Y being HI, W being CG, and Z being H. We conclude that $B \rightarrow H$.

- $A \twoheadrightarrow CG$: We already know that $A \twoheadrightarrow CGHI$ and $A \twoheadrightarrow HI$. By the difference rule, $A \twoheadrightarrow CGHI - HI$. Since $CGHI - HI = CG$, $A \twoheadrightarrow CG$.

6.3.3 Fourth Normal Form

Let us return to our *BC-scheme* example in which *customer-name* $\twoheadrightarrow$ *street*, and *customer-city* holds, but no nontrivial functional dependencies hold. We saw earlier that, although *BC-scheme* is in BCNF, it is not an ideal design since we must repeat a customer's address information for each loan. We shall see that we can use the given multivalued dependency to improve the database design, by decomposing *BC-scheme* into a *fourth normal form* (4NF) decomposition.

A relation scheme R is in 4NF with respect to a set D of functional and multivalued dependencies if for all multivalued dependencies in D^+ of the form $X \twoheadrightarrow Y$, where $X \subseteq R$ and $Y \subseteq R$, at least one of the following hold:

- $X \twoheadrightarrow Y$ is trivial multivalued dependency.

- X is a superkey for scheme R.

A database design is in 4NF if each member of the set of relation schemes comprising the design is in 4NF.

Note that the definition of 4NF differs from the definition of BCNF only in the use of multivalued dependencies instead of functional dependencies. Every 4NF scheme is in BCNF. To see that this is so, note that if a scheme R is not in BCNF, then there is a nontrivial functional dependency $X \rightarrow Y$ holding on R, where X is not a key. Since $X \rightarrow Y$ implies $X \twoheadrightarrow Y$ (by the replication rule), R cannot be in 4NF.

The analogy between 4NF and BCNF applies to the algorithm for decomposing a scheme into 4NF. Figure 6.15 shows the 4NF decomposition algorithm. It is identical to the BCNF decomposition algorithm of Figure 6.10 except for the use of multivalued instead of functional dependencies.

If we apply the algorithm of Figure 6.15 to *BC-scheme*, we find that *customer-name* $\twoheadrightarrow$ *loan-number* is a nontrivial multivalued dependency and *customer-name* is not a key for *BC-scheme*. Following the algorithm, we replace *BC-scheme* by two schemes:

(*customer-name, loan-number*)
(*customer-name, street, customer-city*).

result := {*R*};
done := false;
while (**not** *done*) **do**
   if (there is a scheme R_i in *result* that is not in 4NF)
      then begin
            let $X \twoheadrightarrow Y$ be a nontrivial multivalued dependency that holds
            on R_i such that $X \rightarrow R_i$ is not in F^+, and $X \cap Y = \varnothing$;
            result := (*result* − R_i) $\cup$ (R_i − *Y*) $\cup$ (*XY*);
        end
    else *done* := true;

Figure 6.15   4NF decomposition algorithm.

This pair of schemes which are in 4NF eliminates the problem we have encountered with redundancy of *BC-scheme*.

As was the case when we were dealing solely with functional dependencies, we are interested also in decompositions that are lossless-join decompositions and that preserve dependencies. The following fact about multivalued dependencies and lossless joins shows that the algorithm of Figure 6.15 generates only lossless-join decompositions:

- Let *R* be a relation scheme and *D* a set of functional and multivalued dependencies on *R*. Let R_1 and R_2 form a decomposition of *R*.

- This decomposition is a lossless-join decomposition of *R* if and only if at least one of the following multivalued dependencies is in D^+:

$$R_1 \cap R_2 \twoheadrightarrow R_1$$
$$R_1 \cap R_2 \twoheadrightarrow R_2$$

Recall that we stated earlier that if $R_1 \cap R_2 \rightarrow R_1$ or $R_1 \cap R_2 \rightarrow R_2$, then R_1 and R_2 are a lossless-join decomposition of *R*. The above fact regarding multivalued dependencies is a more general statement about lossless joins. It says that for *every* lossless-join decomposition of *R* into two schemes R_1 and R_2, one of the two dependencies $R_1 \cap R_2 \twoheadrightarrow R_1$ or $R_1 \cap R_2 \twoheadrightarrow R_2$ must hold.

The question of dependency preservation when we have multivalued dependencies is not as simple as for the case in which we have only functional dependencies. Let *R* be a relation scheme and let $R_1, R_2, ..., R_n$

be a decomposition of R. Recall that for a set F of functional dependencies, the restriction F_i of F to R_i is all functional dependencies in F^+ that include *only* attributes of R_i. Now consider a set D of both functional and multivalued dependencies. The *restriction* of D to R_i is the set D_i, consisting of:

- All functional dependencies in D^+ that include only attributes of R_i

- All multivalued dependencies of the form:

$$X \twoheadrightarrow Y \cap R_i$$

where $X \subseteq R_i$ and $X \twoheadrightarrow Y$ is in D^+.

A decomposition of scheme R into schemes R_1, R_2, ..., R_n is a *dependency-preserving decomposition* with respect to a set D of functional and multivalued dependencies if every set of relations $r_1(R_1)$, $r_2(R_2)$, ..., $r_n(R_n)$ such that for all i, r_i satisfies D_i, there exists a relation $r(R)$ that satisfies D and for which $r_i = \Pi_{R_i}(r)$ for all i.

Let us apply the 4NF decomposition algorithm of Figure 6.15 to our example of $R = (A,B,C,G,H,I)$ with $D = \{A \twoheadrightarrow B, B \twoheadrightarrow HI, CG \rightarrow H\}$. We shall then test the resulting decomposition for dependency preservation.

R is not in 4NF. Observe that $A \twoheadrightarrow B$ is not trivial, yet A is not a key. Using $A \twoheadrightarrow B$ in the first iteration of the **while** loop, we replace R with two schemes, (A,B) and (A,C,G,H,I). It is easy to see that (A,B) is in 4NF since all multivalued dependencies that hold on (A,B) are trivial. However, the scheme (A,C,G,H,I) is not in 4NF. Applying the multivalued dependency $CG \twoheadrightarrow H$ (which follows from the given functional dependency $CG \rightarrow H$ by the replication rule), we replace (A,C,G,H,I) by the two schemes (C,G,H) and (A,C,G,I). Scheme (C,G,H) is in 4NF, but scheme (A,C,G,I) is not. To see that (A,C,G,I) is not in 4NF recall that we showed earlier that $A \twoheadrightarrow HI$ is in D^+. Therefore $A \twoheadrightarrow I$ is in the restriction of D to (A,C,G,I). Thus, in a third iteration of the **while** loop, we replace (A,C,G,I) by two schemes (A,I) and (A,C,G). The resulting 4NF decomposition is $\{(A,B), (C,G,H), (A,I), (A,C,G)\}$.

This 4NF decomposition is not dependency-preserving since it fails to preserve the multivalued dependency $B \twoheadrightarrow HI$. Consider the relations of Figure 6.16. Figure 6.16 shows the four relations that may result from the projection of a relation on (A,B,C,G,H,I) onto the four schemes of our decomposition. The restriction of D to (A,B) is $A \twoheadrightarrow B$ and some trivial dependencies. It is easy to see that r_1 satisfies $A \twoheadrightarrow B$ because there is no pair of tuples with the same A value. Observe that r_2 satisfies *all* functional and multivalued dependencies since no two tuples in r_2 have the same

r_1:

A	B
a_1	b_1
a_2	b_1

r_2:

C	G	H
c_1	g_1	h_1
c_2	g_2	h_2

r_3:

A	I
a_1	i_1
a_2	i_2

r_4:

A	C	G
a_1	c_1	g_1
a_2	c_2	g_2

Figure 6.16   Projection of relation r onto a 4NF decomposition of R.

value on any attribute. A similar statement can be made for r_3 and r_4. Therefore, the decomposed version of our database satisfies all the dependencies in the restriction of D. However, there is no relation r on (A,B,C,G,H,I) that satisfies D and decomposes into r_1, r_2, r_3, and r_4. To see this, observe that $r = \bowtie_{i=1}^{4} r_i$ is as shown in Figure 6.17. Relation r does not satisfy $B \twoheadrightarrow HI$. Any relation S containing r and satisfying $B \twoheadrightarrow HI$ must include the tuple $(a_2,b_1,c_2,g_2,h_1,i_1)$. However, Π_{CGH} (S) includes a tuple (c_2,g_2,h_i) that is not in r_2. Thus, our decomposition fails to detect a violation of $B \twoheadrightarrow HI$.

A	B	C	G	H	I
a_1	b_1	c_1	g_1	h_1	i_1
a_2	b_1	c_2	g_2	h_2	i_2

Figure 6.17   A relation $r(R)$ that does not satisfy $B \twoheadrightarrow HI$.

We have seen that if we are given a set of multivalued and functional dependencies, it is advantageous to find a database design that meets the three criteria of:

- 4NF.

- Dependency preservation.

- Lossless join.

If all we have are functional dependencies, the first criteria is just BCNF.

We have seen also that it is not always possible to achieve all three of these criteria. We succeeded in finding such a decomposition for the bank example, but failed for the example of scheme $R = (A,B,C,G,H,I)$.

When we cannot achieve our three goals, we compromise on 4NF, and accept BCNF or even 3NF, if necessary to ensure dependency preservation.

6.4 Normalization Using Join Dependencies

We have seen that the lossless-join property is one of several properties of a good database design. Indeed, this property is essential since, without it, information is lost. When we restrict the set of legal relations to those satisfying a set of functional and multivalued dependencies, we are able to use these dependencies to show that certain decompositions are lossless-join decompositions.

Because of the importance of the concept of lossless join, it is useful to be able to constrain the set of legal relations over a scheme R to those relations for which a given decomposition is a lossless-join decomposition. In this section, we define such a constraint, called a *join dependency*. As has been the case for other types of dependency, join dependencies will lead to another normal form called *project-join normal form* (PJNF).

6.4.1 Join Dependencies

Let R be a relation scheme and $R_1, R_2, ..., R_n$ be a decomposition of R. The join-dependency $*(R_1, R_2, ..., R_n)$ is used to restrict the set of legal relations to those for which $R_1, R_2, ..., R_n$ is a lossless-join decomposition of R. Formally, if $R = \cup_{i=1}^{n} R_i$, we say that a relation $r(R)$ satisfies the *join dependency* $*(R_1, R_2, ..., R_n)$ if:

$$\underset{i=1}{\overset{n}{\Join}} (\Pi_{R_i} (r)) = r$$

A join dependency is *trivial* if one of the R_i is R itself.

Consider the join dependency $*(R_1, R_2)$ on scheme R. This dependency requires that for all legal $r(R)$:

$$r = \Pi_{R_i} (r) \bowtie \Pi_{R_2} (r)$$

Let r contain the two tuples t_1 and t_2 defined as follows:

$$t_1[R_1 - R_2] = (a_1, a_2, \ldots, a_i) \quad t_2[R_1 - R_2] = (b_1, b_2, \ldots, b_i)$$
$$t_1[R_1 \cap R_2] = (a_{i+1}, \ldots, a_j) \quad t_2[R_1 \cap R_2] = (a_{i+1}, \ldots, a_j)$$
$$t_1[R_2 - R_1] = (a_{j+1}, \ldots, a_n) \quad t_2[R_2 - R_1] = (b_{j+1}, \ldots, b_n)$$

Thus, $t_1[R_1 \cap R_2] = t_2[R_1 \cap R_2]$, but t_1 and t_2 have different values on all other attributes. Let us compute $\Pi_{R_1} (r) \bowtie \Pi_{R_2} (r)$. Figure 6.18 shows $\Pi_{R_1} (r)$ and $\Pi_{R_2} (r)$. When we compute the join, we get two additional tuples besides t_1 and t_2, as shown by t_3 and t_4 in Figure 6.19.

If $*(R_1, R_2)$ holds, whenever we have tuples t_1 and t_2 we must also have t_3 and t_4. Thus, Figure 6.19 shows a tabular representation of the join dependency $*(R_1, R_2)$. Compare Figure 6.19 to Figure 6.12, in which we gave a tabular representation of $V \twoheadrightarrow W$. If we let $V = R_1 \cap R_2$ and $W = R_1$, then we can see that the two tabular representations in these figures are the same. Indeed, $*(R_1, R_2)$ is just another way of stating $R_1 \cap R_2 \twoheadrightarrow R_1$. Using the complementation and augmentation rules for multivalued dependencies, we see that $R_1 \cap R_2 \twoheadrightarrow R_1$ implies $R_1 \cap R_2 \twoheadrightarrow R_2$. Thus, $*(R_1, R_2)$ is equivalent to $R_1 \cap R_2 \twoheadrightarrow R_2$. This observation is not surprising in light of the fact we noted earlier that R_1

	$R_1 - R_2$		$R_1 \cap R_2$	
$\Pi_{R_1} (t_1)$	a_1 $\cdots$	a_i	a_{i+1} $\cdots$	a_j
$\Pi_{R_1} (t_2)$	b_1 $\cdots$	b_i	a_{i+1} $\cdots$	a_j

	$R_1 \cap R_2$		$R_2 - R_1$	
$\Pi_{R_2} (t_1)$	a_{i+1} $\cdots$	a_j	a_{j+1} $\cdots$	a_n
$\Pi_{R_1} (t_2)$	a_{i+1} $\cdots$	a_j	b_{j+1} $\cdots$	b_n

Figure 6.18 $\Pi_{R_1} (r)$ and $\Pi_{R_2} (r)$.

	$R_1 - R_2$		$R_1 \cap R_2$		$R_2 - R_1$	
t_1	$a_1 \cdots a_i$		$a_{i+1} \cdots a_j$		$a_{j+1} \cdots a_n$	
t_2	$b_1 \cdots b_i$		$a_{i+1} \cdots a_j$		$b_{j+1} \cdots b_n$	
t_3	$a_1 \cdots a_i$		$a_{i+1} \cdots a_j$		$b_{j+1} \cdots b_n$	
t_4	$b_1 \cdots b_i$		$a_{i+1} \cdots a_j$		$a_{j+1} \cdots a_n$	

Figure 6.19   Tabular representation of $*(R_1, R_2)$.

and R_2 form a lossless-join decomposition of R if and only if $R_1 \cap R_2 \twoheadrightarrow R_2$ or $R_1 \cap R_2 \twoheadrightarrow R_1$.

Every join dependency of the form $*(R_1, R_2)$ is therefore equivalent to a multivalued dependency. However, there are join dependencies that are not equivalent to any multivalued dependency. The simplest example of such a dependency is on scheme $R = (A,B,C)$. The join dependency $*((A,B), (B,C), (A,C))$ is not equivalent to any collection of multivalued dependencies. Figure 6.20 shows a tabular representation of this join dependency. To see that no set of multivalued dependencies logically implies $*((A,B), (B,C), (A,C))$ consider Figure 6.20 as a relation $r(A,B,C)$ as shown in Figure 6.21. Relation r satisfies $*((A,B), (B,C), (A,C))$, as can be verified by computing:

$$\Pi_{AB} (r) \bowtie \Pi_{BC} (r) \bowtie \Pi_{AC} (r)$$

and showing that the result is exactly r. However, r does not satisfy any nontrivial multivalued dependency. To see this, verify that r fails to satisfy any of $A \twoheadrightarrow B$, $A \twoheadrightarrow C$, $B \twoheadrightarrow A$, $B \twoheadrightarrow C$, $C \twoheadrightarrow A$, or $C \twoheadrightarrow B$.

Just as a multivalued dependency is a way of stating the independence of a pair of relationships, a join dependency is a way of stating that a *set* of relationships are all independent. This notion of independence of

A	B	C
a_1	b_1	c_2
a_2	b_1	c_1
a_1	b_2	c_1
a_1	b_1	c_1

Figure 6.20   Tabular representation of $*((A,B), (B,C), (A,C))$.

A	B	C
a_1	b_1	c_2
a_2	b_1	c_1
a_1	b_2	c_1
a_1	b_1	c_1

Figure 6.21   Relation $r(A,B,C)$.

relationships is a natural consequence of the way we generally define a relation. Consider, for example:

$$Borrow\text{-}scheme = (branch\text{-}name, loan\text{-}number, customer\text{-}name, amount)$$

from our banking example. We can define a relation *borrow* (*Borrow-scheme*) as the set of all tuples on *Borrow-scheme* such that:

- The loan represented by *loan-number* is made by the branch named *branch-name*.

- The loan represented by *loan-number* is made to the customer named *customer-name*.

- The loan represented by *loan-number* is in the amount given by *amount*.

The above definition of the *borrow* relation is a conjunction of three predicates: one on *loan-number* and *branch-name*, one on *loan-number* and *customer-name*, and one on *loan-number* and *amount*. Surprisingly, it can be shown that the above intuitive definition of *borrow* logically implies the join dependency *((loan-number, branch-name), (loan-number, customer-name), (loan-number, amount)).

Thus, join dependencies have an intuitive appeal and correspond to one of our three criteria for a good database design.

For functional and multivalued dependencies, we were able to give a system of inference rules that are sound and complete. Unfortunately, no such set of rules is known for join dependencies. It appears to be necessary to consider more general classes of dependencies than join dependencies to construct a sound and complete set of inference rules. The bibliographic notes contain references to recent research in this area.

6.4.2 Project-Join Normal Form

Project-join normal form is defined in a manner similar to BCNF and 4NF, except that join dependencies are used. A relation scheme R is in *project-*

join normal form (PJNF) with respect to a set D of functional, multivalued, and join dependencies if for all join dependencies in D^+ of the form $*(R_1, R_2, ..., R_n)$ where each $R_i \subseteq R$ and $\cup_{i=1}^{n} R_i = R$, at least one of the following holds:

- $*(R_1, R_2, ..., R_n)$ is a trivial join dependency.

- Every R_i is a superkey for R.

A database design is in PJNF if each member of the set of relation schemes comprising the design is in PJNF. PJNF is called *fifth normal form* (5NF) in some of the literature on database normalization.

Let us return to our banking example. Given the join dependency $*((loan\text{-}number, branch\text{-}name), (loan\text{-}number, customer\text{-}name), (loan\text{-}number, amount))$, *Borrow-scheme* is not in PJNF. To put *Borrow-scheme* into PJNF, we must decompose it into the three schemes specified by the join dependency: *(loan-number, branch-name)*, *(loan-number, customer-name)*, and *(loan-number, amount)*.

Because every multivalued dependency is also a join dependency, it is easy to see that every PJNF scheme is also in 4NF. Thus, in general, we may not be able to find a dependency-preserving decomposition for a given scheme into PJNF.

6.5 Domain-Key Normal Form

The approach we have taken toward normalization is to define a form of constraint (functional, multivalued, or join dependency) and then use that form of constraint to define a normal form. Domain-key normal form is based on three notions.

- **Domain declaration**. Let A be an attribute, and let **dom** be a set of values. The domain declaration $A \subseteq$ **dom** requires that the A value of all tuples be values in **dom**.

- **Key declaration**. Let R be a relation scheme with $K \subseteq R$. The key declaration key (K) requires that K be a superkey for R, that is, $K \rightarrow R$. Note that all key declarations are functional dependencies but not all functional dependencies are key declarations.

- **General constraint**. A general constraint is a predicate on the set of all relations on a given scheme. The dependencies we have studied in this chapter are examples of a general constraint. In general, a general constraint is a predicate expressed in some agreed-upon form, such as first-order logic.

We now give an example of a general constraint that is not a functional, multivalued, or join dependency. Suppose that all accounts whose number begins with 9 are special high-interest accounts with a minimum balance of $2500. Then we would include as a general constraint "If the first digit of $t[account\text{-}number]$ is 9, then $t[balance] \geq 2500$."

Domain declarations and key declarations are easy to test in a practical database system. General constraints, however, may be extremely costly (in time and space) to test. The purpose of a domain-key normal form database design is to allow the general constraints to be tested using only domain and key constraints.

Formally, let **D** be a set of domain constraints and let **K** be a set of key constraints for a relation scheme R. Let **G** denote the general constraints for R. Scheme R is in *domain-key normal form* (DKNF) if $D \cup K$ logically imply **G**.

Let us return to the general constraint we gave above on accounts. The constraint implies that our database design is not in DKNF. To create a DKNF design, we need two schemes in place of *Account-info-scheme*:

> *Regular-acct-scheme* = (*branch-name, account-number, balance*)
> *Special-acct-scheme* = (*branch-name, account-number, balance*)

We retain all the dependencies we had on *Account-info-scheme* as general constraints. The domain constraints for *Special-acct-scheme* require that:

- The account number begins with 9.

- The balance is greater than 2500.

The domain constraints for *Regular-acct-scheme* require that the account number not begin with 9. The resulting design is in DKNF although the proof of this fact is beyond the scope of this text.

Let us compare DKNF to the other normal forms we have studied. Under the other normal forms, we did not take into consideration domain constraints. We assumed (implicitly) that the domain of each attribute was some infinite domain such as the set of all integers or the set of all character strings. We allowed key constraints (indeed, we allowed functional dependencies). For each normal form, we allowed a restricted form of general constraint (a set of functional, multivalued, or join dependencies). Thus, we can rewrite the definitions of PJNF, 4NF, BCNF, and 3NF in a manner which shows them to be special cases of DKNF.

The following is a DKNF-inspired rephrasing of our definition of PJNF. Let $R = (A_1, A_2, ..., A_n)$ be a relation scheme. Let $\text{dom}(A_i)$ denote the domain of attribute A_i, and let all these domains be infinite. Then all domain constraints **D** are of the form $A_i \subseteq \text{dom}(A_i)$. Let the general constraints be a set **G** of functional, multivalued, or join dependencies. If F

is the set of functional dependencies in G, let the set K of key constraints be those nontrivial functional dependencies in F^+ of the form $X \rightarrow R$. Scheme R is in PJNF if and only if it is in DKNF with respect to D, K, G.

A consequence of DKNF is that all insertion and deletion anomalies are eliminated.

DKNF represents an "ultimate" normal form because it allows arbitrary constraints rather than dependencies, yet it allows efficient testing of these constraints. Of course, if a scheme is not in DKNF we may be able to achieve DKNF via decomposition, but such decompositions, as we have seen, are not always dependency-preserving decompositions. Thus, while DKNF is a goal of a database designer, it may have to be sacrificed in a practical design.

6.6 Atomic Values

Conspicuous by their absence from our discussion of 3NF, 4NF, etc. are first and second normal forms. The reason for this is that second normal form is of historical interest only. We, therefore, do not discuss it formally in this chapter. Rather, we define it and let the reader experiment with it in Exercise 6.25. Although we have not mentioned first normal form, we have assumed it since we introduced the relational model in Chapter 3. We now, finally, make our assumption explicit.

A relation scheme R is in *first normal form* (1NF) if the domains of all attributes of R are atomic. A domain is *atomic* if elements of the domain are considered to be indivisible units.

For example, the set of integers is an atomic domain, but the set of all sets of integers is a nonatomic domain. The distinction is that we do not normally consider integers to have subparts, but we consider sets of integers to have subparts, namely, the integers comprising the set. The important issue in 1NF is not the domain itself, but the way we use domain elements in our database. The domain of all integers would be nonatomic if we considered each integer to be an ordered list of digits.

In all our examples, we have assumed atomic domains. We have made this assumption not only for the relational model but also for the entity-relationship, network, and hierarchical models. Because this assumption is so natural, we have chosen not to draw attention to it until now.

The reason we mention 1NF at all is that recent developments in database theory and practice have called into question the legitimacy of assuming 1NF. We shall see several examples of this in Chapter 15. For now, we consider a document retrieval system. For each document, we store the following information:

- Document title.
- Author list.

title	author-list	date			keywords
		day	month	year	
salesplan	{Smith, Jones}	1 April 79			{profit, strategy}
status report	{Jones, Frick}	17 June 85			{profit, personnel}

Figure 6.22   Non-1NF document relation.

- Date.

- Keywords list.

We can see that if we define a relation for the above information, several domains will be nonatomic.

- **Authors**. A document may have a set of authors. Nevertheless, we may want to find all documents of which Jones was one of the authors. Thus we are interested in a subpart of the domain element "set of authors."

- **Keywords**. If we store a set of keywords for a document, we expect to be able to retrieve all documents whose keywords include one or more keywords. Thus, we view the domain of *keyword list* as nonatomic.

- **Date**. Unlike *keywords* and *authors*, *date* does not have a set-valued domain. However, we may view *date* as consisting of the subfields day, month, and year. This makes the domain of *date* nonatomic.

Figure 6.22 shows an example document relation. This relation can be represented in 1NF, but the resulting relation is awkward (see Figure 6.23). Since we must have atomic domains in 1NF, yet want access to individual

title	author	day	month	year	keyword
salesplan	Smith	1	April	79	profit
salesplan	Jones	1	April	79	profit
salesplan	Smith	1	April	79	strategy
salesplan	Jones	1	April	79	strategy
status report	Jones	17	June	85	profit
status report	Frick	17	June	85	profit
status report	Jones	17	June	85	personnel
status report	Frick	17	June	85	personnel

Figure 6.23   1NF version of non-1NF relation in Figure 6.22.

authors and to individual keywords, we need one tuple for each (keyword, author) pair. The *date* attribute is replaced in the 1NF version by three attributes: one for each subfield of *date*.

Much of the awkwardness of the relation in Figure 6.23 is removed if we assume that:

- *title* $\twoheadrightarrow$ *author*.
- *title* $\twoheadrightarrow$ *keyword*.
- *title* $\rightarrow$ *day month year*.

Then, we can decompose the relation into 4NF using the schemes:

- (*title, author*)
- (*title, keyword*)
- (*title, day, month, year*)

Figure 6.24 shows the projection of the relation of Figure 6.23 onto the above decomposition.

Although 1NF can represent our example document database adequately, the non-1NF representation may be an easier-to-understand model for the typical user of a document retrieval system. Users of such

title	*author*
salesplan	Smith
salesplan	Jones
status report	Jones
status report	Frick

title	*keyword*
salesplan	profit
salesplan	strategy
status report	profit
status report	personnel

title	*day*	*month*	*year*
salesplan	1	April	79
status report	17	June	85

Figure 6.24   4NF version of 1NF relation in Figure 6.23.

systems think of the database in terms of our non-1NF design. The 4NF design would require users to include joins in their queries, thereby complicating interaction with the system. We could define a view that eliminates the need for users to write joins in their query. However in such a view, we lose the one-to-one correspondence between tuples and documents.

Once we realize that there are new applications of database systems that benefit from a non-1NF representation, we need to define new normal forms and criteria for goodness of a design. These issues are the subject of current research (see the bibliographic notes) and are beyond the scope of this text. Chapter 14 provides some additional insight into the issues involved in non-1NF relation databases.

6.7 Alternative Approaches to Database Design

In this section, we reexamine normalization of relation schemes with an emphasis on the impact of normalization on the design of practical database systems.

We have taken the approach of starting with a single relation scheme and decomposing it. One of our goals in choosing a decomposition was that the decomposition be a lossless-join decomposition. In order to consider losslessness, we assumed that it is valid to talk about the join of all the relations of the decomposed database.

Consider the database of Figure 6.25, showing a *borrow* relation decomposed in PJNF. In Figure 6.25, we represent a situation in which we have not yet determined the amount of loan 58, but wish to record the remainder of the data on the loan. If we compute the natural join of these relations we discover that all tuples referring to loan 58 disappear. In other words, there is no *borrow* relation corresponding to the relations of Figure 6.25. We refer to the tuples that "disappear" in computing the join as

branch-name	loan-number
Round Hill	58

loan-number	amount

loan-number	customer-name
58	Johnson

Figure 6.25   Decomposition in PJNF.

dangling tuples. Formally, let $r_1(R_1)$, $r_2(R_2)$, ..., $r_n(R_n)$ be a set of relations. A tuple of relation r_i is a *dangling tuple* if t is not in the relation:

$$\Pi_{R_i} \left(\underset{j=1}{\overset{n}{\bowtie}} \, r_j \right)$$

Dangling tuples may occur in practical database applications. They represent incomplete information, as in our example where we wish to store data about a loan still in the process of being negotiated. The relation $\bowtie_{j=1}^{n} r_j$ is called a *universal relation* since it involves all the attributes in the "universe" defined by $\cup_{j=1}^{n} R_j$.

The only way we can write a universal relation for the example of Figure 6.25 is to include *null values* in the universal relation. We saw in Chapter 3 that null values present serious difficulties. Ongoing research regarding null values and universal relations is discussed in the bibliographic notes. Because of the difficulty of managing null values, it may be desirable to view the relations of the "decomposed" design as representing "the" database, rather than the universal relation whose scheme we decomposed during the normalization process.

Note that not all incomplete information can be entered into the database of Figure 6.25, without resorting to the use of null values. For example, we cannot enter a loan number unless we know at least one of the following:

- The customer name.
- The branch name.
- The amount of the loan.

Thus, a particular decomposition defines a restricted form of incomplete information that is acceptable in our database.

The normal forms that we have defined generate good database designs from the point of view of representation of incomplete information. Returning again to the example of Figure 6.25, we would not want to allow the storage of the following fact: "there is a loan (whose number is unknown) to Jones in the amount of $100." Since *loan-number* → *customer-name amount*, the only way we can relate *customer-name* and *amount* is through *loan-number*. If we do not know the loan number, we cannot distinguish this loan from other loans with unknown numbers.

In other words, we do not want to store data for which the key attributes are unknown. Observe that the normal forms we have defined do not allow us to store that type of information unless we use null values. Thus, our normal forms allow representation of acceptable incomplete information via dangling tuples while prohibiting the storage of undesirable incomplete information.

If we allow dangling tuples in our database, we may prefer to take an alternative view of the database design process. Instead of decomposing a universal relation, we may *synthesize* a collection of normal form schemes from a given set of attributes. We are interested in the same normal forms regardless of whether we use decomposition or synthesis. The decomposition approach is better understood and more widely used. The bibliographic notes provide references to research into the synthesis approach.

Another consequence of our approach to database design is that attribute names must be unique in the universal relation. We cannot use *name* to refer to both *customer-name* and to *branch-name*. It is generally preferable to use unique names, as we have done. Nevertheless, if we defined our relation schemes directly rather than in terms of a universal relation, we could obtain relations on schemes such as the following for our banking example:

> *branch-loan (name, number)*
> *loan-customer (number, name)*
> *loan (number, amount)*

Observe that with the above relations, such expressions as *branch-loan* ⋈ *loan-customer* are meaningless. Indeed, the expression *branch-loan* ⋈ *loan-customer* finds loans made by branches to customers with the same name as the name of the branch.

However, in a language like SQL, there is no natural join operation, so in a query involving *branch-loan* and *loan-customer*, references to *name* must be disambiguated by prefixing the relation name. In such environments, the multiple roles for *name* (as branch name and as customer name) are less troublesome and may be simpler for some users.

We feel that the *unique role assumption*, that each attribute name has a unique meaning in the database, is generally preferable to the reuse of the same name in multiple roles. When the unique role assumption is not made, the database designer must be especially careful when constructing a normalized relational database design.

6.8 Summary

In this chapter we have presented criteria for a good database design:

- Lossless join.
- Dependency preservation.
- PJNF, BCNF, 4NF, or 3NF.

We have shown how to achieve these goals and how to find a good compromise when not all the criteria can be achieved.

In order to represent these criteria, we defined several types of data dependencies:

- Functional dependencies.

- Multivalued dependencies.

- Join dependencies.

We studied the properties of these dependencies with emphasis on what dependencies are logically implied by a set of dependencies.

DKNF is an idealized normal form that may be difficult to achieve in practice. Yet, DKNF has desirable properties that should be included to the extent possible in a good database design.

In the latter sections, we reexamined our basic assumptions about the relational model to provide insight into why particular design approaches have won acceptance and to indicate the trends in relational database design represented by current research activity.

In reviewing the issues we have discussed in this chapter, it is worthwhile to observe that the reason we could define rigorous approaches to relational database design is that the relational data model rests on a firm mathematical foundation. This is one of the primary advantages of the relational model as compared with the other data models we have studied.

Exercises

6.1 Explain what is meant by:

- repetition of information.

- inability to represent information.

- loss of information.

Explain why any one of these properties may indicate a bad relational database design.

6.2 List all functional dependencies satisfied by the relation of Figure 6.26.

6.3 Use the definition of functional dependency to argue that each of Armstrong's axioms (reflexivity, augmentation, and transitivity) are sound.

A	B	C
a_1	b_1	c_1
a_1	b_1	c_2
a_2	b_1	c_1
a_2	b_1	c_3

Figure 6.26   Relation of Exercise 6.2

6.4 Explain how functional dependencies can be used to indicate that:

- A one-to-one relationship set exists between entity sets *student* and *advisor*.

- A many-to-one relationship set exists between entity sets *student* and *advisor*.

6.5 Consider the following proposed rule for functional dependencies: If $X \rightarrow Y$ and $Z \rightarrow Y$ then $X \rightarrow Z$. Prove that this rule is *not* sound by showing a relation r which satisfies $Z \rightarrow Y$ and $Z \rightarrow Y$ but does not satisfy $X \rightarrow Z$.

6.6 Use Armstrong's Axioms to prove the soundness of the union rule. (Hint: Use the augmentation rule to show that if $X \rightarrow Y$ then $X \rightarrow XY$. Apply the augmentation rule again using $X \rightarrow Z$ and then apply the transitivity rule.)

6.7 Use Armstrong's Axioms to prove the soundness of the decomposition rule.

6.8 Use Armstrong's Axioms to prove the soundness of the pseudotransitivity rule.

6.9 Compute the closure of the following set F of functional dependencies for relation scheme $R = (A, B, C, D, E)$.

$$A \rightarrow BC$$
$$CD \rightarrow E$$
$$B \rightarrow D$$
$$E \rightarrow A$$

List the candidate keys for R.

6.10 Using the functional dependencies of Exercise 6.9, compute B^+.

6.11 Consider the following algorithm to compute X^+.

```
result := ∅;
/* fdcount is an array whose ith element contains the number
    of attributes on the left side of the ith FD that are
    not yet known to be in X⁺ */
for i := 1 to | F| do
    begin
        fdcount [i] := size of left side of ith FD;
    end
/* appears is an array with one entry for each attribute.  The
    entry for attribute A is a list of integers.  Each integer
    i on the list indicates that A appears on the left side
    of the ith FD */
for each attribute A do
    begin
        appears [A] := NIL ;
        for i := 1 to | F|  do
            begin
                let V → W  denote the ith FD;
                if A ∈ V  then add A to appears [A];
            end
    end
addin (X);
return (result);
addin (X);
for each attribute A in X do
    begin
        if A ∉ result  then
            begin
                for each element  i of appears [A] do
                    begin
                        fdcount [i] := fdcount [i] − 1;
                        if fdcount [i] := 0 then
                            begin
                                let V → W  denote the ith FD;
                                addin (W);
                            end
                    end
            end
    end
```

Show that this algorithm is more efficient than the one presented
in the text and that it computes X^+ correctly.

6.12 Suppose we decompose the scheme R of Exercise 6.9 into:

$$(A, B, C)$$
$$(A, D, E).$$

Show that this is a lossless-join decomposition if the set F of functional dependencies of Exercise 6.9 hold.

6.13 Show that the following decomposition of the scheme R of Exercise 6.9 is not a lossless-join decomposition.

$$(A, B, C)$$
$$(C, D, E)$$

Hint: Give an example of a relation r on scheme R such that

$$\Pi_{A, B, C}\,(r) \bowtie \Pi_{C, D, E}\,(r) \neq r$$

6.14 Let $R_1, R_2, \ldots, R_n$ be a decomposition of scheme U. Let $u(U)$ be a relation and let $r_i = \Pi_{R_I}\,(u)$. Show that

$$u \subseteq \bowtie_{i=1}^{n} r_i$$

6.15 Show that the decomposition in Exercise 6.12 is not a dependency preserving decomposition.

6.16 List the three design goals for relational databases and explain why they are desirable.

6.17 Why are certain functional dependencies called *trivial* functional dependencies?

6.18 List all the multivalued dependencies satisfied by the relation of Figure 6.26.

6.19 Give a lossless-join decomposition of the scheme R of Exercise 6.9 into BCNF.

6.20 Give an example of a scheme R' and set F' of functional dependencies such that there are at least two distinct lossless-join decompositions of R' into BCNF.

6.21 In designing a relational database, why might we choose a non-BCNF design?

6.22 Show that the coalescence rule is sound. (Hint: Apply the definition of $X \twoheadrightarrow Y$ to a pair of tuples t_1 and t_2 such that $t_1[X] = t_2[X]$. Observe that since $W \cap Y = \emptyset$, then if two tuples have the same value on $R - Y$ then they have the same value on W.)

6.23 Give a lossless-join, dependency-preserving decomposition of the scheme R of Exercise 6.9 into 3NF.

6.24 Show that if a relation scheme is in BCNF then it is also in 3NF.

6.25 A functional dependency $X \to Y$ is called a *partial* dependency if there is a proper superset Z of X such that $Z \to Y$. We say that Y is *partially dependent* on Z. A relation scheme R is in *second normal form* (2NF) if each attribute A in R either:

- appears in a candidate key

- is not partially dependent on a candidate key.

Show that every 3NF scheme is in 2NF. (Hint: show that every partial dependency is a transitive dependency).

6.26 Explain why first normal form is acceptable for data-processing applications.

6.27 Give an example other than that of Section 6.6 to show why we may prefer not to design a 1NF scheme.

6.28 Use the definition of multivalued dependency to argue that the following axioms are sound:

- the complementation rule.

- the multivalued augmentation rule.

- the multivalued transitivity rule.

6.29 Use the definitions of functional and multivalued dependencies to show the soundness of the replication rule.

6.30 Use the axioms for functional and multivalued dependencies to show that the following rules are sound:

- the multivalued union rule.

- the intersection rule.

- the difference rule.

6.31 Let $R = (A, B, C, D, E)$ and let M be the following set of multivalued dependencies

$$A \twoheadrightarrow BC$$
$$B \twoheadrightarrow CD$$
$$E \twoheadrightarrow AD$$

List the nontrivial dependencies in M^+.

6.32 Give a lossless-join decomposition of scheme R in Exercise 6.31 into 4NF.

6.33 Give an example of a relation scheme R and a set of dependencies such that R is in BCNF but not in 4NF.

6.34 Explain why 4NF is a more desirable normal form than BCNF.

6.35 Give an example of relation scheme R and a set of dependencies such that R is in 4NF but not in PJNF.

6.36 Explain why PJNF is a more desirable normal form than 4NF.

6.37 Rewrite the definitions of 4NF and BCNF using the notions of domain constraints and general constraints.

6.38 Explain why DKNF is a highly desirable normal form, yet one that if difficult to achieve in practice.

6.39 Given the three goals of relational database design, is there any reason to design a database scheme that is in 2NF but in no higher normal form?

6.40 Consider a non-1NF scheme $R = (A, B, C, S)$, where dom (S) is the set of relations on scheme (X, Y, Z). Let r be a relation on R that satisfies $A \rightarrow S$. Let s be a relation on (A, B, C, X, Y, Z) containing the same information as r. Show that s satisfies $A \twoheadrightarrow XYZ$.

6.41 Let a *prime* attribute be one that appears in at least one candidate key. Let X and Y be sets of attributes such that $X \rightarrow Y$ holds, but $Y \rightarrow X$ does not hold. Let A be an attribute that is not in X and not in Y and for which $Y \rightarrow A$ holds. We say that A is *transitively dependent* on X. We can restate our definition of 3NF as follows.

- A relation scheme R is in 3NF with respect to a set F of functional dependencies if there are no non-prime attributes A in R for which A is transitively dependent on a key for R.

Show that this new definition is equivalent to the original one.

6.42 Explain how dangling tuples may arise and what problems they may cause.

6.43 Show that the coalescence rule is sound. (Hint: This exercise involves several steps. Suppose that $t_1[X] = t_2[X]$. We need to show that $t_1[Z] = t_2[Z]$. Apply the definition of the multivalued dependency $X \twoheadrightarrow Y$ to t_1 and t_2, thus defining two new tuples, t_3 and t_4. Using set theory, state those equalities that hold between attribute values of these 4 tuples. Using a few of these equalities, it can be shown that $t_1[Z] = t_2[Z]$).

Bibliographic Notes

The first discussion of relational database design theory appeared in an early paper by Codd [1970]. During the 1970's a large number of dependencies and normal forms were introduced. Codd [1970] defined functional dependencies. Armstrong's axioms were introduced in Armstrong [1974]. Codd [1972a] introduced first, second and third normal forms. The requirement of 1NF was questioned by Makinouchi [1977]. A relational algebra for non-1NF relations appears in Jaeschke and Schek [1982] and Fischer and Thomas [1983]. Roth et al. [1984] presents a relational calculus for non-1NF relations. A non-1NF version of SQL called SQL/NF appears in Roth et al. [1985].

BCNF was introduced in Codd [1972a]. The desirability of BCNF is discussed in Bernstein and Goodman [1980b]. Beeri et al. [1977] give a set of axioms for functional and multivalued dependencies and prove that their axioms are sound and complete. Our axiomatization is based on theirs. Biskup et al. [1979] give the algorithm we used to find a lossless-join dependency-preserving decomposition into 3NF. Fundamental results on the lossless-join property appear in Aho et al. [1979b].

The notions of PJNF and DKNF are from Fagin [1979] and Fagin [1981], respectively. The synthesis approach to database design is discussed in Bernstein [1976].

Maier [1983] presents the theory of relational databases in detail. Ullman [1982a] presents a more theoretic coverage of many of the normal forms presented here. See Maier [1983] for additional dependencies.

Join dependencies were introduced by Rissanen [1979]. Sciore [1982] gives a set of axioms for a class of dependencies that properly includes the join dependencies. In addition to their use in PJNF, join dependencies are central to the definition of universal relation databases [Fagin et al. 1982]. This use of join dependencies has led to a large amount of research into *acyclic* database schemes. Intuitively, a scheme is acyclic if every pair of attributes if related in a unique way. Formal treatment of acyclic schemes appears in Fagin [1983], and Beeri et al. [1983].

File and System Structure

In preceding chapters, we have emphasized the higher-level models of a database. At the *conceptual* or *logical* level, the database was viewed as a collection of tables (the relational model), as a collection of record types and sets (the network model), or as a forest of tree structures (the hierarchical model). The logical model of the database is the correct level for database *users* to focus on. The goal of a database system is to simplify and facilitate access to data. Users of the system should not be burdened unnecessarily with the physical details of the implementation of the system.

Nevertheless, a major factor in a user's satisfaction or lack thereof with a database system is its performance. If the response time for a request is too long, the value of the system is diminished. The performance of a system depends on the efficiency of the data structures used to represent the data in the database and on how efficiently the system is able to operate on these data structures. As is the case elsewhere in computer systems, a tradeoff must be made not only between space and time, but also between the efficiency of one kind of operation versus that of another.

In this chapter as well as in Chapter 8 we describe various methods for implementing the data models and languages presented in preceding chapters. We shall define various data structures that will allow fast access to data. We shall consider several alternative structures, each best suited to a different kind of access to data. The final choice of data structure needs to be made based upon the expected use of the system and the physical characteristics of the specific machine.

7.1 Overall System Structure

In this section, we divide a database system into modules that deal with each of the responsibilities of the overall system. Some of the functions of the database system may be provided by the computer's operating system. In most cases, the operating system provides only the most basic services and the database system must build on that base. Thus, our discussion of the design of a database system will include consideration of the interface between the database system and the operating system.

A database system consists of a number of functional components, including:

- **The file manager**, which manages the allocation of space on disk storage and the data structures used to represent information stored on disk.

- **The buffer manager**, which is responsible for the transfer of information between disk storage and main memory.

- **The query parser**, which translates statements in a query language into a lower-level language.

- **The strategy selector**, which attempts to transform a user's request into an equivalent but more efficient form, thus finding a good strategy for executing the query.

- **The authorization and integrity manager**, which tests for the satisfaction of integrity constraints (such as key constraints) and checks the authority of users to access Data.

- **The recovery manager**, which ensures that the database remains in a consistent (correct) state despite system failures.

- **The concurrency controller**, which ensures that concurrent interactions with the database proceed without conflicting with each other.

In addition, several data structures are required as part of the physical system implementation, including:

- **Data files**, which store the database itself.

- **System data files**, which store information about the structure of the database. Authorization information, such as key constraints, is kept here. The data dictionary is stored here.

- **Indices**, which provide for fast access to data items holding particular values.

- **Statistical data**, which store information about the data in the database. This information is used by the strategy selector.

Figure 7.1 shows these components and the connections among them.

In this chapter, we shall discuss how the file manager, buffer manager, data files, and system data files can be implemented. In Chapter 8, we show how indices can be implemented. In Chapter 9, we study how the query parser, the strategy selector, and statistical data are implemented. Chapters 10 and 11 describe the recovery manager and concurrency control schemes respectively. Chapter 13 describes authorization and integrity management.

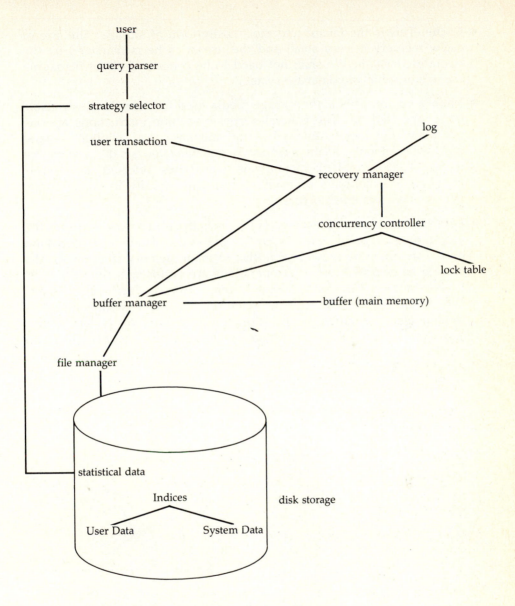

Figure 7.1   System structure.

7.2 Physical Storage Media

Several types of data storage exist in most computer systems. These storage media are classified by the speed with which data can be accessed, by the cost per unit of data to buy the memory, and by how "reliable" they are. Among the media typically available are:

- **Cache**. This is the fastest and most costly form of storage. The size of cache memory is very small and the use of cache is managed by the operating system. We shall not need to be concerned about managing cache storage in the database system.

- **Main memory**. This is the storage media used for data that is available to be operated on. The general-purpose machine instructions operate on main memory. Although main memory may contain several megabytes of data, main memory is generally too small to store the entire database. Main memory is sometimes referred to as *core* memory. The contents of main memory are usually lost if a power failure or system crash occurs.

- **Direct-access storage** (disk storage). This is the primary medium for the long-term storage of data. Typically, the entire database is stored on disk. Data must be moved from disk to main memory in order for the data to be operated on. After operations are performed, the data must be returned to disk. Disk storage is referred to as *direct-access* storage because it is possible to read data on disk in any order (unlike sequential-access storage). Disk storage usually survives power failures and system crashes. Disk storage devices themselves may fail and destroy data, but such failures are significantly less frequent than system crashes.

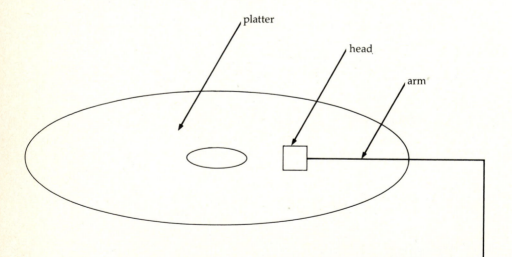

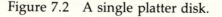

Figure 7.2   A single platter disk.

- **Sequential-access storage** (tape storage). This is storage used primarily for backup and archival data. Although tape is much cheaper than disk, access to data is much slower, since the tape must be read sequentially from the beginning. This form of storage is used primarily for recovery from disk failures (see Chapter 10). Tape devices are less complex than disks; thus they are more reliable.

Since disk storage is of central importance in database implementation, we shall examine the characteristics of disks in more detail. Figure 7.2 shows a simple disk. The head is a device which stays close to the surface to the platter and reads or writes information encoded magnetically on the platter. The platter is organized into concentric tracks of data as shown in Figure 7.3. The *arm* can be positioned over any one of the tracks. The platter is spun at a high speed. To read or write information, the arm is positioned over the correct track; and, when the data to be accessed passes under the head, the read or write operation is performed.

Since the platter rotates at a high speed, it does not take very long for the contents of an entire track to pass under the head. This amount of time is referred to as the *disk latency time*. Relative to the latency time, it takes a long time to reposition the arm. The time for repositioning the arm, the *seek time*, grows as the distance that the arm must move increases. It is useful to store related information on the same track or on physically close tracks whenever possible in order to minimize the seek time.

The disk shown in Figures 7.2 and 7.3 is a very simple one. It is typical of disks in early computer systems and in personal computers. Medium-

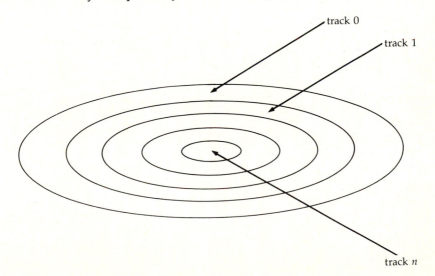

Figure 7.3   Structure of a platter.

and large-scale computers have high-capacity disks with multiple platters. Such a device is pictured in Figure 7.4. Multiple-platter disks are called disk packs when we wish to distinguish them from single-platter disks. Henceforth, when we use the term *disk*, we shall be referring to multiple-platter disks.

All the disk arms are moved as a unit by the *actuator*. Each arm has two heads: one to read and write the top surface of the platter below it, and one to read and write the bottom surface of the platter above it. At any moment, the set of tracks over which the heads are located form a *cylinder*. This cylinder holds the data that is accessible without any movement of the actuator. That is, all data within this cylinder is accessible within the disk latency time. Just as it is efficient to store related data in a single track or a collection of close tracks, so it is efficient to store related data in the same cylinder, or, if this is not possible, in cylinders that are close to each other.

Data is transferred between disk and main memory in units called *blocks*. A block is a contiguous sequence of bytes from a single track of one platter. Block sizes range from 512 bytes to several thousand bytes. If

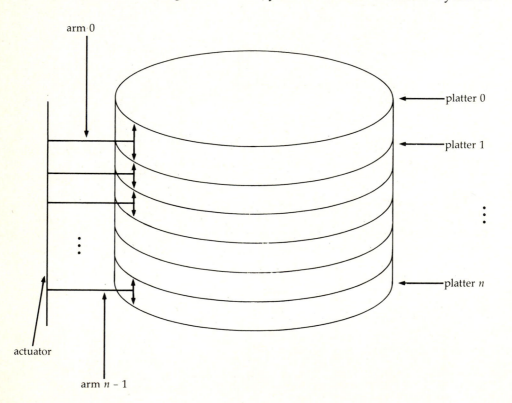

Figure 7.4   A disk pack.

several blocks from a cylinder need to be transferred from disk to main memory, we may be able to save access time be requesting the blocks in the order in which they will pass under the heads. If the desired blocks are on different cylinders, it is advantageous to request the blocks in an order that minimizes actuator movement. The simplest way to optimize block access time is to organize the blocks on disk in a way that corresponds closely to the manner in which we expect data to be accessed. However, it may be costly to maintain such an organization as data is inserted into and deleted from the database. In other cases, it is impossible to organize data in a way that corresponds closely to the manner in which it is accessed. Such situations arise if an optional organization for one application is especially bad for another application sharing the same data. We shall examine these issues in the next section as we study the storage of data in disk files provided by the underlying operating system.

7.3 File Organization

A *file* is organized logically as a sequence of records. These records are mapped onto disk blocks. Files are provided as a basic construct in operating systems, so we shall assume the existence of an underlying *file system*. We need to consider ways of representing logical data models in terms of files.

Although blocks are of a fixed size determined by the physical properties of the disk and by the operating system, record sizes vary. In a relational database, tuples of distinct relations are generally of different sizes. In a network database, it is likely that the owner record type is of a different size than the member record type.

One approach to mapping the database to files is to use several files and store records of only one fixed length in any given file. An alternative is to structure our files in such a way that we can accommodate multiple lengths for records. Files of fixed-length records are easier to implement than files of variable-length records. Many of the techniques used for them can be applied to the variable-length case. Thus, we begin by considering a file of fixed-length records.

7.3.1 Fixed-Length Records

As an example, let us consider a file of *deposit* records for our bank database. Each record of this file is defined as follows:

> **type** *deposit* = **record**
>> *branch-name* : char (20);
>> *account-number* : integer;
>> *customer-name* : char (20);
>> *balance* : real;
>
> **end**

record 0	Perryridge	102	Hayes	400
record 1	Round Hill	305	Turner	350
record 2	Mianus	215	Smith	700
record 3	Downtown	101	Johnson	500
record 4	Redwood	222	Lindsay	700
record 5	Perryridge	201	Williams	900
record 6	Brighton	217	Green	750
record 7	Downtown	110	Peterson	600
record 8	Perryridge	218	Lyle	700

Figure 7.5   File containing *deposit* records.

If we assume that each character occupies a byte, an integer occupies 4 bytes, and a real 8 bytes, our *deposit* record is 52 bytes long. A simple approach is to use the first 52 bytes for the first record, the next 52 bytes for the second record, and so on (Figure 7.5). However, there are two problems with this simple approach:

- It is difficult to delete a record from this structure. The space occupied by the record to be deleted must be filled with some other record of the file, or we must have a way of marking deleted records so that they can be ignored.

- Unless the block size happens to be a multiple of 52 (which is unlikely), some records will cross block boundaries. That is, part of the record will be stored in one block and part in another. It would thus require two block accesses to read or write such a record.

record 0	Perryridge	102	Hayes	400
record 1	Round Hill	305	Turner	350
record 3	Downtown	101	Johnson	500
record 4	Redwood	222	Lindsay	700
record 5	Perryridge	201	Williams	900
record 6	Brighton	217	Green	750
record 7	Downtown	110	Peterson	600
record 8	Perryridge	218	Lyle	700

Figure 7.6   File of Figure 7.5 with record 2 deleted.

When a record is deleted, we could move the record that came after it into the space formerly occupied by the deleted record, etc., until every record following the deleted record has been moved ahead (Figure 7.6). Such an approach requires moving a large number of records. It might be better simply to move the last record of the file into the space occupied by the deleted record, as shown in Figure 7.7.

It is undesirable to move records in order to occupy the space freed by a deleted record, since this requires additional block accesses. Since insertions tend to be more frequent than deletions, it is acceptable to leave the space occupied by the deleted record open, and wait for a subsequent insertion before reusing the space. A simple marker on a deleted record is not sufficient since it is hard to find this available space when an insertion is being done. Thus, we need to introduce additional structure.

At the beginning of the file, we allocate a certain number of bytes as a *file header*. The header will contain a variety of information about the file. For now, all we need to store there is the address of the first record whose contents are deleted. We use this first record to store the address of the second available record, etc. Intuitively, we may think of these stored addresses as *pointers* since they "point" to the location of a record. Figure 7.8 shows the file of Figure 7.5 after records 1, 4, and 6 have been deleted.

Upon insertion of a new record, we use the record pointed to by the header. We change the header pointer to point to the next available record. If no space is available, we add the record to the end of the file.

The use of pointers requires careful programming. If we move or delete a record to which another record contains a pointer, that pointer becomes incorrect in the sense that it no longer points to the desired record. Such pointers are called *dangling pointers* and, in effect, point to garbage. In order to avoid the dangling-pointer problem, we must avoid moving or deleting records that are pointed to by other records. We say that such records are *pinned*.

record 0	Perryridge	102	Hayes	400
record 1	Round Hill	305	Turner	350
record 8	Perryridge	218	Lyle	700
record 3	Downtown	101	Johnson	500
record 4	Redwood	222	Lindsay	700
record 5	Perryridge	201	Williams	900
record 6	Brighton	217	Green	750
record 7	Downtown	110	Peterson	600

Figure 7.7   File of Figure 7.5 with record 2 deleted.

header					
record 0		Perryridge	102	Hayes	400
record 1					
record 2		Mianus	215	Smith	700
record 3		Downtown	101	Johnson	500
record 4					
record 5		Perryridge	201	Williams	900
record 6					
record 7		Downtown	110	Peterson	600
record 8		Perryridge	218	Lyle	700

Figure 7.8   File of Figure 7.5 after deletion of records 1, 4, and 6.

Insertion and deletion for files of fixed-length records are quite simple to implement because the space made available by a deleted record is exactly the space needed to insert a record. If we allow records of variable length in a file, this is no longer the case. An inserted record may not fit in the space left free by a deleted record or it may fill only part of that space.

7.3.2 Variable-Length Records

Variable-length records arise in database systems in several ways:

- Storage of multiple record types in a file.
- Record types that allow variable lengths for one or more fields.
- Record types that allow repeating fields.

There are a number of different techniques for implementing variable-length records which are described below. For purposes of illustration, we shall use one example to demonstrate the various implementation techniques. We consider a different representation of the *deposit* information stored in the file of Figure 7.5, in which we use one variable-length record for each branch name and all of the account information for that branch. The format of the record is:

```
type deposit-list = record
                branch-name : char (20);
                account-info : array [1 .. ∞] of
                            record;
                                account-number : integer;
                                customer-name : char (20);
                                balance : real;
                            end
        end
```

0	Perryridge	102	Hayes	400	201	Williams	900	218	Lyle	700	⊥
1	Round Hill	305	Turner	350	⊥						
2	Mianus	215	Smith	700	⊥						
3	Downtown	101	Johnson	500	110	Peterson	600	⊥			
4	Redwood	222	Lindsay	700	⊥						
5	Brighton	217	Green	750	⊥						

Figure 7.9   Byte string representation of variable-length records.

We define *account-info* as an array with an arbitrary number of elements so that there is no limit to how large a record can be (up to, of course, the size of the disk!).

Byte String Representation

A simple method for implementing variable-length records is to attach a special *end-of-record* (⊥) symbol to the end of each record. We can then store each record as a string of consecutive bytes. Figure 7.9 shows such an organization to represent the file of fixed-length records of Figure 7.5 using variable-length records.

The byte string representation has several disadvantages. The most serious of these are:

- It is not easy to reuse space occupied formerly by a deleted record. Although techniques exist to manage insertion and deletion, they lead to a large number of small fragments of disk storage that are wasted.

- There is no space, in general, for records to grow longer. If a variable-length record becomes longer, it must be moved, and movement is costly if the record is pinned.

Thus, the byte string representation is not usually used for implementing variable-length records.

Fixed-Length Representation

In order to implement variable-length records efficiently in a file system, we use one or more fixed-length records to represent one variable-length record.

There are two techniques for implementing files of variable-length records using fixed-length records.

- **Reserved space**. If there is a maximum record length that is never exceeded, we may use fixed-length records of that length. Unused space (for records shorter than the maximum space) is filled with a special null, or "end-of-record" symbol.

- **Pointers**. The variable-length record is represented by a list of fixed-length records, chained together via pointers.

If we choose to apply the reserved-space method to our account example, we need to select a maximum record length. Figure 7.10 shows how the file of Figure 7.5 would be represented if we allow a maximum of three accounts per branch. A record in this file is of the *account-list* type, but with the array containing exactly three elements. Those branches with fewer than three accounts (for example, Round Hill) have records with null fields. We use the symbol ⊥ to represent this in Figure 7.10. In practice, a particular value that can never represent real data is used (for example, a negative "account number" or a "name" beginning with a "*").

The reserved-space method is useful when most records are of length close to the maximum. Otherwise, a significant amount of space may be wasted. In our bank example, it may be the case that some branches have many more accounts than others. This leads us to consider use of the pointer method. To represent the file using the pointer method, we add a pointer field as we did in Figure 7.8. The resulting structure is shown in Figure 7.11.

In effect, the file structures of Figures 7.8 and 7.11 are the same except that, in Figure 7.8, we used pointers only to chain deleted records together, while in Figure 7.11, we chain together all records pertaining to the same branch.

A disadvantage to the structure of Figure 7.11 is that we waste space in all records except the first in a chain. The first record needs to have the *branch-name* value, but subsequent records do not. Nevertheless, we need to include a field for *branch-name* in all records, lest the records not be of

0	Perryridge	102	Hayes	400	201	Williams	900	218	Lyle	700
1	Round Hill	305	Turner	350	⊥	⊥	⊥	⊥	⊥	⊥
2	Mianus	215	Smith	700	⊥	⊥	⊥	⊥	⊥	⊥
3	Downtown	101	Johnson	500	110	Peterson	600	⊥	⊥	⊥
4	Redwood	222	Lindsay	700	⊥	⊥	⊥	⊥	⊥	⊥
5	Brighton	217	Green	750	⊥	⊥	⊥	⊥	⊥	⊥

Figure 7.10   File of Figure 7.5 using the reserved-space method.

0		Perryridge	102	Hayes	400
1		Round Hill	305	Turner	350
2		Mianus	215	Smith	700
3		Downtown	101	Johnson	500
4		Redwood	222	Lindsay	700
5			201	Williams	900
6		Brighton	217	Green	750
7			110	Peterson	600
8			218	Lyle	700

Figure 7.11   File of Figure 7.5 using the pointer method.

fixed length. This wasted space is significant since we expect, in practice, that each branch has a large number of accounts. To deal with this problem, we allow two kinds of block in our file:

- **Anchor block**, which contains the first record of a chain.

- **Overflow block**, which contains records other than those that are the first record of a chain.

Thus, all records *within a block* have the same length, even though not all records in the file have the same length. Figure 7.12 shows this file structure.

Perryridge	102	Hayes	400	Anchor
Round Hill	305	Turner	350	Block
Mianus	215	Smith	700	
Downtown	101	Johnson	500	
Redwood	222	Lindsay	700	
Brighton	217	Green	750	

201	Williams	900	Overflow
218	Lyle	700	Block
110	Peterson	600	

Figure 7.12   Anchor block and overflow block organization.

7.3.3 Organization of Records into Blocks

A file may be viewed as a collection of records. However, since data is transferred between disk storage and main memory in units of a block, it is worthwhile to assign records to blocks in such a way that a single block contains related records. If we assign records to blocks randomly, it will usually be the case that a different block must be accessed for each record accessed. On the other hand, if we can access several of the records desired using only one block access, we have saved some disk accesses. Since disk accesses are usually the bottleneck in the performance of a database system, careful assignment of records to blocks can pay significant performance dividends.

Earlier, we described a file structure in which all account information for a branch appeared in one (variable-length) record. Our fixed-length record representations of this file structure used several records to represent a variable-length record. If we can store several of these records together in a block, we reduce the number of block accesses required to read a variable-length record. It is easy to group records together this way if the database never changes. Suppose, however, that a new account is opened at the Perryridge branch. If we are using the structure shown in Figure 7.12, we would like to add the record for this account to the same block as the other Perryridge branch accounts. It is likely to be the case, however, that the block is filled with account records for other branches. We must either move one of those records or we must abandon our goal of grouping together records representing a single variable-length record. Neither option is desirable.

As an alternative, let us consider a structure which uses slightly more space than the structure of Figure 7.12, but allows for improved efficiency in accessing data. We assign one *bucket* to each *branch-name* value. The bucket holds the entire variable-length record for the corresponding *branch-name* value. A bucket consists of as many blocks as necessary to represent the data, but buckets never share blocks. Figure 7.13 shows a bucket file structure for the *deposit* file. The buckets are structured slightly differently from the previous fixed-length record structures we have used:

- The first record in the bucket holds the *branch-name* value for the bucket.

- Subsequent bucket records hold the repeating fields. There is no need to repeat the *branch-name* since it is the same for all records in the bucket. For the same reason, there is no need to chain records together since they represent only one variable-length record. (We may still use pointer chains to facilitate space recovery after deletion.)

Observe that there are two different record lengths in the bucket. The first record holds a *branch-name* value. All other records hold three fields:

Block 0	Perryridge		
	102	Hayes	400
	201	Williams	900
	218	Lyle	700

Block 1	Round Hill		
	305	Turner	350

Block 2	Mianus		
	215	Smith	700

Block 3	Downtown		
	101	Johnson	500
	110	Peterson	600

Block 4	Redwood		
	222	Lindsay	700

Block 5	Brighton		
	217	Green	750

Figure 7.13   A bucket file structure.

account-number, *customer-name*, and *balance*. Since every bucket must have *exactly* one record holding the *branch-name* value, there is no problem managing insertion and deletion of records from the bucket using any of the techniques we described for fixed-length records.

In the example of Figure 7.13, each bucket occupies exactly one block. If we expand our example to a more realistic one in which a branch has thousands of accounts, a bucket may require several blocks. We chain blocks of a bucket together using methods similar to those we used earlier to chain records together. We allocate a fixed amount of space at the beginning of each block as a *block header* and use it to store the bucket-chain pointers. Figure 7.14 shows part of a file structure for an expanded bank database. We have omitted the internal structure of each block except for the block header.

As a bucket grows due to insertion of records, new blocks may need to be added to it. As records are deleted, a block may become empty. As we did for deleted records, we can maintain a chain of available blocks and reuse them for buckets that expand beyond their current set of blocks.

The reuse of blocks appears to be a good idea from the standpoint of space efficiency. However, this strategy is not the best from the standpoint of time efficiency. When a bucket is searched, each block must be read. In order to minimize the time that this search takes, we need to minimize the time it takes to transfer these blocks into main memory. Thus, we would like the blocks for a bucket to be stored on the same cylinder of the disk, or on adjacent cylinders. If a block becomes empty, we would prefer that it

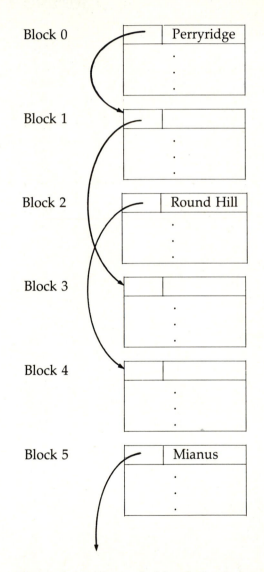

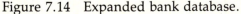

Figure 7.14   Expanded bank database.

be reused by the bucket that formerly contained it, rather than have it reused by another bucket. Such a policy could result in a large number of empty blocks, but this occurs only if deletion is more frequent than insertion. Since almost all database applications have at least as many insertions as deletions, the amount of wasted space is likely to be low.

In practice, it is not possible to maintain a perfect placement of block on disk without leaving an excessive amount of space empty. Eventually, buckets will overflow their cylinder or cylinders and no room may be available on nearby cylinders. In such cases, any available space may be used. If the bucket becomes sufficiently fragmented that performance begins to suffer, the database can be reorganized. The database is copied to tape and reloaded with the blocks relocated so that buckets are no longer fragmented and reasonable room for bucket growth exists. It is usually necessary to forbid user access to the database during such reorganizations.

7.4 Buffer Management

We have already discussed the need to use disk storage for the database, and the need to transfer blocks of data between main memory and disk. A major goal of the file structures presented above is to minimize the number of blocks that must be accessed. Another way to reduce the number of disk accesses is to keep as many blocks as possible in main memory. The goal is to maximize the chance that when a block is accessed, it is already in main memory and, thus, no disk access is required.

Since it is not possible to keep all blocks in main memory, we need to manage the allocation of the space available in main memory for the storage of blocks. The *buffer* is that part of main memory available for storage of copies of disk blocks. There is always a copy kept on disk of every block, but the copy on disk may be an older version of the block than the version in the buffer. The subsystem responsible for the allocation of buffer space is called the *buffer manager*.

The buffer manager intercepts all requests made by the rest of the system for blocks of the database. If the block is already in the buffer, the requestor is passed the address of the block in main memory. If the block is not in the buffer, the buffer manager reads the block in from disk in to the buffer, and passes the address of the block in main memory to the requestor. Thus, the buffer manager is transparent to those system programs that issue disk block requests. Readers familiar with operating system concepts will note that the buffer manager appears to be nothing more than a virtual memory manager as found in most operating systems. However, in order to serve the database system well, the buffer manager must use more sophisticated techniques than typical virtual memory management schemes:

- **Replacement strategy**. When there is no room left in the buffer, a block must be removed from the buffer before a new one can be read in. Typical operating systems use a least recently used (LRU) scheme, in which the block that was referenced least recently is written back to disk and removed from the buffer. This simple approach can be improved upon for database application.

- **Pinned blocks**. In order for the database system to be able to recover from crashes (Chapter 10), it is necessary to restrict those times when a block may be written back to disk. A block that is not allowed to be written back to disk is said to be *pinned*. Although most operating systems do not provide support for pinned blocks, such a feature is essential for the implementation of a database system that is resilient to crashes.

- **Forced output of blocks**. There are situations in which it is necessary to write the block back to disk even though the buffer space it occupies is not needed. This is called the *forced output* of a block. We shall see the reason for requiring force output in Chapter 10. The requirement is due to the fact that main memory contents and thus buffer contents are lost in a crash while data on disk usually survives a crash.

We now discuss these issues in more detail.

The goal of a replacement strategy for blocks in the buffer is the minimization of accesses to the disk. For general-purpose programs, it is not possible to predict accurately which blocks will be referenced. Therefore, operating systems use the past pattern of block references as a predictor of future references. The assumption that is generally made is that blocks that have been referenced recently are likely to be referenced again. Therefore, if a block must be replaced, the least recently referenced block is replaced. This is called the LRU block replacement scheme.

LRU is an acceptable replacement scheme in operating systems. However, a database system is able to predict the pattern of future references more accurately than an operating system. A user request to the database system involves several steps. The database system is often able to determine in advance which blocks will be needed by each of the steps required to perform the user-requested operation. Thus, unlike operating systems, which must rely on the past to predict the future, database systems may have information regarding at least the short-term future.

To illustrate how information about future block access allows for improvement over the LRU strategy, consider the processing of the relational algebra expression

$$borrow \bowtie customer.$$

Assume that the strategy chosen to process this request is given by the following pseudocode program:

> **for each** tuple *b* of *borrow* **do**
>   **for each** tuple *c* of *customer* **do**
>   **if** *b*[*customer-name*] = *c*[*customer-name*]
>   **then begin**
>   let *x* be a tuple defined as follows:
>   *x*[*branch-name*] := *b*[*branch-name*]
>   *x*[*loan-number*] := *b*[*loan-number*]
>   *x*[*customer-name*] := *b*[*customer-name*]
>   *x*[*amount*] := *b*[*amount*]
>   *x*[*street*] := *c*[*street*]
>   *x*[*customer-city*] := *c*[*customer-city*]
>   include tuple *x* as part of result of *borrow* ⋈ *customer*
>   **end**
>   **end**
> **end**

Assume that the two relations of this example are stored in separate files. In this example, we can see that once a tuple of *borrow* has been processed, it is not needed again. Therefore, once processing of an entire block of *borrow* tuples is completed, that block is no longer needed in main memory, despite the fact that it has been used very recently. The buffer manager should be instructed to free the space occupied by a *borrow* block as soon as the last tuple has been processed. This buffer management strategy is called the *toss-immediate* strategy.

Now consider blocks containing *customer* tuples. We need to examine every block of *customer* tuples once for each tuple of the *borrow* relation. When processing of a *customer* block is completed, we know that it will not be accessed again until all other *customer* blocks have been processed. Thus, the most recently used *customer* block will be the last block to be re-referenced, and the least recently used *customer* block is the block that will be referenced next. This is the exact opposite of the assumptions that form the basis for the LRU strategy. Indeed, the optimal strategy for block replacement is the most recently used (MRU) strategy. If a *customer* block must be removed from the buffer, the MRU strategy chooses the most recently used block.

In order for the MRU strategy to work correctly for our example, the system must pin the *customer* block currently being processed. After the last *customer* tuple has been processed, the block is unpinned and it becomes the most recently used block.

In addition to using knowledge that the system may have about the request being processed, the buffer manager can use statistical information regarding the probability that a request will reference a particular relation, DBTG-set, etc. The data dictionary is a most frequently accessed part of the database. Thus, the buffer manager should try not to remove data dictionary blocks from main memory unless other factors dictate otherwise. In the next chapter, we discuss indices for files. Since an index for a file may be accessed more frequently than the file itself, the buffer manager should, in general, not remove index blocks from main memory if alternatives are available.

The ideal database block replacement strategy needs knowledge of the database operations being performed. No single strategy is known that handles all of the possible scenarios well. Indeed a surprisingly large number of database systems use LRU despite its faults. The exercises explore some alternative strategies.

The strategy used by the buffer manager for block replacement is influenced by other factors besides the time at which the block will be referenced again. If the system is processing requests by several users concurrently, the concurrency control subsystem (Chapter 11) may need to delay certain requests in order to ensure the preservation of database consistency. If the buffer manager is provided with information by the concurrency control subsystem as to which requests are being delayed, the buffer manager can use this information to alter its block replacement strategy. Specifically, blocks needed by active (nondelayed) requests can be retained in the buffer at the expense of blocks needed by the delayed requests.

The crash recovery subsystem (Chapter 10) imposes very stringent constraints on block replacement. If a block has been modified, the buffer manager is not allowed to write the new version of the block in the buffer back to disk since this would destroy the old version. Instead, the block manager must seek permission from the crash recovery subsystem before writing out a block. The crash recovery subsystem may demand that certain other blocks be force-output before it will grant permission to the buffer manager to output the block it requested. In Chapter 10, we define precisely the interaction between the buffer manager and the crash recovery subsystem.

7.5 Mapping Relations to Files

Many relational database systems store each relation in a separate file. This allows the database system to take full advantage of the file system provided as part of the operating system. It is usually the case that tuples of a relation can be represented as fixed-length records. (Note that we are assuming first normal form). Thus, relations can be mapped to a simple file structure. This simple implementation of a relational database system is well suited to database systems designed for personal computers. In such systems, the size of the database is small, so less is gained from a sophisticated file structure. Furthermore, in many personal computers, small overall size of the object code for the database system is essential. A simple file structure reduces the amount of code needed to implement the system.

This simple approach to relational database implementation becomes less satisfactory as the size of the database increases. We have seen that there are performance advantages to be gained from careful assignment of records to blocks and from careful organization of the blocks themselves. Thus, it is apparent that a more complicated file structure may be beneficial, even if we retain the strategy of storing each relation in a separate file.

However, many large-scale database systems do not rely directly on the underlying operating system for file management. Instead one large operating system file is allocated to the database system. All relations are stored in this one file, and the management of this file is left to the database system. To see the advantage of storing many relations in one file, consider the following SQL query for the bank database:

> **select** account-number, customer-name, street, customer-city
> **from** deposit, customer
> **where** deposit.customer-name = customer.customer-name

The above query computes a join of the *deposit* and *customer* relations. Thus, for each tuple of *deposit*, the system must locate the *customer* tuples with the same value for *customer-name*. Ideally, these records will be located with the help of *indices*, which we shall discuss in Chapter 8. Regardless of how these records are located, however, they need to be transferred from disk into main memory. In the worst case, each record will reside on a different block, forcing us to do one block read for each record required by the query.

As a concrete example, consider the *deposit* and *customer* relations of Figures 7.15 and 7.16, respectively. In Figure 7.17, we show a file structure designed for efficient execution of queries involving *deposit* ⋈ *customer* . The *deposit* tuples for each *customer-name* are stored near the *customer* tuple for the corresponding *customer-name*. This structure mixes tuples of two relations together, but allows for efficient processing of the join. When a

branch-name	account-number	customer-name	balance
Perryridge	102	Hayes	400
Mianus	220	Hayes	600
Round Hill	503	Hayes	700
Round Hill	305	Turner	350

Figure 7.15   The *deposit* relation.

customer-name	street	customer-city
Hayes	Main	Harrison
Turner	Putnam	Stamford

Figure 7.16   The *customer* relation.

tuple of the *customer* relation is read, the entire block containing that tuple is copied from disk into main memory. Since the corresponding *deposit* tuples are stored on the disk near the *customer* tuple, the block containing the *customer* tuple contains tuples of the *deposit* relation needed to process the query. If a customer has so many accounts that the *deposit* records do not fit in one block, the remaining records appear on nearby blocks. This file structure, called *clustering*, allows us to read many of the required records using one block read. Thus, we are able to process this particular query more efficiently.

Our use of clustering has enhanced processing of a particular join, *deposit* ⋈ *customer* , but it results in slowing processing of other types of query. For example:

select *
from *customer*

requires more block access than in the scheme under which we stored each relation in a separate file. Instead of several *customer* records appearing in a block, each record is located in a distinct block. Indeed, simply finding all of the *customer* records is not possible without some additional structure. In order to locate all tuples of the *customer* relation in the structure of Figure 7.17, we need to chain all the records of that relation together using pointers, as shown in Figure 7.18.

The determination of when clustering is to be used depends upon the types of query that the database designer believes to be most frequent.

Hayes	Main	Harrison	
Perryridge	102	Hayes	400
Mianus	220	Hayes	600
Round Hill	503	Hayes	700
Turner	Putnam	Stamford	
Round Hill	305	Turner	350

Figure 7.17   Clustering file structure.

Careful use of clustering can produce significant performance gains in query processing.

So far, we have considered only the representation of the relations themselves. A relational database system needs to maintain data *about* the relations. This information is called the *data dictionary*. Among the types of information the system must store are:

- Names of the relations.

- Names of the attributes of each relation.

- Domains of attributes.

- Names of views defined on the database, and the definition of those views.

- Integrity constraints for each relation (for example, key constraints).

In addition to the above items many systems keep data on users of the system:

- Names of authorized users.

- Accounting information about users.

In systems that use highly sophisticated structures to store relations, statistical and descriptive data about relations may be kept:

- Number of tuples in each relation.

- Method of storage used for each relation (for example, clustered or nonclustered).

In the next chapter, in which we study indices, we shall see a need to store information about each index on each relation:

Hayes	Main	Harrison	
Perryridge	102	Hayes	400
Mianus	220	Hayes	600
Round Hill	503	Hayes	700
Turner	Putnam	Stamford	
Round Hill	305	Turner	350

Figure 7.18   Clustering file structure with pointer chains.

- Name of the index.

- Name of the relation being indexed.

- Attributes that the index is on.

- Type of index.

All this information is, in effect, a miniature database. Some database systems store this information using special-purpose data structures and code. It is generally preferable to store the data about the database in the database itself. By using the database to store system data, we simplify the overall structure of the system and allow the full power of the database to be used to permit fast access to system data.

The exact choice of how to represent system data using relations must be made by the system designer. One possible representation is:

System-catalog-scheme = (*relation-name, number-of-attributes*)
Attribute-scheme = (*attribute-name, relation-name, domain-type, position*)
User-scheme = (*user-name, encrypted-password, group*)
Index-scheme = (*index-name, relation-name, index-type, index-attributes*)
View-scheme = (*view-name, definition*)

Several alternative designs that are used in actual relational database systems appear in Chapter 15.

7.6 Mapping Networks to Files

A network database consists of records and links. We have already seen several ways of storing records within files. In the relational model, there are no explicit pointers. The only pointers that need to appear in a physical representation of a relational database are part of the data structures used to represent variable-length records, buckets, etc. In the network model, however, pointers appear explicitly in the form of links.

Links are implemented by adding *pointer-fields* to records that are associated via a link. Each record must have one pointer field for each link with which it is associated. To illustrate this, consider the data-structure diagram of Figure 7.19 and a sample database corresponding to it (Figure 7.20). Figure 7.21 shows the sample instance with pointer fields to

Figure 7.19   Data-structure diagram.

Beck	Maple	San Francisco		200	55

256	100 000

Katz	North	San Jose

347	667

Doner	Sidehill	Palo Alto

301	10 533

Figure 7.20   Sample database corresponding to diagram of Figure 7.19.

represent the links. Each line in Figure 7.20 is replaced in Figure 7.21 by two pointers.

Since the *CustAcct* link is many-to-many, each record may be associated with an arbitrary number of records. Thus, it is not possible to limit the number of pointer fields in a record. Therefore, even if a record itself is of fixed length, the actual record used in the physical implementation is a variable-length record.

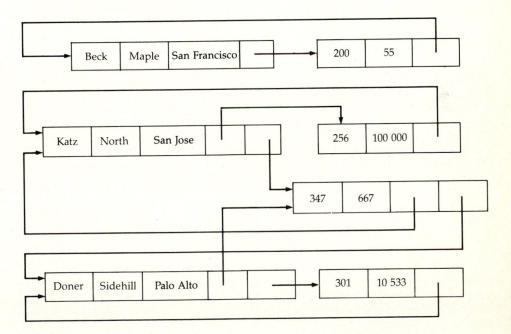

Figure 7.21   Implementation of instance of Figure 7.20.

These complications led the architects of the DBTG model to restrict links to be either one-to-one or one-to-many. We shall see that, under this restriction, the number of pointers needed is reduced and it is possible to retain fixed-length records. To illustrate the implementation of the DBTG model, let us assume that the *CustAcct* link is one-to-many and represented by the DBTG-set *CustAcct* as defined below:

> **set name is** *CustAcct*
> **owner is** *customer*
> **member is** *account*

A sample database corresponding to this scheme is shown in Figure 7.22.

An *account* record may be associated with only one *customer* record. Thus, we need only one pointer in the *account* record to represent the *CustAcct* relationship. However, a *customer* record may be associated with many *account* records. Rather than using multiple pointers in the *account* record, we can use a *ring structure* to represent the entire occurrence of the DBTG-set *CustAcct*. In a ring structure, the records of both the owner and member type for a set occurrence are organized into a circular list. There is one circular list for each set occurrence (that is, for each record of the owner type).

Figure 7.23 shows the ring structure for the example instance of Figure 7.22. Let us examine the DBTG-set occurrence owned by the Camp record. There are two member-type (*account*) records. Rather than containing one pointer to each member record, the owner (Camp) record contains a pointer to only the "first" member record (account 226). This member record contains a pointer to the next member record (account 177). Since the record for account 177 is the "last" member record, it contains a pointer to the owner record.

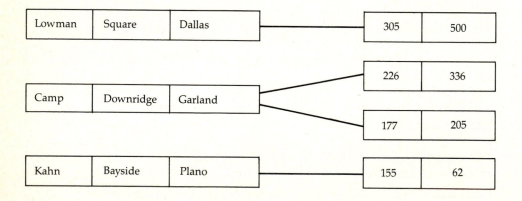

Figure 7.22   Sample database for *CustAcct* DBTG-set.

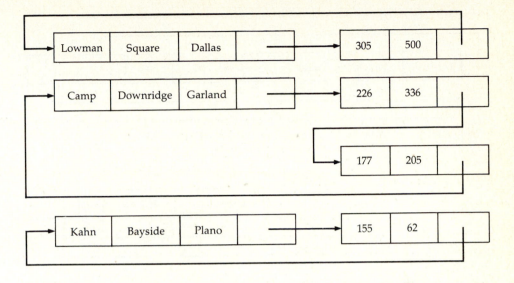

Figure 7.23 Ring structure for instance of Figure 7.22.

If we represent DBTG-sets using the ring structure, a record contains exactly one pointer for each DBTG-set it is involved in, regardless of whether it is of the owner type or member type. Thus, fixed-length records can be represented within a ring structure without the need to resort to variable-length records. This structural simplicity is offset by added complexity in accessing records within a set. To find a particular member record of a set occurrence, the pointer chain must be traversed to navigate from the owner record to the desired member record. Under the implementation scheme we presented earlier, there is a pointer from the owner to each member.

The ring structure implementation strategy for the DBTG model provided the motivation for the DBTG data retrieval facility. Recall the statements

and
$$\textbf{find first } \textit{<record type>} \textbf{ within } \textit{<set type>}$$
$$\textbf{find next } \textit{<record type>} \textbf{ within } \textit{<set type>}$$

The terms **first** and **next** in these statements refer to the ordering of records given by the ring-structure pointers. Thus, once the owner has been found, it is easy to do a **find first** since all the system must do is follow a pointer. Similarly, all the system must do in response to a **find next** is follow the ring-structure pointer.

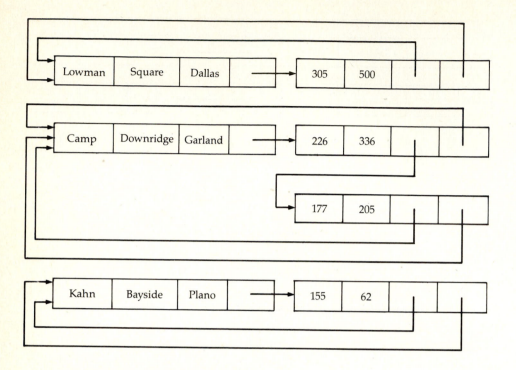

Figure 7.24   Ring structure of Figure 7.23 with owner pointers.

The **find owner** statement of the DBTG query language is reflected in a modified form of the ring structure in which every member-type record contains a second pointer, which points to the owner record. This structure is illustrated in Figure 7.24. Under this implementation strategy, a record has one pointer for each DBTG-set for which it is of the owner type and two pointers (a *next-member* pointer and an *owner* pointer) for each DBTG-set for which it is of the member type. This strategy allows for efficient execution of a **find owner** statement. Under our earlier strategy, it is necessary to traverse the ring structure until we find the owner.

The physical placement of records is important for an efficient implementation of a network database, as is the case for a relational database.

The statements **find first, find next,** and **find owner** are designed for processing a sequence of records within a particular DBTG-set occurrence. Since these are the most frequently used statements in a DBTG query, it is desirable to store records of a DBTG-set occurrence physically close to each other on disk. To specify the strategy that the system is to use to store a DBTG-set, a **placement** clause is added to the definition of the member record type.

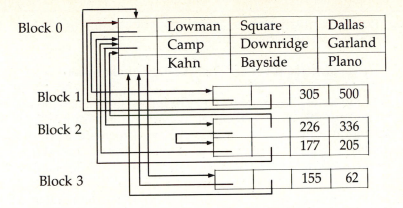

Figure 7.25   Clustered record placement for instance of Figure 7.22.

Consider the DBTG-set *CustAcct* and the example instance shown in Figure 7.22. If we add the clause:

placement clustered via *CustAcct*

to the definition of record type *account* (the member record type *CustAcct* of the DBTG-set), the system will store members of each set occurrence close to each other physically on disk. To the extent possible, members of a set occurrence will be stored in the same block. Figure 7.25 illustrates this storage strategy for the example instance for Figure 7.22.

The clustered placement strategy does not require the owner record of a DBTG-set to be stored near the set's members. This allows for the storage of each record type in a distinct file. If we are willing to store more than one record type in a file, we can specify that owner and member records are to be stored close to each other physically on disk. This is done by

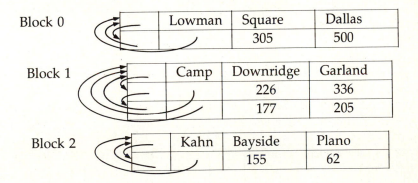
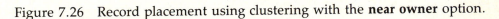

Figure 7.26   Record placement using clustering with the **near owner** option.

adding the clause **near owner** to the **placement** clause. For our example of the *CustAcct* set, we would add the clause

placement clustered via *CustAcct* **near owner**

to the definition of the record type *account*. Figure 7.26 illustrates this storage strategy. By storing member records in the same block as the owner, we reduce the number of block accesses required to read an entire set occurrence. This form of storage is analogous to the clustering file structure we proposed earlier for the relational model. This similarity is not surprising since queries that require traversal of DBTG-set occurrences under the network model require natural joins under the relational model.

7.7 Mapping Hierarchies to Files

A hierarchical database scheme is a collection of tree-structure diagrams. For each diagram there is exactly one instance. A straightforward technique for implementing the instance of a tree-structure diagram is to associate one pointer with a record for each child that the record has. To illustrate this, consider the database tree of Figure 7.27. Figure 7.28 shows an implementation of this database using parent-to-child pointers. Parent-child pointers, however, are not an ideal structure for the implementation of hierarchical databases since a parent record may have an arbitrary number of children. Thus, fixed-length records become variable-length records once the parent-child pointers are added.

Instead of parent-child pointers, we may use *leftmost-child* and *next-sibling* pointers. A record has only two pointers. The leftmost-child pointer points to one child. The next-sibling pointer points to another child of the same parent. Figure 7.29 shows this structure for the database tree of Figure 7.27. Under this structure, every record has exactly two pointers. Thus fixed-length records retain their fixed length when we add the necessary pointers.

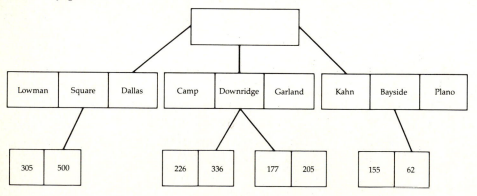

Figure 7.27   Sample database tree.

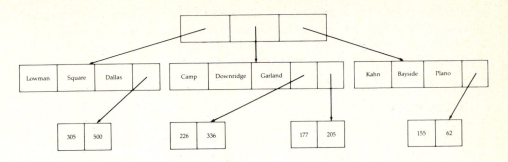

Figure 7.28   Implementation with parent-child pointers.

Observe that several pointer fields are unused in Figure 7.29. In general, the last child of a parent has no next sibling, thus its next sibling field is set to null. Rather than place nulls in such fields it is useful to place pointers there to facilitate the preorder traversal required to process queries on hierarchical databases. We place a pointer in the next sibling field of the rightmost siblings to the next record in preorder. Figure 7.30 shows this modification to the structure of Figure 7.29. Using these pointers, it is possible to process a tree instance in preorder simply by following pointers. For this reason the pointers are sometimes referred to as *preorder threads*.

A parent pointer is often added to records in an implementation of a hierarchical database. This pointer facilitates the processing of queries that give a value for a child record and request a value from the corresponding parent record. If we include parent pointers, there are a total of exactly three pointer fields added to each record.

In order to see how we can best locate records of a hierarchical database physically on disk, we draw an analogy between the parent-child relationship within a hierarchy and the owner-member relationship within a DBTG-set. In both cases, a one-to-many relationship is being represented. We desire to store the members and the owners of a set

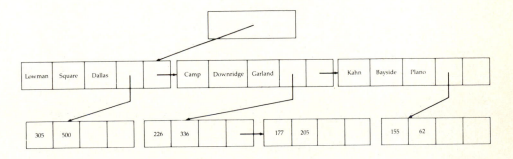

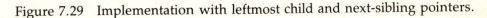

Figure 7.29   Implementation with leftmost child and next-sibling pointers.

occurrence together. Similarly, we desire to store child records and their parent physically close on disk. This form of storage allows a sequence of **get first**, **get next**, and **get next within parent** statements to be executed with a minimal number of block accesses.

7.8 Summary

A major factor in a user's satisfaction or lack thereof with a database system is its performance. If the response time for a request is too long, the value of the system is diminished. The performance of a system depends on the efficiency of the data structures used to represent the data in the database and on how efficiently the system is able to operate on these data structures. As is the case elsewhere in computer systems, a tradeoff must be made not only between space and time, but also between the efficiency of one kind of operation versus that of another.

Several types of data storage exist in most computer systems. These storage media are classified by the speed with which data can be accessed, by the cost per unit of data to buy the memory, and by how "reliable" they are. Among the media typically available are: cache, main memory, direct-access storage (disk storage), and sequential-access storage (tape storage).

A *file* is organized logically as a sequence of records which are mapped onto disk blocks. One approach to mapping the database to files is to use several files and store records of only one fixed length in any given file. An alternative is to structure files in such a way that they can accommodate multiple lengths for records. There are a number of different techniques for implementing variable-length records including the pointer method and the reserved-space method.

Since data is transferred between disk storage and main memory in units of a block, it is worthwhile to assign file records to blocks in such a way that a single block contains related records. If we can access several

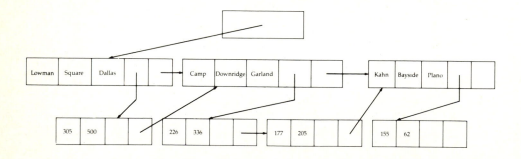

Figure 7.30   Implementation using preorder threads.

of the records desired using only one block access, we have saved some disk accesses. Since disk accesses are usually the bottleneck in the performance of a database system, careful assignment of records to blocks can pay significant performance dividends.

One way to reduce the number of disk accesses is to keep as many blocks as possible in main memory. Since it is not possible to keep all blocks in main memory, we need to manage the allocation of the space available in main memory for the storage of blocks. The *buffer* is that part of main memory available for storage of copies of disk blocks. The subsystem responsible for the allocation of buffer space is called the *buffer manager*.

A database system consists of a number of functional components, including the file manager, the buffer manager, the query parser, the strategy selector, the recovery manager, and the concurrency controller. In addition, several data structures are required as part of the physical system implementation, including data files, system data files, indices, and statistical data.

Exercises

7.1 List the physical storage media available on your local computer and the speed with which data can be accessed on each medium.

7.2 Define the term *dangling pointer*.

7.3 Define the term *pinned record*.

7.4 Consider the deletion of record 5 from the file of Figure 7.7. compare the relative merits of the following techniques for implementing the deletion:

- Move record 6 to the space occupied by record 5 and move record 7 to the space occupied by record 6.

- Move record 7 to the space occupied by record 5.

- Mark record 5 as deleted and move no records.

7.5 Show the structure of the file of Figure 7.8 after each step of the following series of steps:

- insert (Brighton, 323, Silver, 1600)

- delete record 2

- insert (Brighton, 626, Gray, 2000)

7.6 Give an example of a database application in which the reserved space method of representing variable-length records is preferable to the pointer method.

7.7 Give an example of a database application in which the pointer method of representing variable length records is preferable to the reserved space method.

7.8 Show that structure of the file of Figure 7.10 after each step of the following series of steps:

- insert (Mianus, 101, Thompson, 2800)
- insert (Brighton, 323, Silver, 1600)
- delete (Perryridge, 102, Hayes, 400)

7.9 What happens if we attempt to insert the record

(Perryridge, 929, Glenn, 3000)

into the file of Figure 7.10?

7.10 Show the structure of the file of Figure 7.11 after each step of the following series of steps:

- insert (Mianus, 101, Thompson, 2800)
- insert (Brighton, 323, Silver, 1600)
- delete (Perryridge, 102, Hayes, 400)

7.11 Explain why the allocation of records to blocks is an important issue in database system performance.

7.12 If a block becomes empty as a result of deletions, for what purposes should the block be re-used? Why? If possible, determine the buffer management strategy used by the operating system running on your local computer system. Discuss how useful this strategy would be for the implementation of database systems.

7.13 Give an example of a relational algebra expression and a query processing strategy such that:

- MRU is preferable to LRU
- LRU is preferable to MRU

7.14 List some advantages and disadvantages of each of the following strategies for storing a relational database:

- store each relation in one file
- store the entire database in one file

7.15 Consider a relational database with two relations:

> *course (course-name, room, instructor)*
> *enrollment (course-name, student-name, grade)*

Define instances of these relations for three courses, each having five students. Give a file structure of these relations that uses clustering.

7.16 Is it possible in general to have two clustering indices on the same relation for different search keys? Explain.

7.17 Give a network data structure diagram for the database of Exercise 7.16. Give a ring file structure for the network database instance you defined in Exercise 7.16.

7.18 Give a tree structure diagram for the database of Exercise 7.16. Give a file structure for the hierarchical database instance you defined in Exercise 7.16.

Bibliographic Notes

There are several papers describing the overall system structure of specific database systems. Astrahan et al. [1976] discusses System R. Chamberlin et al. [1981] reviews System R in retrospect. Stonebraker et al. [1976] describes the implementation of Ingres. Specific references to functional components of a database system (recovery, concurrency, etc.) appear in the bibliographic notes of subsequent chapters.

Wiederhold [1983], Bohl [1981], and Trivedi et al. [1980] discuss the physical properties of disks. Basic data structures are discussed in Knuth [1973], Aho et al. [1983], and Horowitz and Sahni [1976]. Textbook discussions of file organization for database systems include Teorey and Fry [1982] and Ullman [1982a].

Buffer management is discussed in most operating system texts including Peterson and Silberschatz [1985]. Stonebraker [1981] discusses the relationship between database system buffer managers and operating system buffer managers.

8

Indexing and Hashing

Many queries reference only a small proportion of the records in a file. For example, the query "Find all accounts at the Perryridge branch" references only a fraction of the account records. It is inefficient for the system to have to read every record and check the *branch-name* field for the name "Perryridge." Ideally, the system should be able to locate these records directly. In order to allow these forms of access, we design additional structures that we associate with files. We shall consider two general approaches to this problem: the construction of indices and the construction of hash functions.

8.1 Basic Concepts

An index for a file works in much the same way as a catalog in a library. If we are looking for a book by a particular author, we look in the author catalog and a card in the catalog tells us where to find the book. To assist us in searching the catalog, the cards are kept in alphabetic order, so we do not have to check every card to find the one we want.

In real-world databases, indices of the type described above may be too large to be handled efficiently. Instead, more sophisticated indexing techniques may be used. We shall discuss some of these techniques subsequently. As an alternative to indexing, techniques using *hash functions* may be used. We shall consider several techniques for both hashing and indexing. No one technique is the best. Rather, each technique is best suited to particular database applications. Each technique must be evaluated based on:

- **Access time**. The time it takes to find a particular data item, using the technique in question.

- **Insertion time**. The time it takes to insert a new data item. This includes the time it takes to find the correct place to insert the new data item as well as the time it takes to update the index structure.

- **Deletion time**. The time it takes to delete a data item. This includes the time it takes to find the item to be deleted as well as the time it takes to update the index structure.

- **Space overhead**. The additional space occupied by an index structure. Provided that the amount of additional space is moderate, it is usually worthwhile to sacrifice the space to achieve improved performance.

It is often the case that we desire to have more than one index or hash function for a file. Returning to the library example, we note that most libraries maintain several card catalogs: for author, for subject, and for title. The attribute or set of attributes used to look up records in a file is called a *search key*. Note that this definition of *key* differs from that of primary key, candidate key, and superkey. This duplicate meaning for key is (unfortunately) well established in practice. Using the above notion of a search key, we see that if there are several indices on a file there are several search keys.

8.2 Index-Sequential Files

Index-sequential files are one of the oldest index schemes used in database systems. As the name suggests, index-sequential files consist of a sequential file and an index. They are designed for applications that require both

- Sequential processing of the entire file.
- Random access to individual records.

8.2.1 Sequential File

A *sequential file* is designed for efficient processing of records in sorted order based on some search key. To permit fast retrieval of records in search-key order, records are chained together by pointers. The pointer in each record points to the next record in search-key order. Furthermore, in order to minimize the number of block accesses in sequential file processing, records are stored physically in search-key order, or as close to search-key order as possible.

Figure 8.1 shows a sequential file of *deposit* records taken from our banking example. In the example of Figure 8.1, the records are stored in search-key order, using *branch-name* as the search key. It is difficult to maintain physical sequential order as records are inserted and deleted, since it is costly to move many records as a result of a single insertion or deletion. Deletion can be managed using pointer chains, as we saw in Chapter 7. For insertion, we apply the following rules:

1. Locate the record in the file that comes before the record to be inserted in search-key order.

Brighton	217	Green	750
Downtown	101	Johnson	500
Downtown	110	Peterson	600
Mianus	215	Smith	700
Perryridge	102	Hayes	400
Perryridge	201	Williams	900
Perryridge	218	Lyle	700
Redwood	222	Lindsay	700
Round Hill	305	Turner	350

Figure 8.1   Sequential file for *deposit* records.

2. If there is a free record (that is, space left after a deletion) within the same block as this record, insert the new record there. Otherwise insert the new record in an *overflow block*. In either case, adjust the pointers so as to chain the records together in search-key order.

Figure 8.2 shows the file of Figure 8.1 after the insertion of the record (North Town, 888, Adams, 800). The structure in Figure 8.2 allows for fast insertion of new records, but it forces sequential file-processing applications to process records in an order that does not match the physical order of the records.

If relatively few records need to be stored in overflow blocks, there is little problem with this approach. Eventually, however, the correspondence between search-key order and physical order may be

Brighton	217	Green	750
Downtown	101	Johnson	500
Downtown	110	Peterson	600
Mianus	215	Smith	700
Perryridge	102	Hayes	400
Perryridge	201	Williams	900
Perryridge	218	Lyle	700
Redwood	222	Lindsay	700
Round Hill	305	Turner	350
North Town	888	Adams	800

Figure 8.2   Sequential file after an insertion.

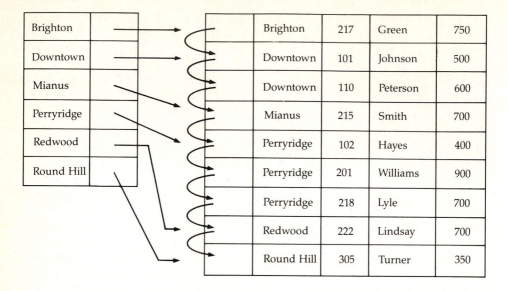

Figure 8.3   Dense index.

totally lost, and sequential processing becomes significantly less efficient. At this point, the file should be *reorganized* so that it is once again physically in sequential order. Such reorganizations are costly and are done during times when the system load is low. The frequency with which reorganizations are needed depends on the frequency of insertion of new records. In the extreme case in which insertions rarely occur, it is possible always to keep the file in physically sorted order. In such a case, the pointer field shown in Figure 8.1 is not needed.

8.2.2 Index File

We have seen how the sequential file structure meets the requirement of fast sequential access to all records of the file in one particular search-key order. In order to allow fast random access, an index structure is used. There are two types of index that may be used:

- **Dense index**. An index record appears for every search-key value in the file. The record contains the search-key value and a pointer to the record.

- **Sparse index**. Index records are created for only some of the records. To locate a record, we find the index record with the largest search-key value that is less than or equal to the search-key value we are looking for. We start at the record pointed to by that index record and follow the pointers in the file until we find the desired record.

Figures 8.3 and 8.4 show dense and sparse indices, respectively, for the *deposit* file. Suppose we are looking up records for the Perryridge branch. Using the dense index of Figure 8.3, we follow the pointer directly to the first Perryridge record. We process this record, and follow the pointer in that record to locate the next record in search-key (*branch-name*) order. We continue processing records until we encounter a record for a branch other than Perryridge. If we are using the sparse index (Figure 8.4), we do not find an index entry for Perryridge. Since the last entry (in alphabetic order) before Perryridge is Mianus, we follow that pointer. We then read the *deposit* file in sequential order until we find the first Perryridge record, and begin processing at that point.

As we have seen, it is generally faster to locate a record if we have a dense index rather than a sparse index. However, sparse indices have an advantage over dense indices in that they require less space and they impose less maintenance overhead for insertions and deletions.

There is a trade-off that the system designer must make between access time and space overhead. Although the decision regarding this trade-off is dependent on the specific application, a good compromise is to have a sparse index with one index entry per block. In Figure 8.5, we show the block structure of the *deposit* file and a sparse index with one entry per block. The reason this design is a good trade-off is that the dominant cost in processing a database request is the time it takes to bring a block from disk into main memory. Once we have brought the block in, the time to scan the entire block is negligible. Using this sparse index, we

Brighton				
Mianus				
Redwood				

Brighton	217	Green	750
Downtown	101	Johnson	500
Downtown	110	Peterson	600
Mianus	215	Smith	700
Perryridge	102	Hayes	400
Perryridge	201	Williams	900
Perryridge	218	Lyle	700
Redwood	222	Lindsay	700
Round Hill	305	Turner	350

Figure 8.4   Sparse index.

locate the block containing the record we are seeking. Thus, unless the record is on an overflow block, we minimize block accesses while keeping the size of the index (and thus, our space overhead) as small as possible.

For the above technique to be fully general, we must consider the case where records for one search-key value occupy several blocks. It is easy to modify our scheme to handle this (see Exercise 8.4).

Even if we use a sparse index, the index itself may become too large for efficient processing. It is not unreasonable, in practice, to have a file with 100,000 records, with 10 records stored in each block. If we have one index record per block, the index has 10,000 records. Index records are smaller than data records, so let us assume 100 index records fit on a block. Thus, our index occupies 100 blocks.

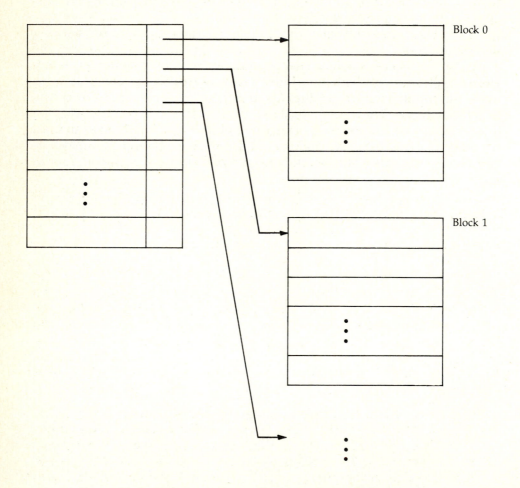

Figure 8.5   Sparse index with one index record per block.

If an index is sufficiently small to be kept in main memory, search time is low. However, if the index is so large that it must be kept on disk, a search results in several disk block reads. If the index occupies b blocks, and binary search is used, we may read as many as $1 + \log_2(b)$ blocks. For our 100-block index, this means 7 block reads. Note that if overflow blocks have been used, binary search will not be possible. In that case, a sequential search is typically used which requires b block reads. Thus, the process of searching the index may be costly.

To deal with this problem, we treat the index just as we would treat any other sequential file, and we construct a sparse index on the index, as shown in Figure 8.6. To locate a record, we first use binary search on the outer index to find the record for the largest search-key value less than or equal to the one we desire. The pointer points to a block of the inner index. We scan this block until we find the record which has the largest search-key value less than or equal to the one we desire. The pointer in this record points to the block of the file that contains the record for which we are looking.

Using the two levels of indexing, we have read only one index block rather than 7, if we assume that the outer index is already in main memory. If our file is extremely large, even the outer index may grow too large to fit in main memory. In such a case, we can create yet another level of index. Indeed, we can repeat this process as many times as necessary. In practice, however, it is generally the case that two levels are sufficient, and situations requiring more than three levels are extremely rare. Frequently, each level of index corresponds to a unit of physical storage. Thus, we may have indices and the track, cylinder, and disk levels.

Regardless of what form of index is used, every index must be updated whenever a record is either inserted into or deleted from the file. We describe algorithms for updating single-level indices below:

- **Deletion**. In order to delete a record, it is necessary to look up the record to be deleted. If the deleted record was the last record with its particular search-key value, then we delete the search-key value from the index. For dense indices, we delete a search-key value similarly to record deletion in a file. For sparse indices, we delete a key value by replacing its entry in the index (if one exists) with the next search-key value (in search-key order). If the next search-key value already has an index entry, we delete the entry.

- **Insertion**. Perform a lookup using the search-key value appearing in the record to be inserted. If the index is dense, and the search-key value does not appear in the index, insert it. If the index is sparse, no change needs to be made to the index unless a new block is created. In this case, the first search-key value (in search-key order) appearing in the new block is inserted into the database.

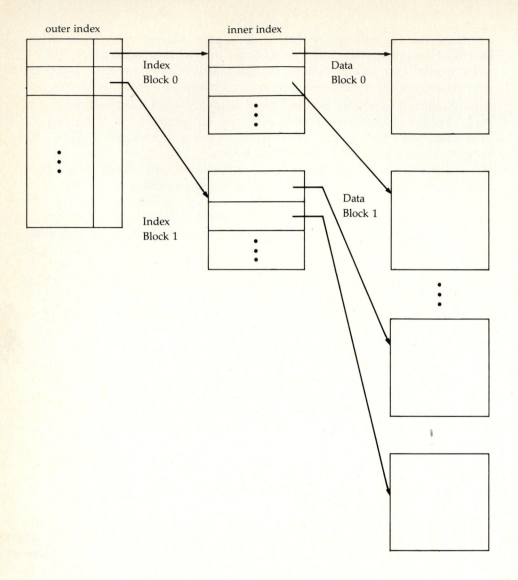

Figure 8.6   Two-level sparse index.

8.2.3 Secondary Indices

In a standard index-sequential file, only one index is maintained. If we choose to include several indices on different search keys, the index whose search key specifies the sequential order of the file is the *primary index*. The other indices are called *secondary indices*. The search key of a primary index is usually (though not necessarily) the primary key.

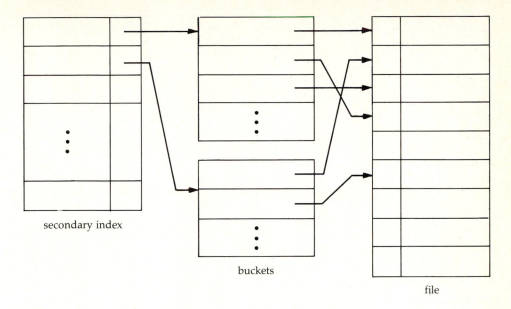

secondary index

buckets

file

Figure 8.7   Secondary index.

Secondary indices may be structured differently from primary indices. Figure 8.7 shows the structure of a secondary index using an extra level of indirection. The pointers do not point directly to the file. Instead, they point to a *bucket* which contains pointers to the file. A bucket is a collection of one or more blocks chained together as in Chapter 7.

This approach allows all the pointers for one secondary search-key value to be stored together. This is useful in certain types of queries for which we may do considerable processing using only the pointers. For primary keys, we can obtain all the pointers for one primary search-key value using a sequential scan.

A sequential scan in primary-key order is efficient because records are stored physically in an order that approximates primary-key order. However, we cannot (except in rare special cases) store a file physically in both primary-key order and in key order based upon a secondary key. Because secondary-key order and physical-key order differ, if we attempt to scan the file sequentially in secondary-key order, the reading of each record is likely to require the reading of a new block from disk.

By storing pointers in a bucket as shown in Figure 8.7, we eliminate the need for extra pointers in the records themselves and eliminate the need for sequential scans in secondary-key order.

It is desirable to use dense rather than sparse secondary indices. To see this, consider the index of Figure 8.8 on the secondary-key *customer-name*.

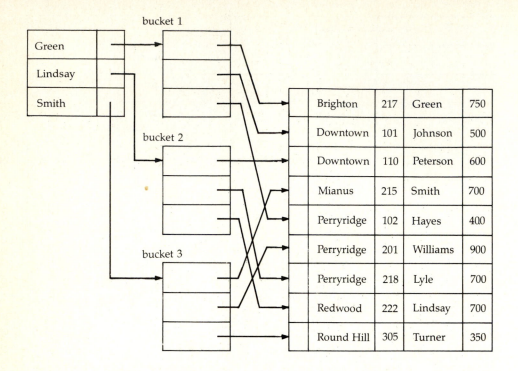

Figure 8.8   Secondary index on *customer-name*.

If we are performing a lookup on Peterson, we must read all three records pointed to by entries in bucket 2. Only one entry points to a record for which the *customer-name* value is Peterson, yet three records needed to be read. Since the file is not ordered physically by *customer-name*, we expect this lookup to require three disk block reads. Contrast this example with our earlier example of the sparse primary index of Figure 8.4. Since the file is stored physically in *branch-name* order, we expect only one block read for a lookup.

By using a dense secondary index rather than a sparse one, we eliminate the need to read records with a secondary-search-key value other than the one on which we are performing a lookup.

The procedure described earlier for deletion and insertion can be applied to an indexed file with multiple indices. Whenever the file is modified, *every* index must be updated.

Secondary indices improve the performance of queries that use keys other than the primary one. However, they impose a serious overhead on modification of the database. The designer of a database decides which secondary indices are desirable based on an estimate of the relative frequency of queries and modifications.

8.3 B$^+$-Tree Indexed Files

The primary disadvantage of the indexed-sequential file organization is that performance degrades as the file grows. Although this degradation can be remedied by reorganization of the file, it is undesirable to perform such reorganizations frequently. The B$^+$-*tree file structure* is the most widely used of several file structures that maintain their efficiency despite insertion and deletion of data. A B$^+$-tree index takes the form of a *balanced* tree in which every path from the root of the tree to a leaf of the tree is of the same length. Each node in the tree has between $\lceil n/2 \rceil$ and n children, where n is fixed for a particular tree.

We shall see that the B$^+$-tree structure imposes some overhead on insertion and deletion as well as some added space overhead. Nevertheless, this overhead is acceptable for files with a high frequency of modification since the cost of file reorganization is avoided.

A B$^+$-tree index is a multilevel index, but it has a structure that differs from that of the multilevel indexed-sequential index. We consider first the structure of the leaf nodes of a B$^+$-tree. A typical leaf node is shown in Figure 8.9. It contains up to $n - 1$ search-key values $K_1, K_2, ..., K_{n-1}$ and n pointers $P_1, P_2, ..., P_n$. Pointer P_n has a special purpose which we shall discuss shortly. For $1 \le i < n$, P_i points to the bucket for records with search-key value K_i. The search-key values within a leaf node are kept in sorted order; thus, if $i < j$, then $K_i < K_j$. Figure 8.10 shows one leaf node of a B$^+$ tree for the *deposit* file, in which we have chosen n to be 3. It is possible also for P_i to point to the first record having search-key value K_i, with a pointer chain used to link all records with the same search-key value. An alternative is for P_i to point to a bucket containing pointers to each record with search-key value K_i. This organization is desirable if we have several indices on the same file. In Figure 8.10, we are assuming a bucket for each search-key value.

Now that we have seen the structure of a leaf node, let us consider how search-key values are assigned to particular nodes. Each leaf can hold up to $n - 1$ values. We allow leaf nodes to contain as few as $\lceil (n - 1)/2 \rceil$ values, where $\lceil x \rceil$ denotes the greatest integer not less than x (that is, we round upward). The range of values in each leaf do not overlap. Thus if L_i and L_j are leaf nodes and $i < j$, then every search-key value in L_i is less than every search-key value in L_j.

P_1	K_1	P_2	$\cdots$	P_{n-1}	K_{n-1}	P_n

Figure 8.9   Typical leaf node of a B$^+$-tree.

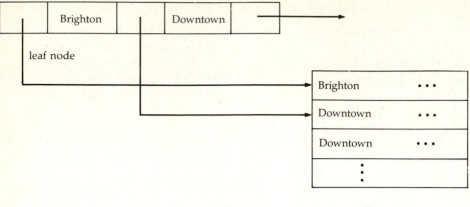

deposit file

Figure 8.10   A leaf node for *deposit* B^+-tree index ($n = 3$).

Now we can explain the use of the pointer P_n. Since there is a linear order on the leaves based upon the search-key values they contain, we use P_n to chain the leaf nodes together in search-key order. This allows for efficient sequential processing of the file.

The nonleaf nodes of the B^+-tree form a multilevel index on the leaf nodes. The structure of nonleaf nodes is the same as for leaf nodes except that all pointers are pointers to tree nodes. A node may hold up to n pointers, but must hold at least $\lceil n/2 \rceil$ pointers. Let us consider a node containing m pointers. If $1 < i < m$, pointer P_i points to the subtree containing search-key values less than K_i and greater than or equal to K_{i-1}. Pointer P_m points to the part of the subtree containing those key values greater than or equal to K_{m-1}, and pointer P_1 points to the part of the subtree containing those search-key values less than K_1.

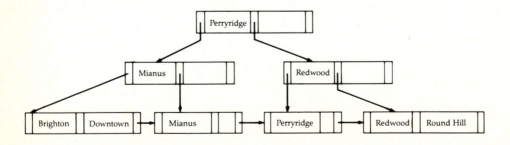

Figure 8.11 B^+-tree for *deposit* file with $n = 3$.

The requirement that each node hold at least $\lceil n/2 \rceil$ pointers is imposed at all levels of the tree except for the root. Figure 8.11 shows a complete B$^+$-tree for the *deposit* file (with $n = 3$). For simplicity, we have omitted the pointers to the file itself. As an example of a B$^+$-tree for which the root must have less than $\lceil n/2 \rceil$ values, we show a B$^+$-tree for the *deposit* file in Figure 8.12 with $n = 5$. It is always possible to construct a B$^+$-tree, for any n, in which all nonroot nodes contain at least $\lceil n/2 \rceil$ pointers.

The examples we have given of B$^+$-trees have all been balanced. That is, the length of every path from the root to a leaf node is the same. This property is a requirement for a B$^+$-tree. Indeed, the "B" in B$^+$-tree stands for "balanced." It is the balance property of B$^+$-trees that ensures good performance for lookup, insertion, and deletion.

Let us consider how queries are processed using a B$^+$-tree. Suppose we wish to find all records with search-key value of k. First, we examine the root node and look for the smallest search-key value greater than k. Assume this search-key value is K_i. We follow pointer P_i to another node. If $K < K_1$, then we follow P_1 to another node. If we have m pointers in the node, and $K \geq K_{m-1}$, then we follow P_m to another node. Once again, we look for the smallest search-key value greater than k and follow the corresponding pointer. Eventually, we reach a leaf node, at which point the pointer directs us to the desired records.

Thus, in processing a query, a path is traversed in the tree from the root to some leaf node. If there are K search-key values in the file, this means the path is no longer than $\log_{\lceil n/2 \rceil}(K)$. In practice, this means that only a few nodes need to be accessed even if the file is extremely large. Typically, a node is made to be the same size as a block. Thus, it is reasonable for n to be between 10 and 100 (or even larger). Even if we have one million search-key values in the file, a lookup requires that only between 3 and 6 nodes be accessed.

Insertion and deletion are more complicated than lookup since it may be necessary to *split* a node that becomes too large as the result of an insertion or to *combine* nodes if a node becomes too small (fewer than $\lceil n/2 \rceil$ pointers). Furthermore, when a node is split or a pair of nodes are

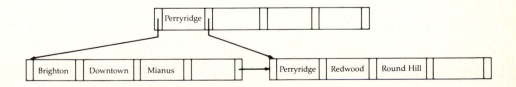

Figure 8.12   B$^+$-tree for *deposit* file with $n = 5$.

combined, we must ensure that balance is preserved. To introduce the idea behind insertion and deletion in a B^+-tree, let us assume temporarily that nodes never become too large nor too small. Under this assumption, insertion and deletion are as defined below.

- **Insertion**. Using the same technique as for lookup, we find the leaf node in which the search-key value would appear. If the search-key value already appears in the leaf node, we add the new record to the bucket. If the search-key value does not appear, we insert the value in the leaf node, and position it so that the search keys are still in order. We then create a new bucket and insert the new record.

- **Deletion**. Using the same technique as for lookup, we find the record to be deleted, and remove it from its bucket. If the bucket becomes empty as a result of deletion, we remove the search-key value from the leaf node.

We now consider an example in which a node must be split. Assume that we wish to insert a record with a *branch-name* value of Clearview into the B^+-tree of Figure 8.11. Using the algorithm for lookup, we find that Clearview should appear in the node containing Brighton and Downtown. There is no room to insert the search-key value Clearview. Therefore, the node is *split* into two nodes. Figure 8.13 shows the two leaf nodes that result from inserting Clearview and splitting the node containing Brighton and Downtown. In general, we take the n search-key values (the $n - 1$ values in the leaf node plus the value being inserted) and put the first $\lceil (n - 1)/2 \rceil$ in the existing node and the remaining values in a new node.

Having split a leaf node, we must insert the new leaf node into the B^+-tree structure. In our example, the new node has Downtown as its smallest search-key value. We need to insert this search-key value into the parent of the leaf node that was split. The B^+-tree of Figure 8.14 shows the result of the insertion. The search-key value Downtown was inserted into the parent. It was possible to perform this insertion because there was room for an added search-key value. If this were not the case, the parent would have had to be split. In the worst case, all nodes along the path to the root must be split. If the root itself is split, the entire tree becomes deeper.

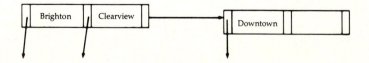

Figure 8.13   Split of leaf node on insertion of Clearview.

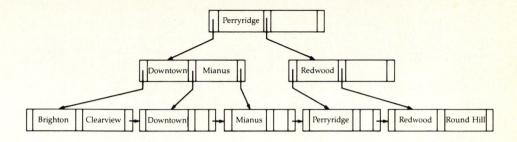

Figure 8.14   Insertion of "Clearview" into the B$^+$-tree of Figure 8.11.

The general technique for insertion into a B$^+$-tree is to determine the leaf node l into which insertion must occur. If a split results, insert the new node into the parent of node l. If this insertion causes a split, proceed recursively until either an insertion does not cause a split or until a new root is created.

We now consider deletions that cause tree nodes to contain too few pointers. First, let us delete "Downtown" from the B$^+$-tree of Figure 8.14. We locate the entry for Downtown using our lookup algorithm (Figure 8.11). When we delete the entry for Downtown from its leaf node, the leaf becomes empty. Since, in our example $n = 3$ and $0 < \lceil (n - 1)/2 \rceil$, this node must be eliminated from the B$^+$-tree. To delete a leaf node, we must delete the pointer to it from its parent. In our example, this leaves the parent node, which formerly contained three pointers, with only two pointers. Since $2 \geq \lceil n/2 \rceil$, the node is still sufficiently large and the deletion operation is complete. The resulting B$^+$-tree is shown in Figure 8.15.

When a deletion is made to a parent of a leaf node, it is possible that the parent node itself becomes too small. This is exactly what happens if we delete "Perryridge" from the B$^+$-tree of Figure 8.15. Deletion of the

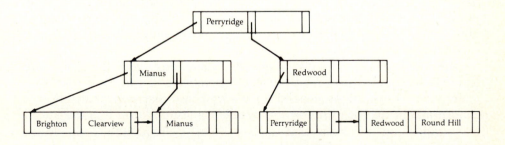

Figure 8.15   Deletion of "Downtown" from the B$^+$-tree of Figure 8.14.

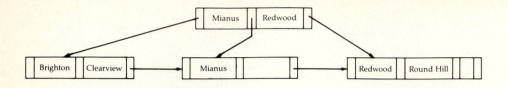

Figure 8.16   Deletion of "Perryridge" from the B^+-tree of Figure 8.15.

Perryridge entry causes a leaf node to become empty. When we delete the pointer to this node in its parent, the parent is left with only one pointer. Since $n = 3$, $\lceil n/2 \rceil = 2$ and thus only one pointer is too few. However, since the node contains useful information, we cannot simply delete it. Instead, we look at the sibling node (containing the one search key, Mianus). This sibling node has room to accommodate the information contained in our now-too-small node, so we coalesce these nodes, so that the sibling node now contains the keys "Mianus" and "Redwood." The other node (the node containing only the search key "Redwood") now contains redundant information and can be deleted from its parent (which happens to be the root in our example). Figure 8.16 shows the result. Notice that the root became empty after the deletion, so the depth of the B^+-tree has been decreased by 1.

It is not always possible to coalesce nodes. To illustrate this, let us delete "Perryridge" from the B^+-tree of Figure 8.14. In this example, the "Downtown" entry is still part of the tree. Once again, the leaf node containing "Perryridge" becomes empty. The parent of the leaf node becomes too small (only one pointer). However, in this example, the sibling node already contains the maximum number of pointers, three. Thus, it cannot accommodate an additional pointer. The solution in this case it to *redistribute* the pointers so that each sibling has two pointers. The result is shown in Figure 8.17. Note that the redistribution of values necessitates a change of a search-key value in the parent of the two siblings. In general, to delete a value in a B^+-tree, we perform a lookup on the value and delete it. If the node is too small, we delete it from its parent. This results in recursive application of the deletion algorithm until either the root is reached, a parent remains adequately full after deletion, or coalescence is applied.

Although insertion and deletion operations on B^+-trees are complicated, they require relatively few operations. It can be shown that the number of operations needed for a worst-case insertion or deletion is proportional to the logarithm of the number of search keys. It is the speed of operation on B^+-trees that makes them a frequently used index structure in database implementations.

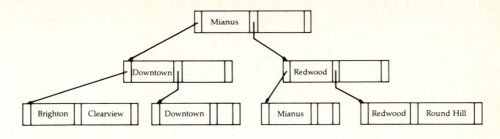

Figure 8.17   Deletion of "Perryridge" from the B⁺-tree of Figure 8.14.

8.4 B-Tree Index Files

B-tree indices are similar to B⁺-tree indices. The primary distinction between the two approaches is that a B-tree eliminates the redundant storage of search-key values. In the B⁺-tree of Figure 8.14, the search keys "Downtown," "Mianus," "Redwood," and "Perryridge" appear twice. Every search-key value appears in some leaf node.

A corresponding B-tree allows search-key values to appear only once. Figure 8.18 shows a B-tree that is representing the same search keys as the B⁺-tree of Figure 8.14. Since search keys are not repeated in the B-tree, we are able to store the index using fewer tree nodes than in the corresponding B⁺-tree index. However, since search keys that appear in nonleaf nodes appear nowhere else in the B-tree, we are forced to include an additional pointer field for each search key in a nonleaf node. These additional pointers are the bucket pointers for the associated search key.

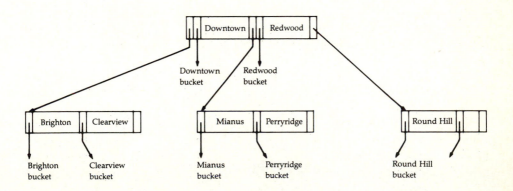

Figure 8.18   B-tree equivalent of B⁺-tree in Figure 8.14.

A generalized B-tree leaf node appears in Figure 8.19a and a nonleaf node appears in Figure 8.19b. The pointers P_i are the tree pointers that we used also for B^+-trees. The pointers B_i in the nonleaf nodes are the bucket pointers.

B-trees offer an additional advantage over B^+-trees besides the lack of redundant storage of search keys. In a lookup on a B^+-tree, it is necessary in all cases to traverse a path from the root of the tree to some leaf node. However, in a B-tree, it is possible in some cases to find the desired value before reading a leaf node. Thus lookup is slightly faster in a B-tree, though, in general, lookup time is still proportional to the logarithm of the number of search keys.

These advantages of B-tree over B^+-trees are offset by several disadvantages.

- Leaf and nonleaf nodes are of the same size in a B^+-tree. In a B-tree, the nonleaf nodes are larger. This complicates storage management for the index.

- Deletion in a B-tree is more complicated. In a B^+-tree, the deleted entry always appears in a leaf. In a B-tree it is possible that the deleted entry appears in a nonleaf node. The proper value must be selected as a replacement from the subtree of the node containing the deleted entry. Specifically, if search key K_i is deleted, the smallest search key appearing in the subtree of pointer P_{i+1} must be moved to the field formerly occupied by K_i.

The advantages of B-trees are marginal for large indices. Thus, the structural simplicity of a B^+-tree is preferred by many database system implementors. Details of the insertion and deletion algorithms for B-trees are explored in the exercises.

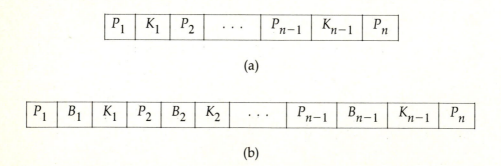

(a)

(b)

Figure 8.19   Typical nodes of a B-tree: (a) leaf node and (b) nonleaf node.

8.5 Static Hash Functions

One disadvantage of index schemes is that we must traverse an index structure in order to locate data. The technique of *hashing* allows us to avoid traversing an index structure. It involves the computation of the address of a data item directly by computing a function on the search-key value of the desired record. Formally, let K denote the set of all search-key values, and B the set of all addresses. A *hash function h* is a function from K to B.

The principle behind hashing is that although the set K of all possible search keys is large (perhaps infinite), the set $\{K_1, K_2, ..., K_n\}$ of search keys actually stored in the database is much smaller than K. We do not know at design time which search-key values will be stored in the database, but we know that there are too many possible values to justify allocating one bucket for every possible value. We *do* know, however, at design time approximately how many search-key values will be stored in the database. We choose the number of buckets to correspond to the number of search-key values we expect to have stored in the database. It is the hash function that defines the assignment of search-key values to particular buckets.

Hash functions require careful design. A bad hash function may result in lookup taking time proportional to the number of search keys in the file. A well-designed function gives an average-case lookup time that is a (small) constant, independent of the number of search keys in the file. This is accomplished by ensuring that, on average, records are distributed uniformly among the buckets.

Let h denote a hash function. To perform a lookup on a search-key value K_i, we simply compute $h(K_i)$ and search the bucket with that address. Suppose that two search keys, K_5 and K_7 have the same hash value, that is, $h(K_5) = h(K_7)$. If we perform a lookup on K_5, the bucket $h(K_5)$ contains records with search-key values K_5 and records with search-key values K_7. Thus, we have to check the search-key value of every record in the bucket to verify that the record is one that we want.

The worst possible hash function maps all search-key values to the same bucket. This is a bad function because all records in the file are in the same bucket, and thus lookup requires that every record in the file be scanned. An ideal hash function maps every search-key value to a distinct bucket. Such a function is ideal because every record in the bucket searched as a result of a lookup is a record with the desired search-key value.

Since we do not know at design time precisely which search-key values will be stored in the file, a good hash function to choose is one that assigns search-key values to buckets such that:

- The distribution is uniform. That is, each bucket is assigned the same number of search-key values from the set of all possible search-key values.

- The distribution is random. That is, in the average case, each bucket will have nearly the same number of values assigned to it.

To illustrate the principles involved in choosing a hash function, let us attempt to choose a hash function for the *deposit* file using the search key *branch-name*. The hash function we choose must have desirable properties not only on the example *deposit* file we have been using, but also on a *deposit* file of realistic size for a large bank with many branches.

Assume that we decide to have 26 buckets and define a hash function that maps names beginning with the ith letter of the alphabet to the ith bucket. This hash function has the virtue of simplicity, but it fails to provide a uniform distribution since we expect more branch names to begin with such letters as "*B*" or "*R*" than "*Q*" or "*X*," for example.

Typical hash functions perform some computation on the internal binary machine representation of characters in the search key. A simple hash function of this type is to compute the sum, modulo the number of buckets allocated of the binary representations of characters of a key. Figure 8.20 shows the application of such a scheme, using ten buckets, to the *deposit* file, under the assumption that the ith letter in the alphabet is represented by the integer i.

Insertion is almost as simple as lookup. If the search-key value of the record to be inserted is K_i, we compute $h(K_i)$ to locate the bucket into which the new record is to be inserted.

Deletion is equally straightforward. If the search-key value of the record to be deleted is K_i, we compute $h(K_i)$ and search the corresponding bucket for that record.

The form of hash structure we have described above is sometimes referred to as *open hashing*. Under an alternative approach to hashing called *closed hashing*, all records are stored in one bucket and the hash function computes addresses within the bucket. Closed hashing is used frequently in the construction of symbol tables for compilers and assemblers, but open hashing is preferred for database systems. The reason for this is that deletion under closed hashing is troublesome. Typically, compilers and assemblers perform only lookup and insertion operations on their symbol tables. However, in a database system, it is important to be able to handle deletion as well as insertion. Thus, closed hashing is of only minor importance in database implementation.

An important drawback to the form of hashing we have described above is that the hash function must be chosen when we implement the system and cannot be changed easily thereafter. Since the function h maps search-key values to a fixed set B of bucket addresses, we waste space if B

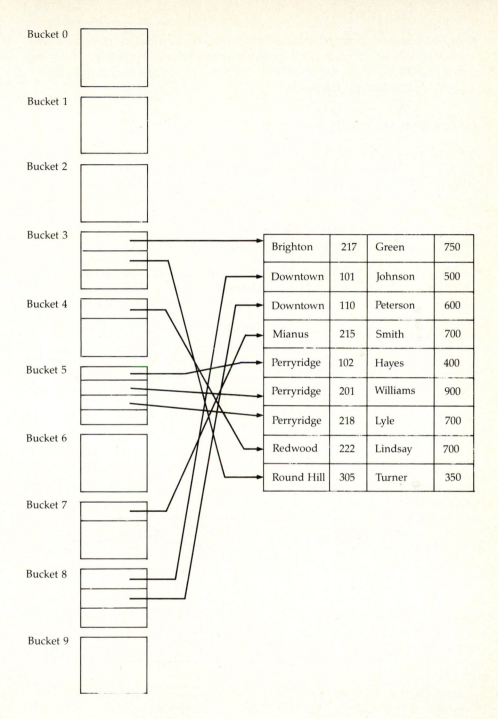

Figure 8.20   Hash table for *deposit* file using *branch-name* as the key.

is excessively large. If B is too small, our buckets contain records of many different search-key values, and performance suffers. Typically, choosing the size of B to be twice the number of search-key values in the file gives a good space/performance trade-off.

8.6 Dynamic Hash Functions

As we have seen, the need to fix the set B of bucket addresses is a serious problem with the static hashing technique of the previous section. Most databases grow larger over time. If we are to use static hashing for such a database, we face three classes of options:

- Choose a hash function based on the current file size. This will result in performance degradation as the database grows.

- Choose a hash function based on the anticipated size of the file at some point in the future. Although this avoids performance degradation, a significant amount of space is wasted initially.

- Periodically reorganize the hash structure in response to file growth. Such a reorganization involves the choice of a new hash function, recomputing the hash function on every record in the file, and generating new bucket assignments. This is a massive reorganization which is costly in terms of time. Furthermore, it is necessary to forbid access to the file during reorganization.

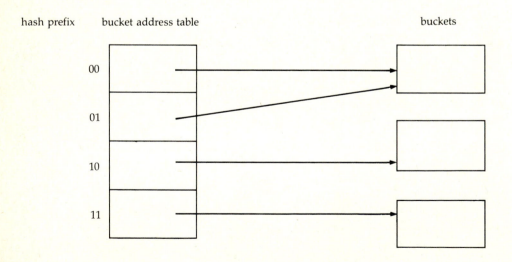

Figure 8.21   Sample extendible hash structure.

There are several hashing techniques that allow the hash function to be modified dynamically in order to accommodate the growth or shrinkage of the database. These techniques are called *dynamic hash functions*. Below, we describe one form of dynamic hashing called *extendible hashing*. The bibliographic notes provide references to other forms of dynamic hashing.

Extendible hashing copes with changes in database size by splitting and coalescing buckets as the database grows and shrinks. As a result, space efficiency is retained. The splitting and coalescing of buckets imposes some performance overhead. However, since the reorganization is performed on only one bucket at a time, the resulting overhead is acceptably low.

We now describe how extendible hashing works. We choose a hash function h with the desirable properties of uniformity and randomness. However, this hash function generates values over a relatively large range. This range is b-bit binary integers. A typical value for b is 32.

We do not create a bucket for each hash value. Indeed, 2^{32} is over 4 billion, and that many buckets is unreasonably large for all but the largest databases. Instead, we create buckets on demand, as records are inserted into the file. We do not use the entire b bits of the hash initially. At any point, we use i bits, where $0 \le i \le b$. These i bits are used as an offset into a table of bucket addresses. The value of i grows and shrinks with the size of the database.

To locate the bucket containing search-key value K_j, we compute $h(K_j)$, take the first i high-order bits, look at the corresponding table entry for this bit string, and follow the bucket pointer in the table entry. Figure 8.21 shows a hash structure with $i = 2$. Note that several table entries point to the same bucket in the figure.

We illustrate the operation of insertion using our example *deposit* file. We assume that initially the file is empty, and we insert the records one by one. Figure 8.22 shows the 32-bit hash values on *branch-name*.

branch-name	h(*branch-name*)
Brighton	0010 1101 1111 1011 0010 1100 0011 0000
Clearview	1101 0101 1101 1110 0100 0110 1001 0011
Downtown	1010 0011 1010 0000 1100 0110 1001 1111
Mianus	1000 0111 1110 1101 1011 1111 0011 1010
Perryridge	1111 0001 0010 0100 1001 0011 0110 1101
Redwood	1011 0101 1010 0110 1100 1001 1110 1011
Round Hill	0101 1000 0011 1111 1001 1100 0000 0001

Figure 8.22   Hash function for *branch-name*.

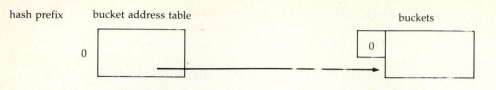

Figure 8.23   Initial extendible hash structure.

The initial, empty hash structure is shown in Figure 8.23. The "0" appearing next to the one bucket in the figure indicates that 0 bits of the hash $h(K)$ are required to determine the correct bucket for K. This number will, of course, change as the file grows. In order to illustrate all the features of extendible hashing using a small example, we shall make the unrealistic assumption that a bucket can hold only two records.

Let us insert the record (Perryridge, 102, Hayes, 400). The bucket address table contains a pointer to the one bucket and the record is inserted. Next let us insert the record (Round Hill, 305, Turner, 350). This record is also placed in the one bucket of our structure.

When we attempt to insert the next record (Downtown, 101, Johnson, 500), we find that the bucket is full. We split the bucket, placing those records whose search key has a hash beginning with 1 in a new bucket, and leaving the other records in the original bucket. Figure 8.24 shows the state of our structure after the split. Notice that a "1" appears next to each bucket indicating that 1 bit of the hash is needed to determine the correct bucket.

Next, we insert (Redwood, 222, Lindsay, 700). Since the first bit of h(Redwood) is 1, we must insert this record into the bucket pointed to by the "1" entry in the bucket address table. Once again, we find the bucket full. In order to split the bucket, we need to increase the number of bits

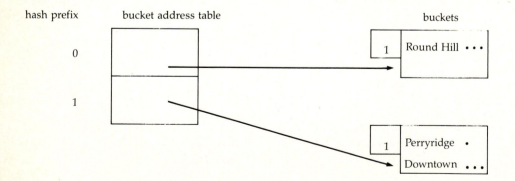

Figure 8.24   Hash structure after three insertions.

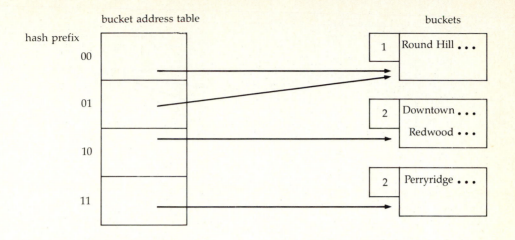

Figure 8.25   Hash structure after four insertions.

we use from the hash. We now use two bits, allowing us $2^2 = 4$ buckets. This necessitates doubling the size of the bucket address table to four entries, as shown in Figure 8.25. Since the bucket of Figure 8.24 for hash prefix 0 was not split, the two entries of the bucket address table of 00 and 01 both point to this bucket.

For each record in the bucket of Figure 8.24 for hash prefix 1 (the bucket being split), we examine the first 2 bits of the hash to determine which bucket of the new structure should hold it.

We continue in this manner until we have inserted all of the *deposit* records of Figure 8.26. The resulting structure is shown in Figure 8.27.

Let us now examine the advantages and disadvantages of extendible hashing as compared with the other schemes we have discussed. The main advantage to extendible hashing is that performance does not degrade as the file grows. Furthermore, there is minimal space overhead. Although

Brighton	217	Green	750
Downtown	101	Johnson	500
Mianus	215	Smith	700
Perryridge	102	Hayes	400
Redwood	222	Lindsay	700
Round Hill	305	Turner	350
Clearview	117	Throggs	295

Figure 8.26   *deposit* records.

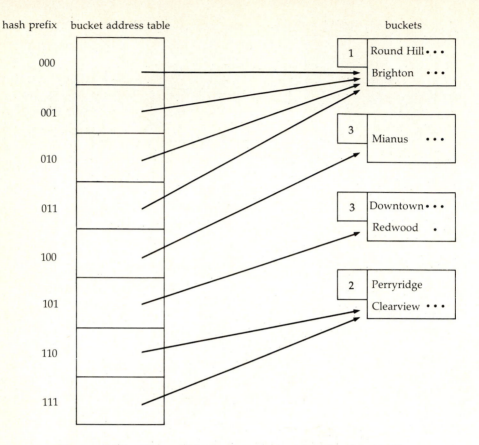

hash prefix   bucket address table   buckets

Figure 8.27   Extendible hash structure for the *deposit* file.

the bucket address table is additional overhead, it contains one pointer for each hash value for the current prefix length. This table is thus small. The main space savings of extendible hashing over other forms of hashing is that no buckets need be reserved for future growth; rather, buckets can be allocated dynamically.

Lookup in an extendible hash table involves an additional level of indirection since we must access the bucket address table before accessing the bucket itself. This extra reference has only a minor impact on performance. Although the hash structures we discussed earlier do not have this extra level of indirection, they lose their minor performance advantage as they become full.

Thus, extendible hashing appears to be a highly attractive technique provided we are willing to accept the added complexity involved in its implementation. References to a more detailed description of the implementation of extendible hashing appear in the bibliographic notes.

8.7 Comparison of Indexing and Hashing

We have seen several indexing schemes and several hashing schemes. Each scheme has advantages in certain situations. A database system implementor could provide many schemes and leave the final decision of which schemes to use to the database designer. However, such an approach requires the implementor to write more code, adding both to the cost of the system and the space that the system occupies. Instead, most database systems use only a few or just one form of indexing or hashing.

In order to make a wise choice, the implementor or the database designer must consider the following issues:

- Is the cost of periodic reorganization of the index or hash structure acceptable?

- What is the relative frequency of insertion and deletion?

- Is it desirable to optimize average access time at the expense of increasing the worst-case access time?

- What types of queries are users likely to pose?

We have already examined the first three of the above issues in discussing the relative merits of specific indexing techniques and again in our discussion of hashing techniques. The fourth issue, the expected type of query, is critical to the choice of indexing or hashing.

If most queries are of the form:

$$\textbf{select } A_1, A_2, ..., A_n$$
$$\textbf{from } r$$
$$\textbf{where } A_i = C$$

then, to process this query, the system will perform a lookup on an index or hash structure for attribute A_i, for value C. For queries of this form, a hashing scheme is preferable. An index lookup requires time proportional to the log of the number of values in R for A_i. In a hash structure, however, the average lookup time is a constant independent of the size of the database. The only advantage to an index over a hash structure for this form of query is that the worst-case lookup time is proportional to the number of values in R for A if hashing is used, while, if an index is used, the worst-case lookup time is proportional to the log of the number of values.

Index techniques are preferable to hashing in cases where a range of values is specified in the query. Such a query takes the following form:

> select $A_1, A_2, ..., A_n$
> from r
> where $A_i \leq C_2$ and $A_i \geq C_1$

In other words, the above query finds all records with A_i values between C_1 and C_2.

Let us consider how we would process this query using an index. First, we perform a lookup on value C_1. Once we have found the bucket for value C_1, we follow the pointer chain in the index to read the next bucket in alphabetic order and continue in this manner until we reach C_2.

If instead of an index we have a hash structure, we can perform a lookup on C_1 and locate the corresponding bucket, but it is not easy, in general, to determine the next bucket that must be examined. The difficulty arises from the fact that a good hash function assigns values randomly to buckets. Thus, there is no simple notion of "next bucket." The reason we cannot chain buckets together into alphabetic order is that each bucket is assigned many search-key values. Although, at any time, a bucket contains only a few values, the number of *possible* values is large. Since these values are randomly distributed, no chain of buckets can be guaranteed to represent search-key order.

If we want to support range queries using a hash structure, we must choose a hash function that *preserves order*. That is, if K_1 and K_2 are search-key values and $K_1 < K_2$, then $h(K_1) < h(K_2)$. Such a function ensures that the buckets are in key order. An order-preserving hash function that meets our requirements of uniformity and randomness is difficult to find in many cases. Our earlier example of a hash function on names that used the first letter of the name to identify 1 of 26 buckets preserved order but failed to provide uniformity. Consider a hash function on *balance* that maps a record to 1 of 100 buckets by computing *balance*/1000 and dropping the values to the right of the decimal. All records for which *balance*/1000 > 100 are put in bucket 100. This hash function preserves order but fails to provide uniformity since we believe that there are many more small accounts (less than $10,000) than large accounts.

Because of the difficulty in finding good hash functions that preserve order, most systems use indexing in preference to hashing unless it is known in advance that range queries will be infrequent.

8.8 Multiple-Key Access

Until now, we have assumed implicitly that only one index (or hash table) is used to process a query on a relation. However, for certain types of queries it is advantageous to use multiple indices if they exist.

Assume the *deposit* file has two indices, one for *branch-name* and one for *customer-name*. Note that since there are multiple indices on *deposit*, the buckets will contain pointers to the records in the file rather than contain the records themselves. Consider the following query, "Find the balance in all of Williams' account at the Perryridge branch."

> **select** *balance*
> **from** *deposit*
> **where** *branch-name* = "Perryridge" **and** *customer-name* = "Williams"

There are three strategies possible for processing this query:

- Use the index on *branch-name* to find all records pertaining to the Perryridge branch. Examine each such record to see if *customer-name* = "Williams."

- Use the index on *customer-name* to find all records pertaining to Williams. Examine each such record to see if *branch-name* = "Perryridge."

- Use the index on *branch-name* to find *pointers* to all records pertaining to the Perryridge branch. Use the index on *customer-name* to find pointers to all records pertaining to Williams. Take the intersection of these two sets of pointers. Those pointers that are in the intersection point to records pertaining to both Williams and Perryridge.

The third strategy is the only one of the three that takes advantage of the existence of multiple indices. However, even this strategy may be poor if all of the following hold:

- There are a large number of records pertaining to the Perryridge branch.

- There are a large number of records pertaining to Williams.

- There are only a small number of records pertaining to *both* Williams and to the Perryridge branch.

If these conditions hold, we must scan a large number of pointers to produce a small result.

To speed the processing of multiple search-key queries, several special structures can be maintained. We shall consider two such structures: the *grid structure* and *partitioned hash functions*.

A grid structure for queries on two search keys is a two-dimensional array, indexed by the values for the search keys. Figure 8.28 shows part of a grid structure for the *deposit* file. To perform a lookup to answer our example query, we look for the entry in the "Williams" row and the

"Perryridge" column. That entry contains pointers to all records with *customer-name* = "Williams" and *branch-name* = "Perryridge."

No special computations need be performed, and only the records needed to answer the query are accessed.

The grid structure is suitable also for queries involving one search key. Consider the query

> **select** *
> **from** *deposit*
> **where** *branch-name* = "Perryridge"

The pointers that appear in the Perryridge column point to all the records pertaining to Perryridge.

It is conceptually simple to extend the grid structure approach to any number of search keys. If we want our structure to be used for queries on *n* keys, we construct an *n*-dimensional array as our grid structure.

Grid structures provide significant improvement in the processing time for multiple-key queries. However, they impose a space overhead as well as a performance overhead on record insertion and deletion.

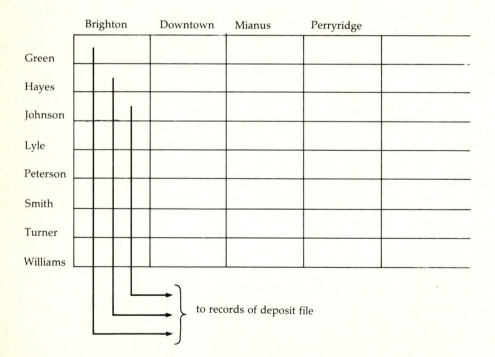

Figure 8.28   Grid structure for *deposit* file.

An alternative approach to multiple-key queries is the use of a partitioned hash function. Suppose we wish to construct a structure suitable for queries on the *deposit* file involving *customer-name* and *branch-name*. We construct a hash structure for the key (*customer-name*, *branch-name*). The only difference between the structure we shall create and those we saw earlier is that we impose an additional constraint on the hash function *h*. Hash values are split into two parts. The first part depends only on the *customer-name* part of the search-key value and the second part of the hash value depends only on the *branch-name* part of the search-key value. The hash function in called *partitioned* because the hash values are partitioned into a partition that depends on each element of the key.

Figure 8.29 shows a sample hash function on this search key. In this sample function, the first 3 bits depend on *customer-name* and the final 3 bits depend on *branch-name*. Thus, the hash values for (Hayes, Perryridge) and (Hayes, Mianus) agree on the first 3 bits and the hash values for (Johnson, Downtown) and (Peterson, Downtown) agree on the last 3 bits.

The partitioned hash function of Figure 8.29 can be used to answer the query "Find the balance in all of Williams' accounts at the Perryridge branch." We simply compute *h*(Williams, Perryridge) and access the hash structure. The same hash structure is suitable for a query involving only one of the the two search keys. To find all records pertaining to the Perryridge branch, we compute *part* of the partitioned hash. Since we have only the *branch-name* value, we are able to compute only the last 3 bits of the hash. For the value "Perryridge," these 3 bits are 101. We access the hash structure and scan those buckets for which the last 3 bits of the hash value are 101. In the example of Figure 8.29, we access the buckets for hash values 110101, 000101, and 001101.

As was the case for the grid file, partitioned hashing extends to an arbitrary number of attributes. There are several improvements we can make in partitioned hashing if we know how frequently a user will specify

search-key value	hash value
(Green, Brighton)	101 111
(Hayes, Perryridge)	110 101
(Johnson, Downtown)	111 001
(Lyle, Perryridge)	000 101
(Peterson, Downtown)	010 001
(Smith, Mianus)	011 111
(Turner, Round Hill)	011 000
(Williams, Perryridge)	001 101
(Hayes, Mianus)	110 011

Figure 8.29   Partitioned hash function for key (*customer-name, branch-name*).

each attribute in a query. The bibliographic notes reference these techniques.

Several other hybrid techniques for processing multiple-key queries exist. Such techniques may be useful in applications where the system implementor knows that most queries will be of a restricted form. References to some of the more interesting techniques appear in the bibliographic notes.

8.9 Summary

Many queries reference only a small proportion of the records in a file. In order to reduce the overhead in searching for these records, *indices* can be constructed for the files that store the database.

Index-sequential files are one of the oldest index schemes used in database systems. Index-sequential files consist of a sequential file and an index. They are designed for applications that require both sequential processing of the entire file and random access to individual records. To permit fast retrieval of records in search-key order, records are chained together by pointers. In order to allow fast random access, an index structure is used. There are two types of index that may be used, dense index and sparse index.

In a standard index-sequential file, only one index is maintained. If several indices on different search keys are used, the index whose search key specifies the sequential order of the file is the *primary index*. The other indices are called *secondary indices*. Secondary indices improve the performance of queries that use search keys other than the primary one. However, they impose a serious overhead on modification of the database.

The primary disadvantage of the indexed-sequential file organization is that performance degrades as the file grows. To overcome this deficiency, a B$^+$-*tree index* can be used. A B$^+$-tree index takes the form of a *balanced* tree in which every path from the root of the tree to a leaf of the tree is of the same length. Lookup in this scheme is quite straightforward and efficient. However, insertion and deletion are more complicated. Nevertheless, the number of operations required for insertion and deletion on B$^+$-trees is proportional to the logarithm of the size of the database.

B-tree indices are similar to B$^+$-tree indices. The primary distinction between the two approaches is that a B-tree eliminates the redundant storage of search-key values. The major disadvantage is that leaf and nonleaf nodes are not of the same size which complicates storage management for the index.

One disadvantage of index schemes is that we must traverse an index structure to locate data. The technique of *hashing* allows us to avoid traversing an index structure. It involves the computation of the address of a data item directly by computing a function on the search-key value of the desired record. Since we do not know at design time precisely which search-key values will be stored in the file, a good hash function to choose is one that assigns search-key values to buckets such that the distribution is both uniform and random.

A *static hashing function* is one in which the set of bucket addresses is fixed. Such a function cannot accommodate easily databases that grow significantly larger over time. There are several hashing techniques that allow the hash function to be modified dynamically. These are called *dynamic hash functions*. One such type of function is *extendible hashing* which copes with changes in database size by splitting and coalescing buckets as the database grows and shrinks.

Exercises

8.1 In the sequential file organization, why is an overflow *block* used even if there is, at the moment, only one overflow record?

8.2 When is it preferable to use a dense index rather than a sparse index?

8.3 Since indices speed query processing, why might indices not be kept on several search-keys? List as many reasons as possible.

8.4 Generalize the structure of Figure 8.5 for a situation in which it is possible that the records for one search-key value occupy several blocks.

8.5 What is the difference between a primary index and a secondary index?

8.6 Construct a B^+-tree for the following set of key values:

$$(2, 3, 5, 7, 11, 17, 19, 23, 29, 31)$$

under the assumption that the number of search-key values that fit in one node is:

a. 3

b. 5

c. 7

8.7 For each B^+-tree of Exercise 8.6, show the steps involved in the following queries:

- find records with a search-key value of 11
- find records with a search-key value between 7 and 17.

8.8 For each B^+-tree of Exercise 8.6, show the form of the tree after each of the following series of operations:

- insert 9
- insert 10
- insert 8
- delete 23
- delete 19

8.9 Repeat Exercise 8.6 for a B-tree.

8.10 Explain the distinction between closed and open hashing and discuss the relative merits of both techniques in database applications.

8.11 If a hash structure is used on a search key for which range queries are likely, what property should the hash function have?

8.12 Suppose that we are using extendible hashing on a file containing records with the following search-key values:

$$2, 3, 5, 7, 11, 17, 19, 23, 29, 31.$$

Show the extendible hash structure for this file if the hash function is $h(x) = x \bmod 8$ and buckets can hold three records.

8.13 Show how the extendible hash structure of Exercise 8.12 changes as the result of each of the following steps:

- delete 11
- delete 31
- insert 1
- insert 15

Bibliographic Notes

The basic data structures used in indexing and hashing are covered in several texts including Aho et al. [1983], Horowitz and Sahni [1976], and Knuth [1973].

B-tree indices are discussed in Bayer [1972], Bayer and McCreight [1972], and Nievergelt [1974], and Held and Stonebraker [1978]. Bayer and

Schkolnick [1977] analyze the problem of managing a B-tree index for a file updated concurrently by several processes. Other discussions of concurrency control within B-trees and similar data structures include those of Lehman and Yao [1981], Kung and Lehman [1980], and Ford and Calhoun [1984]. Knuth [1973] analyzes a large number of different hashing techniques. An empirical study of insertion and deletion on trees appears in Eppinger [1983]. Several alternative tree and tree-like search structures have been proposed. Tries are trees whose structure is based on the "digits" of keys (for example, a dictionary thumb-index, which has one entry for each letter). Such trees may not be balanced in the sense of a B-tree. Tries are discussed by Orestein [1982], Litwin [1981], and Fredkin [1960]. Related work includes the digital B-trees of Lomet [1981].

There are several proposed dynamic hashing schemes. Linear hashing was introduced by Litwin [1978, 1980]. Larson [1982] presents a performance analysis of linear hashing. Extendible hashing was introduced by Fagin et al. [1979]. Partitioned hash functions have been applied to several index structures. The grid file structure appears in Nievergelt et al. [1984], and Hinrichs [1985]. Partial match retrieval uses a partitioned hash function to limit the number of buckets to be searched in processing a multiple-key query [Rivest 1976, Burkhard 1976, 1979, and Ullman 1982a]. King et al. [1983] uses a combination of extendible hashing and partitioned hash functions in an index structure designed for multiple key queries that include subset queries (as in keyword-based retrieval). Optimal choice of partitioning for a partitioned hash function is discussed in Bolour [1979] and Aho and Ullman [1979]. Other techniques for multi-key queries include those of Lum [1974], Lum and Ling [1970], and Shneiderman [1976].

Query Processing

In the preceding sections, we have considered how to structure the data in the database. These decisions are made at the time the database is designed. Although it is possible to change this structure, it is relatively costly to do so. Thus, when a query is presented to the system, it is necessary to find the best method of finding the answer using the existing database structure. There are a large number of possible strategies for processing a query, especially if the query is complex. Nevertheless, it is usually worthwhile for the system to spend a substantial amount of time on the selection of a strategy. Typically, strategy selection can be done using information available in main memory, with little or no disk accesses. The actual execution of the query will involve many accesses to disk. Since the transfer of data from disk is slow relative to the speed of main memory and the central processor of the computer system, it is advantageous to spend a considerable amount of processing to save disk accesses.

9.1 Query Interpretation

Given a query, there are generally a variety of methods for computing the answer. For example, we saw that in SQL a query could be expressed in several different ways. Each way of expressing the query "suggests" a strategy for finding the answer. However, we do not expect users to write their queries in a way that suggests the most efficient strategy. Thus, it becomes the responsibility of the system to transform the query as entered by the user into an equivalent query which can be computed more efficiently. This "optimizing," or more accurately, improving of the strategy for processing a query, is called *query optimization*. There is a close analogy between code optimization by a compiler and query optimization by a database system. We shall study the issues involved in efficient query processing both in high-level languages and at the level of physical access to the data.

Query optimization is an important issue in any database system since the difference in execution time between a good strategy and a bad one may be huge. In the network model and the hierarchical model, query optimization is left, for the most part, to the application programmer. Since the data manipulation language statements are embedded in a host programming language, it is not easy to transform a network or hierarchical query to an equivalent one unless one has knowledge about the entire application program.

Since a relational query can be expressed entirely in a relational query language without the use of a host language, it is possible to optimize queries automatically. Since the most useful optimization techniques apply to the relational model, we shall emphasize the relational model in this chapter. The bibliographic notes reference techniques for optimization of network and hierarchical queries.

Before query processing can begin, the system must translate the query into a usable form. Languages such as SQL are suitable for human use, but ill-suited to be the system's internal representation of a query. A more useful internal representation of query is one based on the relational algebra. The only difference between the form of the relational algebra we shall use here and that of Chapter 3 is that we shall add redundant parentheses to indicate the order of operation evaluation.

Thus, the first action the system must take on a query is to translate the query into its internal form. This translation process is similar to that done by the parser of a compiler. In the process of generating the internal form of the query, the parser checks the syntax of the user's query, verifies that the relation names appearing in the query are names of relation in the database, etc. If the query was expressed in terms of a view, the parser replaces all references to the view name with the relational algebra expression to compute a view.

The details of the parser are beyond the scope of this text. Parsing is covered in most compiler texts (see the bibliographic notes).

Once the query has been translated to an internal relational algebra form, the optimization process begins. The first phase of optimization is done at the relational algebra level. An attempt is made to find an expression that is equivalent to the given expression but that is more efficient to execute. The next phase involves the selection of a detailed strategy for processing the query. A choice must be made as to exactly how the query will be executed. A choice of specific indices to use must be made. The order in which tuples are processed must be determined. The final choice of a strategy is based primarily on the number of disk accesses required.

9.2 Equivalence of Expressions

The relational algebra is a procedural language. Thus, each relational algebra expression represents a particular sequence of operations. We have already seen that there are several ways to express a given query in the relational algebra. The first step in selecting a query processing strategy is to find a relational algebra éxpression that is equivalent to the given query and is efficient to execute.

We use our bank example to illustrate optimization techniques. In particular, we shall use the relations *customer* (*Customer-scheme*), *deposit* (*Deposit-scheme*), and *branch* (*Branch-scheme*). As was the case earlier, we define our relation scheme as follows:

Customer-scheme = (*customer-name, street, customer-city*)
Deposit-scheme = (*branch-name, account-number, customer-name, balance*)
Branch-scheme = (*branch-name, assets, branch-city*)

9.2.1 Selection Operation

Let us consider the relational algebra expression we wrote in Chapter 3 for the query "Find the assets and name of all banks who have depositors living in Port Chester":

$$\Pi_{branch\text{-}name,\ assets} (\sigma_{customer\text{-}city}\ =\ \text{``Port Chester''}$$
$$(customer \bowtie deposit \bowtie branch))$$

This expression constructs a large relation, *customer* $\bowtie$ *deposit* $\bowtie$ *branch* . However, we are interested in only a few tuples of this relation (those pertaining to residents of Port Chester), and in only two of the eight attributes of this relation. The large intermediate result:

$$customer \bowtie deposit \bowtie branch$$

is probably too large to be kept in main memory and thus must be stored on disk. This means that in addition to the disk accesses required to read the relations *customer*, *deposit*, and *branch*, the system will need to access disk to read and write intermediate results. Clearly, we could process the query more efficiently if there were a way to reduce the size of the intermediate result.

Since we are concerned only about tuples for which *customer-city* = "Port Chester," we need not consider those tuples of the *customer* relation that do not have *customer-city* = "Port Chester." By reducing the number of tuples of the *customer* relation that we need to access, we reduce the size of the intermediate result. Our query is now represented by the relational algebra expression:

$$\Pi_{branch\text{-}name,\ assets} (\ (\sigma_{customer\text{-}city}\ =\ \text{``Port Chester''}\ (customer))$$
$$\bowtie deposit \bowtie branch)$$

The above example suggests the following rule for transforming relational algebra queries:

- Perform selection operations as early as possible.

In our example, we recognized that the selection operator pertained only to the *customer* relation, so we performed the selection on *customer* directly.

Suppose that we modify our original query to restrict attention to customers with a balance over \$1000. The new relational algebra query is

$$\Pi_{branch\text{-}name,\ assets}\ (\sigma_{customer\text{-}city\ =\ \text{``Port Chester''}\ \wedge\ balance\ >\ 1000}$$
$$(customer \bowtie deposit \bowtie branch))$$

We cannot apply the selection:

$$customer\text{-}city = \text{``Port Chester''} \wedge balance > 1000$$

directly to the *customer* relation, since the predicate involves attributes of *customer* and *deposit*. However, the *branch* relation does not involve either *customer-city* or *balance*. If we decide to process the join as:

$$((customer \bowtie deposit) \bowtie branch)$$

then we can rewrite our query as:

$$\Pi_{branch\text{-}name,\ assets}$$
$$((\sigma_{customer\text{-}city\ =\ \text{``Port Chester''}\ \wedge\ balance\ >\ 1000}\ (customer \bowtie deposit))$$
$$\bowtie\ branch)$$

Let us examine the subquery:

$$\sigma_{customer\text{-}city\ =\ \text{``Port Chester''}\ \wedge\ balance\ >\ 1000}\ (customer \bowtie deposit)$$

We can split the selection predicate into two, forming the expression:

$$\sigma_{customer\text{-}city\ =\ \text{``Port Chester''}}\ (\sigma_{balance\ >\ 1000}\ (customer \bowtie deposit))$$

Both of the above expressions select tuples with *customer-city* = "Port Chester" and *balance* > 1000. However, the latter form of the expression provides a new opportunity to apply the "perform selections early" rule. We now rewrite our query as:

$$(\sigma_{customer\text{-}city\ =\ \text{``Port Chester''}}\ (customer)) \bowtie (\sigma_{balance\ >\ 1000}\ (deposit))$$

We now add a second transformation rule:

• Replace expressions of the form:

$$\sigma_{P_1 \wedge P_2}(e)$$

by

$$\sigma_{P_1}(\sigma_{P_2}(e))$$

where P_1 and P_2 are predicates and e is a relational algebra expression.

An easy way to remember this transformation is by noting the following equivalences among relational algebra expressions:

$$\sigma_{P_1}(\sigma_{P_2}(e)) = \sigma_{P_2}(\sigma_{P_1}(e)) = \sigma_{P_1 \wedge P_2}(e)$$

9.2.2 Natural Join Operation

By modifying queries so that selections are done early, we reduce the size of temporary results. Another way to reduce the size of temporary results is to choose an optimal ordering of the join operations. We mentioned in Chapter 3 that natural join is associative. Thus, for all relations r_1, r_2, and r_3:

$$(r_1 \bowtie r_2) \bowtie r_3 = r_1 \bowtie (r_2 \bowtie r_3)$$

although these expressions are equivalent, the costs of computing them may differ. Consider again the expression:

$$\Pi_{branch\text{-}name, \; assets}((\sigma_{customer\text{-}city \, = \, \text{``Port Chester''}}(customer)) \\ \bowtie deposit \bowtie branch)$$

We could choose to compute $deposit \bowtie branch$ first and then join the result with:

$$\sigma_{customer\text{-}city \, = \, \text{``Port Chester''}}(customer)$$

However, $deposit \bowtie branch$ is likely to be a large relation since it contains one tuple for every account. However,

$$\sigma_{customer\text{-}city\ =\ \text{``Port Chester''}}\ (customer)$$

is probably a small relation. To see this, note that since the bank has a large number of widely distributed branches, it is likely that only a small fraction of the bank's customers live in Port Chester. If we compute:

$$(\sigma_{customer\text{-}city\ =\ \text{``Port Chester''}}\ (customer)) \bowtie deposit$$

first, we obtain one tuple for each account held by a resident of Port Chester. Thus, the temporary relation we must store is smaller than if we compute $deposit \bowtie borrow$ first.

There are other options to consider for evaluating our query. We do not care about the order in which attributes appear in a join, since it is easy to change the order before displaying the result. Thus, for all relations r_1 and r_2:

$$r_1 \bowtie r_2 = r_2 \bowtie r_1$$

That is, natural join is commutative.

Using this fact, we can consider rewriting our relational algebra expression as

$$\Pi_{branch\text{-}name,\ assets}\ (((\sigma_{customer\text{-}city\ =\ \text{``Port Chester''}}\ (customer))$$
$$\bowtie branch) \bowtie deposit)$$

That is, we could join $\sigma_{customer\text{-}city\ =\ \text{``Port Chester''}}\ (customer)$ with $branch$ as the first join operation performed. Note, however, that there are no attributes in common between *Branch-scheme* and *Customer-scheme*, so the join is really just a cartesian product. If there are c customers in Port Chester and b branches, this cartesian product generates bc tuples, one for every possible pair of customers and branches (without regard for whether or not the customer has an account at the branch). Thus, it appears that this cartesian product will produce a large temporary relation. As a result, we would reject this strategy. However, if the user had entered the above expression, we could use the associativity and commutativity of natural join to transform this expression to the more efficient expression we used earlier.

9.2.3 Projection Operation

We now consider another technique for reducing the size of temporary results. The projection operation, like the selection operation, reduces the size of relations. Thus, whenever we need to generate a temporary relation, it is advantageous to apply any projections that are possible. This suggests a companion to the "perform selections early" rule we stated earlier:

- Perform projections early.

Consider the following form of our example query:

$$\Pi_{branch\text{-}name,\ assets}\ (((\sigma_{customer\text{-}city}\ =\ \text{"Port Chester"}\ (customer))$$
$$\bowtie\ deposit)\ \bowtie\ branch)$$

When we compute the subexpression:

$$((\sigma_{customer\text{-}city}\ =\ \text{"Port Chester"}\ (customer))\ \bowtie\ deposit)$$

we obtain a relation whose scheme is:

    (*customer-name, customer-city, branch-name, account-number, balance*)

We can eliminate several attributes from the scheme. The only attributes we must retain are those that:

- Appear in the result of the query or
- Are needed to process subsequent operations.

By eliminating unneeded attributes, we reduce the number of columns of the intermediate result. Thus, the size of the intermediate result is reduced. In our example, the only attribute we need is *branch-name*. Therefore, we modify the expression to:

$$\Pi_{branch\text{-}name,\ assets}\ ((\ \Pi_{branch\text{-}name}\ (((\sigma_{customer\text{-}city}\ =\ \text{'Port Chester'}\ (customer))$$
$$\bowtie\ deposit))\ \bowtie\ branch)$$

9.2.4 Other Operations

The example we have used involves a sequence of natural joins. We chose this example because natural joins arise frequently in practice and because natural joins are one of the more costly operations in query processing. However, we note that equivalences similar to those presented above hold for the union and set difference operations. We list some of these equivalences below:

$$\sigma_P(r_1 \cup r_2) = \sigma_P(r_1) \cup \sigma_P(r_2)$$
$$\sigma_P(r_1 - r_2) = \sigma_P(r_1) - r_2 = \sigma_P(r_1) - \sigma_P(r_2)$$
$$(r_1 \cup r_2) \cup r_3 = r_1 \cup (r_2 \cup r_3)$$
$$r_1 \cup r_2 = r_2 \cup r_1$$

We have seen several techniques for generating more efficient relational algebra expressions for a query. For queries whose structure is more complex than those of our example there may be a large number of possible strategies that appear to be efficient. Some query processors simply choose from such a set of strategies based on certain heuristics. Others retain all promising strategies and perform the latter phases of query optimization for each strategy. The final choice of strategy is made only after the details of each strategy have been worked out and an estimate is made of the processing cost of each strategy.

9.3 Estimation of Query-Processing Cost

The strategy we choose for a query depends upon the size of each relation and the distribution of values within columns. In the example we have used in this chapter, the fraction of customers who live in Port Chester has a major impact on the usefulness of our techniques. In order to be able to choose a strategy based on reliable information, database systems may store statistics for each relation r. These statistics include:

1. n_r, the number of tuples in the relation r.

2. S_r, the size of a record (tuple) of relation r in bytes (for fixed-length records).

3. $V(A,r)$, the number of distinct values that appear in the relation r for attribute A.

The first two statistics allow us to estimate accurately the size of a cartesian product. The cartesian product $r \times s$ contains $n_r n_s$ tuples. Each tuple of $r \times s$ occupies $s_r s_s$ bytes.

The third statistic is used to estimate how many tuples satisfy a selection predicate of the form:

$$<attribute\text{-}name> = <value>$$

However, in order to perform such an estimation, we need to know how often each value appears in a column. If we assume that each value appears with equal probability, then $\sigma_{A = a}(r)$ is estimated to have

n_r /$V(A,r)$ tuples. However, it may not always be realistic to assume that each value appears with equal probability. The *branch-name* attribute in the *deposit* relation is an example of such a case. There is one tuple in the *deposit* relation for each amount. It is reasonable to expect that the large branches have more accounts than smaller branches. Therefore certain *branch-name* values appear with greater probability than others.

Despite the fact that our uniform distribution assumption is not always true, it is a good approximation of reality in many cases. Therefore, many query processors make such an assumption when choosing a strategy. For simplicity, we shall assume a uniform distribution for the remainder of this chapter.

Estimation of the size of a natural join is somewhat more complicated than estimation of the size of a selection or a cartesian product. Let $r_1(R_1)$ and $r_2(R_2)$ be relations. If $R_1 \cap R_2 = \emptyset$, then $r_1 \bowtie r_2$ is the same as $r_1 \times r_2$, and we can use our estimation technique for cartesian products. If $R_1 \cap R_2$ is a key for R_1, then we know that a tuple of r_2 will join with exactly one tuple from r_1. Therefore, the number of tuples in $r_1 \bowtie r_2$ is no greater than the number of tuples in r_2.

The most difficult case to consider is when $R_1 \cap R_2$ is a key for neither R_1 nor R_2. In this case, we use the third statistic and assume, as before, that each value appears with equal probability. Consider a tuple t of r_1, and assume $R_1 \cap R_2 = \{A\}$. We estimate that there are $n_{r_2}/V(A,r_2)$ tuples in r_2 with an A value of $t[A]$. So tuple t produces

$$\frac{n_{r_2}}{V(A,r_2)}$$

tuples in $r_1 \bowtie r_2$. Considering all of the tuples in r_1, we estimate that there are

$$\frac{n_{r_1} n_{r_2}}{V(A,r_2)}$$

tuples in $r_1 \bowtie r_2$. Observe that if we reverse the roles of r_1 and r_2 in the above estimate, we obtain an estimate of $n_{r_1} n_{r_2} / V(A,r_1)$ tuples in $r_1 \bowtie r_2$. These two estimates differ if $V(A,r_1) \neq V(A,r_2)$. If this situation occurs, there are likely to be some dangling tuples that do not participate in the join. Thus, the lower of the two estimates is probably the better one.

The above estimate of join size may be too high if the $V(A, r_1)$ A values in r_1 have few values in common with the $V(A, r_2)$ A values in r_2. However, it is unlikely that our estimate will be very far off in practice since dangling tuples are likely to be only a small fraction of the tuples in a real-world relation. If dangling tuples appear frequently, then a correction factor could be applied to our estimates.

If we wish to maintain accurate statistics, then every time a relation is modified, it is necessary also to update the statistics. This is a substantial amount of overhead. Therefore, most systems do not update the statistics on every modification. Instead, statistics are updated during periods of light load on the system. As a result, the statistics used for choosing a query processing strategy may not be accurate. However, if the interval between the update of the statistics is not too long, the statistics will be sufficiently accurate to provide a good estimation of the size of the results of expressions.

Statistical information about relations is particularly useful when several indices are available to assist in the processing of a query, as we shall see in Section 9.4.

9.4 Estimation of Costs of Access Using Indices

The cost estimates we have considered for relational algebra expressions did not consider the affects of indices and hash functions on the cost of evaluating an expression. The presence of these structures, however, has a significant influence on the choice of a query-processing strategy.

- Indices and hash functions allow fast access to records containing a specific value on the index key.

- Indices (though not most hash functions) allow the records of a file to be read in sorted order. In Chapter 8, we pointed out that it is efficient to read the records of a file in an order corresponding closely to physical order. If an index allows the records of a file to be read in an order that corresponds to the physical order of records, we call that index a *clustering index*. Clustering indices allow us to take advantage of the physical clustering of records into blocks.

The detailed strategy for processing a query is called an *access plan* for the query. A plan includes not only the relational operations to be performed but also the indices to be used and the order in which tuples are to be accessed and the order in which operations are to be performed.

Of course, the use of indices imposes the overhead of access to those blocks containing the index. We need to take these blocks accesses into account when we estimate the cost of a strategy that involves the use of indices.

In this section, we consider queries involving only one relation. We use the selection predicate to guide us in the choice of the best index to use in processing the query.

As an example of the estimation of the cost of a query using indices assume that we are processing the query:

> **select** *account-number*
> **from** *deposit*
> **where** *branch-name* = "Perryridge" **and** *customer-name* = "Williams"
>   **and** *balance* > 1000

Assume that we have the following statistical information about the *deposit* relation:

- 20 tuples of *deposit* fit in one block.

- $V(deposit, branch-name) = 50$.

- $V(deposit, customer-name) = 200$.

- $V(deposit, balance) = 5000$.

- The *deposit* relation has 10,000 tuples.

Let us assume that the following indices exist on *deposit*:

- A clustering, B^+-tree index for *branch-name*.

- A nonclustering, B^+-tree index for *customer-name*.

As before, we shall make the simplifying assumption that values are distributed uniformly.

Since $V(deposit, branch-name) = 50$, we expect that $10000/50 = 200$ tuples of the *deposit* relation pertain to the Perryridge branch. If we use the index on *branch-name*, we will need to read these 200 tuples and check each one for satisfaction of the **where** clause. Since the index is a clustering index, $200/20 = 10$ block reads are required to read the *deposit* tuples. In addition, several index blocks must be read. Assume the B^+-tree index stores 20 pointers per node. This means that the B^+-tree index must have between 3 and 5 leaf nodes. With this number of leaf nodes, the entire tree has a depth of 2, so at most 2 index blocks must be read. Thus the above strategy requires 12 total block reads.

We conclude that it is preferable to use the index for *branch-name*.

If we use the index for *customer-name*, we estimate the number of block accesses as follows. Since $V(deposit, customer-name) = 200$, we expect that $10000/200 = 50$ tuples of the *deposit* relation pertain to Williams. However, since the index for *customer-name* is nonclustering, we anticipate that one block read will be required for each tuple. Thus, 50 block reads are required, just to read the *deposit* tuples. Let us assume that 20 pointers fit into one node of the B$^+$-tree index for *customer-name*. Since there are 200 customer names, the tree has between 11 and 20 leaf nodes. So, as was the case for the other B$^+$-tree index, the index for *customer-name* has a depth of 2 and 2 block accesses are required to read the necessary index blocks. Therefore, this strategy requires a total of 52 block reads. We conclude that it is preferable to use the index for *branch-name*.

Observe that if both indices were nonclustering, we would prefer to use the index for *customer-name* since we expect only 50 tuples with *customer-name* = "Williams" versus 200 tuples with *branch-name* = "Perryridge." Without the clustering property, our first strategy would have required 200 bock accesses to read the data plus 2 index block accesses for a total of 202 block reads. However, because of the clustering property of the *branch-name* index, it is actually less expensive in this example to use the *branch-name* index.

We did not consider using the *balance* attribute and the predicate *balance* > 1000 as a starting point for a query processing strategy for two reasons:

- There is no index for *balance*.

- The selection predicate on *balance* involves a "greater than" comparison. In general, equality predicates are more selective than "greater than" predicates. Since we have an equality predicate available to us (indeed, we have two), we prefer to start by using such a predicate since it is likely to select fewer tuples.

Estimation of the cost of access using indices allows us to estimate the complete cost, in terms of block accesses, of a plan. For a given relational algebra expression, it may be possible to formulate several plans. The access plan selection phase of a query optimizer chooses the best plan for a given expression.

We have seen that different plans may have significant differences in cost. It is possible that a relational algebra expression for which a good plan exists may be preferable to an apparently more efficient algebra expression for which only inferior plans exist. Thus, it is often worthwhile for a large number of strategies to be evaluated down to the access plan level before a final choice of query-processing strategy is made.

9.5 Join Strategies

Earlier, we estimated the *size* of the result of a relational algebra expression involving a natural join. In this section, we apply our techniques for estimating the cost of processing a query to the problem of estimating the *cost* of processing a join. We shall see that several factors influence the selection of an optimal strategy:

- The physical order of tuples in a relation.

- The presence of indices and the type of index (clustering or nonclustering).

- The cost of computing a temporary index for the sole purpose of processing one query.

Let us begin by considering the expression

$$deposit \bowtie customer$$

and assume that we have no indices whatsoever. Let:

- $n_{deposit} = 10,000$.

- $n_{customer} = 200$.

9.5.1 Simple Iteration

If we are not willing to create an index, we must examine every possible pair of tuples t_1 in *deposit* and t_2 in *customer*. Thus, we examine $10000 * 200 = 2000000$ pairs of tuples.

If we execute this query cleverly, we can reduce the number of block accesses significantly. Suppose that we use the procedure of Figure 9.1 for computing the join. We read each tuple of *deposit* once. This may require as many as 10,000 block accesses. However, if the tuples of *deposit* are stored together physically, fewer accesses are required. If we assume that 20 tuples of *deposit* fit in one block, then reading *deposit* requires $10000/20 = 500$ block accesses.

```
for each tuple d in deposit do
    begin
        for each tuple c in customer do
            begin
                test pair (d,c) to see if a tuple should be added to the result
            end
    end
```

Figure 9.1   Procedure for computing join.

```
        for each block Bd of deposit do
      begin
         for each block Bc of customer do
            begin
               for each tuple b in Bd do
                  begin
                     for each tuple c in Bc do
                        begin
                           test pair (b,c) to see if a tuple
                           should be added to the result
                        end
                  end
            end
      end
```

Figure 9.2   Procedure to compute *deposit* $\bowtie$ *customer* .

We read each tuple of *customer* once for each tuple of *deposit*. This suggests that we read each tuple of *customer* 10,000 times. Since $n_{customer} = 200$, we could make as many as 2,000,000 accesses to read *customer* tuples. As was the case for *deposit*, we can reduce the required number of accesses significantly if we store the *customer* tuples together physically. If we assume that 20 *customer* tuples fit in one block, then only 10 accesses are required to read the entire *customer* relation. Thus, only 10 accesses per tuple of *deposit* rather than 200 are required. This implies that only 100,000 block accesses are needed to process the query.

9.5.2 Block-Oriented Iteration

A major savings in block accesses results if we process the relations on a per-block basis rather than a per-tuple basis. Again, assuming that *deposit* tuples are stored together physically and that *customer* tuples are stored together physically, we can use the procedure of Figure 9.2 to compute *deposit* $\bowtie$ *customer* . This procedure performs the join by considering an entire block of *deposit* tuples at once. We still must read the entire *deposit* relation at a cost of 500 accesses. However, instead of reading the *customer* relation once for each *tuple* of *deposit*, we read the *customer* relation once for each *block* of *deposit*. Since there are 500 blocks of *deposit* tuples and 10 blocks of *customer* tuples, reading *customer* once for every block of *deposit* tuples requires $10 \times 500 = 5000$ block accesses. Thus, the total cost in terms of block accesses is 5500 accesses (5000 accesses to *customer* blocks plus 500 accesses to *deposit* blocks). Clearly, this is a significant improvement over the number of accesses that were necessary for our initial strategy.

Our choice of *deposit* for the outer loop and *customer* for the inner loop was arbitrary. If we had used *customer* as the relation for the outer loop and *deposit* for the inner loop, the cost of our final strategy would have been slightly lower (5010 block accesses). See Exercise 9.10 for a derivation of these costs.

A major advantage to the use of the smaller relation (*customer*) in the inner loop is that it may be possible to store the entire relation in main memory temporarily. This speeds query processing significantly since it is necessary to read the inner loop relation only once. If *customer* is indeed small enough to fit in main memory, out strategy requires only 500 blocks to read *deposit* plus 10 blocks to read *customer* for a total of only 510 block accesses.

9.5.3 Merge-Join

In those cases in which neither relation fits in main memory, it is still possible to process the join efficiently if both relations happen to be stored in sorted order on the join attributes. Suppose that both *customer* and *deposit* are sorted by *customer-name*. We can then perform a *merge-join* operation. To compute a merge-join, we associate one pointer with each relation. These pointers point initially to the first tuple of the respective relations. As the algorithm proceeds, the pointers move through the relation. A group of tuples of one relation with the same value on the join attributes is read. Then the corresponding tuples (if any) of the other relation are read. Since the relations are in sorted order, tuples with the same value on the join attributes are in consecutive order. This allows us to read each tuple only once. In the case in which the tuples of the relations are stored together physically, this algorithm allows us to compute the join by reading each block exactly once. For our example of *deposit* ⋈ *customer* there is a total of 510 block accesses. This is as good as the earlier join method we presented for the special case in which the entire *customer* relation fit in main memory. The algorithm of Figure 9.3 does not require the entire relation to fit in main memory. Rather, it suffices to keep all tuples with the same value for the join attributes in main memory. This is usually feasible even if both relations are large.

A disadvantage of the merge-join method is the requirement that both relations be sorted physically. However, it may be worthwhile to sort the relations in order to allow a merge-join to be performed.

9.5.4 Use of an Index

Frequently, the join attributes form a search key for an index as one of the relations being joined. In such a case, we may consider a join strategy that uses such an index. The simple strategy of Figure 9.1 is more efficient if an index exists on *customer* for *customer-name*. Given a tuple *d* in *deposit*, it is

```
        pd := address of first tuple of deposit;
        pc := address of first tuple of customer;
        while (pc ≠ null) do
          begin
              t_c := tuple to which pc points;
              s_c := {t_c};
              set pc to point to next tuple of customer;
              done := false;
              while (not done) do
                begin;
                    t_c' := tuple to which pc points;
                    if t_c' [customer-name] = t_c[customer-name]
                      then begin
                              S_i := S_c ∪ {t_c'};
                              set pc to point to next tuple of customer;
                          end
                      else done := true;
                end
              t_d := tuple to which pd points;
              set pd to point to next tuple of deposit;
              while (t_d[customer-name] < t_c[customer-name]) do
                begin
                    t_d := tuple to which pd points;
                    set pd to point to next tuple of deposit;
                end
              while (t_d[customer-name] = t_c[customer-name]) do
                begin
                    for each t in S_c do
                      begin
                          compute t ⋈ t_d and add this to result;
                      end
                    set pd to point to next tuple of deposit;
                    td := tuple to which pd points;
                end
          end
        end.
```

Figure 9.3   Merge-join.

no longer necessary to read the entire *customer* relation. Instead, the index is used to look up tuples in *customer* for which the *customer-name* value is $d[customer-name]$.

Without use of an index, and without special assumptions about the physical storage of relations, it was shown that as many as 2 million accesses might be required. Using the index, but without making any assumptions about physical storage, the join can be computed with significantly fewer block accesses. We still need 10,000 accesses to read *deposit*. However, for each tuple of deposit only an index lookup is required. If we assume (as before) that $n_{customers} = 200$, and that 20 pointers fit in one block, then this lookup requires at most 2 index block accesses plus a block access to read the *customer* tuple itself. We access 3 blocks per tuple of *deposit* instead of 200. Adding this to the 10,000 accesses to read *deposit*, we find that the total cost of this strategy is 40,000 accesses.

Although a cost of 40,000 accesses appears high, we must remember that we achieved more efficient strategies only when we assumed that tuples were stored physically together. If this assumption does not hold for the relations being joined, then the strategy we just presented is highly desirable. Indeed the savings (160,000 accesses saved) is enough to justify creation of the index. Even if we create the index for the sole purpose of processing this one query and erase the index afterwards, we may perform fewer accesses than if we use the strategy of Figure 9.1.

9.5.5 Three-Way Join

Let us now consider a join involving three relations:

$$branch \bowtie deposit \bowtie customer$$

Assume that $n_{deposit}$ and $n_{customer}$ are as above and that $n_{branch} = 50$. Not only do we have a choice of strategy for join processing, but also we have a choice of which join to compute first. There are many possible strategies to consider. We shall analyze several of them below and leave others to the exercises.

- **Strategy 1**. Let us first compute the join (*deposit* $\bowtie$ *customer*) using one of the strategies we presented above. Since *customer-name* is a key for *customer*, we know that the result of this join has at most 10,000 tuples (the number of tuples in *deposit*). If we build an index on *branch* for *branch-name*, we can compute:

$$branch \bowtie (deposit \bowtie customer)$$

by considering each tuple t of (*deposit* $\bowtie$ *customer*) and looking up the tuple in *branch* with a *branch-name* value of $t[branch-name]$. Since *branch-name* is a key for *branch*, we know that we must examine only one *branch* tuple for each of the 10,000 tuples in (*deposit* $\bowtie$ *customer*). The exact number of block accesses required by this strategy depends on the way we compute (*deposit* $\bowtie$ *customer*) and on the way in which *branch* is stored physically. Several exercises examine the costs of various possibilities.

- **Strategy 2**. Compute the join without constructing any indices at all. This requires checking $50 * 10000 * 200$ possibilities, a total of 100,000,000.

- **Strategy 3**. Instead of performing two joins, we perform the pair of joins at once. The technique is first to build two indices:

    On *branch* for *branch-name*.

    On *customer* for *customer-name*.

Next we consider each tuple t in *deposit*. For each t, we look up the corresponding tuples in *customer* and the corresponding tuples in *branch*. Thus, we examine each tuple of *deposit* exactly once.

Strategy 3 represents a form of strategy we have not considered before. It does not correspond directly to a relational algebra operation. Instead, it combines two operations into one special-purpose operation. Using strategy 3, it is often possible to perform a join of three relations more efficiently than it is using two joins of two relations. The relative costs depend on the way in which the relations are stored, the distribution of values within columns, and the presence of indices. The exercises provide an opportunity to compute these costs in several examples.

9.6 Structure of the Query Optimizer

We have seen only some of the many query processing strategies used in database systems. Most systems implement only a few strategies and, as a result, the number of strategies to be considered by the query optimizer is limited. Other systems consider a large number of strategies. For each strategy a cost estimate is computed.

In order to simplify the strategy selection task, a query may be split into several subqueries. This not only simplifies strategy selection but also allows the query optimizer to recognize cases where a particular subquery appears several times in the same query. By performing such subqueries only once, time is saved both in the query optimizing phase and in the execution of the query itself. Recognition of common subqueries is analogous to the recognition of *common subexpressions* in many optimizing compilers for programming languages.

Clearly, examination of the query for common subqueries and the estimation of the cost of a large number of strategies impose a substantial overhead on query processing. However, the added cost of query optimization is usually more than offset by the savings at query execution time. Therefore, most commercial systems include relatively sophisticated optimizers. The bibliographic notes give references to descriptions of query optimizers of actual database systems.

9.7 Summary

There are a large number of possible strategies for processing a query, especially if the query is complex. Strategy selection can be done using information available in main memory, with little or no disk accesses. The actual execution of the query will involve many accesses to disk. Since the transfer of data from disk is slow relative to the speed of main memory and the central processor of the computer system, it is advantageous to spend a considerable amount of processing to save disk accesses.

Given a query, there are generally a variety of methods for computing the answer. It is the responsibility of the system to transform the query as entered by the user into an equivalent query which can be computed more efficiently. This "optimizing," or, more accurately, improving of the strategy for processing a query is called *query optimization*.

The first action the system must take on a query is to translate the query into its internal form which (for relational database systems) is usually based on the relational algebra. In the process of generating the internal form of the query, the parser checks the syntax of the user's query, verifies that the relation names appearing in the query are names of relation in the database, etc. If the query was expressed in terms of a view, the parser replaces all references to the view name with the relational algebra expression to compute the view.

Each relational algebra expression represents a particular sequence of operations. The first step in selecting a query-processing strategy is to find a relational algebra expression that is equivalent to the given expression and is efficient to execute. There are a number of different rules for transforming relational algebra queries, including:

- Perform selection operations as early as possible.

- Perform projections early.

The strategy we choose for a query depends upon the size of each relation and the distribution of values within columns. In order to be able to choose a strategy based on reliable information, database systems may store statistics for each relation r. These statistics include:

- The number of tuples in the relation r.

- The size of a record (tuple) of relation r in bytes (for fixed-length records).

- The number of distinct values that appear in the relation r for a particular attribute.

The first two statistics allow us to estimate accurately the size of a cartesian product. The third statistic allows us to estimate how many tuples satisfy a simple selection predicate.

Statistical information about relations is particularly useful when several indices are available to assist in the processing of a query. The presence of these structures has a significant influence on the choice of a query-processing strategy.

Queries involving a natural join may be processed in several ways, depending on the availability of indices and the form of physical storage used for the relations. If tuples of a relation are stored together physically, a *block-oriented* join strategy may be advantageous. If the relations are sorted, a *merge-join* may be desirable. It may be more efficient to sort a relation prior to join computation (so as to allow use of the merge-join strategy). It may also be advantageous to compute a temporary index for the sole purpose of allowing a more efficient join strategy to be used.

Exercises

9.1 At what point during query processing does optimization occur?

9.2 Why is it not desirable to force users to make an explicit choice of a query processing strategy? Are there cases in which it *is* desirable for users to be aware of the costs of competing query processing strategies?

9.3 Consider the following SQL query for our bank database:

> **select** *customer-name*
> **from** *deposit S*
> **where** (**select** *branch-name*
>   **from** *deposit T*
>   **where** *S.customer-name = T.customer-name*)
>   **contains**
>   (**select** *branch-name*
>   **from** *branch*
>   **where** *branch-city =* "Brooklyn")

Write an efficient relational algebra expression that is equivalent to this query. Justify your choice.

9.4 Consider the following SQL query for our bank database:

> **select** $T.branch\text{-}name$
> **from** $branch$ T, $branch$ S
> **where** $T.assets > S.assets$ **and**
> $S.branch\text{-}city = \text{“Brooklyn”}$

Write an efficient relational algebra expression that is equivalent to this query. Justify your choice.

9.5 Show that the following equivalences hold, and explain how they can be applied to improve the efficiency of certain queries:

a. $\sigma_P(r_1 \cup r_2) = \sigma_P(r_1) \cup \sigma_P(r_2)$

b. $\sigma_P(r_1 - r_2) = \sigma_P(r_1) - r_2 = \sigma_P(r_1) - \sigma_P(r_2)$

c. $(r_1 \cup r_2) \cup r_3 = r_1 \cup (r_2 \cup r_3)$

d. $r_1 \cup r_2 = r_2 \cup r_1$

9.6 Consider the relations $r_1(A,B,C)$, $r_2(C,D,E)$, and $r_3(E,F)$, with primary keys A, C, and E respectively. Assume that r_1 has 1000 tuples, r_2 has 1500 tuples and r_3 has 750 tuples. Estimate the size of $r_1 \bowtie r_2 \bowtie r_3$, and give an efficient strategy for computing the join.

9.7 Consider the relations $r_1(A,B,C)$, $r_2(C,D,E)$, and $r_3(E,F)$ of Exercise 9.6 again, but now assume there are no primary keys except the entire scheme. Let $V(C,r_1)$ be 900, $V(C,r_2)$ be 1100, $V(E,r_2)$ be 50, and $V(E,r_3)$ be 100. Assume that r_1 has 1000 tuples, r_2 has 1500 tuples and r_3 has 750 tuples. Estimate the size of $r_1 \bowtie r_2 \bowtie r_3$, and give an efficient strategy for computing the join.

9.8 Clustering indices may allow faster access to data than a nonclustering index. When must we create a nonclustering index despite the advantages of a clustering index?

9.9 What are the advantages and disadvantages of hash functions relative to B^+-tree indices? How might the type of index available influence the choice of a query processing strategy?

9.10 Recompute the cost of the strategy of Section 9.5.2 using *deposit* as the relation of the inner loop and *customer* as the relation of the output loop (thereby reversing the roles they played in the example of Section 9.5.2).

9.11 Explain the difference between a clustering index and a nonclustering index.

9.12 Let relations $r_1(A,B,C)$ and $r_2(C,D,E)$ have the following properties:

- r_1 has 20,000 tuples.
- r_2 has 45,000 tuples.
- 25 tuples of r_1 fit on one block.
- 30 tuples of r_2 fit on one block.

Estimate the number of block accesses required using each of the following join strategies for $r_1 \bowtie r_2$:

- Simple iteration.
- Block-oriented iteration.
- Merge-join

9.13 Consider relations r_1 and r_2 of Exercise 9.12 along with a relation $r_3(E,F)$. Assume that r_3 has 30,000 tuples and that 40 tuples of r_3 fit on one block. Estimate the costs of the 3 strategies of Section 9.5.5 for computing $r_1 \bowtie r_2 \bowtie r_3$.

Bibliographic Notes

Some the ideas used in query optimization are derived from solutions to similar problems in code optimization as performed by compilers of standard programming languages. There are several texts that present optimization from a programming languages point of view, including [Aho et al. 1986], and [Tremblay and Sorenson 1985]. Selinger et al. [1979] describes access path selection in System R. Kim [1981, 1982] describe join strategies and the optimal use of available main memory. These papers discuss many of the strategies that we presented in this chapter. Wong and Youssefi [1976] introduce a technique called *decomposition*, which is used in the Ingres database system. The Ingres decomposition strategy motivated the third strategy we presented for three-way joins. In Ingres, an extension of this technique is used to choose a strategy for general queries. Ingres and System R are discussed in more detail in Chapter 15.

If an entire group of queries is considered, it is possible to discover *common subexpressions* that can be evaluated once for the entire group. Finkelstein [1982], and Hall [1976] consider optimization of a group of queries and the use of common subexpressions. When queries are generated through views, it is often the case that more relations are joined than is necessary to compute the query. A collection of techniques for join minimization have been grouped under the name *tableau optimization*. The notion of a tableau was introduced by Aho et al. [1979a, 1979c]. Ullman [1982a] and Maier [1983] provide a textbook coverage of tableaux.

Theoretical results on the complexity of the computation of relational algebra operations appear in [Gotlieb 1975], [Pecherer 1975], and [Blasgen and Eswaren 1976]. A survey of query processing techniques appears in [Jarke and Koch 1984].

An actual query processor must translate statements in the query language into an internal form suitable for the analysis we have discussed in this chapter. Parsing query languages differs little from parsing of traditional programming languages. Most compiler texts (including [Aho et al. 1986], and [Tremblay and Sorenson 1985]) cover the main parsing techniques. A more theoretical presentation of parsing and language translation is given by Aho and Ullman [1972, 1973].

Query processing for distributed database systems use some concepts from this chapter. Techniques specific to distributed systems appear in Chapter 12 and the bibliographic notes to that chapter.

Crash Recovery

A computer system, like any other mechanical or electrical device, is subject to failure. There are a variety of causes of such failure, including:

- **Disk crash**. The information residing on the disk is lost.

- **Power failure**. The information stored in main memory and general-purpose registers is lost.

- **Software errors**. The results generated may be incorrect, resulting in erroneous output to the user and the database system itself entering an inconsistent state.

There are other sources for failure such as a fire breaking out in the machine room, sabotage, or even a "black hole" passing through the building in which the computer system is residing. In each of these cases, information concerning the database system is lost.

An integral part of a database system is a recovery scheme which is responsible for the detection of failures and the restoration of the database to a consistent state that existed prior to the occurrence of the failure.

10.1 Failure Classification

There are various types of failure that may occur in a system, each of which needs to be dealt with in a different manner. The simplest type of failure to deal with is one which does not result in the loss of information in the system. The ones that are more difficult to deal with are those that do result in loss of information.

10.1.1 Storage Types

There are various types of storage media which are distinguished by their relative speed, capacity, and resilience to failure.

- **Volatile storage**. Information residing in volatile storage does not usually survive system crashes. Examples of such storage are main and cache memory.

- **Nonvolatile storage**. Information residing in nonvolatile storage usually survives system crashes. Examples of such storage are disk and magnetic tapes. Disk is used for online storage while tapes are used for archival storage. Disks are more reliable than main memory but less reliable than magnetic tapes. Both, however, are subject to failure (for example, head crash) which may result in loss of information.

- **Stable storage**. Information residing in stable storage is *never* lost (this should be taken with a grain of salt, since theoretically we cannot guarantee this). To implement an approximation of such storage, we need to replicate information in several nonvolatile storage media (usually disk) with independent failure modes, and update the information in a controlled manner as will be discussed in Section 10.9.

10.1.2 Failure Types

A recovery scheme must be invoked as a result of various types of failures. In this chapter we will consider only the following four types of failure.

- **Logical errors**. The program can no longer continue with its normal execution due to internal conditions such as bad input, data not found, overflow, or resource limit exceeded.

- **System errors**. The system has entered an undesirable state (e.g., deadlock), as a result of which the program cannot continue with its normal execution. The program, however, can be reexecuted at a later time.

- **System crash**. The hardware malfunctions, causing the loss of the content of volatile storage. The content of nonvolatile storage remains intact.

- **Disk failure**. A disk block loses its content as a result of either head crash or failure during a data transfer operation.

In Sections 10.2 through 10.7, we deal only with recovery from the first three types of failure. In Section 10.8, we consider what can be done in the case of the fourth type of failure.

10.1.3 Storage Structure and Operations

The database system resides in nonvolatile storage (usually a disk). The database is partitioned into fixed-length storage units called *blocks* which are the unit of both storage allocation and data transfer. Programs executing the various database applications read information from the disk to main memory and then write the information out back onto the disk.

The read and write operations are done in block units. The blocks residing on the disk are referred to as *physical blocks*, while the blocks residing temporarily in main memory are referred to as *buffer blocks*.

Block movements between the disk and main memory are initiated through the following two operations:

- **input**(X), which transfers the physical block in which data item X resides to main memory.

- **output**(X), which transfers the buffer block on which X resides to the disk and replaces the appropriate physical block there.

This scheme is illustrated in Figure 10.1.

Application programs interact with the database system through the following two operations:

- **read**(X,x_i), which assigns the value of data item X to the local variable x_i. This operation is executed as follows:

  1. If the block on which X resides is not in main memory, then issue **input**(X).

  2. Assign to x_i the value of X from the buffer block.

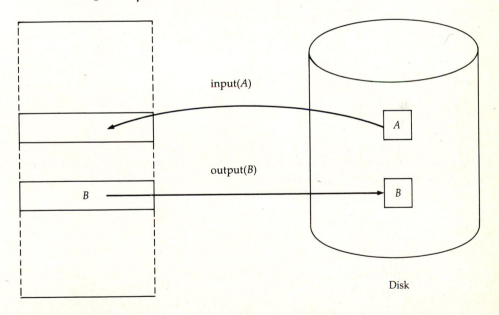

Figure 10.1   Block storage operations.

- **write**(X,x_i), which assigns the value of local variable x_i to data item X in the buffer block. This operation is executed as follows:

  1. If the block on which X resides is not in main memory, then issue **input**(X).

  2. Assign the value of x_i to X in the buffer block for X.

Note that both operations may require the transfer of a block from disk to main memory. They do not, however, require the transfer of a block from main memory to disk.

A buffer block is eventually written out to the disk either because the buffer manager needs the memory space for other purposes, or because the database system wishes to reflect the change to X on the disk. We shall say that the database system *force outputs* the buffer block of X if it issues an **output**(X).

When a program needs to access a data item X for the first time, it must execute **read**(X,x_i). All updates to X are then performed on x_i. After the program accesses X for the last time, it must execute **write**(X,x_i) in order to reflect the change to X in the database itself.

The **output**(X) operation need not take effect immediately after the **write**(X,x_i) is executed, since the block on which X resides may contain other data items that are still being accessed. Thus, the actual output takes place later. Notice that if the system crashes after the **write**(X,x_i) operation was executed but before **output**(X) was executed, the new value of X is never written to disk and, thus, is lost.

10.1.4 A Banking Example

Consider a somewhat simplified banking system consisting of several accounts and a set of application programs that access and update those accounts. Let P be a program that transfers \$50 from account A to account B. This program may be defined as:

$$
\begin{aligned}
P: \quad &\textbf{read}(A,a_1) \\
&a_1 := a_1 - 50 \\
&\textbf{write}(A,a_1) \\
&\textbf{read}(B,b_1) \\
&b_1 := b_1 + 50 \\
&\textbf{write}(B,b_1)
\end{aligned}
$$

Suppose that just prior to the execution of program P, the values of accounts A and B are \$1000 and \$2000, respectively. Further suppose that the main memory contains the buffer block of A, but not that of B (see Figure 10.2). When **read**(A,a_1) is executed, the action that takes place is to assign the value \$1000 to a_1. When **read**(B,b_1) is executed, however, the system must first bring the physical block of B to main memory (see Figure 10.3), and only then is b_1 assigned the value \$2000.

During the execution of P, the values of a_1 and a_2 are changed to \$950 and \$2050, respectively. Thus, after the write operations are executed, the state of the system is as depicted in Figure 10.4. Note that at this point (in this example), the **output**(A) and **output**(B) operations have not yet been executed. Therefore, the values of A and B on the buffer and physical blocks differ.

Several errors may be encountered during the execution of program P that may prevent P from completing successfully.

- **Logical error**. If, for example, accounts A or B do not exist in the database.

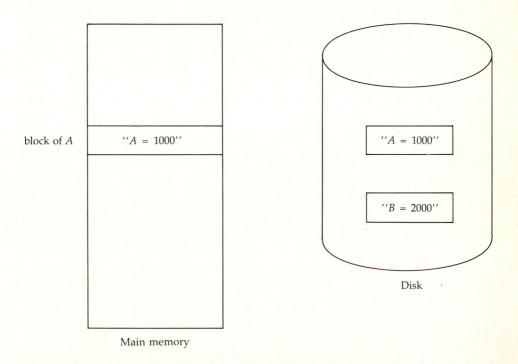

block of A "$A = 1000$"   "$A = 1000$"

                                              "$B = 2000$"

                                              Disk

Main memory

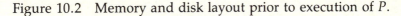

Figure 10.2   Memory and disk layout prior to execution of P.

- **System error**. If, for example, there is a parity check during the execution of P.

- **System crash**. If a system crash occurs, then the content of main memory is lost; in particular the buffer blocks for A and B and the local variables a_1 and b_1 are lost.

- **Disk failure**. Several of the physical blocks on the disk are damaged, resulting in erroneous information being transferred to main memory when **input**(A) is executed.

10.2 Transactions

Consider again our simplified banking system of Section 10.1.4 with a program P that transfers $50 from account A to account B. Let the current value of accounts A and B be $1000 and $2000, respectively. Suppose that program P executed to completion. Then, the final value of accounts A and B after this program executed is $950 and $2050, respectively. Thus, the sum of A and B is unchanged by this execution.

Suppose that during the execution of program P a failure has occurred that prevented P from completing its execution successfully. Further,

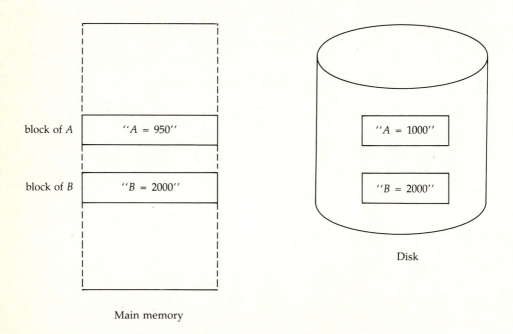

block of A "A = 950"   "A = 1000"

block of B "B = 2000"   "B = 2000"

Main memory   Disk

Figure 10.3   Memory and disk layout during the execution of P.

suppose that this happened after the **output**(*A*) operation was executed but before the **output**(*B*) operation was executed. In this case, the value of accounts *A* and *B* reflected in the database are $950 and $2000. We have destroyed $50 as a result of this failure. In particular, we note that the sum *A* + *B* is no longer preserved.

What we are pointing out is that, as the result of the failure, the state of the system no longer reflects a real state of the world that the database is supposed to capture. We term such a state as *inconsistent* state. Obviously, we must ensure that such inconsistencies are not visible in a database system. Note, however, that the system must at some point be in an inconsistent state. Even if program *P* executed to completion, there exists a point at which the value of account *A* is $950 and the value of account *B* is $2000, which is clearly an inconsistent state. This state, however, is eventually replaced by the consistent state where the value of account *A* is $950, and the value of account *B* is $2050.

The main point is in the way we define program units. This leads us to the concept of *transaction*, which is a program unit whose execution preserves the consistency of the database. If, before a transaction executes, the database is in a consistent state then, when the transaction completes its execution, the database is in a consistent state. We want the database to be in a consistent state whenever a transaction starts. In order to ensure

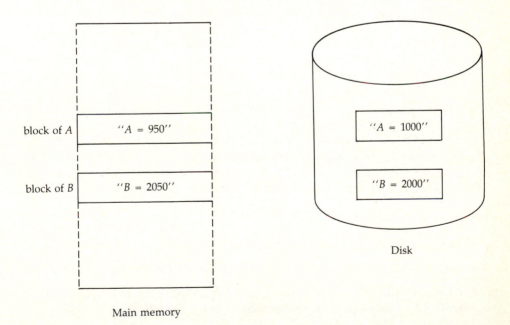

block of *A*   "*A* = 950"   "*A* = 1000"

block of *B*   "*B* = 2050"   "*B* = 2000"

Disk

Main memory

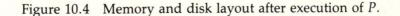

Figure 10.4   Memory and disk layout after execution of *P*.

that this is the case, we require that transactions be *atomic*, that is, either all the instructions associated with it are executed to completion, or none are performed. It is the responsibility of the recovery scheme to ensure the atomicity property.

Note that it is the responsibility of the programmer to define properly the various programs so that each preserves the consistency of the database. For example, the program to transfer funds from account A to account B could be defined to be composed of two separate programs, one which debits account A, and the other which credits account B. The execution of these two programs one after the other will indeed preserve consistency. However, each program by itself does not transform the database from a consistent state to a new consistent state.

A transaction is a program unit that accesses and possibly updates various data items. Each one of these items is read precisely once by the transaction and possibly is written at most once by the transaction if it updates that data item.

As pointed out in Section 10.1.1, a transaction may not always complete its execution successfully. Such a transaction is termed *aborted*. In order to ensure the atomicity property, an aborted transaction must have no affect on the state of the database. Thus, the state of the database must be restored to the state it was in just before the transaction in question started executing. We say that such a transaction has been *rolled back*. It is part of the responsibility of the recovery scheme to manage transaction aborts.

A transaction which successfully completes its execution is termed *committed*. A committed transaction that performs updates transforms the database into a new consistent state.

The effect of a committed transaction cannot be undone by aborting the transaction. It can only be undone by writing and executing a *compensating* transaction. The introduction of such transactions is usually the responsibility of the user, not the database system itself.

We need to be more precise about what is meant by "successful completion" of a transaction. To do so, we establish a simple abstract model. A transaction must be in one of the following states:

- **Active**, the initial state.

- **Partially committed**, after the last statement has been reached.

- **Failed**, after discovering that normal execution can no longer proceed.

- **Aborted**, after the transaction has been rolled back and the database restored to its state prior to the start of the transaction.

- **Committed**, after "successful" completion.

The state diagram corresponding to a transaction is depicted in Figure 10.5.

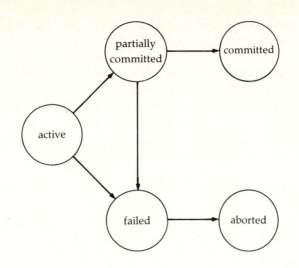

Figure 10.5   State diagram of a transaction.

We say that a transaction has committed only if it has entered the committed state. Similarly, we say that a transaction has aborted only if it has entered the aborted state. Furthermore, such a transaction will be said to have *terminated*. Once a transaction has terminated, a new transaction can be processed. (We shall defer to Chapter 11 consideration of cases where several transactions are being processed concurrently.)

A transaction starts in the active state. When it reaches its last statement it enters the partially committed state. At this point, the transaction has completed its execution, but it is still possible that it may have to be aborted since the actual output may not have been output to disk yet, and thus a hardware failure may preclude its successful completion. We, therefore, must be cautious when dealing with *observable external writes*, that is, those writes that cannot be "erased" (such as those to a terminal or printer). Most systems allow such writes to take place only after the transaction has entered the commit state. One way to implement such a scheme is to store any value associated with such external writes temporarily in a nonvolatile storage, and to perform the actual writes only at commit time. A committed transaction will then always be able to complete its external writes except in case of disk failure. If we wish to ensure that even a disk crash will not prevent an observable external write, an approximation of stable storage may be used.

A transaction enters the failed state after it is determined that the transaction can no longer proceed with its normal execution (for example, due to hardware or logical errors). Such a transaction must be rolled back.

Once this is accomplished, the transaction enters the aborted state. At this point in time the system has two options:

- **Restart the transaction.** This can take place only if the transaction was aborted as a result of some hardware or software error which was not created due to the internal logic of the transaction. A restarted transaction is considered to be a new transaction.

- **Kill the transaction.** This usually takes place because of some internal logical error which can be corrected only by rewriting the application program.

A transaction enters the committed state if it has partially committed and it is guaranteed that it will never be aborted. In the following, we describe various schemes for ensuring this property.

10.3 Incremental Log with Deferred Updates

Consider again our simplified banking system and transaction T that transfers $50 from account A to account B with initial values of A and B being $1000 and $2000, respectively. Suppose that a system crash has occurred during the execution of T after **output**(A) has taken place, but before **output**(B) was executed. Since the memory contents were lost, we do not know the fate of the transaction and, thus, could invoke one of two possible recovery procedures.

- **Reexecute** T. This will result in the value of A becoming $900 rather than $950. Thus, the system enters an inconsistent state.

- **Do not reexecute** T. The current system state is values of $950 and $2000 for A and B, respectively. Thus, we have entered an inconsistent state.

In either case, the database is left in an inconsistent state and thus this simple recovery scheme does not work.

The difficulty is that we have modified the database without having assurance that the transaction will indeed commit. This suggests the following new recovery scheme.

During the execution of a transaction all the write operations are deferred until the transaction partially commits. All updates are recorded on a system-maintained file, called the *log*. When a transaction partially commits, the information on the log associated with the transaction is used in executing the deferred writes. If the system crashes before the transaction completes its execution, or, if the transaction aborts, then the information on the log is simply ignored.

The execution of transaction T_i proceeds as follows. Before T_i starts its execution a record <T_i **start**> is written to the log. During its execution, any **write**(X, x_j) operation by T_i results in the writing of a new record to the log. Each such record consists of the following fields:

- Transaction name (that is, T_i).

- Data item name (that is, X).

- New value of the data item (that is, the current value of x_j).

Finally, when T_i partially commits, a record <T_i **commit**> is written to the log.

When transaction T_i partially commits, the records associated with it in the log are used in executing the deferred writes. Since a failure may occur while this updating is taking place, we must ensure that, prior to the start of these updates, all the log records are written out to stable storage. Once this has been accomplished, the actual updating can take place. At this point, the transaction enters the committed state.

To illustrate this, let us reconsider our simplified banking system. Let T_0 be a transaction that transfers \$50 from account A to account B. This transaction may be defined as follows,

$$T_0: \textbf{read}(A, a_1)$$
$$a_1 := a_1 - 50$$
$$\textbf{write}(A, a_1)$$
$$\textbf{read}(B, b_1)$$
$$b_1 := b_1 + 50$$
$$\textbf{write}(B, b_1)$$

Let T_1 be a transaction that withdraws \$100 from account C. This transaction can be defined as

$$T_1: \textbf{read}(C, c_1)$$
$$c_1 := c_1 - 100$$
$$\textbf{write}(C, c_1)$$

Suppose that these transactions are executed one after the other in the order T_0 followed by T_1, and that the value of accounts A, B, and C before the execution took place was \$1000, \$2000, and \$700, respectively.

The portion of the log containing the relevant information concerning these two transactions is presented in Figure 10.6.

There are various orders in which the actual outputs can take place to both the database system and the log as a result of the execution of T_0 and T_1. One such order is presented in Figure 10.7. Note that the value of A is changed in the database only after the record $<T_0,A,950>$ has been placed in the log.

Using the log, the system can handle any failure which does not result in the loss of information on nonvolatile storage. The recovery scheme uses the following recovery procedure:

- **redo**(T_i), which sets the value of all data items updated by transaction T_i to the new values.

The set of data items updated by T_i and their respective new values can be found in the log.

The **redo** operation must be *idempotent*; that is, executing it several times must be equivalent to executing it once. This is required in order to guarantee correct behavior even if a failure occurs during the recovery process.

After a failure has occurred, the recovery subsystem consults the log to determine which transactions need to be redone. Transaction T_i needs to be redone if the log contains both the record $<T_i$ **starts**$>$ and the record $<T_i$ **commits**$>$. Thus, if the system crashes after the transaction completes its execution, the information in the log is used in restoring the state of the system to a previous consistent state.

To illustrate this, let us return to our banking example with transactions T_0 and T_1 executed one after the other in the order T_0 followed by T_1. Figure 10.6 shows the log that results from the complete execution of T_0 and T_1. Let us suppose that the system crashes before the completion of the transactions and see how the recovery technique restores

$<T_0$ **starts**$>$
$<T_0,A,950>$
$<T_0,B,2050>$
$<T_0$ **commits**$>$
$<T_1$ **starts**$>$
$<T_1,C,600>$
$<T_1$ **commits**$>$

Figure 10.6   Portion of the system log corresponding to T_0 and T_1.

Log   Database

$<T_0$ **starts**$>$

$<T_0,A,950>$

$<T_0,B,2050>$

$<T_0$ **commits**$>$

$A = 950$

$B = 2050$

$<T_1$ **starts**$>$

$<T_1,C,600>$

$<T_1$ **commits**$>$

$C = 600$

Figure 10.7   State of system log and database corresponding to T_0 and T_1.

the database to a consistent state. Assume that the crash occurs just after the log record for the step:

$$\mathbf{write}(B,b_1)$$

of transaction T_0 has been written to stable storage. The log at the time of the crash is as shown in Figure 10.8a. When the system comes back up, no recovery action need be taken, since no commit record appears in the log. The values of accounts A and B remain \$1000 and \$2000, respectively.

Now, let us assume the crash comes just after the log record for the step:

$$\mathbf{write}(C,c_1)$$

of transaction T_1 has been written to stable storage. The log at the time of the crash is as shown in Figure 10.8b. When the system comes back up, recovery action needs to be taken for T_0 since the record:

$$<T_0 \textbf{ commits}>$$

appears in the log. The operation **redo**(T_0) is performed. After this operation takes place, the values of accounts A and B are \$950 and \$2050, respectively. The value of account C remains \$700.

Assume a crash occurs just after the log record

$$<T_1 \textbf{ commits}>$$

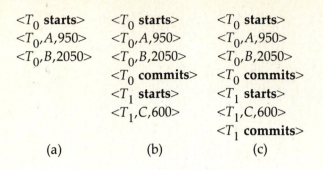

Figure 10.8   Three snapshots of the same system log.

is written to stable storage. When the system comes back up, two commit records are in the log: one for T_0 and one for T_1. Therefore, the operations **redo**(T_0) and **redo**(T_1) must be performed. After these operations take place, the values of accounts A, B, and C are \$950, \$2050, and \$600, respectively.

Finally, let us consider a case in which a second system crash occurs during recovery from the first crash. Some changes may have been made to the database as a result of the **redo** operations, but it may be the case that not all changes have been made. When the system comes up after the second crash, recovery proceeds exactly as in the above examples. For each commit record:

$$<T_i \textbf{ commits}>$$

found in the log, the operation **redo**(T_i) is performed. In other words, the recovery actions are restarted from the beginning. Since **redo** writes values to the database independent of the values currently in the database, the result of a successful second attempt at **redo** is the same as if **redo** had succeeded the first time.

10.4 Incremental Log with Immediate Updates

Another technique for recovery is to apply all the updates directly to the database and keep an *incremental log* of all the changes to the system state. If a crash occurs, the information in the log is used in restoring the state of the system to a previous consistent state.

Before a transaction T_i starts its execution, a record $<T_i$ **start**$>$ is written to the log. During its execution, any **write**(X,x_j) operation by T_i is *preceded* by the writing of a new record to the log. Each such record consists of the following fields:

- Transaction name (that is, T_i).

- Data item name (that is, X).

- Old value of the data item.

- New value of the data item.

When T_i partially commits, a record $<T_i$ **commit**$>$ is written to the log.

Since the information in the log is used in reconstructing the state of the database, we cannot allow the actual update to the database to take place before the corresponding log record is written out to stable storage. We therefore require that prior to executing an **output**(X) operation, the log records corresponding to X be written onto stable storage. We shall return to this issue in Section 10.6.

To illustrate this, let us reconsider our simplified banking system with transactions T_0 and T_1 executed one after the other in the order T_0 followed by T_1. The portion of the log containing the relevant information concerning these two transactions is presented in Figure 10.9.

One possible order in which the actual outputs took place to both the database system and the log as a result of the execution of T_0 and T_1 is described in Figure 10.10.

Using the log, the system can handle any failure which does not result in the loss of information on nonvolatile storage. The recovery scheme utilizes two recovery procedures:

- **undo**(T_i), which restores the value of all data items updated by transaction T_i to the old values.

- **redo**(T_i), which sets the value of all data items updated by transaction T_i to the new values.

$$<T_0 \text{ starts}>$$
$$<T_0, A, 1000, 950>$$
$$<T_0, B, 2000, 2050>$$
$$<T_0 \text{ commits}>$$
$$<T_1 \text{ starts}>$$
$$<T_1, C, 700, 600>$$
$$<T_1 \text{ commits}>$$

Figure 10.9   Portion of the system log corresponding to T_0 and T_1.

The set of data items updated by T_i and their respective old and new values can be found in the log.

The **undo** and **redo** operations must be idempotent in order to guarantee correct behavior even if a failure occurs during the recovery process.

After a failure has occurred, the recovery scheme consults the log to determine which transactions need to be redone and which need to be undone. This classification of transactions is accomplished as follows:

- Transaction T_i needs to be undone if the log contains the record $<T_i$ **starts**$>$ but does not contain the record $<T_i$ **commits**$>$.

- Transaction T_i needs to be redone if the log contains both the record $<T_i$ **starts**$>$ and $<T_i$ **commits**$>$.

To illustrate this, let us return to our banking example with transaction T_0 and T_1 executed one after the other in the order T_0 followed by T_1. Let us suppose that the system crashes before the completion of the transactions. We shall consider three cases. The logs for each of our examples appear in Figures 10.11a to c.

First, let us assume that the crash occurs just after the log record for the step:

$$\textbf{write}(B, b_1)$$

of transaction T_0 has been written to stable storage. Figure 10.11a shows the log at the time of the crash. When the system comes back up, it finds

Log	Database
$<T_0$ **starts**$>$	
$<T_0, A, 1000, 950>$	
$<T_0, B, 2000, 2050>$	
	$A = 950$
	$B = 2050$
$<T_0$ **commits**$>$	
$<T_1$ **starts**$>$	
$<T_1, C, 700, 600>$	
	$C = 600$
$<T_1$ **commits**$>$	

Figure 10.10   State of system log and database corresponding to T_0 and T_1.

the record $<T_0$ **starts**$>$ in the log, but no corresponding $<T_0$ **commits**$>$ record. This means that transaction T_0 must be undone, so an **undo**(T_0) is performed. As a result, the values in accounts A and B are restored to ~~$950,~~ $1000, and $2000, respectively.

Next, let us assume that the crash comes just after the log record for the step:

$$\textbf{write}(C, c_1)$$

of transaction T_1 has been written to stable storage. Figure 10.11b shows the log at the time of the crash. When the system comes back up, two recovery actions need to be taken. The operation **undo**(T_1) must be performed since the record $<T_1$ **starts**$>$ appears in the log, but there is no record $<T_1$ **commits**$>$. The operation **redo**(T_0) must be performed since the log contains both the record $<T_0$ **starts**$>$ and the record $<T_0$ **commits**$>$. At the end of the entire recovery procedure, the values of accounts A, B, and C are $950, $2050, and $700, respectively.

Finally, let us assume that the crash occurs just after the log record:

$$<T_1 \textbf{ commits}>$$

has been written to stable storage. When the system comes back up, both T_0 and T_1 need to be redone since the records $<T_0$ **starts**$>$ and $<T_0$ **commits**$>$ appear in the log as do the records $<T_1$ **starts**$>$ and $<T_1$ **commits**$>$. After the recovery procedures **redo**(T_0) and **redo**(T_1) are performed, the values in accounts A, B, and C are $950, $2050, and $600, respectively.

$<T_0$ **starts**$>$	$<T_0$ **starts**$>$	$<T_0$ **starts**$>$
$<T_0,A,1000,950>$	$<T_0,A,1000,950>$	$<T_0,A,1000,950>$
$<T_0,B,2000,2050>$	$<T_0,B,2000,2050>$	$<T_0,B,2000,2050>$
	$<T_0$ **commits**$>$	$<T_0$ **commits**$>$
	$<T_1$ **starts**$>$	$<T_1$ **starts**$>$
	$<T_1,C,700,600>$	$<T_1,C,700,600>$
		$<T_1$ **commits**$>$
(a)	(b)	(c)

Figure 10.11   Three snapshots of the same system log.

10.5 Checkpoints

When a system failure occurs, it is necessary to consult the log in order to determine those transactions that need to be redone and those that need to be undone. In principle, the entire log needs to be searched in order to determine this. There are two major difficulties with this approach:

- The searching process is time-consuming.

- Most of the transactions that need to be redone have already actually written their updates into the database and do not really need to be redone. Redoing them will cause no harm but will cause recovery to take longer.

In order to reduce these types of overhead, we introduce the concept of *checkpoints*. During execution, the system maintains the log as described above. In addition, however, the system periodically performs checkpoints, which requires the following sequence of actions to take place:

1. Output all log records currently residing in main memory onto stable storage.

2. Output all modified buffer blocks to the disk.

3. Output a log record <**checkpoint**> onto stable storage.

With the checkpoint mechanism, we can refine our previous recovery schemes. After a failure has occurred, the recovery scheme examines the log to determine the last transaction T_i that started executing before the last checkpoint took place. Such a transaction can be found by searching the log backwards to find the first <**checkpoint**> record and then finding the subsequent <T_i **start**> record.

Once transaction T_i has been identified, the **redo** and **undo** operations need to be applied only to transaction T_i and all transactions T_j that started executing after transaction T_i. The operations that are required are as follows:

- For all transactions T_k such that the record <T_k **commits**> appears in the log, execute **redo**(T_k).

- For all transactions T_k that have no <T_k **commits**> record in the log, execute **undo**(T_k).

Obviously, the **undo** operation need not be applied when the *log with the deferred update* scheme is being employed.

To illustrate this, consider the set of transactions $\{T_0, T_1, ..., T_{100}\}$ executed in the order of the subscripts. Suppose that the last checkpoint took place during the execution of transaction T_{67}. Thus only transactions $T_{67}, T_{68}, ..., T_{100}$ need to be considered during the recovery scheme. Each of these needs to be redone if it has committed; otherwise it needs to be undone.

10.6 Buffer Management

In this section, we consider several subtle details that are essential to the implementation of a crash recovery scheme that ensures data consistency and imposes a minimal amount of overhead on interactions with the database.

In the abstract transaction model we have been using, we assume that whenever an **input**(X) operation is executed, there is room in main memory for that block. In real systems, this may not always be the case. Operating systems that provide *virtual memory* deal with this situation by choosing some block in main memory and issuing an **output** operation to write that block to disk. This provides space in main memory for the **input** to succeed. In Chapter 7, we considered how database buffer managers might choose a block to be written back to disk.

The strategy of outputing blocks to disk that is typically used by operating systems conflicts with the requirements of our crash recovery scheme. We impose the additional requirement that all log records pertaining to a block be written to stable storage before that block is output to disk.

Consider, again, our banking example with transactions T_0 and T_1. Suppose that the state of the log is as shown in Figure 10.12 and that transaction T_0 issues a **read**(B,b_1). Assume that the physical block on which B resides is not in main memory, and that main memory is full. Suppose that the block on which A resides is chosen to be output to disk. If the system outputs this block to disk and then a crash occurs, the values in the database for accounts A, B, and C are $950, $2000, and $700, respectively.

$<T_0$ **starts**$>$
$<T_0,A,1000,950>$

Figure 10.12   Banking example log.

This is an inconsistent database state. As we noted earlier, the log record

$$<T_0, A, 1000, 950>$$

must be output to stable storage prior to the output of the block on which A resides.

The above example leads us to state the following rule for buffer management in database systems:

- Before executing an output operation on a block in main memory, all log records pertaining to data on that block must be force output to stable storage, if they are not already in stable storage.

When log records are output to stable storage, it is advantageous to output entire blocks of log records since it is typically as costly to output a block as to output a part of a block. This allows us to reduce the overhead of log output operations since the force output of a log record causes other log records to be output at zero cost.

The same observation applies to log records written prior to a transaction entering the committed state.

10.7 Shadow Paging

An alternative to log-based crash recovery techniques is *shadow paging*. Under certain circumstances, shadow paging may require fewer disk accesses than the log-based methods discussed above. There are, however, disadvantages to the shadow-block approach, as we shall see.

As before, the database is partitioned into some number of fixed-length blocks which are referred to as *pages*. The term page is borrowed from operating systems since we are using a paging scheme for memory management. Let us assume there are n pages, numbered 1 through n. (In practice n may be in the hundreds of thousands.) These pages need not be stored in any particular order on disk (there are many reasons for this, as we saw in Chapter 7). However, there must be a way to find the ith page of the database for any given i. This is accomplished using a *page table* as shown in Figure 10.13. The page table has n entries, one for each database page. Each entry contains a pointer to a page on disk. The first entry contains a pointer to the first page of the database, the second entry points to the second page, etc. The example in Figure 10.13 shows that the logical order of database pages need not correspond to the physical order in which the pages are placed on disk.

The key idea behind the shadow-paging technique is to maintain *two* page tables during the life of a transaction, the *current* page table and the *shadow* page table. When the transaction starts, both page tables are

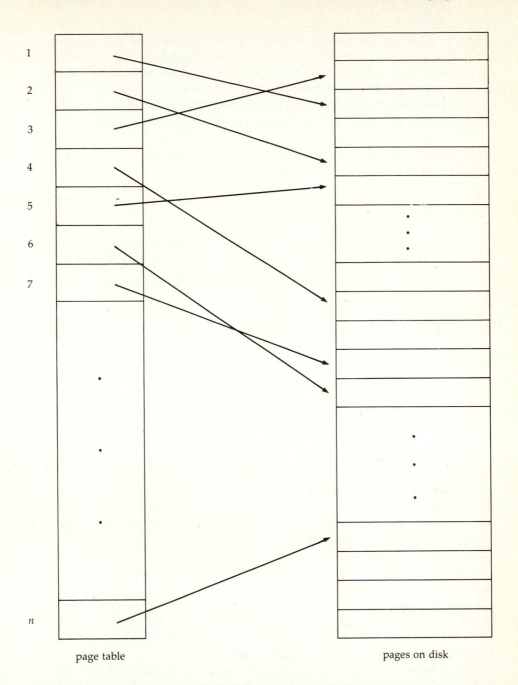

Figure 10.13   Sample page table.

identical. The shadow page table is never changed during the duration of the transaction. The current page table may be changed when a transaction performs a write operation. All **input** and **output** operations use the current page table to locate database pages on disk.

Suppose the transaction performs a **write**(X,x_j) operation and that X resides on the ith page. The write operation is executed as follows:

1. If the ith page (that is, the page on which X resides) is not already in main memory, then issue **input**(X).

2. If this is the first write performed on the ith page by this transaction, then modify the current page table as follows:

   a. Find an unused page on disk. Typically, the database system has access to a list of unused (free) pages, as we saw in Chapter 7.

   b. Delete the page found in step 2a from the list of free page frames.

   c. Modify the current page table so that the ith entry points to the page found in step 2a.

3. Assign the value of x_j to X in the buffer page.

Let us compare the above action for a write operation to that described in Section 10.1.3. The only difference is that we have added a new step. Steps 1 and 3 above correspond to steps 1 and 2 in Section 10.1.3. The added step, step 2 above, manipulates the current page table. Figure 10.14 shows the shadow and current page tables for a transaction performing a write to the fourth page of a database consisting of 10 pages.

Intuitively, the shadow page approach to recovery is to store the shadow page table in nonvolatile storage so that the state of the database prior to the execution of the transaction may be recovered in the event of a crash, or transaction abort. When the transaction commits, the current page table is written to nonvolatile storage. The current page table then becomes the new shadow page table and the next transaction is allowed to begin execution. It is important that the shadow page table be stored in nonvolatile storage since it provides our only means of locating database pages. The current page table may be kept in main memory (volatile storage). We do not care if the current page table is lost in a crash, since the system recovers using the shadow page table.

Successful recovery requires that we find the shadow page table on disk after a crash. A simple way of doing this is to choose one fixed location in stable storage that contains the disk address of the shadow page table. When the system comes back up after a crash, we copy the shadow page table into main memory and use it for subsequent transaction

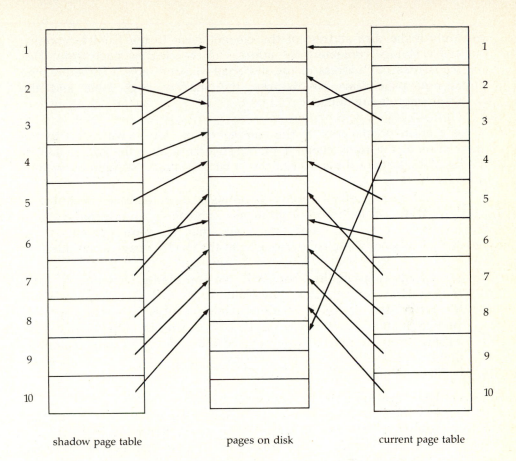

shadow page table   pages on disk   current page table

Figure 10.14   Shadow and current page tables.

processing. Because of our definition of the **write** operation, we are guaranteed that the shadow page table points to the database pages corresponding to the state of the database prior to any transaction that was active at the time of the crash. Thus, aborts are automatic. Unlike our log-based schemes, no **undo** operations need be invoked.

In order to commit a transaction, we must do the following:

1. Ensure that all buffer pages in main memory that have been changed by the transaction are output to disk. (Note that these output operations will not change database pages pointed to by some entry in the shadow page table.)

2. Output the current page table to disk. Note that we must not overwrite the shadow page table since we may need it for recovery from a crash.

3. Output the disk address of the current page to the fixed location in stable storage containing the address of the shadow page table. This overwrites the address of the old shadow page table. Therefore, the current page table has become the shadow page table and the transaction is committed.

If a crash occurs prior to the completion of step 3, we revert to the state prior to the transaction. If the crash occurs after the completion of step 3, the effects of the transaction will be preserved. No **redo** operations need be invoked.

Shadow paging offers several advantages over log-based techniques. The overhead of log-record output is eliminated, and recovery from crashes is significantly faster (since no **undo** or **redo** operations are needed). However, there are drawbacks to the shadow page technique:

- **Data fragmentation**. In Chapter 7, we considered strategies to keep related database pages close physically on the disk. This locality allows for faster data transfer. Shadow paging causes database pages to change location when they are updated. As a result, either we lose the locality property of the pages or we must resort to more complex, higher-overhead schemes for physical storage management. (See the bibliographic notes for references.)

- **Garbage collection**. Each time a transaction commits, the database pages containing the old version of data changed by the transaction become inaccessible. In Figure 10.14, the page pointed to by the fourth entry of the shadow page table will become inaccessible once the transaction of that example commits. Such pages are considered *garbage* since they are not part of free space and do not contain usable information. Garbage may be created also as a side-effect of crashes. Periodically, it is necessary to find all the garbage pages and add them to the list of free pages. This process, called *garbage collection*, imposes additional overhead and complexity on the system. There are several standard algorithms for garbage collection. See the bibliographic notes for references.

In addition to the drawbacks of shadow paging we have just mentioned, shadow paging is more difficult than logging to adapt to systems that allow several transactions to execute concurrently. In such systems, some logging is typically required even if shadow paging is used. System R, for example, uses a combination of shadow paging and a logging scheme similar to that presented in Section 10.4. It is possible to use the log-based schemes of this chapter with minor changes in a concurrent database system without the use of shadow paging, as will be discussed in Chapter 11.

10.8 Failure with Loss of Nonvolatile Storage

Until now, we have considered only the case where a failure results in the loss of information residing in volatile storage while the content of the nonvolatile storage remains intact. Although failures in which the content of nonvolatile storage is lost are rare, we nevertheless need to be prepared to deal with this type of failure. In this section, we discuss only disk-type storage. Our discussions apply as well to other nonvolatile storage types.

The basic scheme is to *dump* the entire content of the database to stable storage periodically, say once a day. For example, we may dump the database to one or more magnetic tapes. If a failure occurs that results in the loss of physical database blocks, the most recent dump is used in restoring the database to a previous consistent state. Once this has been accomplished, the log is used to bring the database system to the most recent consistent state.

More precisely, no transaction may be active during the dump procedure and a procedure similar to checkpointing must take place.

1. Output all log records currently residing in main memory onto stable storage.

2. Output all buffer blocks onto the disk.

3. Output a log record <**dump**> onto the stable storage.

Once this has been accomplished, the dumping procedure may start. It is crucial that during this procedure no transaction execution can take place.

To recover from the loss of nonvolatile storage, the log is consulted and all the transactions that have committed since the last dump occurred are redone. Notice that no **undo** operations need to be executed.

10.9 Stable Storage Implementation

As pointed out in Section 10.1.1, information residing in stable storage is *never* lost. To implement such a storage, we need to replicate the needed information in several nonvolatile storage media (usually disk) with independent failure modes, and update the information in a controlled manner to ensure that failure during data transfer does not damage the needed information. For the remainder of this section, we will discuss the issue of how one can protect the storage media from failure during data transfer.

Block transfer to and from memory and disk storage can result in:

- **Successful completion**. The transferred information arrived safely at its destination.

- **Partial failure**. A failure occurred in the midst of transfer and the target block has incorrect information.

- **Total failure**. The failure occurred sufficiently early during the transfer so that target block remains intact.

We require that if a data-transfer failure occurs, the system detects it and invokes a recovery procedure to restore the block to a consistent state. To do so, the system must maintain two physical blocks for each logical database block. An output operation is executed as follows:

1. Write the information onto the first physical block.

2. When the first write successfully completes, write the same information onto the second physical block.

3. The output is completed only after the second write successfully completes.

During recovery, each pair of physical blocks is examined. If both are the same and no detectable error exists, then no further actions are necessary. If one block contains a detectable error, then replace its content with the value of the second block. If both blocks contain no detectable error, but they differ in content, then replace the content of one of them (whichever) with the value of the other. This recovery procedure ensures that a write to stable storage either succeeds completely or results in no change. The attempt to write to stable storage succeeds only if all copies are written.

10.10 Summary

A computer system, like any other mechanical or electrical device, is subject to failure. There are a variety of causes of such failure, including disk crash, power failure, and software errors. In each of these cases, information concerning the database system is lost. An integral part of a database system is a recovery scheme which is responsible for the detection of failures and the restoration of the database to a state that existed prior to the occurrence of the failure.

There are various types of failure that may occur in a system, including logical errors, system errors, system crash, and disk failure. Each of these must be dealt with in a different manner. The simplest type of failure to deal with is one which does not result in the loss of information in the system. The ones that are more difficult to deal with are those that do result in loss of information.

In case of failure, the state of the database system may no longer be consistent; that is, it may not reflect a state of the world that the database is supposed to capture. To preserve consistency, we require that each transaction be atomic; that is, either all the instructions associated with it are executed to completion, or none are performed. It is the responsibility of the recovery scheme to ensure the atomicity property.

There are three different schemes for ensuring atomicity.

- **Incremental log with deferred updates**. During the execution of a transaction all the write operations are deferred until the transaction partially commits. All updates are recorded on the system log which must be kept in stable storage. When a transaction partially commits, the information on the log associated with the transaction is used in executing the deferred writes. If the system crashes before the transaction completes its execution, or, if the transaction aborts, then the information on the log is simply ignored. Using the log, the system can handle any failure which does not result in the loss of information on nonvolatile storage. In particular, after a failure has occurred the recovery scheme consults the log and each committed transaction is redone. In order to reduce the overhead of searching the log and redoing transactions, the *checkpointing* technique can be used.

- **Incremental log with immediate updates**. All updates are applied directly to the database and an *incremental log* of all the changes to the system state is kept in stable storage. If a crash occurs, the information in the log is used in restoring the state of the system to a previous consistent state. This is accomplished by using the **undo** and **redo** operation. As before, the log can be used to handle any failure which does not result in the loss of information on nonvolatile storage, and the checkpointing technique can be used to reduce the overhead of searching the log and performing undo and redo operations.

- **Shadow paging**. Two page tables are maintained during the life of a transaction: the *current* page table and the *shadow* page table. When the transaction starts, both page tables are identical. The shadow page table is never changed during the duration of the transaction. The current page table may be changed when a transaction performs a **write** operation. All **input** and **output** operations use the current page table to locate database pages on disk. When the transaction partially commits, the shadow page table is discarded and the current table becomes the new page table. If the transaction aborts, the current page table is simple discarded.

In order to recover from failures that result in the loss of nonvolatile storage, the entire contents of the database need to be dumped onto stable storage periodically, say once a day. If a failure occurs that results in the loss of physical database blocks, the most recent dump is used in restoring the database to a previous consistent state. Once this has been accomplished, the log is used to bring the database system to the most recent consistent state.

Exercises

10.1 Compare the two log-based recovery schemes in terms of ease of implementation and overhead cost.

10.2 Suppose that you have been hired to implement a recovery scheme on a new database system. Which of the three recovery schemes discussed in this chapter (Sections 10.3, 10.4, and 10.5) would you choose? How might your choice depend on the particular application?

10.3 Explain the purpose of the checkpoint mechanism. How often should a database management system do a checkpoint?

10.4 Compare the shadow paging recovery scheme with the log-based recovery schemes in terms of ease of implementation and overhead cost.

10.5 Explain the difference between the three storage types -- volatile, non-volatile, and stable in terms of cost.

10.6 Stable storage cannot really be implemented.

    a. Explain why.

    b. How do database systems deal with this problem?

10.7 Explain the recovery procedure that needs to take place after a disk crash.

10.8 Explain the reasons why recovery of interactive transactions is more difficult to deal with than recovery of batch transactions. Is there a simple way to deal with this difficulty?

10.9 What is the purpose of compensating transactions? Present two examples of their use.

10.10 If immediate update is used in a system, show by an example how an inconsistent database state could result if log records for a transaction are not force-output to disk prior to committing that transaction.

10.11 Suppose that we allow transactions to be nested within other transactions. Discuss the modifications that need to be made in each of the recovery schemes covered in this chapter.

10.12 Consider a database consisting of 10 consecutive disk blocks (block 1, block 2, ..., block 10). Show a possible physical ordering of the blocks after the following updates, assuming that shadow paging is used, and the buffer in main memory can hold only 3 blocks, and a LRU strategy is used for buffer management.

> read block 3
> read block 7
> read block 5
> read block 3
> read block 1
> modify block 1
> read block 10
> modify block 5

Bibliographic Notes

Two early papers presenting some initial theoretical work in the area of recovery are Davies [1972] and Bjork [1973].

Most of the recovery mechanisms introduced in this chapter are based on those used in System R. An overview of the recovery scheme of that system is presented by Gray et al. [1981a]. The shadow paging mechanism of System R is described by Lorie [1977].

Discussions concerning analytic models for rollback and recovery strategies in database systems are offered by Chandy et al. [1975]. A fast transaction oriented logging scheme is presented by Reuter [1980].

Two tutorial and survey papers covering various recovery techniques for database systems are presented by Gray [1978] and Verhofstadt [1978]. A comprehensive presentation of the principles of recovery is offered by Haerder and Reuter [1983]. Basic textbook discussions are offered by Ullman [1982a] and Date [1983].

Recent work in the theory of transaction processing has involved long-duration transactions and nested transactions. Moss [1981] and Lynch [1983] discuss nested transactions. Gray [1981] discusses long-duration transactions and alternatives to the transaction model presented in this chapter.

11

Concurrency Control

One of the most important concepts in modern systems is undoubtedly *multiprogramming*. By having several transactions executing at the same time, the processor may be shared among them. This scheme improves the overall efficiency of the computer system by getting more work done in less time.

The idea of multiprogramming is relatively simple. A transaction is executed until it must wait, typically for the completion of some input or output request. In a uniprogrammed computer system, the processor would just sit idle. All of this waiting time is wasted; no useful work is accomplished. With multiprogramming, we try to use this time productively. Several transactions are available for execution at one time. When a transaction has to wait, the system takes the processor away from that transaction and gives it to another transaction. The benefits of multiprogramming are increased processor utilization and higher total transaction *throughput*, that is, the amount of work which is accomplished in a given time interval.

There are two complementary schemes for implementing multiprogramming: noninteractive systems (batch systems) and interactive systems (time-sharing systems). Interactive transactions tend to be composed of many short transactions where the user waits for the result. Accordingly, the *response* time of interactive transactions should be quite short, on the order of seconds at most. Since each transaction tends to be short, only a small amount of processor time is needed for each user. Since the system switches rapidly from one user to the next, each user is given the impression that he has his own computer, while it is actually one computer shared among many users.

Thus, in a multiprogramming environment several transactions may be executed concurrently. As we shall see in this chapter, it is necessary for the system to control the interaction among the concurrent transactions in order to prevent them from destroying the consistency of the database. This control is achieved through a variety of mechanisms which we will refer to as *concurrency control* schemes.

To simplify notation, we shall deviate from our transaction definition syntax of Chapter 10 and drop the temporary local variable of the **read** and

write operations. We shall assume that the temporary local variable has the same name as that of the datum being accessed. Thus, for the remainder of this book, we shall use **read**(Q) and **write**(Q) for **read**(Q,q) and **write**(Q,q).

11.1 Serializability

Consider the simplified banking system of Chapter 10 consisting of several accounts and a set of transactions that access and update those accounts. Let T_0 and T_1 be two transactions that transfer funds from one account to another. Transaction T_0 transfers \$50 from account A to account B and is defined as:

$$
\begin{aligned}
T_0: \quad &\textbf{read}(A); \\
&A := A - 50; \\
&\textbf{write}(A); \\
&\textbf{read}(B); \\
&B := B + 50; \\
&\textbf{write}(B).
\end{aligned}
$$

Transaction T_1 transfers 10 percent of the balance from account A to account B and is defined as:

$$
\begin{aligned}
T_1: \quad &\textbf{read}(A); \\
&temp := A * 0.1; \\
&A := A - temp; \\
&\textbf{write}(A); \\
&\textbf{read}(B); \\
&B := B + temp; \\
&\textbf{write}(B).
\end{aligned}
$$

Let the current value of accounts A and B be \$1000 and \$2000, respectively. Suppose that the two transactions are executed one at a time in the order T_0 followed by T_1. This execution sequence is represented in Figure 11.1. The final value of accounts A and B after this execution takes place is \$855 and \$2145, respectively. Thus, the total amount of money in accounts A and B, that is, the sum $A + B$, is preserved after the execution of both transactions.

Similarly, if the transactions are executed one at a time in the order T_1 followed by T_0, then the corresponding execution sequence is that of Figure 11.2. Again, as expected, the sum $A + B$ is preserved, and the final value of accounts A and B is \$850 and \$2150, respectively.

The execution sequences described above are called *schedules*. They represent the order in which instructions are executed in the system in

T_0	T_1
read(*A*)	
A := *A* − 50	
write(*A*)	
read(*B*)	
B := *B* + 50	
write(*B*)	
	read(*A*)
	temp := *A* * 0.1
	A := *A* − *temp*
	write(*A*)
	read(*B*)
	B := *B* + *temp*
	write(*B*)

Figure 11.1   Schedule 1.

chronological ordering. Clearly, a schedule must preserve the order in which the instructions appear in each individual transaction. For example, in transaction T_0, the instruction **write**(*A*) must appear before the instruction **read**(*B*), in any valid schedule. In the following, we shall refer to the first execution sequence (T_0 followed by T_1) as schedule 1, and the second execution sequence (T_1 followed by T_0) as schedule 2.

T_0	T_1
	read(*A*)
	temp := *A* * 0.1
	A := *A* − *temp*
	write(*A*)
	read(*B*)
	B := *B* + *temp*
	write(*B*)
read(*A*)	
A := *A* − 50	
write(*A*)	
read(*B*)	
B := *B* + 50	
write(*B*)	

Figure 11.2   Schedule 2.

The schedules described above are called *serial schedules*. Each serial schedule consists of a sequence of instructions from various transactions where the instructions belonging to one single transaction appear together in that schedule. Thus, for a set of n transactions there exists $n!$ different legal serial schedules.

When several transactions are executed in parallel, the corresponding schedule need no longer be serial. Thus, the number of possible schedules for a set of n transactions is much larger than $n!$. Returning to our previous example, suppose that the two transactions are executed in parallel. Several execution sequences are possible since the various instructions from both transactions may now be interleaved. One such possible schedule is shown in Figure 11.3. After this execution takes place, we arrive at a state where the final values of accounts A and B are $950 and $2100, respectively. This is an incorrect result, since we have gained $50 in the process of the concurrent execution. Indeed, the sum $A + B$ is not preserved by the execution of the two transactions.

Not all parallel executions result in an incorrect state. To illustrate this, consider the nonserial schedule of Figure 11.4. Upon execution of this schedule, we arrive at the same state as the one in which the transactions are executed serially in the order T_0 followed by T_1. The sum $A + B$ is indeed preserved.

The first nonserial schedule, schedule 3, resulted in the system entering a final state which is an *inconsistent* state. As pointed out, we have expected that the sum $A + B$ be preserved after the execution of both transactions. Indeed, this was the case for the two possible serial

T_0	T_1
read(A)	
$A := A - 50$	
	read(A)
	$temp := A * 0.1$
	$A := A - temp$
	write(A)
	read(B)
write(A)	
read(B)	
$B := B + 50$	
write(B)	
	$B := B + temp$
	write(B)

Figure 11.3   Schedule 3.

schedules, schedules 1 and 2. Nevertheless, this consistency requirement is not met in schedule 3.

We require that a transaction be a program that preserves consistency. That is, each transaction, when executed alone, transfers the system from one consistent state into a new consistent state. During its execution, however, the system may temporarily enter an inconsistent state as we saw in Chapter 10. A natural way to define correctness in a concurrent system is to require that the outcome of processing a set of transactions concurrently be the same as one produced by running these transactions serially in some order. A system that ensures this property is said to ensure *serializability*.

The "same outcome" notion depends on the type of operations a transaction performs on a data item between the time the transaction reads the data item and the time the transaction writes the data item out. If the outcome of the execution of a pair of operations is the same regardless of the order of execution, those operations are said to *commute*. In general, it is difficult to determine whether two operations commute. For this reason we will not interpret the type of operations that a transaction can perform on a particular data item Q. We thus assume that between the execution of a **read**(Q) and **write**(Q) instruction, a transaction may perform an arbitrary sequence of operations on Q. Thus, from our point of view, the significant operations of a transaction are only its read and write instructions.

In order to formalize the concept of serializability, we need to define the notion of *equivalent* schedules. We shall say that two schedules S_1 and S_2 are *computationally equivalent*, written $S_1 \equiv S_2$, if:

T_0	T_1
read(A)	
$A := A - 50$	
write(A)	
	read(A)
	$temp := A * 0.1$
	$A := A - temp$
	write(A)
read(B)	
$B := B + 50$	
write(B)	
	read(B)
	$B := B + temp$
	write(B)

Figure 11.4   Schedule 4.

1. The set of transactions that participate in S_1 and S_2 are the same.

2. For each data item Q, if in S_1, transaction T_i executes **read**(Q) and the value of Q read by T_i was written by T_j, then the same will hold in S_2.

3. For each data item Q, if in S_1, transaction T_i executes the last **write**(Q) instruction, then the same holds also in S_2.

Condition 1 ensures that the same set of transactions participate in both schedules. Condition 2 ensures that each transaction reads the same values in both schedules and, therefore, performs the same computation. Condition 3, coupled with condition 2, ensures that both schedules result in the same final system state.

Returning to our previous examples, we note that schedule 1 $\neq$ schedule 2, since in schedule 1, the value of account A read by transaction T_1 was produced by T_0, while this is not the case in schedule 2. However, schedule 1 $\equiv$ schedule 4 because the values of account A and B read by transaction T_1 were produced by T_0 in both schedules.

It is possible to have two schedules that produce the same outcome that are not equivalent under our definition. For example, consider transaction T_2 that transfers \$10 from account B to account A. Let schedule 5 be as defined in Figure 11.5, and let schedule 6 be the serial schedule T_0 followed by T_2. We claim that schedule 5 $\neq$ schedule 6, since in schedule 5, the value of account B read by transaction T_0 was produced by T_2, while this is not the case in schedule 6. However, the final values of accounts A

T_0	T_2
read(A)	
$A := A - 50$	
write(A)	
	read(B)
	$B := B - 10$
	write(B)
read(B)	
$B := B + 50$	
write(B)	
	read(A)
	$A := A + 10$
	write(A)

Figure 11.5   Schedule 5.

and B after the execution of either schedule 5 or schedule 6 are the same, namely $960 and $2040, respectively.

The reason for this is that we are not willing to interpret the types of operations that can be performed on data items. Under this assumption, our definition of computational equivalence is indeed both necessary and sufficient for schedule equivalence. To illustrate this, consider again transactions T_0 and T_1. These two transactions have the same read and write operations and in the same order. Nevertheless, the serial schedule $<T_0,T_1>$ does not produce the same outcome as the serial schedule $<T_1,T_0>$, as was evident from schedules 1 and 2.

Given the notions of equivalent schedules, we can now define formally the concept of *serializability*. Let $\{T_0, T_1, ..., T_n\}$ be the set of transactions participating in a schedule S. We shall say that S is serializable if there exists a serial schedule S' such that $S \equiv S'$.

In Section 11.2, we describe an algorithm for determining whether a schedule is serializable. In Sections 11.3 through 11.7, we describe various mechanisms for ensuring serializability.

11.2 Testing for Serializability

Suppose that we are given a particular schedule S, and we wish to determine whether this schedule is serializable. In this section, we shall present two different methods for determining this.

11.2.1 Read before Write

Consider a system where a transaction must read a data item before it can write into it. We shall show that in such a system there exists a simple and efficient algorithm to determine serializability.

To do so, we construct a directed graph, called a *precedence graph*. This graph consists of a pair $G = (V,E)$ where V is a set of vertices and E is a

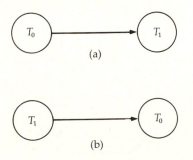

Figure 11.6   Precedence graph for schedules 1 and 2.

set of edges. The set of vertices consists of all the transactions participating in the schedule. The set of edges consists of all edges $T_i \rightarrow T_j$ for which the following two conditions hold:

- T_i executes "**write**(Q)" before T_j executes "**read**(Q)".

- T_i executes "**read**(Q)" before T_j executes "**write**(Q)".

If an edge $T_i \rightarrow T_j$ exists in the precedence graph, this implies that in any serial schedule S' equivalent to S, T_i must appear before T_j.

For example, the precedence graph for schedule 1 is shown in Figure 11.6a. It contains the single edge $T_0 \rightarrow T_1$ since all the instructions of T_0 are executed before the first instruction of T_1 is executed. Similarly, Figure 11.6b shows the precedence graph for schedule 2 with the single edge $T_1 \rightarrow T_0$, since all the instructions of T_1 are executed before the first instruction of T_0 is executed.

The precedence graph for schedule 3 is depicted in Figure 11.7. It contains the edge $T_0 \rightarrow T_1$ because T_0 executes "**read**(A)" before T_1 executes "**write**(A)". It also contains the edge $T_1 \rightarrow T_0$ because T_1 executes "**read**(B)" before T_0 executes "**write**(B)".

If the precedence graph for S has a cycle, then the schedule S is not serializable. If the graph contains no cycles, then the schedule S is serializable. The serializability order can be obtained through *topological sorting*, which determines a linear order consistent with the partial order of the precedence graph. There are, in general, several possible linear orders which can be obtained through a topological sorting. For example, the graph of Figure 11.8a has two acceptable linear orderings as illustrated in Figure 11.8b and c.

Thus, in order to test for serializability, we need to construct the precedence graph and invoke a cycle detection algorithm. Since finding a cycle in a graph requires on the order of n^2 operations, where n is the number of nodes in the graph (that is, the number of transactions), we have a practical scheme for determining serializability.

Returning to our previous examples, note that the precedence graphs for schedules 1 and 2 (Figure 11.6) indeed do not contain cycles. The

Figure 11.7   Precedence graph for schedule 3.

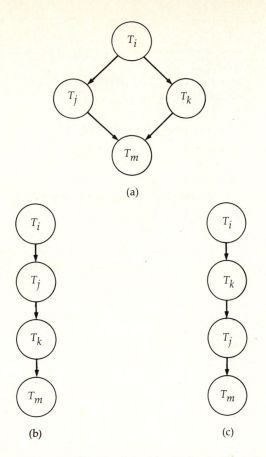

Figure 11.8   Illustration of topological sorting.

precedence graph of schedule 3 (Figure 11.7), on the other hand, contains a cycle, indicating that the schedule is not serializable.

11.2.2 Unconstrained Writes

Consider a system where a transaction writes a data item without first reading that item. We shall show that for such a system there is no efficient algorithm for determining serializability.

In the case where a read must precede a write, we know that if two transactions, T_i and T_j, access a data item Q, and at least one of these transactions writes Q, then either the edge $T_i \rightarrow T_j$, or the edge $T_j \rightarrow T_i$ is inserted in the precedence graph. This, however, is no longer the case when writes can be issued without being preceded by a read. As we shall see shortly, this is the cause of our inability to come up with an efficient algorithm for testing for serializability.

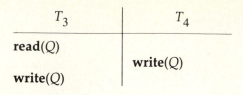

Figure 11.9   Schedule 7.

Consider schedule 7 of Figure 11.9 consisting of only the significant operations (that is, the reads and writes) of transactions T_3 and T_4. This schedule is not serializable since it is not equivalent to either the serial schedule $<T_3,T_4>$ or the serial schedule $<T_4,T_3>$. Since T_3 reads Q before T_4 writes Q, T_3 must appear before T_4 in the serializability order. Therefore, the edge $T_3 \rightarrow T_4$ must be inserted in the precedence graph. Similarly, since T_3 executes the last **write**(Q), T_3 must appear after T_4 in the serializability order. Therefore, the edge $T_4 \rightarrow T_3$ must be inserted in the precedence graph. Since the precedence graph contains a cycle, we know that the schedule is not serializable.

From the above example, it appears that the edge $T_i \rightarrow T_j$ must be inserted in the precedence graph if, in the corresponding schedule, T_i writes Q after T_j writes Q. This, however, is not always the case. To illustrate this, suppose that we augment schedule 7 with transaction T_5 and thus obtain schedule 8 depicted in Figure 11.10. If we follow our previous rules for forming edges in the precedence graph, we get the graph of Figure 11.11. This graph contains a cycle, and thus it appears that the schedule is not serializable. Close examination, however, reveals that the above schedule is equivalent to the serial schedule $<T_3,T_4,T_5>$. The edge $T_4 \rightarrow T_3$ should *not* have been inserted in the graph, since the values of item Q produced by T_3 and T_4 were never used by any other transaction, and T_5 produced a new final value of Q. The **write**(Q) instructions of T_3 and T_4 are called *useless writes*.

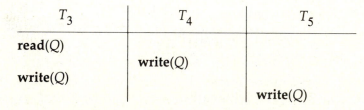

Figure 11.10   Schedule 8.

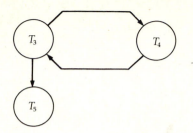

Figure 11.11   Precedence graph for schedule 8.

What we have pointed out above is that we cannot simply use the precedence graph scheme sketched above when we allow unconstrained writes. We need to develop a scheme for deciding whether an edge needs to be inserted in a precedence graph.

Let S be a schedule. Suppose that transaction T_j reads the value of data item Q written by T_i. Clearly, if S is serializable, then in any serial schedule S' that is equivalent to S, T_i must precede T_j. Suppose now that in schedule S transaction T_k executed a **write**(Q). Then in schedule S', T_k must either precede T_i or follow T_j. It cannot appear between T_i and T_j since otherwise T_j would not read the value of Q written by T_i and thus we would have $S \neq S'$.

The above constraints cannot be expressed in terms of the simple precedence graph model previously discussed. The difficulty stems from the fact that we know that in the above example one of the pair of edges $T_k \rightarrow T_i$, $T_j \rightarrow T_k$ must be inserted in the graph, but we have not yet formed the rule for determining the appropriate choice.

To do so, we need to extend the precedence graph to include labeled edges. We term such a graph a *labeled precedence graph*. As before, the nodes of the graph are the transactions participating in the schedule. The rules for inserting labeled edges are described below.

Let S be a schedule consisting of transactions $\{T_0, T_1, \ldots, T_n\}$. Let T_b and T_f be two dummy transactions such that T_b issues **write**(Q) for each Q in S, and T_f issues **read**(Q) for each Q in S. We construct a new schedule S' from S by inserting T_b at the beginning of S and appending T_f to the end of S. We construct the labeled precedence graph for schedule S' as follows:

1. Add an edge $T_i \overset{0}{\rightarrow} T_j$, if transaction T_j reads the value of data item Q written by transaction T_i.

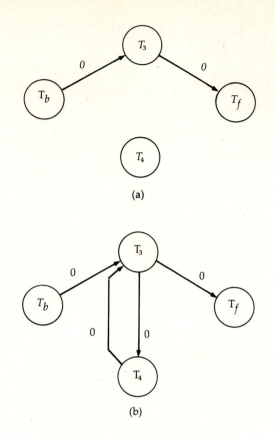

Figure 11.12   Labeled precedence graph of schedule 7.

2. Remove all the edges incident on useless transactions. A transaction T_i is *useless* if there exists no path, in the precedence graph, from T_i to transaction T_f.

3. For each data item Q such that:

   - T_j reads the value of Q written by T_i.

   - T_k executes **write**(Q) and $T_k \neq T_b$.

   do the following:

   a. If $T_i = T_b$ and $T_j \neq T_f$, then insert the edge $T_j \overset{0}{\rightarrow} T_k$ in the labeled precedence graph.

    b. If $T_i \neq T_b$ and $T_j = T_f$, then insert the edge $T_k \xrightarrow{0} T_i$ in the labeled precedence graph.

    c. If $T_i \neq T_b$ and $T_j \neq T_f$, then insert the pair of edges $T_k \xrightarrow{p} T_i$, and $T_j \xrightarrow{p} T_k$ in the labeled precedence graph where p is a unique integer larger than 0 not used before for labeling edges.

Rule (c) reflects the fact that if T_i writes a data item that T_j reads, then a transaction T_k that writes the same data item must come before T_i or after T_j. Rules (a) and (b) are special cases that result from the fact that T_b and T_f are necessarily the first and last transactions, respectively. When we apply rule (c), we are *not* requiring T_n to be *both* before T_i *and* after T_j. Rather we have a choice of where T_n may appear in an equivalent serial ordering.

To illustrate this, consider again schedule 7 (Figure 11.9). The graph constructed in steps 1 and 2 is depicted in Figure 11.12a. It contains the edge $T_b \xrightarrow{0} T_3$ since T_3 reads the value of Q written by T_b. It contains the edge $T_3 \xrightarrow{0} T_f$ since T_3 was the last transaction that wrote Q and, thus, T_f read that value. The final graph corresponding to schedule 7 is depicted in Figure 11.12b. It contains the edge $T_3 \xrightarrow{0} T_4$ as a result of step 3a. It contains the edge $T_4 \xrightarrow{0} T_3$ as a result of step 3b.

Consider now schedule 8 (Figure 11.10). The graph constructed in steps 1 and 2 is depicted in Figure 11.13a. The final graph is shown in Figure 11.13b. It contains the edges $T_3 \xrightarrow{0} T_4$ and $T_3 \xrightarrow{0} T_5$ as a result of step 3a. It contains the edges $T_3 \xrightarrow{0} T_5$ (already in the graph) and $T_4 \xrightarrow{0} T_5$ as a result of step 3b.

Finally, consider the schedule of Figure 11.14. This schedule is serializable since it is equivalent to the serial schedule $<T_3, T_4, T_5>$. The corresponding labeled precedence graph, constructed in steps 1 and 2, is depicted in Figure 11.15a. The final graph is depicted in Figure 11.15b. The edges $T_3 \xrightarrow{0} T_4$ and $T_3 \xrightarrow{0} T_5$ were inserted as a result of rule 3a. The pair of edges $T_3 \xrightarrow{1} T_4$ and $T_5 \xrightarrow{1} T_3$ were inserted as the result of a *single* application of rule 3c.

The graphs depicted in Figures 11.12 and 11.15 contain the following two minimal cycles, respectively:

- $T_3 \xrightarrow{0} T_4 \xrightarrow{0} T_3$
- $T_3 \xrightarrow{0} T_5 \xrightarrow{1} T_3$

The graph in Figure 11.13b, on the other hand contains no cycles.

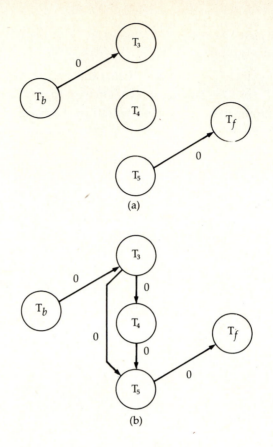

Figure 11.13   Labeled precedence graph of schedule 8.

If the graph contains no cycle, the corresponding schedule is serializable. Indeed, the graph of Figure 11.13 contains no cycle and its corresponding schedule 8 is serializable. However, if the graph contains a cycle this does *not* necessarily imply that the corresponding schedule is not

T_3	T_4	T_5
read(Q)		
	write(Q)	
		read(Q)
write(Q)		
		write(Q)

Figure 11.14   Schedule 9.

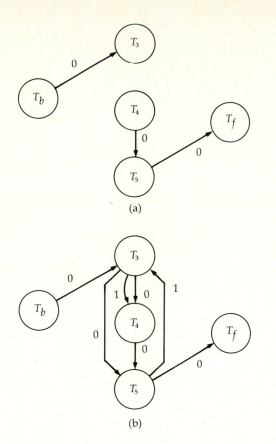

Figure 11.15   Labeled precedence graph of schedule 9.

serializable. Indeed, the graph of Figure 11.12 contains a cycle and its corresponding schedule 7 is not serializable. The graph of Figure 11.15, on the other hand, contains a cycle, but its corresponding schedule 9 is serializable.

How, then do we determine whether a schedule is serializable or not? The answer simply lies in an appropriate interpretation of the precedence graph. Suppose that there are n distinct edge pairs. That is, we applied rule 3c n times in the construction of the precedence graph. Then there exists 2^n different graphs, where each graph contains only one edge from each pair. If any one of these graphs is acyclic, then the corresponding schedule is serializable. The serializability order is determined by the removal of the dummy transactions T_b and T_f, and the topological sorting of the remaining acyclic graph.

Returning to the graph of Figure 11.15b, since there is exactly one distinct pair, there are two different graphs that need to be considered.

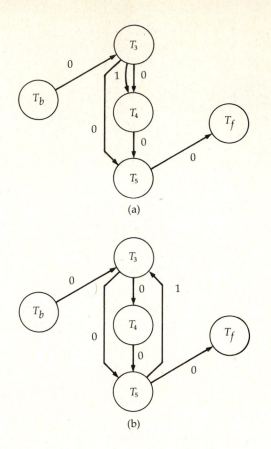

Figure 11.16   Two distinct precedence graphs.

The two graphs are depicted in Figure 11.16. Since the graph of Figure 11.16b is acyclic, we know that the corresponding schedule 9 is serializable.

The algorithm described above requires exhaustive testing of all possible distinct graphs. It has been shown that the problem of testing for an acyclic graph in this set falls in the class of *NP*-complete problems (see the bibliographic notes for references to discussion of the theory of *NP*-complete problems). An algorithm for an *NP*-complete problem will almost certainly run in exponential time as a function of the size of the problem.

11.3 Locking

One way to ensure serializability is to require that access to data items be done in a mutually exclusive manner; that is, while one transaction accesses a data item, no other transaction can modify that data item. The most common method used to implement this is to allow a transaction to access a data item only if it is currently holding a lock on that item.

There are various modes in which a data item may be locked. In this section, we restrict our attention to two modes:

- **Shared**. If a transaction T has obtained a shared mode lock (denoted by S) on item Q, then T can read this item but it cannot write Q.

- **Exclusive**. If a transaction T has obtained an exclusive mode lock (denoted by X) on item Q, then T can both read and write Q.

We require that every transaction request a lock in an appropriate mode on data item Q depending on the type of operations it will perform on Q.

Given a set of lock modes, we can define a *compatibility function* on them as follows. Let A and B represent arbitrary lock modes. Suppose that a transaction T_i requests a lock of mode A on item Q on which transaction T_j ($T_i \neq T_j$) currently holds a lock of mode B. If transaction T_i can be granted a lock on Q immediately, in spite of the presence of the mode B lock, then we say mode A is *compatible* with mode B. Such a function can be represented conveniently by a matrix. The compatibility relation between the two modes of locking used in this section is given by the matrix COMP of Figure 11.17. An element, say COMP(A,B), of the matrix has the value *true* if and only if mode A is compatible with mode B.

Note that shared mode is compatible with shared mode, but not with exclusive mode. At any time, several shared mode locks can be held simultaneously (by different transactions) on a particular data item. A subsequent exclusive mode lock request has to wait until the currently held shared mode lock is released.

A transaction requests a shared lock on data item Q by executing the LS(Q) instruction. Similarly, an exclusive lock is requested through the LX(Q) instruction. A data item Q may be unlocked via the UN(Q) instruction.

In order to access a data item, transaction T_i must first lock it. If the data item is already locked by another transaction in an incompatible mode, then T_i must *wait* until all incompatible locks held by other transactions have been released. Transaction T_i may unlock a data item which it had locked at some earlier point.

	S	X
S	true	false
X	false	false

Figure 11.17 Lock compatibility matrix COMP.

It should be noted that a transaction must hold a lock on a data item as long as it accesses it. Moreover, it is not always desirable for a transaction to unlock a data item immediately after its last access of that data item, since serializability may not be ensured.

To illustrate this, consider again our simplified banking system. Let A and B be two accounts that are accessed by transactions T_6 and T_7. Transaction T_6 transfers \$50 from account B to account A, and is defined as:

$$
\begin{aligned}
T_6: \ & LX(B); \\
& \textbf{read}(B); \\
& B := B - 50; \\
& \textbf{write}(B); \\
& UN(B); \\
& LX(A); \\
& \textbf{read}(A); \\
& A := A + 50; \\
& \textbf{write}(A); \\
& UN(A).
\end{aligned}
$$

Transaction T_7 displays the total amount of money in accounts A and B, that is, the sum $A + B$, and is defined as:

$$
\begin{aligned}
T_7: \ & LS(A); \\
& \textbf{read}(A); \\
& UN(A); \\
& LS(B); \\
& \textbf{read}(B); \\
& UN(B); \\
& \textbf{display}(A + B).
\end{aligned}
$$

Suppose that the values of accounts A and B are \$100 and \$200, respectively. If these two transactions are executed serially, either in order T_6, T_7 or the order T_7, T_6, then transaction T_7 will display the value \$300. If, however, these transactions are executed concurrently, then schedule 10, as shown in Figure 11.18, is possible. In this case, transaction T_7 displays \$250, which is incorrect. The reason for this is that the transaction T_6 has unlocked the data item too early as a result of which T_7 saw an inconsistent state.

Suppose now that unlocking is delayed to some later point, say, the end of the transaction. Transaction T_8, below, corresponds to T_6 with unlocking delayed and is defined as:

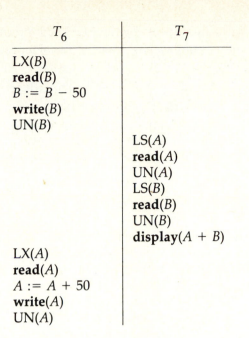

T_6	T_7
LX(B)	
read(B)	
B := B − 50	
write(B)	
UN(B)	
	LS(A)
	read(A)
	UN(A)
	LS(B)
	read(B)
	UN(B)
	display(A + B)
LX(A)	
read(A)	
A := A + 50	
write(A)	
UN(A)	

Figure 11.18   Schedule 10.

T_8: LX(B);
        read(B);
        B := B − 50;
        write(B);
        LX(A);
        read(A);
        A := A + 50;
        write(A);
        UN(B);
        UN(A).

Transaction T_9 below, corresponds to T_7 with unlocking delayed and is defined as:

T_9: LS(A);
        read(A);
        LS(B);
        read(B);
        display(A + B);
        UN(A);
        UN(B);

Consider the partial schedule of Figure 11.19 for T_8 and T_9. Since T_8 is holding an exclusive mode lock on B and T_9 is requesting a shared mode lock on B, T_9 is waiting for T_8 to unlock B. Similarly, since T_9 is holding a shared mode lock on A and T_8 is requesting an exclusive mode lock on A, T_8 is waiting for T_9 to unlock A. Thus, we have arrived at a state where neither of these transactions can ever proceed with its normal execution. This situation is called *deadlock*. When deadlock occurs, the system must roll back one of the two transactions. Once a transaction has been rolled back, the data items that were locked by that transaction are unlocked. These data items are then available to the other transaction, which can continue with its execution. We shall return to the issue of deadlock handling in Section 11.8.

What we have pointed out here is that locking should be used cautiously. On one hand, if one tries to maximize concurrency by unlocking data items as soon as possible, we may get inconsistent states. On the other hand, if one does not unlock a data item before locking another data item, deadlocks may occur.

We shall require that each transaction in the system follow a set of rules, called a *locking protocol*, indicating when a transaction may lock and unlock each of the data items. Locking protocols restrict the number of possible schedules. The set of all such schedules is a proper subset of all possible serializable schedules. We shall present several locking protocols that allow only serializable schedules. Before doing so, we need a few definitions.

Let $\{T_0, T_1, \ldots, T_n\}$ be a set of transactions participating in a schedule S. We say that T_i *precedes* T_j in S, written $T_i \rightarrow T_j$, if there exists a data item Q, such that T_i has held lock mode A on Q and T_j has held lock mode B on Q later, and $\text{COMP}(A,B) = $ false. If $T_i \rightarrow T_j$, then this implies that in any equivalent serial schedule T_i must appear before T_j.

T_8	T_9
LX(B)	
read(B)	
$B := B - 50$	
write(B)	
	LS(A)
	read(A)
	LS(B)
LX(A)	

Figure 11.19   Schedule 11.

We say that a schedule S is *legal* under a given locking protocol if S is a possible schedule for a set of transactions following the rules of the locking protocol. We can state the following definition: A locking protocol *ensures serializability* if and only if for all legal schedules, the associated $\rightarrow$ relation is acyclic.

11.3.1 The Two-Phase Locking Protocol

One protocol that ensures serializability is the *two-phase locking protocol*. This protocol requires that each transaction issue lock and unlock requests in two phases:

- **Growing phase**. A transaction may obtain locks but may not release any lock.

- **Shrinking phase**. A transaction may release locks but may not obtain any new locks.

Initially, a transaction is in the growing phase. The transaction acquires locks as needed. Once the transaction releases a lock, it enters the shrinking phase and no more lock requests may be issued.

For example, transactions T_8 and T_9 are two-phase. On the other hand, transactions T_6 and T_7 are not two-phase.

The two-phase locking protocol ensures serializability (see Exercise 11.5). It does not, however, ensure freedom from deadlock. To demonstrate this, observe that transactions T_8 and T_9 are two-phase, but in schedule 11 (Figure 11.19) they are deadlocked.

If T_i is a non-two-phase transaction, it is always possible to find another transaction T_j that is two-phase such that there is a nonserializable schedule possible for T_i and T_j.

Consider the following two transactions for which we have shown only some of the significant read and write operations. Transaction T_{10} is defined as:

$$T_{10}: \quad \textbf{read}(a_1);$$
$$\textbf{read}(a_2);$$
$$. . .$$
$$\textbf{read}(a_n);$$
$$\textbf{write}(a_1).$$

while transaction T_{11} is defined as:

$$T_{11}: \quad \textbf{read}(a_1);$$
$$\textbf{read}(a_2);$$
$$\textbf{display}(a_1 + a_2).$$

If we employ the two-phase locking protocol, then T_{10} must lock a_1 in exclusive mode. Therefore, any concurrent execution of both transactions amounts to a serial execution. Notice, however, the T_{10} needs an exclusive lock on a_1 only at the end of its execution, when it writes a_1. Thus, if T_{10} could initially lock a_1 in *shared* mode, and then later change the lock to exclusive mode, we could get more parallelism, since T_{10} and T_{11} could access a_1 and a_2 simultaneously.

This observation leads us to a refinement of the basic two-phase locking protocol, in which lock *conversions* are allowed. We shall provide a mechanism for upgrading a shared lock to an exclusive lock, and downgrading an exclusive lock to a shared lock. We denote conversion from shared to exclusive modes by UP, and from exclusive to shared by DN. Lock conversion cannot be allowed to occur arbitrarily. Rather, upgrading can take place only in the growing phase, while downgrading can take place only in the shrinking phase.

Returning to our example, transactions T_{10} and T_{11} can run concurrently under the refined two-phase locking protocol as shown in the incomplete schedule of Figure 11.20, where only some of the locking instructions are shown.

Note that a transaction attempting to upgrade a lock on an item Q may be forced to wait. This occurs if Q is currently locked by *another* transaction in shared mode.

We now describe a simple scheme that can be used to generate the appropriate lock instructions for a transaction. When a transaction T_i issues a **read**(Q) operation the system issues an LS(Q) instruction followed by the

T_{10}	T_{11}
LS(a_1)	
	LS(a_1)
LS(a_2)	
	LS(a_2)
LS(a_2)	
LS(a_4)	
	UN(a_1)
	UN(a_2)
LS(a_n)	
UP(a_1)	

Figure 11.20   Incomplete schedule with a lock conversion.

read(Q) instruction. When T_i issues a **write**(Q) operation, the system checks to see whether T_i already holds a shared lock on Q. If the answer is yes, then the system issues a UP(Q) instruction followed by the **write**(Q) instruction. Otherwise, the system issues an LX(Q) instruction followed by the **write**(Q) instruction.

It is possible that there are serializable schedules for a set of transactions that cannot be obtained through the two-phase locking protocol. However, in order to do better than two-phase locking, we need either to have additional information about the transactions, or to impose some structure or ordering upon the set of data items in the database.

11.3.2 Graph-Based Protocols

As was pointed out above, in the absence of information concerning the manner in which data items are accessed, the two-phase locking protocol is both necessary and sufficient for ensuring serializability. Thus, if we wish to develop protocols that are not two-phase, we need to have some additional information on how each transaction will access the database. There are various models that differ in the amount of such information provided. The simplest model requires that we have prior knowledge as to the order in which the database items will be accessed. Given such information, it is possible to construct locking protocols that are not two-phase but, nevertheless, ensure serializability.

To acquire such prior knowledge, we impose a partial ordering $\rightarrow$ on the set $\mathbf{D} = \{d_1, d_2, \ldots, d_h\}$ of all data items. If $d_i \rightarrow d_j$, then any transaction accessing both d_i and d_j must access d_i before accessing d_j. This partial ordering may be the result of either the logical or physical organization of the data, or it may be imposed solely for the purpose of concurrency control.

The partial ordering implies that the set $\mathbf{D}$ may be now viewed as a directed acyclic graph, called a *database graph*. In this section, for the sake of simplicity, we will restrict our attention only to graphs that are rooted trees. We will present a simple protocol, called the *tree protocol*, which is restricted to employ only *exclusive* locks. References to other, more complex graph-based locking protocols are provided in the bibliographic notes.

In the tree protocol, the only lock instruction allowed is LX. Each transaction T_i can lock a data item at most once and must observe the following rules:

1. The first lock by T_i may be on any data item.

2. Subsequently, a data item Q can be locked by T_i only if the parent of Q is currently locked by T_i.

3. Data items may be unlocked at any time.

4. A data item that has been locked and unlocked by T_i cannot subsequently be relocked by T_i.

As we stated earlier, all schedules that are legal under the tree protocol are serializable.

To illustrate this protocol, consider the database graph of Figure 11.21. The following four transactions follow the tree protocol on this graph. We have shown only the lock and unlock instructions:

T_{12} : LX(B); LX(E); UN(E); LX(D); UN(B); LX(G); UN(D); UN(G).
T_{13} : LX(D); LX(H); UN(D); LX(J); UN(J); UN(H).
T_{14} : LX(B); LX(E); UN(E); UN(B).
T_{15} : LX(D); LX(H); UN(D); UN(H).

One possible schedule in which these four transactions participated is depicted in Figure 11.22. Note that during its execution, transaction T_{12} holds locks on two *disjoint* subtrees.

Observe that the schedule of Figure 11.21 is serializable. It can be shown not only that the tree protocol ensures serializability, but also that it ensures freedom from deadlock.

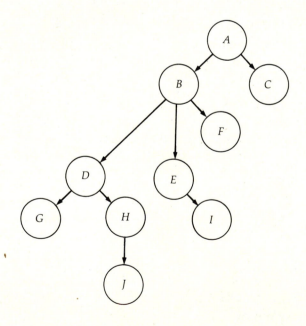

Figure 11.21   Tree structured database graph.

The tree locking protocol has the advantage over the two-phase locking protocol that unlocking may occur earlier, resulting in less waiting time, and thus concurrency is enhanced. In addition, since it is deadlock-free, no rollbacks are required. The protocol has the disadvantage that in some cases more data items need to be locked, thus increasing the locking overhead and creating the possibility of additional waiting time.

11.3.3 Recovery

A database system which allows concurrent execution must, in addition to ensuring serializability, provide a mechanism for recovery in order to ensure the atomicity property of a transaction. In order to ensure this property, the system must employ some form of recovery scheme. The various log-based recovery schemes described in Chapter 10 can be used for this purpose. The main difference is that now several transactions, rather than one, may have to be rolled back as a result of a failure. This phenomenon is called *cascading rollback*.

To illustrate this, consider the partial schedule of Figure 11.23 consisting of three transactions, each of which follows the two-phase

T_{12}	T_{13}	T_{14}	T_{15}
LX(B)			
	LX(D)		
	LX(H)		
	UN(D)		
LX(E)			
UN(E)			
LX(D)			
UN(B)			
		LX(B)	
		LX(E)	
	UN(H)		
LX(G)			
UN(D)			
			LX(D)
			LX(H)
			UN(D)
			UN(H)
		UN(E)	
		UN(B)	
UN(G)			

Figure 11.22   Serial schedule.

locking protocol. Suppose that transaction T_{16} aborted after unlocking A because of some logical error. As a result, T_{16} must be rolled back, and since T_{17} is dependent on T_{16} and T_{18} is dependent on T_{17} we have cascading rollback.

In order to eliminate cascading rollbacks, the system must ensure that transactions can read only committed values, that is, values that were produced by committed transactions. This can be accomplished by requiring that unlocking be performed only after the transaction has reached its last statement. Moreover, the unlocking can occur only after the appropriate log records have been written out to stable storage. Clearly, this reduces concurrency. Moreover, the situation becomes worse as the number of data items that need to be locked by a transaction is larger.

Thus, there are conflicting criteria in selecting a concurrency control scheme: guarding against cascading rollbacks versus increasing parallelism. If a system can ensure that transaction failure will occur relatively infrequently, then cascading rollbacks can be tolerated. Otherwise, they should be guarded against.

11.4 Timestamp Ordering

In the locking protocols described above, the order between every pair of conflicting transactions is determined at execution time when both transactions lock the first data item they have in common in incompatible modes. Another method for determining the serializability order is to select an ordering in advance between every pair of transactions. The most common method for doing so is to use a *timestamp-ordering* scheme.

With each transaction T_i in the system, we associate a unique fixed timestamp, denoted by $TS(T_i)$. This timestamp is assigned by the database system before the transaction T_i starts execution. If a transaction T_i has been assigned timestamp $TS(T_i)$, and a new transaction T_j enters the

T_{16}	T_{17}	T_{18}
LX(A)		
LX(B)		
UN(A)		
	LX(A)	
	UN(A)	
		LX(A)

Figure 11.23   Partial schedule.

system, then $TS(T_i) < TS(T_j)$. There are two simple methods for implementing this scheme:

- Use the value of the system clock as the timestamp; that is, a transaction's timestamp equals the value of the clock when the transaction enters the system.

- Use a logical counter that is incremented after a new timestamp has been assigned; that is, a transaction's timestamp equals the value of the counter when the transaction enters the system.

The timestamps of the transactions determine the serializability order. Thus if $TS(T_i) < TS(T_j)$, then the system must ensure that the produced schedule is equivalent to a serial schedule in which transaction T_i appears before transaction T_j.

To implement this scheme, we associate with each data item Q two timestamp values:

- **W-timestamp**(Q), which denotes the largest timestamp of any transaction that successfully executed **write**(Q).

- **R-timestamp**(Q), which denotes the largest timestamp of any transaction that successfully executed **read**(Q).

These timestamps are updated whenever a new **read**(Q) or **write**(Q) instruction is executed.

The timestamp ordering protocol ensures that any conflicting read and write operations are executed in the timestamp order. This protocol operates as follows:

- Suppose that transaction T_i issues **read**(Q).

  If $TS(T_i) < $ W-timestamp(Q), then this implies that T_i needs to read a value of Q which was already overwritten. Hence the read operation must be rejected and T_i is rolled back.

  If $TS(T_i) \geq $ W-timestamp(Q), then the read is executed, and R-timestamp(Q) is set to the maximum of R-timestamp(Q) and $TS(T_i)$.

- Suppose that transaction T_i issues **write**(Q).

  If $TS(T_i) < $ R-timestamp(Q), then this implies that the value of Q that T_i is producing was previously needed and it was assumed that it would never be produced. Hence, the write operation must be rejected and T_i is rolled back.

If $TS(T_i) <$ W-timestamp(Q), then this implies that T_i is attempting to write an obsolete value of Q. Hence, this write operation can be ignored.

Otherwise, the write is executed, and W-timestamp(Q) is set to the maximum of W-timestamp(Q) and $TS(T_i)$.

A transaction T_i, which is rolled back as a result of the concurrency control scheme, is assigned a new timestamp and is restarted.

To illustrate this protocol, consider the transactions T_{19} and T_{20} defined below. Transaction T_{19} displays the contents of accounts A and B, and is defined as:

$$T_{19}: \textbf{read}(B);$$
$$\textbf{read}(A);$$
$$\textbf{display}(A + B).$$

Transaction T_{20} transfers funds from account A to account B and then displays the contents of both.

$$T_{20}: \textbf{read}(B);$$
$$B := B - 50;$$
$$\textbf{write}(B);$$
$$\textbf{read}(A);$$
$$A := A + 50;$$
$$\textbf{write}(A);$$
$$\textbf{display}(A + B).$$

Suppose that $TS(T_{19}) < TS(T_{20})$. Then the schedule of Figure 11.24 is possible.

We note that the above execution can also be produced by the two-phase locking protocol. There are, however, schedules that are possible under the two-phase locking protocol but are not possible under the timestamp protocol, and vice-versa (see Exercise 11.6).

The timestamp ordering protocol ensures serializability. This follows from the fact that conflicting operations are processed in timestamp order. The protocol ensures freedom from deadlock, since no transaction ever waits.

The timestamp concurrency control scheme defined above may result in cascading rollbacks. If we wish to guard against cascading rollbacks, we

T_{19}	T_{20}
read(B)	
	read(B)
	$B := B - 50$
	write(B)
read(A)	
	read(A)
display($A + B$)	
	$A := A + 50$
	write(A)
	display($A + B$)

Figure 11.24   Serializable schedule.

must ensure that a transaction can read only committed values. This can be achieved by associating a *commit bit* with each transaction T_i and a pointer from each data item written by T_i to that commit bit. Initially the commit bit is set to the value *false*. It is set to the value *true* only after the transaction has committed. A transaction T_j that wishes to read a data item can do so immediately only if the commit bit is set to true; otherwise, it must wait for this event to take place.

11.5 Validation Techniques

In cases where the majority of transactions are read-only transactions, the rate of conflicts among transactions may be very low. Thus, many of these transactions, if executed without the supervision of a concurrency control scheme, would nevertheless leave the system in a consistent state. A concurrency control scheme imposes some overhead of code execution and possible delay of transactions. It may be desirable to use an alternative scheme that imposes less overhead. A difficulty in reducing the overhead is that we do not know in advance which transactions will be involved in a conflict. To do so, we need to provide a scheme for *monitoring* the system.

We assume that each transaction T_i executes in two or three different phases in its lifetime, depending on whether it is a read-only or an update transaction.

1. **Read phase**. During this phase, the execution of transaction T_i takes place. The value of the various data items are read and stored in variables local to T_i. All write operations are performed on temporary local variables, without updating the actual database.

2. **Validation phase**. Transaction T_i performs a validation test to determine whether it can successfully copy the temporary local variable to the database without causing a violation of serializability.

3. **Write phase**. If transaction T_i succeeds in validation (step 2), then the actual updates are applied to the database. Otherwise, T_i is rolled back.

All three phases of concurrently executing transactions can be interleaved.

The read and write phases are self-explanatory. The only phase that needs further discussion is the validation phase. In order to perform the validation test, we need to know when the various phases of transactions T_i took place. We shall, therefore, associate three different timestamps with transaction T_i:

- **Start**(T_i), the time when T_i started its execution.

- **Validation**(T_i), the time when T_i finished its read phase and started its validation phase.

- **Finish**(T_i), the time when T_i finished its write phase.

The serializability order is determined by the timestamp ordering technique using the value of the timestamp Validation(T_i). Thus, the value $TS(T_i) = $ Validation(T_i) and, if $TS(T_j) < TS(T_k)$, then any produced schedule must be equivalent to a serial schedule in which transaction T_j appears before transaction T_k. The reason we have chosen Validation(T_i) rather than Start(T_i) as the timestamp of transaction T_i is because we can expect better response time provided that conflict rates among transactions are indeed low.

The validation test for transaction T_j requires that for all transactions T_i with $TS(T_i) < TS(T_j)$ one of the following two conditions must hold:

1. Finish(T_i) < Start(T_j). Since T_i completes its execution before T_j started, the serializability order is indeed maintained.

2. The set of data items written by T_i does not intersect with the set of data items read by T_j, and T_i completes its write phase before T_j starts its validation phase (Start(T_j) < Finish(T_i) < Validation(T_j)). This condition ensures that the writes of T_i and T_j do not overlap. Since the writes of T_i do not affect the read of T_j, and since T_j cannot affect the read of T_i, the serializability order is indeed maintained.

To illustrate this, consider transactions T_{19} and T_{20}. Suppose that $TS(T_{19}) < TS(T_{20})$. Then the validation phase succeeds producing the schedule depicted in Figure 11.25. Observe that this schedule is serializable, but it cannot be produced either by the two-phase locking protocol or the timestamp ordering scheme.

The validation scheme automatically guards against cascading rollbacks since the actual writes take place only after the transactions issuing the write has committed.

11.6 Multiple Granularity

In the concurrency control schemes described thus far, we have used each individual data item as the unit on which synchronization is performed.

There are circumstances, however, where it would be advantageous to group several data items and treat them as one individual synchronization unit. For example, if a transaction T_i needs to access the entire database, and a locking protocol is used, then T_i must lock each item in the database. Clearly, this is time-consuming. It would be better if T_i could issue a *single* lock request to lock the entire database. On the other hand, if transaction T_j needs to access only a few data items, it should not be required to lock the entire database, since otherwise concurrency is lost.

What is needed is a mechanism to allow the system to define multiple levels of *granularity*. This can be accomplished by allowing data items to be of various sizes and define a hierarchy of data granularities, where the small granularities are nested within larger ones. Such a hierarchy can be represented graphically as a tree. Note that the tree we describe here is significantly different from that used by the tree protocol (Section 11.3.2).

T_{19}	T_{20}
read(B)	
	read(B)
	$B := B - 50$
	write(B)
	read(A)
	$A := A + 50$
	write(A)
read(A)	
display($A + B$)	
	display($A + B$)

Figure 11.25　Serializable schedule.

A nonleaf node of the multiple granularity tree represents the data associated with its descendants. In the tree protocol's tree each node is an independent data item.

To illustrate this, consider the tree of Figure 11.26 consisting of four levels of nodes. The highest level represents the entire database. Below it are nodes of type *area*. Each area in turn has nodes of type *file* as its descendents. Finally, each file has nodes of type *record*.

Each node in the tree can be locked individually. As in the two-phase locking protocol, we shall use *shared* and *exclusive* lock modes. When a transaction locks a node, in either *shared* or *exclusive* mode, this implies that the transaction also locked all the descendents of that node in the same lock mode. For example, if transaction T_i *explicitly* locks file F_c of Figure 11.26, in X mode, then it has locked *implicitly* in X mode all the records belonging to that file. It need not lock the individual records of F_c *explicitly*.

Suppose that transaction T_j wishes to lock record r_{b_6} of file F_b. Since T_i has locked F_b explicitly, it follows that r_{b_6} is also locked (implicitly). But, when T_j issues a lock request for r_{b_6}, r_{b_6} is not explicitly locked! How does the system determine whether T_j can lock r_{b_6} or not? To do so, T_j must traverse the tree from the root to record r_{b_6}. If any node in that path is locked in an incompatible mode, then T_j must be delayed.

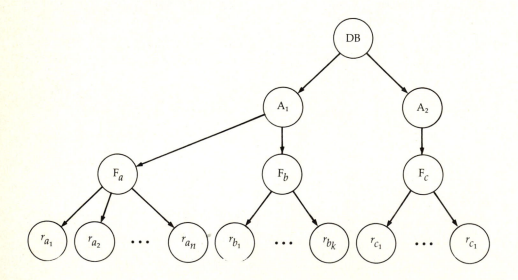

Figure 11.26   Granularity hierarchy.

Suppose now that transaction T_k wishes to lock the entire database. To do so, it simply must lock the root of the hierarchy. Note, however, that T_k should not succeed in locking the root node, since T_i is currently holding a lock on part of the tree (specifically, file F_b). But how does the system determine this? One possibility is to search the entire tree. This, however, defeats the whole purpose of the multiple granularity locking scheme. A more efficient way to achieve this is to introduce a new class of lock modes, called *intention* lock modes. If a node is locked in an intention mode, it implies that explicit locking is being done at a lower level of the tree (that is, at a finer granularity). Intention locks are put on all the ancestors of a node before that node is locked explicitly. Thus, a transaction need not not search the entire tree to determine whether it can lock a node successfully or not. To accomplish this, a transaction wishing to lock a node, say Q, must traverse a path in the tree from the root to Q. While traversing the tree, the transaction locks the various nodes in an intention mode.

There is an intention mode associated with *shared* mode and one with *exclusive* mode. If a node is locked in *intention-shared* mode (denoted by IS), this implies that explicit locking is being done at a lower level of the tree but only with shared-mode locks. Similarly, if a node is locked in *intention-exclusive* mode (denoted by IX), then explicit locking is being done at a lower level with exclusive-mode or shared-mode locks. Finally, if a node is locked in *shared and intention-exclusive* mode (denoted by SIX), this implies that the subtree rooted by that node is locked explicitly in shared mode and that explicit locking is being done at a lower level with exclusive-mode locks. The compatibility function for these lock modes is presented in Figure 11.27.

The multiple granularity locking protocol presented below ensures serializability. Each transaction T_i can lock a node Q, using the following rules:

1. The lock compatibility function of Figure 11.27 must be observed.

	IS	IX	S	SIX	X
IS	true	true	true	true	false
IX	true	true	false	false	false
S	true	false	true	false	false
SIX	true	false	false	false	false
X	false	false	false	false	false

Figure 11.27   Compatibility matrix.

2. The root of the tree must be locked first, and may be locked in any mode.

3. A node Q can be locked by T_i in S or IS mode only if the parent of Q is currently locked by T_i in either IX or IS mode.

4. A node Q can be locked by T_i in X, SIX, or IX mode only if the parent of Q is currently locked by T_i in either IX or SIX mode.

5. T_i can lock a node only if it has not previously unlocked any node (that is, T_i is two-phase).

6. T_i can unlock a node Q only if none of the children of Q are currently locked by T_i.

Observe that the multiple granularity protocol requires that locks be acquired in top-down (root-to-leaf) order, while locks are released in bottom-up (leaf-to-root) order.

To illustrate the protocol, consider the tree of Figure 11.26 and the following transactions:

- Let transaction T_{21} read record r_{a_2} and file F_a. T_{21} needs to lock the database, area A_1 and F_a in IS mode (and in that order), and then lock r_{a_2} in S mode.

- Let transaction T_{22} modify record r_{a_9} in file F_a. T_{22} needs to lock the database, area A_1, and file F_a in IX mode, and then lock r_{a_9} in X mode.

- Let transaction T_{23} read all the records in file F_a. T_{23} needs to lock the database and area A_1 in IS mode and then lock F_a in S mode.

- Let transaction T_{24} read the entire database. T_{24} can do so by locking the database in S mode.

We note that transactions T_{21}, T_{23}, and T_{24} can access the database concurrently. Transaction T_{22} can execute concurrently with T_{21} but not with either T_{23}, or T_{24}.

This protocol enhances concurrency and reduces lock overhead. This is particularly useful in applications that include a mix of:

- Short transactions that access only a few data items.

- Long transactions that produce reports from an entire file or set of files.

There is a similar locking protocol which is applicable to database systems in which data items are organized in the form of a directed acyclic graph. We refer the interested reader to the bibliographic notes for additional references. Deadlock is possible in the protocol presented above as was the case for the two-phase locking protocol. There are techniques to reduce deadlock frequency in the multiple granularity protocol and to eliminate deadlock entirely. These techniques are referenced in the bibliographic notes.

11.7 Multiversion Schemes

The concurrency control schemes discussed thus far ensure serializability by either delaying an operation or aborting the transaction that issued the operation. For example, a *read* operation may be delayed because the appropriate value has not been written yet; or it may be rejected (that is, the issuing transaction must be aborted) because the value it was supposed to read has already been overwritten. These difficulties could be avoided if old copies of each data item are kept in a system.

In *multiversion* database systems, each **write**(Q) operation creates a new version of Q. When a **read**(Q) operation is issued, the system selects one of the versions of Q to be read. The concurrency control scheme must ensure that the selection of the version to be read is done in a manner that ensures serializability. It is also crucial, for performance reasons, that a transaction can determine easily and quickly which version of the data item should be read.

The most common technique used among multiversion schemes is timestamping. With each transaction T_i in the system, we associate a unique static timestamp, denoted by $TS(T_i)$. This timestamp is assigned in the same manner as described in Section 11.4.

With each data item Q, a sequence of versions $<Q_1, Q_2, ..., Q_m>$ is associated. Each version Q_k contains three data fields:

- **Content**, the value of version Q_k.

- **W-timestamp**(Q_k), which denotes the timestamp of the transaction that created version Q_k.

- **R-timestamp**(Q_k), which denotes the largest timestamp of any transaction that successfully read version Q_k.

A transaction, say T_i, creates a new version Q_k of data item Q by issuing a **write**(Q) operation. The content field of the version holds the value written by T_i. The W-timestamp and R-timestamp are initialized to $TS(T_i)$. The R-timestamp value is updated whenever a transaction T_j reads the content of Q_k, and R-timestamp(Q_k) < $TS(T_j)$.

The multiversion timestamp scheme presented below ensures serializability. The scheme operates as follows. Suppose that transaction T_i issues a **read**(Q) or **write**(Q) operation. Let Q_k be a version of Q such that W-timestamp(Q_k) is the largest timestamp $\leq$ TS(T_i).

1. If transaction T_i issues a **read**(Q), then the value returned is that of the content of version Q_k.

2. If transaction T_i issues a **write**(Q), and if TS(T_i) < R-timestamp(Q_k), then transaction T_i is rolled back; otherwise a new version Q_k is created.

The justification for rule 1 is clear. A transaction reads the most recent version that comes before it in time. The second rule forces a transaction to abort if it is "too late" in doing a write. More precisely, if T_i attempts to write a version that some other transaction would have read, then we cannot allow that write to succeed.

The scheme has the desirable property that a read request never fails and is never made to wait. In typical database systems, where reading is a more frequent operation than writing, this advantage may be of major practical significance.

The scheme, however, suffers from two undesirable properties. First, the reading of a data item also requires the updating of the R-timestamp field, resulting in two potential disk accesses rather than one. Second, the conflicts between transactions are resolved through rollbacks rather than waits. This may be quite expensive. An algorithm to alleviate this problem is referenced in the bibliographic notes.

Finally, we note that the multiversion concurrency control scheme does not guard against cascading rollbacks. To eliminate cascading rollback, we can use the same techniques used for the timestamp concurrency control scheme of Section 11.4.

11.8 Deadlock Handling

A system is in a deadlock state if there exists a set of transactions such that every transaction in the set is waiting for another transaction in the set. More precisely, there exists a set of waiting transactions $\{T_0, T_1, ..., T_n\}$ such that T_0 is waiting for a data item which is held by T_1, and T_1 is waiting for a data item which is held by T_2 and ...,and T_{n-1} is waiting for a data item which is held by T_n, and T_n is waiting for a data item which is held by T_0. The only remedy to this undesirable situation is for the system to invoke some drastic action, such as rolling back some of the transactions involved in the deadlock.

There are two principal methods for dealing with the deadlock problem. We can use a *deadlock prevention* protocol to ensure that the system will *never* enter a deadlock state. Alternatively, we can allow the system to enter a deadlock state and then try to recover using a *deadlock detection and recovery* scheme. As we shall see, both methods may result in transaction rollback. Prevention is commonly used if the probability that the system would enter a deadlock state is relatively high; otherwise, detection and recovery should be used.

We note that a detection and recovery scheme requires overhead that includes not only the run time cost of maintaining the necessary information and executing the detection algorithm, but also the potential losses inherent in recovery from a deadlock.

11.8.1 Deadlock Prevention

There are a number of different schemes that can be used for deadlock prevention. The simplest scheme requires that each transaction locks all its data items before it begins execution. Moreover, either all are locked in one step, or none are locked. There are two main disadvantages to these protocols. First, *data item utilization* may be very low, since many of the data items may be locked but unused for a long period of time. Second, *starvation* is possible. A transaction that needs several popular data items may have to wait indefinitely while at least one of the data items that it needs is always allocated to some other transaction.

Another method for preventing deadlocks is to impose a partial ordering of all data items and require that a transaction can lock a data item only in the order specified by the partial order. We have seen one such scheme in the tree protocol.

Another approach for preventing deadlocks is to use preemption and transaction rollbacks. To control the preemption, we assign a unique timestamp to each transaction. These timestamps are used to decide whether a transaction should wait or roll back. If a transaction is rolled back, it retains its *old* timestamp when restarted. Two different deadlock prevention schemes using timestamps have been proposed:

- The **wait-die** scheme is based on a nonpreemptive technique. When transaction T_i requests a data item currently held by T_j, T_i is allowed to wait only if it has a smaller timestamp than that of T_j (that is, T_i is older than T_j). Otherwise, T_i is rolled back (dies). For example, suppose that transactions T_{25}, T_{26}, and T_{27} have timestamps 5, 10, and 15 respectively. If T_{25} requests a data item held by T_{26}, T_{25} will wait. If T_{27} requests a data item held by T_{26}, T_{27} will be rolled back.

- The **wound-wait** scheme is based on a preemptive technique and is a counterpart to the *wait-die* system. When transaction T_i requests a data item currently held by T_j, then T_i is allowed to wait only if it has a larger timestamp than T_j (that is, T_i is younger than T_j). Otherwise, T_j is rolled back (T_j is *wounded* by T_i). Returning to our previous example, with transactions T_{25}, T_{26}, and T_{27}. If T_{25} requests a data item held by T_{26}, then the data item will be preempted from T_{26} and T_{26} will be rolled back. If T_{27} requests a data item held by T_{26}, then T_{27} will wait.

Both schemes avoid starvation. This follows from the fact that at any time, there is a transaction with the smallest timestamp. This transaction *cannot* be required to roll back in either scheme. Since timestamps always increase, and since transactions are *not* assigned new timestamps when they are rolled back, a transaction which is rolled back will eventually have the smallest timestamp. Thus, it will not be rolled back again.

There are, however, significant differences in the way the two schemes operate.

- In the *wait-die* scheme, an older transaction must wait for a younger one to release its data item. Thus the older the transaction gets, the more it tends to wait. By contrast, in the *wound-wait* scheme, an older transaction never waits for a younger transaction.

- In the *wait-die* scheme, if a transaction T_i dies and is rolled back because it requested a data item held by transaction T_j, then T_i may reissue the same sequence of requests when it is restarted. If the data item is still held by T_j, then T_i will die again. Thus T_i may die several times before acquiring the needed data item. Contrast this series of events with what happens in the *wound-wait* scheme. Transaction T_i is wounded and rolled back because T_j requested a data item it holds. When T_i is restarted and requests the data item now being held by T_j, T_i waits. Thus, there may be fewer rollbacks in the *wound-wait* scheme.

The major problem with all these schemes is that some unnecessary rollbacks may occur.

11.8.2 Deadlock Detection and Recovery

If a system does not employ some protocol that ensures deadlock freedom, then a detection and recovery scheme must be used. An algorithm that examines the state of the system is invoked periodically to determine whether a deadlock has occurred. If it has, then the system must attempt to recover from the deadlock. In order to do so the system must:

- Maintain information about the current allocation of data items to transactions, as well as any outstanding data item requests.

- Provide an algorithm that uses this information to determine whether the system has entered a deadlock state.

- Recover from the deadlock when the detection algorithm determines that a deadlock exists.

In the following, we shall elaborate on the above issues.

Deadlock Detection

Deadlocks can be described precisely in terms of a directed graph called a *wait-for graph*. This graph consists of a pair $G = (V,E)$ where V is a set of vertices and E is a set of edges. The set of vertices consists of all the transactions in the system. Each element in the set E of edges is an ordered pair (T_i,T_j). If $(T_i,T_j) \in E$, then there is a directed edge from transaction T_i to T_j, implying that transaction T_i is waiting for transaction T_j to release a data item that it needs.

When transaction T_i requests a data item currently being held by transaction T_j, then the edge (T_i,T_j) is inserted in the wait-for graph. This edge is removed only when transaction T_j is no longer holding a data item needed by transaction T_i.

A deadlock exists in the system if and only if the wait-for graph contains a cycle. Each transaction involved in the cycle is said to be deadlocked. In order to detect deadlocks, the system needs to maintain the wait-for graph and periodically invoke an algorithm that searches for a cycle in the graph.

To illustrate these concepts consider the wait-for graph in Figure 11.28, which depicts the following situation:

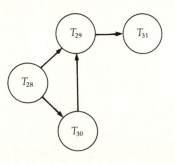

Figure 11.28   Wait-for graph with no cycle.

- Transaction T_{28} is waiting for transactions T_{29} and T_{30}.

- Transaction T_{30} is waiting for transaction T_{29}.

- Transaction T_{29} is waiting for transaction T_{31}.

Since the graph has no cycle, the system is not in a deadlock state.

Suppose now that transaction T_{31} is requesting an item held by T_{30}. The edge (T_{31}, T_{30}) is added to the wait-for graph resulting in a new system state as depicted in Figure 11.29. This time, the graph contains the cycle:

$$T_{29} \rightarrow T_{31} \rightarrow T_{30} \rightarrow T_{29}$$

implying that transactions T_{29}, T_{30}, and T_{31} are all deadlocked.

Consequently, the question arises: When should we invoke the detection algorithm? The answer depends on two factors:

- How often does a deadlock occur?

- How many transactions will be affected by the deadlock?

If deadlocks occur frequently, then the detection algorithm should be invoked more frequently. Data items allocated to deadlocked transactions will be unavailable to other transactions until the deadlock can be broken. In addition, the number of cycles in the graph may also grow. In the worst case, we would invoke the detection algorithm every time a request for allocation cannot be granted immediately.

Recovery from Deadlock

When a detection algorithm determines that a deadlock exists, the system must *recover* from the deadlock. The most common solution is to roll back

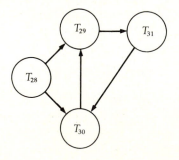

Figure 11.29   Wait-for graph with a cycle.

one or more transactions in order to break the deadlock. To do so, three issues need to be addressed:

- **Selecting a victim**. Given a set of deadlocked transactions, we must determine which transaction (or transactions) to roll back in order to break the deadlock. We should roll back those transactions that will incur the minimum cost. Unfortunately, the term "minimum cost" is not a precise one. Many factors may determine the cost of a rollback, including:

  1. How long the transaction has computed, and how much longer the transaction will compute before completing its designated task.

  2. How many data items the transaction has used.

  3. How many more data items the transaction needs in order to complete.

  4. How many transactions will be involved in the rollback.

- **Rollback**. Once we have decided that a particular transaction must be rolled back, we must determine how far this transaction should be rolled back. The simplest solution is a total rollback: abort the transaction and then restart it. However, it is more effective to roll back the transaction only as far as necessary to break the deadlock. This method, however, requires the system to keep additional information about the state of all the running transactions. We refer the interested reader to the bibliographic notes section for relevant references.

- **Starvation**. In a system where the selecting of victims is based primarily on cost factors, it may happen that the same transaction is always picked as a victim. As a result, this transaction never completes its designated task. This situation is called *starvation*, and needs to be dealt with in any practical system. Clearly, we must ensure that transaction can be picked as a victim only a (small) finite number of times. The most common solution is to include the number of rollbacks in the cost factor.

11.9 Summary

When several transactions execute concurrently in the database, the consistency of data may no longer be preserved. It is necessary for the system to control the interaction among the concurrent transactions, and this control is achieved through one of a variety of mechanisms which are commonly referred to as *concurrency control* schemes.

A transaction is a unit that preserves consistency. We therefore require that any schedule produced by processing a set of transactions concurrently will be computationally equivalent to a schedule produced by running these transactions serially in some order. A system that guarantees this property is said to ensure *serializability*.

In order to determine whether serializability is maintained, we must construct a *precedence graph*. In the case where a transaction must read a data item before it can write into it, testing can be done by searching for a cycle in the graph which can be done in order n^2 time. In the case where a transaction writes onto a data item without first reading that item testing can be done in order 2^n time, by constructing a *labeled precedence graph* and searching for all possible distinct labeled graphs for a cycle.

In order to ensure serializability, a number of different concurrency control schemes can be used. All these do so by either delaying an operation or aborting the transaction that issued the operation. The most common ones are *locking protocols*, *timestamp ordering* schemes, *validation* techniques, and *multiversion* schemes.

A locking protocol is a set of rules which state when a transaction may lock and unlock each of the data items in the database. The *two-phase* locking protocol allows a transaction to lock a new data item only if it has not yet unlocked any data item. The protocol ensures serializability but not deadlock freedom. In the absence of information concerning the manner in which data items are accessed, the two-phase locking protocol is both necessary and sufficient for ensuring serializability.

A timestamp-ordering scheme ensures serializability by selecting an ordering in advance between every pair of transactions. A unique fixed timestamp is associated with each transaction in the system. The timestamps of the transactions determine the serializability order. Thus if the timestamp of transaction T_i is smaller than the timestamp of transaction T_j, then the scheme ensures that the produced schedule is equivalent to a serial schedule in which transaction T_i appears before transaction T_j. This is done by rolling back a transaction whenever such an order is violated.

A validation scheme is an appropriate concurrency control method in the cases where the majority of transactions are read-only transactions, and thus the rate of conflicts among these transactions may be very low. A unique fixed timestamp is associated with each transaction in the system. The serializability order is determined by the timestamp of the transaction. A transaction in this scheme is never delayed. It must, however, pass a validation test, in order to complete. If it does not pass the validation test, it is rolled back to its initial state.

A multiversion concurrency control scheme assumes that each **write**(Q) operation creates a new version of Q. When a **read**(Q) operation is issued, the system selects one of the versions of Q to be read. The concurrency control scheme ensures that the selection of the version to be read is done in a manner that ensures serializability. This is accomplished through the use of timestamps. A read operation always succeeds, while a write operation may result in the rollback of the transaction.

There are circumstances where it would be advantageous to group several data items and treat them as one aggregate data item for purposes of working, resulting in multiple levels of *granularity*. This can be accomplished by allowing data items of various sizes and defining a hierarchy of data items, where the small items are nested within larger ones. Such a hierarchy can be represented graphically as a tree. Locks are acquired in root-to-leaf order, while locks are released in leaf-to-root order. The protocol ensures serializability but not freedom from deadlock.

Various locking protocols including the multiple granularity locking scheme do not guard against deadlocks. One way to prevent deadlock is to use preemption and transaction rollbacks. To control the preemption, we assign a unique timestamp to each transaction. These timestamps are used to decide whether a transaction should wait or roll back. If a transaction is rolled back it retains its *old* timestamp when restarted. The *wait-die* and *wound-wait* schemes are two preemptive schemes. Another method for dealing with deadlock is to use a deadlock detection and recovery scheme. To do so a *wait-for* graph is constructed. A system is in a deadlock state if and only if the wait-for graph contains a cycle. When a detection algorithm determines that a deadlock exists, the system must *recover* from the deadlock. This is accomplished by rolling back one or more transactions in order to break the deadlock.

Exercises

11.1 Explain the concept of transaction atomicity.

11.2 Consider the precedence graph of Figure 11.30. Is the corresponding schedule serializable? Explain your answer.

11.3 Consider the labeled precedence graph of Figure 11.31. Is the corresponding history serializable? Explain your answer.

11.4 Testing for serializability, even in the case of reads before writes, is not a practical method for dealing with the serializability issue. Nevertheless, it is covered in great detail in this chapter. Can you guess why?

11.5 Show that the two-phase locking protocol ensures serializability.

11.6 Show that there are schedules that are possible under the two-phase locking protocol but are not possible under the timestamp protocol, and vice versa.

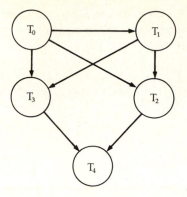

Figure 11.30   Precedence graph.

11.7 Consider the following two transactions

$$T_0: \textbf{read } (A);$$
$$\textbf{read } (B);$$
$$\textbf{if } A = 0 \textbf{ then } B := B + 1;$$
$$T_1: \textbf{read } (B);$$
$$\textbf{read } (A);$$
$$\textbf{if } B = 0 \textbf{ then } A := A + 1;$$

Let the consistency requirement be $A = 0 \lor B = 0$, with $A = B = 0$ the initial values.

a. Show that every serial execution involving these two transactions preserves the consistency of the database.

b. Show a parallel execution of T_0 and T_1 which produces a serializable schedule.

c. Show a parallel execution of T_0 and T_1 which produces a nonserializable schedule.

11.8 Add lock and unlock instructions to transactions T_0 and T_1 of Exercise 11.3 so that they observe the two-phase locking protocol. Can the execution of these transactions result in a deadlock? Show how two-phase locking avoids the nonserializable schedule of Exercise 11.3c.

11.9 Consider the following extension to the tree locking protocol which allows both shared and exclusive locks:

- A transaction can be either a read-only transaction in which case it can request only shared locks, or an update transaction in which case it can request only exclusive locks.

- Each transaction must follow the rules of the tree protocol. Read-only transactions may lock any data item first, while update transactions must lock the root first.

Show that the protocol ensures serializability and deadlock freedom.

11.10 Consider a database organized in the form of a rooted tree. Suppose that we insert a dummy vertex between each pair of vertices. Show that if we follow the tree protocol on the new tree, we get more concurrency than if we follow the tree protocol on the original tree.

11.11 Consider the following graph-based locking protocol which allows only exclusive lock modes and which operates on data graphs which are in the form of a rooted DAG.

- A transaction can lock any vertex first.

- To lock any other vertex, the transaction must be holding a lock on the majority of the parents of the vertex.

Show that the protocol ensures serializability and deadlock freedom.

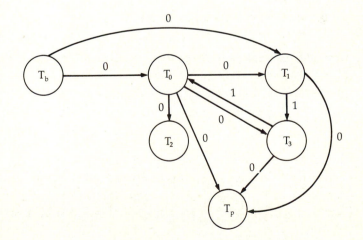

Figure 11.31   Precedence graph.

11.12 Consider the following graph-based locking protocol which allows only exclusive lock modes and which operates on data graphs which are in the form of a rooted DAG.

- A transaction can lock any vertex first.

- To lock any other vertex, the transaction must have visited all the parents of that vertex and must be holding a lock on one of the parents of the vertex.

Show that the protocol ensures serializability and deadlock freedom.

11.13 Consider a database system which includes an atomic **increment** operation in addition to the **read** and **write** operations. Let V be the value of data item X. The operation

$$\textbf{increment}(X) \text{ by } C$$

sets the value of X to $V + C$ in an atomic step. The value of X is not available to the transaction unless it executes a **read**(X). Figure 11.32 shows a lock compatibility matrix for three lock modes: share mode, exclusive mode, and incrementation mode.

a. Show that if all transactions lock data they access in the corresponding mode that two-phase locking ensures serializability.

b. Show that the inclusion of **increment** mode locks allows for increased concurrency. (Hint: Consider check-clearing transactions in our bank example.)

11.14 Consider the validation concurrency control scheme of Section 11.5. Show that by choosing Validation(T_i) rather than Start(T_i) as the timestamp of transaction T_i we can expect better response time provided that conflict rates among transactions is indeed low.

	S	X	I
S	true	false	false
S	false	false	false
I	false	false	true

Figure 11.32   Lock compatibility matrix.

11.15 Consider a variant of the tree protocol called the *forest* protocol. The database is organized as a forest of rooted trees. Each transaction T_i must follow the following rules:

- The first lock in each tree may be on any data item.

- The second, and all subsequent locks in a tree may be requested only if the parent of the requested mode is currently locked.

- Data items may be unlocked at any time.

- A data item may not be re-locked by T_i after it has been unlocked by T_i.

Show that the forest protocol does not ensure serializability.

Bibliographic Notes

The concept of serializability was formulated by Eswaran et al. [1976] in connection to their work on concurrency control for System R. The results concerning serializability testing are due to Papadimitriou et al. [1977] and Papadimitriou [1979]. Additional results are presented by Soisalon-Soinineu and Wood [1982].

The two-phase locking protocol was introduced by Eswaran et al. [1976]. The tree locking protocol is due to Silberschatz and Kedem [1980]. Other non two-phase locking protocols that operate on more general graphs were developed by Yannakakis et al. [1979], Kedem and Silberschatz [1983], and Buckley and Silberschatz [1985]. General discussions concerning locking protocols are offered by Lein and Weinberger [1978], Yannakakis et al. [1979], Yannakakis [1981] and Papadimitriou [1982]. Korth [1983] explores various lock modes which can be obtained from the basic shared and exclusive lock modes. Various algorithms for concurrent access to dynamic search trees were developed by Bayer and Schkolnick [1977], Ellis [1980a, 1980b], Lehman and Yao [1981], and Manber and Ladner [1982]. Exercise 11.9 is from Silberschatz and Kedem [1980]. Exercise 11.10 is from Buckley and Silberschatz [1984]. Exercise 11.11 is from Kedem and Silberschatz [1979]. Exercise 11.12 is from Yannakakis et al. [1980]. Exercise 11.13 is from Korth [1983].

The timestamp-based concurrency control scheme is due to Reed [1983]. An exposition of various timestamp-based concurrency control algorithms is presented by Bernstein and Goodman [1980a]. The validation concurrency control scheme is due to Kung and Robinson [1981].

The locking protocol for multiple granularity data items is due to Gray et al. [1975]. A detailed description is presented by Gray et al. [1976].

Korth [1983] formalizes multiple granularity locking for an arbitrary collection of lock modes (allowing for more semantics than simply read and write). This approach includes a class of lock modes called *update* modes to deal with lock conversion. Carey [1983] extends the multiple granularity idea to timestamp-based concurrency control. An extension of the protocol to ensure deadlock freedom is presented by Korth [1982].

Dijkstra [1965] was one of the first and most influential contributors in the deadlock area. Holt [1971, 1972] was the first to formalize the notion of deadlocks in terms of a graph theoretical model similar to the one presented in this chapter. The timestamp deadlock detection algorithm is due to Rosenkrantz et al. [1978]. An analysis of the probability of waiting and deadlock is presented by Gray et al. [1981b]. Theoretical results concerning deadlocks and serializability are presented by Yannakakis [1981] and Fussell et al. [1981].

Several NP-completeness results exist for concurrency control. Papadimitriou [1979] shows that testing for serializability is NP-complete. Korth [1981] shows that minimizing the number of locks taken by transactions under multiple granularity locking is NP-complete. The theory of NP-completeness is presented in Aho et al. [1974], and Garey and Johnson [1979].

A comprehensive survey paper is presented by Gray [1978]. Textbook discussions are offered by Ullman [1982a] and Date [1983].

Distributed Databases

In a distributed database system, the database is stored on several computers. The computers in a distributed system communicate with each other through various communication media, such as high-speed buses or telephone lines. They do not share main memory, nor do they share a clock.

The processors in a distributed system may vary in size and function. They may include small microcomputers, work stations, minicomputers, and large general-purpose computer systems. These processors are referred to by a number of different names such as *sites*, *nodes*, *computers*, and so on, depending on the context in which they are mentioned. We mainly use the term *site*, in order to emphasize the physical distribution of these systems.

A distributed database system consists of a collection of sites, each of which may participate in the execution of transactions which access data at one site, or several sites. The main difference between centralized and distributed database systems is that, in the former, the data resides in one single location, while in the latter, the data resides in several locations. As we shall see, this distribution of data is the cause of many difficulties that will be addressed in this chapter.

12.1 Structure of Distributed Databases

A distributed database system consists of a collection of sites, each of which maintains a local database system. Each site is able to process *local transactions*, those transactions that access data only in that single site. In addition, a site may participate in the execution of *global* transactions, those transactions that access data in several sites. The execution of global transactions requires communication among the sites.

The sites in the system can be connected physically in a variety of ways. The various topologies are represented as graphs whose nodes correspond to sites. An edge from node A to node B corresponds to a direct connection between the two sites. Some of the most common configurations are depicted in Figure 12.1. The major differences among these configurations involve:

- **Installation cost**. The cost of physically linking the sites in the system.

- **Communication cost**. The cost in time and money to send a message from site *A* to site *B*.

- **Reliability**. The frequency with which a link or site fails.

- **Availability**. The degree to which data can be accessed despite the failure of some links or sites.

As we shall see, these differences play an important role in choosing the appropriate mechanism for handling the distribution of data.

The sites of a distributed database system may be distributed physically either over a large geographical area (such as the United States), or over a small geographical area (such as a single building or a number of adjacent buildings). The former type of network is referred to as a *long-haul* network, while the latter is referred to as a *local-area* network.

Since the sites in long-haul networks are distributed physically over a large geographical area, the communication links are likely to be relatively slow and less reliable as compared with local-area networks. Typical long-haul links are telephone lines, microwave links, and satellite channels. In contrast, since all the sites in local-area networks are close to each other, the communication links are of higher speed and lower error rate than their counterparts in long-haul networks. The most common links are twisted pair, baseband coaxial, broadband coaxial, and fiber optics.

Let us illustrate these concepts by considering a banking system consisting of four branches located in four different cities. Each branch has its own computer with a database consisting of all the accounts maintained at that branch. Each such installation is thus a site. There also exists one single site which maintains information about all the branches of the bank. Suppose that the database systems at the various sites are based on the relational model. Thus, each branch maintains (among others) the relation *deposit(Deposit-scheme)* where

Deposit-scheme = (branch-name, account-number, customer-name, balance)

The site containing information about the four branches maintains the relation *branch(Branch-scheme)*, where

Branch-scheme = (branch-name, assets, branch-city)

There are other relations maintained at the various sites which are ignored for the purpose of our example.

A local transaction is a transaction that accesses accounts in the *one single* site, at which the transaction was initiated. A global transaction, on the other hand, is one which either accesses accounts in a site different

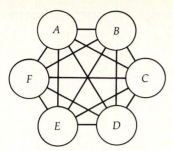

fully connected network

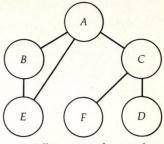

partially connected network

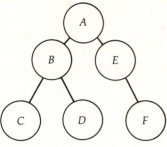

tree structured network

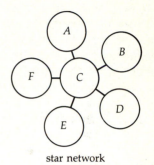

star network

ring network

Figure 12.1   Network topology.

from the one at which the transaction was initiated, or accesses accounts in several different sites. To illustrate the difference between these two types of transactions, consider the transaction to add $50 to account number 177 located at the Valleyview branch. If the transaction was initiated at the Valleyview branch, then it is considered local; otherwise, it is considered global. A transaction to transfer $50 from account 177 to account 305, which is located at the Hillside branch, is a global transaction since accounts in two different sites are accessed as a result of its execution.

What makes the above configuration a distributed database system are the facts that:

- The various sites are aware of each other.

- Each site provides an environment for executing both local and global transactions.

12.2 Trade-offs in Distributing the Database

There are several reasons for building distributed database systems, including sharing of data, reliability and availability, and speedup of query processing. However, along with these advantages come several disadvantages, including software development cost, greater potential for bugs, and increased processing overhead. In this section, we shall elaborate briefly on each of these.

12.2.1 Advantages of Data Distribution

The primary advantage of distributed database systems is the ability to share and access data in a reliable and efficient manner.

Data Sharing and Distributed Control

If a number of different sites are connected to each other, then a user at one site may be able to access data that is available at another site. For example, in the distributed banking system described in Section 12.1, it is possible for a user in one branch to access data in another branch. Without this capability, a user wishing to transfer funds from one branch to another would have to resort to some external mechanism for such a transfer. This external mechanism would, in effect, be a single centralized database.

The primary advantage to accomplishing data sharing by means of data distribution is that each site is able to retain a degree of control over data stored locally. In a centralized system, the database administrator of the central site controls the database. In a distributed system, there is a global database administrator responsible for the entire system. A part of these responsibilities is delegated to the local database administrator for each site. Depending upon the design of the distributed database system, each local administrator may have a different degree of autonomy. This is referred to as *local autonomy*. The possibility of local autonomy is often a major advantage of distributed databases.

Reliability and Availability

If one site fails in a distributed system, the remaining sites may be able to continue operating. In particular, if data are replicated in several sites, a transaction needing a particular data item may find it in several sites. Thus, the failure of a site does not necessarily imply the shutdown of the system.

The failure of one site must be detected by the system, and appropriate action may be needed to recover from the failure. The system must no longer use the services of the failed site. Finally, when the failed site recovers or is repaired, mechanisms must be available to integrate it smoothly back into the system.

Although recovery from failure is more complex in distributed systems than in centralized systems, the ability of most of the system to continue to operate despite the failure of one site results in increased availability. Availability is crucial for database systems used for real-time applications. Loss of access to data by, for example, an airline may result in the loss of potential ticket buyers to competitors.

Speedup of Query Processing

If a query involves data at several sites, it may be possible to split the query into subqueries that can be executed in parallel by several sites. Such parallel computation allows for faster processing of a user's query. In those cases in which data is replicated, queries may be directed by the system to the least heavily loaded sites.

12.2.2 Disadvantages of Data Distribution

The primary disadvantage of distributed database systems is the added complexity required to ensure proper coordination among the sites. This increased complexity takes the form of:

- **Software development cost**. It is more difficult to implement a distributed database system and, thus, more costly.

- **Greater potential for bugs**. Since the sites that comprise the distributed system operate in parallel, it is harder to ensure the correctness of algorithms. The potential exists for extremely subtle bugs. The art of constructing distributed algorithms remains an active and important area of research.

- **Increased processing overhead**. The exchange of messages and the additional computation required to achieve intersite coordination is a form of overhead that does not arise in centralized systems.

In choosing the design for a database system, the designer must balance the advantages against the disadvantages of distribution of data. We shall see that there are several approaches to distributed database design ranging from fully distributed designs to designs which include a large degree of centralization.

12.3 Design of Distributed Databases

The principles of database design that we discussed earlier apply to distributed databases as well. In this section, we focus on those design issues that are specific to distributed databases.

Consider a relation r that is to be stored in the database. There are several issues involved in storing this relation in the distributed database, including:

- **Replication**. The system maintains several identical replicas (copies) of the relation. Each replica is stored in a different site, resulting in data replication. The alternative to replication is to store only one copy of relation r.

- **Fragmentation**. The relation is partitioned into several fragments. Each fragment is stored in a different site.

- **Replication and Fragmentation**. This is a combination of the above two notions. The relation is partitioned into several fragments. The system maintains several identical replicas of each such fragment.

In the following subsections, we elaborate on each of these.

12.3.1 Data Replication

If relation r is replicated, a copy of relation r is stored in two or more sites. In the most extreme case, we have *full replication*, in which a copy is stored in every site in the system.

There are a number of advantages and disadvantages to replication.

- **Availability**. If one of the sites containing relation r fails, then the relation r may be found in another site. Thus, the system may continue to process queries involving r despite the failure of one site.

- **Increased parallelism**. In the case where the majority of access to the relation r results in only the reading of the relation, then several sites can process queries involving r in parallel. The more replicas of r there are, the greater the chance that the needed data is found in the site where the transaction is executing. Hence, data replication minimizes movement of data between sites.

- **Increased overhead on update**. The system must ensure that all replicas of a relation r are consistent since otherwise erroneous computations may result. This implies that whenever r is updated, this update must be propagated to all sites containing replicas, resulting in increased overhead. For example, in a banking system, where account information is replicated in various sites, it is necessary that transactions assure that the balance in a particular account agrees in all sites.

In general, replication enhances the performance of read operations and increases the availability of data to read transactions. However, update transactions incur greater overhead. The problem of controlling concurrent updates by several transactions to replicated data is more complex than the centralized approach to concurrency control that we saw in Chapter 11. We may simplify the management of replicas of relation r by choosing one of them as the *primary copy of r*. For example, in a banking system, an account may be associated with the site in which the account has been opened. Similarly, in an airline reservation system, a flight may be associated with the site at which the flight originates. We shall examine the options for distributed concurrency control in Section 12.7.

12.3.2 Data Fragmentation

If the relation r if fragmented, r is divided into a number of *fragments* r_1, r_2, ..., r_n. These fragments contain sufficient information to reconstruct the original relation r. As we shall see, this reconstruction can take place through the application of either the union operation or a special type of join operation on the various fragments. There are two different schemes for fragmenting a relation: *horizontal* fragmentation and *vertical* fragmentation. Horizontal fragmentation splits the relation by assigning each tuple of r to one or more fragments. Vertical fragmentation splits the relation by decomposing the scheme R of relation r in a special way that we shall discuss. These two schemes can be applied successively to the same relation, resulting in a number of different fragments. Note that some information may appear in several fragments.

Below we discuss the various ways for fragmenting a relation. We shall illustrate these by fragmenting the relation *deposit*, with scheme:

Deposit-scheme = (*branch-name, account-number, customer-name, balance*)

The relation *deposit* (*Deposit-scheme*) is shown in Figure 12.2.

branch-name	account-number	customer-name	balance
Hillside	305	Lowman	500
Hillside	226	Camp	336
Valleyview	117	Camp	205
Valleyview	402	Kahn	10000
Hillside	155	Kahn	62
Valleyview	408	Kahn	1123
Valleyview	639	Green	750

Figure 12.2   Sample *deposit* relation.

Horizontal Fragmentation

The relation r is partitioned into a number of subsets, $r_1, r_2, ..., r_n$. Each subset consists of a number of tuples of relation r. Each tuple of relation r must belong to one of the fragments, so that the original relation can be reconstructed, if needed.

A fragment may be defined as a *selection* on the global relation r. That is, a predicate P_i is used to construct fragment r_i as follows:

$$r_i = \sigma_{P_i}(r)$$

The reconstruction of the relation r can be obtained by taking the union of all fragments, that is,

$$r = \bigcup_{i=1}^{n} r_i$$

To illustrate this, suppose that the relation r is the *deposit* relation of Figure 12.2. This relation can be divided into n different fragments, each of which consists of tuples of accounts belonging to a particular branch. If the

branch-name	account-number	customer-name	balance
Hillside	305	Lowman	500
Hillside	226	Camp	336
Hillside	155	Kahn	62

(a)

branch-name	account-number	customer-name	balance
Valleyview	177	Camp	205
Valleyview	402	Kahn	10000
Valleyview	408	Kahn	1123
Valleyview	639	Green	750

(b)

Figure 12.3   Horizontal fragmentation of relation *deposit*.

banking system has only two branches, Hillside and Valleyview, then there are two different fragments:

$$deposit_1 = \sigma_{branch\text{-}name\, =\, \text{"Hillside"}} (deposit)$$
$$deposit_2 = \sigma_{branch\text{-}name\, =\, \text{"Valleyview"}} (deposit)$$

These two fragments are shown in Figure 12.3. Fragment $deposit_1$ is stored in the Hillside site. Fragment $deposit_2$ is stored in the Valleyview site.

In our example, the fragments are disjoint. By changing the selection predicates used to construct the fragments, we may have a particular tuple of r appear in more than one of the r_i. This is a form of data replication about which we shall say more at the end of this section.

Vertical Fragmentation

In its most simple form, vertical fragmentation is the same as decomposition (see Chapter 6). Vertical fragmentation of $r(R)$ involves the definition of several subsets $R_1, R_2, \ldots, R_n$ of R such that $\cup_{i\,=\,1}^{n} R_i = R$. Each fragment r_i of r is defined by:

$$r_i = \Pi_{R_i} (r)$$

relation r can be reconstructed from the fragments by taking the natural join:

$$r = r_1 \bowtie r_2 \bowtie r_3 \bowtie \cdots \bowtie r_n$$

branch-name	account-number	customer-name	balance	tuple-id
Hillside	305	Lowman	500	1
Hillside	226	Camp	336	2
Valleyview	177	Camp	205	3
Valleyview	402	Kahn	10000	4
Hillside	155	Kahn	62	5
Valleyview	408	Kahn	1123	6
Valleyview	639	Green	750	7

Figure 12.4 The *deposit* relation of Figure 12.2 with tuple-ids.

More generally, vertical fragmentation is accomplished by adding a special attribute called a *tuple-id* to the scheme *R*. A tuple-id is a physical or logical address for a tuple. Since each tuple in *r* must have a unique address, the *tuple-id* attribute is a key for the augmented scheme.

In Figure 12.4, we show the relation *deposit'*, the *deposit* relation of Figure 12.2 with tuple-ids added. Figure 12.5 shows a vertical decomposition of the scheme *Deposit-scheme* ∪ *tuple-id* into:

$$Deposit\text{-}scheme\text{-}3 = (branch\text{-}name, customer\text{-}name, tuple\text{-}id)$$
$$Deposit\text{-}scheme\text{-}4 = (account\text{-}number, balance, tuple\text{-}id)$$

The two relations shown in Figure 12.5 result from computing:

$$deposit_3 = \Pi_{Deposit\text{-}scheme\text{-}3}(deposit')$$
$$deposit_4 = \Pi_{Deposit\text{-}scheme\text{-}4}(deposit')$$

branch-name	customer-name	tuple-id
Hillside	Lowman	1
Hillside	Camp	2
Valleyview	Camp	3
Valleyview	Kahn	4
Hillside	Kahn	5
Valleyview	Kahn	6
Valleyview	Green	7

(a)

account-number	balance	tuple-id
305	500	1
226	336	2
177	205	3
402	10000	4
155	62	5
408	1123	6
639	750	7

(b)

Figure 12.5   Vertical fragmentation of relation *deposit*.

To reconstruct the original *deposit* relation from the fragments, we compute

$$\Pi_{Deposit\text{-}scheme} (deposit_3 \bowtie deposit_4)$$

Note that the expression

$$deposit_3 \bowtie deposit_4$$

is a special from of natural join. The join attribute is *tuple-id*. Since the *tuple-id* value represents an address, it is possible to pair a tuple of *deposit*$_3$ with the corresponding tuple of *deposit*$_4$ by using the address given by the *tuple-id* value. This address allows direct retrieval of the tuple without the need for an index. Thus, this natural join may be computed much more efficiently than typical natural joins.

Although the *tuple-id* attribute is important in the implementation of vertical partitioning, it is important that this attribute not be visible to users. If users are given access to tuple-ids, it becomes impossible for the system to change tuple addresses. Furthermore, the accessibility of internal addresses violates the notion of data independence, one of the main virtues of the relational model.

Mixed Fragmentation

The relation *r* is divided into a number of fragment relations $r_1, r_2, ..., r_n$. Each fragment is obtained as the result of applying either the horizontal fragmentation or vertical fragmentation scheme on relation *r*, or a fragment of *r* which was obtained previously.

To illustrate this, suppose that the relation *r* is the *deposit* relation of Figure 12.2. This relation is divided initially into the fragments *deposit*$_3$ and *deposit*$_4$ as defined above. We can now further divide fragment *deposit*$_3$ using the horizontal fragmentation scheme into the following two fragments:

$$deposit_{3a} = \sigma_{branch\text{-}name\ =\ \text{"Hillside"}} (deposit_3)$$
$$deposit_{3b} = \sigma_{branch\text{-}name\ =\ \text{"Valleyview"}} (deposit_3)$$

Thus relation *r* is divided into three fragments *deposit*$_{3a}$, *deposit*$_{3b}$, and *deposit*$_4$. Each of these may reside in a different site.

12.3.3 Data Replication and Fragmentation

The technique described above for data replication and data fragmentation can be applied successively to the same relation. That is, a fragment can be replicated; replicas can be fragmented; etc. For example, consider a distributed system consisting of sites S_1, S_2, ..., S_{10}. We can fragment *deposit* into *deposit*$_{3a}$, *deposit*$_{3b}$, and *deposit*$_4$, and, for example, store a copy of *deposit*$_{3a}$ in sites S_1, S_3, and S_7, a copy of *deposit*$_{3b}$ at sites S_7 and S_{10}, and a copy of *deposit*$_4$ at sites S_2, S_8, and S_9.

12.4 Transparency and Autonomy

In the previous section, we saw that a relation r may be stored in a variety of ways in a distributed database system. It is essential that the system minimize the degree to which a user needs to be aware of how a relation is stored. As we shall see, a system can hide the details of the distribution of data in the network. We call this *network transparency*.

Network transparency is related, in some sense, to the issue of local autonomy. Network transparency is the degree to which system users may remain unaware of the details of the design of the distributed system. Local autonomy is the degree to which a designer or administrator of one site may be independent of the remainder of the distributed system.

We shall consider the issues of transparency and autonomy from the points of view of:

- Naming of data items.

- Replication of data items.

- Fragmentation of data items.

- Location of fragments and replicas.

12.4.1 Naming and Local Autonomy

Every data item in the database must have a unique name. This property is easy to ensure in a nondistributed database. However, in a distributed database, the various sites must ensure that two sites do not use the same name for distinct data items.

One solution to this problem is to require all names to be registered in a central *name-server*. This approach, however, suffers from several disadvantages:

- The name server may become a bottleneck.

- If the name server crashes, it may not be possible for any site in the distributed system to continue to run.

- There is little local autonomy since naming is controlled centrally.

An alternative approach that results in increased local autonomy is to require that each site prefix its own site identifier to any name it generates. This ensures that no two sites generate the same name (since each site has a unique identifier). Furthermore, no central control is required.

The above solution to the naming problem achieves local autonomy, but fails to achieve network transparency since site identifiers are attached to names. Thus, the *deposit* relation might be referred to as *site17.deposit* rather than simply *deposit*. We shall soon see how to overcome this problem.

Each replica of a data item and each fragment of a data item must have a unique name. It is important that the system be able to determine those replicas that are replicas of the same data item and those fragments that are fragments of the same data item. We adopt the convention of postfixing ".*f1*", ".*f2*", ..., ".*fn*" to fragments of a data item and ".*r1*", ".*r2*", ..., ".*rn*" to replicas. Thus:

$$site17.deposit.f3.r2$$

refers to replica 2 of fragment 3 of *deposit,* and this item was generated by site 17.

12.4.2 Replication and Fragmentation Transparency

It is undesirable to expect users to refer to a specific replica of a data item. Instead, the system should determine which replica to reference on a read request, and update all replicas on a modification request.

When a data item is requested, the specific replica need not be named. Instead, a catalog table is used by the system to determine all replicas for the data item.

Similarly, a user should not be required to know how a data item is fragmented. As we observed earlier, vertical fragments may contain *tuple-ids,* which represent addresses of tuples. Horizontal fragments may involve complicated selection predicates. Therefore, a distributed database system should allow requests to be stated in terms of the unfragmented data items. This presents no major difficulty, since it is always possible to reconstruct the original data item from its fragments. However, it may be inefficient to reconstruct data from fragments. Returning to our horizontal fragmentation of *deposit,* consider the query:

$$\sigma_{branch\text{-}name\,=\,\text{``Hillside''}}\,(deposit)$$

This query could be answered using only the *deposit*$_1$ fragment. However, fragmentation transparency requires that the user not be aware of the existence of fragments $deposit_1$ and $deposit_2$. If we reconstruct $deposit$ prior to processing the above query, we obtain the expression:

$$\sigma_{branch\text{-}name\ =\ \text{``Hillside''}}\ (deposit_1\ \cup\ deposit_2)$$

The optimization of this expression is left to the query optimizer (see Section 12.5.)

12.4.3 Location Transparency

If we have replication and fragmentation transparency provided by the system a large part of the design of the distributed database is hidden from the user. However, the site-identifier component of names forces the user to be aware of the fact that the system is distributed.

Location transparency is achieved by creating a set of alternative names or *aliases* for each user. A user may thus refer to data items by simple names that are translated by the system to complete names.

By using aliases, the user can be unaware of the physical location of a data item. Furthermore, the user is unaffected if the database administrator should decide to move a data item from one site to another.

12.4.4 Complete Naming Scheme

We have seen that a name provided by the user is translated in several steps before it refers to a specific replica of a specific fragment at a specific site. Figure 12.6 shows the complete translation scheme. To illustrate the operation of the scheme, consider a user located in the Hillside branch (site S_1). This user uses the alias *local-deposit* for the local fragment *deposit.f1* of the *deposit* relation. When this user references *local-deposit*, the query processing subsystem looks up *local-deposit* in the alias table and replaces it with $S_1.deposit.f1$. It is possible that $S_1.deposit.f1$ is replicated. If so, the replica table must be consulted in order to choose a replica. This replica could itself be fragmented, requiring examination of the fragmentation table. In most cases, only one or two tables must be consulted. However, the name translation scheme of Figure 12.6 is sufficiently general to deal with any combination of successive replication and fragmentation of relations.

12.4.5 Transparency and Updates to Replicated Data

Providing transparency for users that update the database is somewhat more difficult than providing transparency for readers. The main problem is ensuring that all replicas of a data item are updated and that all affected fragments are updated. In its full generality, the update problem for

    if *name* appears in the alias table
      then *expression* := *map* (*name*)
      else *expression* := *name*;

function *map* (*n*)
if *n* appears in the replica table
    then *n* := name of replica of *n*;
if *n* appears in the fragment table
    then begin
        result := expression to construct fragment;
        for each *n'* **in** *result* **do begin**
        replace *n'* in *result* with *map* (*n'*);
     end
return *result*;

Figure 12.6   Name translation algorithm.

replicated and fragmented data is related to the view update problem that we discussed earlier.

Consider our example of the *deposit* relation and the insertion of the tuple:

$$(Valleyview, 733, Jones, 600)$$

If *deposit* is fragmented horizontally, there is a predicate P_i associated with the *i* th fragment. We apply P_i to the tuple (Valleyview, 733, Jones, 600) to test if that tuple must be inserted in the *i* th fragment. Using our example of *deposit* being fragmented into

$$deposit_1 = \sigma_{branch\text{-}name = \text{"Hillside"}} (deposit)$$

$$deposit_2 = \sigma_{branch\text{-}name = \text{"Valleyview"}} (deposit)$$

the tuple would be inserted into $deposit_2$.

Now consider a vertical fragmentation of deposit into $deposit_3$ and $deposit_4$. The tuple (Valleyview, 733, Jones, 600) must be split into two fragments: one to be inserted into $deposit_3$ and one to be inserted into $deposit_4$.

If the *deposit* relation is replicated, the tuple (Valleyview, 733, Jones, 600) must be inserted in all replicas. This presents a problem if there is concurrent access to the *deposit* relation, since it is possible that one replica is updated earlier than another. We consider this problem in Section 12.7.

12.5 Distributed Query Processing

In Chapter 9, we saw that there are a variety of methods for computing the answer to a query. We saw several techniques for choosing a strategy for processing a query that minimize the amount of time it takes to compute the answer. For centralized systems, the primary criterion for measuring the cost of a particular strategy is the number of disk accesses. In a distributed system, we must take into account several other issues, including:

- The cost of data transmission over the network.

- The potential gain in performance from having several sites process parts of the query in parallel.

The relative cost of data transfer over the network and data transfer to and from disk varies widely depending on the type of network and speed of the disks. Thus, in general, we cannot focus solely on disk costs or on network costs. Rather, we must find a good trade-off between the two. As in Chapter 9, we shall emphasize the relational model although most of our techniques are applicable to the other models.

12.5.1 Replication and Fragmentation

Let us consider an extremely simple query, "Find all the tuples in the *deposit* relation." Although the query is simple, indeed trivial, processing of this query is not trivial, since the *deposit* relation may be fragmented, replicated, or both, as we saw in Section 12.3. If the *deposit* relation is replicated, we have a choice of replica to make. If no replicas are fragmented, we choose the replica for which the transmission cost is lowest. However, if a replica is fragmented, the choice is not as easy to make since several joins or unions need to be computed to reconstruct the *deposit* relation. In this case, the number of strategies for our simple example may be large. Indeed, choosing a strategy may be as complex a task as an arbitrary query.

Fragmentation transparency implies that a user may write a query such as

$$\sigma_{branch\text{-}name\ =\ \text{``Hillside''}}\ (deposit)$$

Since *deposit* is defined as

$$deposit_1\ \cup\ deposit_2$$

the expression that results from the name translation scheme is

$$\sigma_{branch\text{-}name\ =\ \text{``Hillside''}}\ (deposit_1\ \cup\ deposit_2)$$

Using the query optimization techniques of Chapter 9, we can simplify the above expression automatically.

12.5.2 Simple Join Processing

As we saw in Chapter 9, a major aspect of the selection of a query-processing strategy is choosing a join strategy. Consider the relation algebra expression:

$$customer \bowtie deposit \bowtie branch$$

Assume that the three relations are neither replicated nor fragmented and that *customer* is stored at site S_c, *deposit* at S_d, and *branch* at S_b. Let S_I denote the site at which the query was issued. The system needs to produce the result at site S_I. Among the possible strategies for processing this query are the following:

- Ship copies of all three relations to site S_I. Using the techniques of Chapter 9, choose a strategy for processing the entire query locally at site S_I.

- Ship a copy of the *customer* relation to site S_d and compute *customer* $\bowtie$ *deposit* at S_d. Ship *customer* $\bowtie$ *deposit* from S_d to S_b where (*customer* $\bowtie$ *deposit*) $\bowtie$ *branch* is computed. The result of this computation is shipped to S_I.

- Strategies similar to the one above may be devised with the roles of S_c, S_d, S_b exchanged.

It is not the case that one strategy is always the best one. Among the factors that must be considered are the amount of data being shipped, the cost of transmitting a block of data between a pair of sites, and the relative speed of processing at each site. Consider the first two strategies listed above. If we ship all three relations to S_I, and indices exist on these relations, we may need to recreate these indices at S_I. This entails extra processing overhead and extra disk accesses. However, the second strategy has the disadvantage that a potentially large relation (*customer* $\bowtie$ *deposit*) must be shipped from S_d to S_b. This relation repeats the address data for a customer once for each account the customer has. Thus, the second strategy may result in extra network transmission as compared with the first strategy.

12.5.3 Join Strategies that Exploit Parallelism

Let us consider a join of four relations:

$$r_1 \bowtie r_2 \bowtie r_3 \bowtie r_4$$

where relation r_i is stored at site S_i. Assume that the result must be presented at site S_I. There are, of course, many strategies to be considered. One attractive strategy is to compute two joins in parallel. For example, r_1 can be shipped to S_2 and $r_1 \bowtie r_2$ computed at S_2. At the same time, r_3 can be shipped to S_4 and $r_3 \bowtie r_4$ computed at S_4. We are then left with the task of computing:

$$(r_1 \bowtie r_2) \bowtie (r_3 \bowtie r_4)$$

where $(r_1 \bowtie r_2)$ is stored at site S_2 and $(r_3 \bowtie r_4)$ is stored at site S_4. Although we need to compute three natural joins to answer the query $r_1 \bowtie r_2 \bowtie r_3 \bowtie r_4$, the use of parallelism allows the query to be computed by the distributed system in the time it would have taken a single processor to compute two joins.

To achieve even greater parallelism in the above example, site S_2 can ship tuples of $(r_1 \bowtie r_2)$ to S_I as they are produced rather than waiting for the entire join to be computed. Similarly, S_4 can ship tuples of $(r_3 \bowtie r_4)$ to S_I. Once tuples of $(r_1 \bowtie r_2)$ and $(r_3 \bowtie r_4)$ arrive at S_I, site S_I can begin the computation of $(r_1 \bowtie r_2) \bowtie (r_3 \bowtie r_4)$ in parallel with the computation of $(r_1 \bowtie r_2)$ at S_2 and the computation of $(r_3 \bowtie r_4)$ at S_4.

12.5.4 Semijoin Strategies

In situations in which network transmission costs are high, the *semijoin* operator, denoted by $\ltimes$, can be used for efficient processing of queries involving joins. Let r and s be relations on schemes R and S, respectively. The semijoin of r and s, denoted $r \ltimes s$, is

$$\Pi_R (r \bowtie s)$$

Note that, in general, $r \ltimes s \neq s \ltimes r$. The expression $r \ltimes s$ selects those tuples of r that participate in $r \bowtie s$. That is, it selects those tuples t_r in r such that there is a tuple t_s in s such that:

$$t_r[R \cap S] = t_s[R \cap S]$$

We use this fact in a distributed system to avoid the shipment over the network of tuples that are not needed to compute a given join.

Consider the expression $r_1 \bowtie r_2$, where r_1 and r_2 are stored at sites S_1 and S_2, respectively. Let the schemes of r_1 and r_2 be R_1 and R_2. The following is a semijoin strategy for computing $r_1 \bowtie r_2$ and producing the result at S_1.

1. Compute $temp1 = \Pi_{R_1 \cap R_2}(r_1)$ at S_1.

2. Ship $temp1$ from S_1 to S_2.

3. Compute $temp2 = r_2 \ltimes \Pi_{R_1 \cap R_2}(r_1)$ at S_2.

4. Ship $temp2$ from S_2 to S_1.

5. Compute $r_1 \bowtie temp2$ at S_1.

For the above strategy to be correct, $r_1 \bowtie r_2$ must equal:

$$r_1 \bowtie (r_2 \ltimes \Pi_{R_1 \cap R_2}(r_1))$$

To see this, note that the definition of semijoin implies that $r_2 \ltimes \Pi_{R_1 \cap R_2}(r_1)$ is:

$$\Pi_{R_2}(r_2 \bowtie \Pi_{R_1 \cap R_2}(r_1))$$

This is equivalent to:

$$\Pi_{R_2}(r_2 \bowtie r_1)$$

or:

$$r_2 \ltimes r_1$$

Thus,

$$r_1 \bowtie (r_2 \ltimes \Pi_{R_1 \cap R_2}(r_1)) = r_1 \bowtie (\Pi_{R_2}(r_2 \bowtie r_1)) = r_1 \bowtie r_2$$

The strategy thus generates the correct result. Let us now examine why this strategy may be advantageous in a distributed system. Suppose that relatively few tuples of r_1 and r_2 participate in the join. In such a case, $r_2 \ltimes r_1$ has many fewer tuples than r_2. Thus, it is significantly less costly to ship $r_2 \ltimes r_1$ from S_2 to S_1 than to ship all of r_2 from S_2 to S_1. The above semijoin strategy does require the shipment of $\Pi_{R_1 \cap R_2}(r_1)$ from S_1 to S_2, but this cost may be dominated by the savings from the use of the semijoin.

It may appear that semijoin strategies are useful only if there are a large number of dangling tuples. Such situations arise primarily in cases where r_1 or r_2 are not relations in the database but rather the result of a relational algebra expression.

A substantial body of theory has been developed regarding the use of semijoins for query optimization. Some of this theory is referenced in the bibliographic notes.

12.6 Recovery in Distributed Systems

In Chapters 10 and 11, we defined a transaction to be a program unit whose execution preserves the consistency of the database. A transaction must be executed *atomically*. That is, the instructions associated with it are either all executed to completion, or none are performed. In addition, in the case of concurrent execution, the effect of executing a transaction must be the same as if the transaction executed alone in the system.

12.6.1 System Structure

In order to ensure the atomicity property, various recovery and concurrency control schemes were introduced in Chapters 10 and 11. When dealing with a distributed database system, however, it becomes much more complicated to ensure the atomicity property of a transaction. This is due to the fact that several sites may be participating in the execution of the transaction. The failure of one of these sites, or the failure of a communication link connecting these sites, may result in erroneous computations.

It is the function of the *transaction manager* of a distributed database system to ensure that the execution of the various transactions in the distributed system preserves atomicity. Each site has its own local transaction manager. The various transaction managers cooperate to manage global transactions. To understand how such a manager can be implemented, let us define an abstract model of a transaction system. Each site of the system contains two subsystems:

- **Transaction manager**, whose function is to manage the execution of those transactions (or subtransactions) that access data stored in that site. Note that each such transaction may be either a local transaction (that is, a transaction that only executes at that site), or part of a global transaction (that is, a transaction that executes at several sites).

- **Transaction coordinator**, whose function is to coordinate the execution of the various transactions (both local and global) initiated at that site.

The overall system architecture is depicted in Figure 12.7.

The structure of a transaction manager is similar in many respects to the structure used in the centralized system case (Chapters 10 and 11). Each transaction manager is responsible for:

- Maintaining a log for recovery purposes.

- Participating in an appropriate concurrency control scheme to coordinate the parallel execution of the transactions executing at that site.

As we shall see, both the recovery and concurrency schemes need to be modified in order to accommodate the distribution of transactions.

The transaction coordinator subsystem is not needed in the centralized environment, since a transaction accessed data only at one single site. A transaction coordinator, as its name implies, is responsible for coordinating the execution of all the transactions initiated at that site. For each such transaction, the coordinator is responsible for:

- Starting the execution of the transaction.

- Breaking the transaction into a number of subtransactions, and distributing these subtransactions to the appropriate sites for execution.

- Coordinating the termination of the transaction, which may result in the transaction being committed at all sites or aborted at all sites.

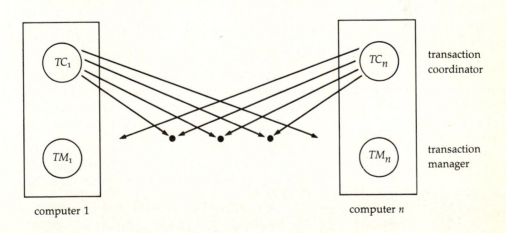

Figure 12.7   System architecture.

12.6.2 Robustness

A distributed system may suffer from the same types of failure that a centralized system does (for example, memory failure, disk crash). There are, however, additional failures that need to be dealt with in a distributed environment, including:

- The failure of a site.
- The failure of a link.
- Loss of messages.
- Network partition.

In order for the system to be robust, it must therefore *detect* any of these failures, *reconfigure* the system so that computation may continue, and *recover* when a processor or a link is repaired.

It is generally not possible to differentiate between link failure, site failure, message loss, and network partition. We can usually detect that a failure has occurred, but we may not be able to identify what kind of failure it is. For example, suppose that site s_1 is not able to communicate with S_2. If could be that S_2 has failed. However, another possibility is that the link between S_1 and S_2 has failed.

Suppose that site S_1 has discovered that a failure has occurred. It must then initiate a procedure that will allow the system to reconfigure and continue with its normal mode of operation.

- If replicated data is stored at the failed site, the catalog should be updated so that queries do not reference the copy at the failed site.

- If transactions were active at the failed site at the time of the failure, these transactions should be aborted. It is desirable to abort such transactions promptly since they may hold locks on data at sites that are still active.

- If the failed site is a central server for some subsystem, an "election" must be held to determine the new server. Examples of central servers include a name server, a concurrency coordinator, or a global deadlock detector.

Since it is, in general, not possible to distinguish between network link failures and site failures, any reconfiguration scheme must be designed to work correctly in case of a partitioning of the network. In particular, the following situations must be avoided:

- Two or more central servers are elected in distinct partitions.
- More than one partition updates a replicated data item.

Reintegration of a repaired site or link into the system also requires some care. When a failed site recovers, it must initiate a procedure to update its system tables to reflect changes made while it was down. If the site had replicas of any data items, it must obtain the current values of these data items and ensure that it receives all future updates. This is more complicated than it seems to be at first glance, since there may be updates to the data items processed during the time the site is recovering.

An easy solution is temporarily to halt the entire system while the failed site rejoins the system. In most applications, this solution is unacceptably disruptive. A preferable solution is to represent the recovery tasks as a series of transactions. The concurrent control subsystem and transaction management subsystem may then be relied upon for proper reintegration of the site.

If a failed link recovers, it is possible that two or more partitions are rejoined. Since a partitioning of the network limits the allowable operations by some or all sites, it is desirable to inform sites promptly of the recovery of the link. This can be done by a message broadcast to all sites. In networks in which broadcast is not feasible, alternative schemes may be used (see the bibliographic notes).

12.6.3 Commit Protocols

In order to assure atomicity, all the sites in which a transaction T executed must agree on the final outcome of the execution. T either commits at all sites, or aborts at all sites. In order to ensure this property, the transaction coordinator of T must execute a *commit protocol*.

There are a number of different commit protocols that can be used. We present the most widely used commit protocol, called *two-phase commit*. Alternatives to two-phase commit are referenced in the bibliographic notes.

Let T be a transaction initiated at site S_i, and let the transaction coordinator at S_i be C_i. When T completes its execution, that is, when all the sites at which T has executed inform C_i that T has completed, then C_i starts the two-phase commit protocol.

- **Phase 1**. C_i adds the record *<prepare T>* to the log and forces it onto stable storage. Once this is done, it sends a *prepare-to-commit* message to all sites at which T executed. Upon receiving such a message, the transaction manager at that site determines whether it is willing to commit its portion of T, or not. If the answer is no, it adds a record *<no T>* to the log and then it responds by sending an *abort T* message to C_i. If the answer is yes, it adds a record *<ready T>* to the log and forces all the log records corresponding to T onto stable storage. Once this is accomplished, it replies with a *ready T* message to C_i.

- **Phase 2**. When C_i receives responses to the *prepare T* message from all the sites, or a prespecified interval of time has elapsed since the *prepare T* message was sent out, C_i can determine whether the transaction T can be committed or aborted. Transaction T can be committed if C_i received a *ready T* message from all the participating sites. Otherwise, transaction T must be aborted. Depending on the verdict, either a record <*commit T*> or a record <*abort T*> is added to the log and forced onto stable storage. At this point, the fate of the transaction has been sealed. Following this, the coordinator sends either a *commit T* or an *abort T* message to all participating sites. When a site receives that message, it records it in the log and sends a message *acknowledge T* to the coordinator. When the coordinator receives the *acknowledge T* message from all the sites, it adds the record <*complete T*> to the log.

Since any site at which T executed could fail at any time, the protocol is designed so that the transaction T will be aborted in all cases prior to the time that *all* sites involved in the execution of T have recorded changes made by T in stable storage. The *ready T* message is, in effect, a promise by a site to follow the coordinator's order to commit T or abort T. The only means by which a site can make such a promise is if the needed information is stored in stable storage. Otherwise, if the site crashes after sending *ready T*, it may be unable to make good on its promise.

Since unanimity is required to commit a transaction, the fate of T is sealed as soon as at least one site responds *abort T*. Since the coordinator site S_i is one of the sites at which T executed, the coordinator can decide unilaterally to abort T. The final verdict regarding T is determined at the time the coordinator writes that verdict (commit or abort) to the log and forces it to stable storage. The final *acknowledge T* messages are not a necessary part of two-phase commit.

We now examine in detail how two-phase commit responds to various types of failures.

- **Failure of participating site**. When a participating site S_k recovers from a failure, it must examine its log to determine the fate of those transactions that were in the midst of execution when the failure occurred. Let T be one such transaction. We consider each of the possible cases below.

    The log contains a <*commit T*> record. In this case, the site executes **redo**(T).

    The log contains an <*abort T*> record. In this case, the site executes **undo**(T).

    The log contains a <*ready T*> record. In this case, the site must consult C_i to determine the fate of T. If C_i is up, it notifies S_k as to

whether T committed or aborted. In the former case, it executes
redo(T), while in the latter case, it executes **undo**(T). If C_i is down,
S_k must try to find the fate of T from other sites. It does so by
sending a *query-status* T message to all the sites in the system.
Upon receiving such a message, a site must consult its log to
determine whether T has executed there, and if so, whether T
committed or aborted. It then notifies S_k about this outcome. If no
site has the appropriate information (that is, whether T committed
or aborted), S_k must periodically resend the *query-status* message
until a site recovers that contains the needed information. Until the
outcome of T is determined, S_k must remain in the *ready* T state.
This may require that locks held by T at S_k not be released. Note
that the site at which C_i resides always has the needed
information.

The log contains no control records concerning T. In this case, S_k
knows that C_i has aborted T since S_k has not responded to the
prepare T message from C_i, and thus by our algorithm C_i must abort
T. Hence, S_k must execute **undo**(T).

- **Failure of the coordinator**. When the coordinator fails, a decision must
  be made as to whether to commit or abort each transaction that was
  being coordinated by the failed coordinator.

  Transaction T can be committed only if there exists an active site
  that contains a *<commit T>* record in its log.

  Transaction T can be aborted only if there exists an active site that
  contains either a *<no T>* or an *<abort T>* record in the log.

If neither of the above can be established, then the fate of transaction T
cannot be determined and this must be postponed until the
coordinator recovers.

- **Failure of a link**. When a link fails, all the messages that are in the
  process of being routed through the link do not arrive at their
  destination intact. From the viewpoint of the sites connected
  throughout that link, it appears that the other sites have failed. Thus
  our previous schemes apply here as well.

- **Network partition**. When a network partitions, two possibilities exist.

  The coordinator and all of its participants remain in one partition.
  In this case, this failure has no effect on the commit protocol.

The coordinator and its participants belong to several partitions. In this case, messages between the participant and the coordinator are lost, reducing the case to a link failure discussed above.

12.7 Concurrency Control

In Chapter 11, we discussed various concurrency control schemes which can be used in a centralized system. In this section, we show how some of these schemes can be modified so that they can be used in a distributed environment.

12.7.1 Locking Protocols

The various locking protocols described in Chapter 11 can be used in a distributed environment. The only change that needs to be incorporated is in the way we implement the lock manager. Below, we present several possible schemes, the first of which deals with the case where no data replication is allowed. The other schemes are applicable to the more general case where data can be replicated in several sites. As in Chapter 11, we shall assume the existence of the *shared* and *exclusive* lock modes.

Nonreplicated Scheme

If no data is replicated in the system, then the locking schemes described in Section 11.4 can be applied as follows. Each site maintains a local lock manager whose function is to administer the lock and unlock requests for those data items that are stored in that site. When a transaction wishes to lock data item X at site S_i, it simply sends a message to the lock manager at site S_i requesting a lock (in a particular lock mode). If data item X is locked in an incompatible mode, then the request is delayed until it can be granted. Once it has been determined that the lock request can be granted, the lock manager sends a message back to the initiator of the request indicating that the lock request has been granted.

The scheme has the advantage of simple implementation. It requires two message transfers for handling lock requests, and one message transfer for handling unlock requests. However, deadlock handling is more complex. Since the lock and unlock requests are no longer made at one single site, the various deadlock handling algorithms discussed in Chapter 11 must be modified, as will be discussed in Section 12.8.

Single-Coordinator Approach

The system maintains one *single* lock manager that resides in one *single* chosen site, say S_i. All lock and unlock requests are made at site S_i. When a transaction needs to lock a data item, it sends a lock request to S_i. The lock manager determines whether the lock can be granted immediately. If so, it sends a message to that effect to the site at which the lock request was initiated. Otherwise, the request is delayed until it can be granted, at which time, a message is sent to the site at which the lock request was initiated. The transaction can read the data item from *any* one of the sites at which a replica of the data item resides. In the case of a write, all the sites where a replica of the data item resides must be involved in the writing.

The scheme has the following advantages.

- **Simple implementation**. This scheme requires two messages for handling lock requests, and one message for handling unlock requests.

- **Simple deadlock handling**. Since all lock and unlock requests are made at one site, the deadlock handling algorithms discussed in Chapter 11 can be applied directly to this environment.

The disadvantages of this scheme include the following:

- **Bottleneck**. The site S_i becomes a bottleneck since all requests must be processed there.

- **Vulnerability**. If the site S_i fails, the concurrency controller is lost. Either processing must stop, or a recovery scheme such as those of Section 12.9 must be used.

A compromise between the advantages and disadvantages noted above can be achieved via a *multiple-coordinator approach* in which the lock manager function is distributed over several sites.

Each lock manager administers the lock and unlock requests for a subset of the data items. Each lock manager resides in a different site. This reduces the degree to which the coordinator is a bottleneck, but it complicates deadlock handling, since the lock and unlock requests are not made at one single site.

Majority Protocol

The majority protocol is a modification of the nonreplicated data scheme that we presented earlier. The system maintains a lock manager at each site. Each manager manages the locks for all the data items or replicas of data items stored at that site. When a transaction wishes to lock a data item X, which is replicated in n different sites, it must send a lock request to more than half of the n sites in which X is stored. Each lock manager determines whether the lock can be granted immediately (as far as it is concerned). As before, the response to the request is delayed until it can be granted. The transaction does not operate on X until it has successfully obtained a lock on a majority of the replicas of X.

This scheme has the advantage of dealing with replicated data in a decentralized manner. This avoids the drawbacks of central control. However, it suffers from the following disadvantages:

- **Implementation**. This scheme is more complicated to implement than the previous schemes. It requires $2(n/2 + 1)$ messages for handling lock requests, and $(n/2 + 1)$ messages for handling unlock requests.

- **Deadlock handling**. Since the lock and unlock requests are not made at one site, the deadlock-handling algorithms discussed in Chapter 11 must be modified, as will be discussed in Section 12.8. In addition, it is possible for a deadlock to occur even if only one data item is being locked. To illustrate this, consider a system with four sites and full replication. Suppose that transactions T_1 and T_2 wish to lock data item Q in exclusive mode. Transaction T_1 may succeed in locking Q at sites S_1 and S_3 while transaction T_2 may succeed in locking Q at sites S_2 and S_4. Each then must wait to acquire the third lock, and hence a deadlock has occurred.

Biased Protocol

This protocol is based on a model similar to that of the majority protocol. The difference is that requests for shared locks are given more favorable treatment than requests for exclusive locks. The system maintains a lock manager at each site. Each manager manages the locks for all the data items stored at that site. We differentiate between the way *shared* and *exclusive* locks are handled.

- **Shared locks**. When a transaction needs to lock data item X, it simply requests a lock on X from the lock manager at one site containing a replica of X.

- **Exclusive locks**. When a transaction needs to lock data item X, it requests a lock on X from the lock manager at all sites containing a replica of X.

As before, the response to the request is delayed until it can be granted.

The scheme has the advantage of imposing less overhead on read operations than does the majority protocol. This is especially significant in common cases in which the frequency of read is much greater than the frequency of write. However, the additional overhead on writers is a disadvantage. Furthermore, the biased protocol shares the majority protocol's disadvantage of complexity in handling deadlock.

Primary Copy

In the case of data replication, we may choose one of the replicas as the primary copy. Thus, for each data item X, the primary copy of X must reside in precisely one site, which we call the *primary site of X*.

When a transaction needs to lock a data item X, it requests a lock at the primary site of X. As before, the response to the request is delayed until it can be granted.

Thus, we are able to handle concurrency control for replicated data in a manner similar to that in which we handled unreplicated data. This allows for a simple implementation. However, if the primary site of X fails, X is inaccessible even though other sites containing a replica may be accessible.

12.7.2 Timestamping

The principal idea behind the timestamping scheme discussed in Section 11.4 is that each transaction is given a *unique* timestamp that is used in deciding the serialization order. Our first task, then, in generalizing the centralized scheme to a distributed scheme is to develop a scheme for generating unique timestamps. Once this has been accomplished, our previous protocols can be directly applied to the nonreplicated environment.

Generating Unique Timestamps

There are two primary methods for generating unique timestamps, one centralized and one distributed. In the centralized scheme, a single site is chosen for distributing the timestamps. The site can use a logical counter or its own local clock for this purpose.

In the distributed scheme, each site generates a unique local timestamp using either a logical counter or the local clock. The global unique timestamp is obtained by concatenating the unique local timestamp with the site identifier, which must be unique (Figure 12.8). The order of concatenation is important! We use the site identifier in the least significant position in order to ensure that the global timestamps generated in one site

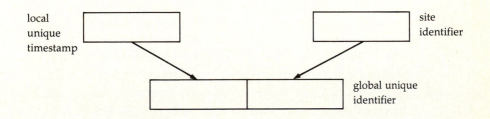

Figure 12.8   Generating unique timestamps.

are not always greater than those generated in another site. Compare this technique for generating unique timestamps with the one we saw earlier for generating unique names.

We may still have a problem if one site generates local timestamps at a faster rate than other sites. In such a case, the fast site's logical counter will be larger than that of other sites. Therefore, all timestamps generated by the fast site will be larger than those generated by other sites. What is needed is a mechanism to ensure that local timestamps are generated fairly across the system. To accomplish this, we define within each site S_i a *logical clock* (LC_i), which generates the unique local timestamp. The logical clock can be implemented as a counter that is incremented after a new local timestamp is generated. To ensure that the various logical clocks are synchronized, we require that a site S_i advance its logical clock whenever a transaction T_i with timestamp $<x,y>$ visits that site and x is greater than the current value of LC_i. In this case, site S_i advances its logical clock to the value $x + 1$.

If the system clock is used to generate timestamps, then timestamps are assigned fairly provided that no site has a system clock that runs fast or slow. Since clocks may not be perfectly accurate, it is necessary that a technique similar to that used for logical clocks be used to ensure that no clock gets very far ahead or behind another clock.

Concurrency Control Schemes

The basic timestamp scheme introduced in Section 11.5 can be extended in a straightforward manner to a distributed system. As in the centralized case, cascading rollbacks may result if no mechanism is used to prevent a transaction from reading a data item value which is not yet committed. To eliminate cascading rollbacks, we can combine the basic timestamp scheme of Section 9.5 with the two-phase commit protocol of Section 12.6 to obtain a protocol that ensures serializability with no cascading rollbacks. We leave the development of such an algorithm as an exercise for the reader.

The basic timestamp scheme described above suffers from the undesirable property that conflicts between transactions are resolved through rollbacks rather than waits. To alleviate this problem, we can buffer the various read and write operations (that is, *delay* them) until a time when we are assured that these operations can take place without causing aborts. A **read**(x) operation by T_i must be delayed if there exists a transaction T_j that will perform a **write**(x) operation but has not yet done so, and $TS(T_j) < TS(T_i)$. Similarly, a **write**(x) operation by T_i must be delayed if there exists a transaction T_j that will perform either **read**(x) or **write**(x) operation and $TS(T_j) < TS(T_i)$. There are various methods for ensuring this property. One such method, called the *conservative timestamp* *ordering scheme*, requires each site to maintain a **read** and **write** queue consisting of all the **read** and **write** requests, respectively, that are to be executed at the site and which must be delayed in order to preserve the above property. We shall not present the scheme here. Rather, we shall leave the development of the algorithm as an exercise for the reader.

12.8 Deadlock Handling

The deadlock prevention and detection algorithms presented in Section 11.9 can be used in a distributed system, provided that some modifications are made. For example, the tree protocol can be used by defining a *global* tree among the system data items. Similarly, the timestamp-ordering approach could be directly applied to a distributed environment, as we saw in Section 12.7.2.

Deadlock prevention may result in some unnecessary waiting and rollback. Furthermore, some of the deadlock prevention techniques may require more sites to be involved in the execution of a transaction than would otherwise be the case.

If we allow deadlocks to occur and rely on deadlock detection, the main problem in a distributed system is deciding how to maintain the wait-for graph. We describe several common techniques to deal with this issue. These schemes require that each site keep a *local* wait-for graph. The nodes of the graph correspond to all the transactions (local as well as nonlocal) that are currently either holding or requesting any of the items local to that site. For example, in Figure 12.9 we have a system consisting of two sites, each maintaining its local wait-for graph. Note that transactions T_2 and T_3 appear in both graphs, indicating that the transactions have requested items at both sites.

These local wait-for graphs are constructed in the usual manner for local transactions and data items. When a transaction T_i on site S_1 needs a

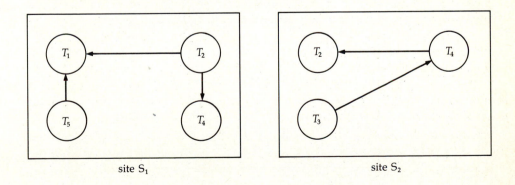

site S_1 site S_2

Figure 12.9   Local wait-for graphs.

resource held by transaction T_j in site S_2, a request message is sent by T_i to site S_2. The edge $T_i \rightarrow T_j$ is then inserted in the local wait-for graph of site S_1.

Clearly, if any local wait-for graph has a cycle, deadlock has occurred. On the other hand, the fact that there are no cycles in any of the local wait-for graphs does not mean that there are no deadlocks. To illustrate this problem, consider the local wait-for graphs of Figure 12.9. Each wait-for graph is acyclic; nevertheless, a deadlock exists in the system. A deadlock exists because the *union* of the local wait-for graphs contains a cycle. This graph is shown in Figure 12.10.

There are a number of different methods for organizing the wait-for graph in a distributed system. Several common schemes are described below.

12.8.1 Centralized Approach

In the centralized approach, a global wait-for graph (union of all the local graphs) is constructed and maintained in a *single* site, the deadlock detection coordinator. Since there is communication delay in the system, we must distinguish between two types of wait-for graphs. The *real* graph describes the real but unknown state of the system at any instance in time, as would be seen by an omniscient observer. The *constructed* graph is an approximation generated by the controller during the execution of its algorithm. Obviously, the constructed graph must be generated in such a way that whenever the detection algorithm is invoked, the reported results are correct in a sense that, if a deadlock exists it is reported promptly, and if it reports a deadlock, then the system is indeed in a deadlock state.

The global wait-for graph may be constructed:

• Whenever a new edge is inserted or removed in one of the local wait-for graphs.

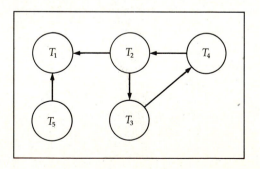

Figure 12.10   Global wait-for graph for Figure 12.9.

- Periodically, when a number of changes have occurred in a local wait-for graph.

- Whenever the coordinator needs to invoke the cycle detection algorithm.

When the deadlock detection algorithm is invoked, the coordinator searches its global graph. If a cycle is found, a victim is selected to be rolled back. The coordinator must notify all the sites that a particular transaction has been selected as victim. The sites, in turn, roll back the victim transaction.

We note that in this scheme unnecessary rollbacks may result, as a result of two situations:

- *False cycles* may exist in the global wait-for graph. To illustrate this point, consider a snapshot of the system represented by the local wait-for graphs of Figure 12.11. Suppose that T_2 releases the resource it is holding in site S_1, resulting in the deletion of the edge $T_1 \to T_2$ in S_1.

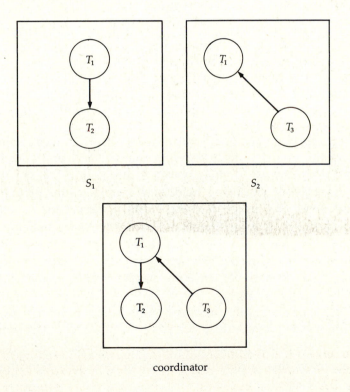

coordinator

Figure 12.11   False cycles in the global wait-for graph.

Transaction T_2 then requests a resource held by T_3 at site S_2, resulting in the addition of the edge $T_2 \rightarrow T_3$ in S_2. If the *insert* $T_2 \rightarrow T_3$ message from S_2 arrives before the *remove* $T_1 \rightarrow T_2$ message from S_1, the coordinator may discover the false cycle $T_1 \rightarrow T_2 \rightarrow T_3$ after the *insert* (but before the *remove*). Deadlock recovery may be initiated, although no deadlock has occurred.

- Unnecessary rollbacks may also result when a *deadlock* has indeed occurred and a victim has been picked, while at the same time one of the transactions was aborted for reasons unrelated to the deadlock. For example, suppose that site S_1 in Figure 12.9 decides to abort T_2. At the same time, the coordinator has discovered a cycle and picked T_3 as a victim. Both T_2 and T_3 are now rolled back, although only T_2 needed to be rolled back.

We note that the same problems exist in solutions employing the other option.

12.8.2 Fully Distributed Approach

In the *fully distributed* deadlock detection algorithm, all controllers share the responsibility for detecting deadlock equally. In this scheme, every site constructs a wait-for graph which represents a part of the total graph, depending on the dynamic behavior of the system. The idea is that if a deadlock exists, a cycle will appear in (at least) one of the partial graphs. Below we present one such algorithm which involves construction of partial graphs in every site.

Each site maintains its own local wait-for graph. A local wait-for graph differs from the one described above in that we add one additional node T_{ex} to the graph. An arc $T_i \rightarrow T_{ex}$ exists in the graph if T_i is waiting for a data item in another site being held by *any* transaction. Similarly, an arc $T_{ex} \rightarrow T_j$ exists in the graph if there exists a transaction at another site which is waiting to acquire a resource currently being held by T_j in this local site.

To illustrate this, consider the two local wait-for graphs of Figure 12.9. The addition of the node T_{ex} in both graphs results in the local wait-for graphs shown in Figure 12.12.

If a local wait-for graph contains a cycle which does not involve node T_{ex}, then the system is in a deadlock state. If, however, there exists a cycle involving T_{ex}, then this implies that there is a *possibility* of a deadlock. In order to ascertain this, a distributed deadlock detection algorithm must be invoked.

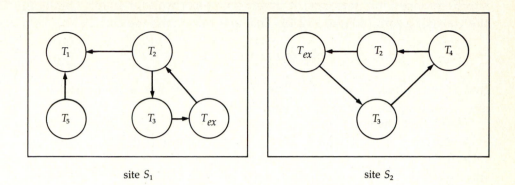

site S_1

site S_2

Figure 12.12   Local wait-for graphs.

Suppose that site S_i contains a cycle in its local wait for graph involving node T_{ex}. This cycle must be of the form:

$$T_{ex} \rightarrow T_{k_1} \rightarrow T_{k_2} \rightarrow \cdots \rightarrow T_{k_n} \rightarrow T_{ex}$$

which indicates that transaction T_{k_n} in S_i is waiting to acquire a data item in some other site, say S_j. Upon discovering this cycle, site S_i sends to site S_j a deadlock detection message containing information about that cycle.

When a site S_j receives this deadlock detection message, it updates its local wait-for graph with the new information it has obtained. When this is done, it searches the newly constructed wait-for graph for a cycle not involving T_{ex}. If one exists, a deadlock is found and an appropriate recovery scheme is invoked. If a cycle involving T_{ex} is discovered, then S_j transmits a deadlock detection message to the appropriate site, say S_k. Site S_k, in return, repeats the above procedure. Thus, after a finite number of rounds, either a deadlock is discovered, or the deadlock detection computation halts.

To illustrate this, consider the local wait-for graphs of Figure 12.12. Suppose that site S_1 discovers the cycle:

$$T_{ex} \rightarrow T_2 \rightarrow T_3 \rightarrow T_{ex}$$

Since T_3 is waiting to acquire a data item in site S_2, a deadlock detection message describing that cycle is transmitted from site S_1 to site S_2. When site S_2 receives this message, it updates its local wait-for graph obtaining the wait-for graph of Figure 12.13. This graph contains the cycle:

$$T_2 \rightarrow T_3 \rightarrow T_4 \rightarrow T_2$$

that does not include node T_{ex}. Therefore, the system is in a deadlock state and an appropriate recovery scheme must be invoked.

Note that the outcome would be the same if site S_2 discovered the cycle first in its local wait-for graph and it sent the deadlock detection message to site S_1. In the worst case, both sites discover the cycle at about the same time, and two deadlock detection messages will be sent, one by S_1 to S_2 and another by S_2 to S_1. This results in unnecessary message transfer and overhead in updating the two local wait-for graphs and searching for cycles in both graphs.

To reduce message traffic, we assign to each transaction T_i a unique identifier, which we denote by $ID(T_i)$. When site S_k discovers that its local wait-for graph contains a cycle involving node T_{ex} of the form

$$T_{ex} \rightarrow T_{K_1} \rightarrow T_{K_2} \rightarrow \cdots \rightarrow T_{K_n} \rightarrow T_{ex}$$

it will send a deadlock detection message to another site only if

$$ID(T_{K_n}) < ID(T_{K_1})$$

Otherwise, site S_k continues with its normal execution leaving the burden of initiating the deadlock detection algorithm to some other site.

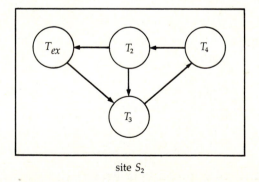

site S_2

Figure 12.13   Local wait-for graph.

To illustrate this, consider again the wait-for graphs maintained at sites S_1 and S_2 of Figure 12.12. Suppose that

$$ID\ (T_1) < ID\ (T_2) < ID\ (T_3) < ID\ (T_4)$$

Let both sites discover these local cycles at about the same time. The cycle in site S_1 is of the form

$$T_{ex} \rightarrow T_2 \rightarrow T_3 \rightarrow T_{ex}$$

Since $ID\ (T_3) > ID\ (T_2)$, site S_1 does not send a deadlock detection message to site S_2.

The cycle in site S_2 is of the form

$$T_{ex} \rightarrow T_3 \rightarrow T_4 \rightarrow T_2 \rightarrow T_{ex}$$

Since $ID\ (T_2) < ID\ (T_3)$, site S_2 does send a deadlock detection message to site S_1, which upon receiving the message updates its local wait-for graph. It then searches for a cycle in the graph and discovers that the system is in a deadlock state.

12.9 Coordinator Selection

Some of the algorithms we have presented above require the use of a coordinator. If the coordinator fails due to the failure of the site at which it resides, the system can continue execution only by restarting a new coordinator on some other site. This can be accomplished by maintaining a backup to the coordinator that is ready to assume responsibility if the coordinator fails. Another approach is to choose the new coordinator after the coordinator has failed. The algorithms that determine where a new copy of the coordinator should be restarted are called *election* algorithms.

12.9.1 Backup Coordinators

A *backup coordinator* is a site which, in addition to other tasks, maintains enough information locally to allow it to assume the role of coordinator with minimal disruption of the distributed system. All messages directed to the coordinator are received by both the coordinator and its backup. The backup coordinator executes the same algorithms and maintains the same internal state information (such as, for a concurrency coordinator, the lock table) as the actual coordinator. The only difference in function between the coordinator and its backup is that the backup does not take any action that affects other sites. Such actions are left to the actual coordinator.

In the event that the backup coordinator detects the failure of the actual coordinator, it assumes the role of coordinator. Since the backup has all of the information available to it that the failed coordinator had, processing can proceed without interruption.

The prime advantage to the backup approach is the ability to continue processing immediately. If a backup were not ready to assume the coordinator's responsibility, it would be necessary for a newly appointed coordinator to seek information from all sites in the system so that it could execute the coordination tasks. Frequently, the only source of some of the requisite information is the failed coordinator. In this case, it may be necessary to abort several (or all) active transactions and restart them under the aegis of the new coordinator. Thus, the backup coordinator approach avoids a substantial amount of delay while the distributed system recovers from a coordinator failure.

The disadvantage to the backup coordinator approach is the overhead of duplicate execution of the coordinator's tasks. Furthermore, a coordinator and its backup need to communicate regularly to ensure that their activities are synchronized.

Thus, the backup coordinator approach involves overhead during normal processing in order to allow fast recovery from a coordinator failure. In the next section, we consider a lower-overhead recovery scheme that requires somewhat more effort in order to recover from a failure.

12.9.2 Election Algorithms

Election algorithms require that a unique identification number be associated with each active site in the system. For ease of notation, we shall assume that the identification number of site S_i is i. Also, to simplify our discussion, we assume that the coordinator resides always at the site with the largest identification number. The goal of an election algorithm is to chose a site for the new coordinator. Hence, when a coordinator fails, the algorithm must elect that active site with the largest identification number. This number must be sent to each active site in the system. Additionally, the algorithm must provide a mechanism by which a site recovering from a crash may identify the current coordinator.

There are a number of different election algorithms. These usually differ in terms of the network configuration. In this section, we present one of these algorithms, the *bully* algorithm.

Suppose that site S_i sends a request that is not answered by the coordinator within a prespecified time interval T. In this situation, it is assumed that the coordinator has failed, and S_i tries to elect itself as the site for the new coordinator.

Site S_i sends an election message to every site with a higher identification number. Site S_i then waits for a time interval T for an answer from any one of these sites.

If no response is received within time T, it is assumed that all sites with numbers greater than i have failed, and S_i elects itself as the site for the new coordinator and sends a message to inform all active sites with identification numbers less than i that S_i is the site at which the new coordinator resides.

However, if an answer is received, S_i begins a time interval T, waiting to receive a message informing it that a site with a higher identification number has been elected. (Some other site is electing itself coordinator, and should report the results within time T'.) If no message is sent within T', then the site with a higher number is assumed to have failed, and site S_i restarts the algorithm.

After a failed site recovers, it immediately begins execution of the same algorithm. If there are no active sites with higher numbers, the recovered site forces all sites with lower numbers to let it become the coordinator site, even if there is a currently active coordinator with a lower number. It is for this reason that the algorithm is termed the *bully* algorithm.

12.10 Summary

A distributed database system consists of a collection of sites, each of which maintains a local database system. Each site is able to process *local transactions*, those transactions that access data only in that single site. In addition, a site may participate in the execution of *global* transactions, those transactions that access data in several sites. The execution of global transactions requires communication among the sites.

There are several reasons for building distributed database systems, including sharing of data, reliability and availability, and speedup of query processing. However, along with these advantages come several disadvantages, including software development cost, greater potential for bugs, and increased processing overhead. The primary disadvantage of distributed database systems is the added complexity required to ensure proper coordination among the sites.

There are several issues involved in storing a relation in the distributed database, including replication and fragmentation. It is essential that the system minimize the degree to which a user needs to be aware of how a relation is stored.

A distributed system may suffer from the same types of failure that a centralized system does. There are, however, additional failures that need to be dealt with in a distributed environment, including the failure of a site, the failure of a link, loss of messages, and network partition. Each of these need to be considered when designing a distributed recovery scheme. In order for the system to be robust, it must therefore *detect* any of these failures, *reconfigure* the system so that computation may continue, and *recover* when a processor or a link is repaired.

In order to assure atomicity, all the sites in which a transaction T executed must agree on the final outcome of the execution. T either commits at all sites or aborts at all sites. In order to ensure this property, the transaction coordinator of T must execute a *commit protocol*. There are a number of different commit protocols that can be used; the one most widely used is the *two-phase commit* protocol.

The various concurrency control schemes which can be used in a centralized system can be modified so that they can be used in a distributed environment. In the case of locking protocols, the only change that needs to be incorporated is in the way we implement the lock manager. There are a variety of different ways of doing so. One or more central coordinators may be used. If instead a distributed approach is taken, replicated data must be treated specially. There are several protocols for doing this including the majority, biased, and primary-copy protocols. In the case of timestamping and validation schemes, the only needed change is in developing a mechanism for generating unique *global* timestamps. This can be done by either concatenating a local timestamp with the site identification, or by advancing local clocks whenever a message arrives with a larger timestamp.

The primary method for dealing with deadlocks in a distributed environment is deadlock detection. The main problem is in deciding how to maintain the wait-for graph. There are a number of different methods for organizing the wait-for graph including a centralized approach, a hierarchical approach, and a fully distributed approach.

Some of the distributed algorithms require the use of a coordinator. If the coordinator fails due to the failure of the site at which it resides, the system can continue execution only by restarting a new copy of the coordinator on some other site. This can be accomplished by maintaining a backup to the coordinator that is ready to assume responsibility if the coordinator fails. Another approach is to choose the new coordinator after the coordinator has failed. The algorithms that determine where a new copy of the coordinator should be restarted are called *election* algorithms.

Exercises

12.1 Discuss the relative advantages of centralized and distributed databases.

12.2 How might a distributed database designed for a local-area network differ from one designed for a long-haul network?

12.3 When it is useful to have replication or fragmentation of data? Explain.

12.4 Explain the notions of transparency and autonomy. Why are they desirable from a human-factors standpoint?

12.5 Consider a relation

employee (name, address, salary, plant-number)

that is fragmented horizontally by *plant-number*. Assume each fragment has two replicas: one stored at the New York site and one stored locally at the plant site. Describe a good query processing strategy for the following queries, entered at the San Jose site.

a. Find all employees at the Boca plant.

b. Find the average salary of all employees.

c. Find the highest paid employee at each of the following sites: Toronto, Edmonton, Vancouver, Montreal.

d. Find the lowest paid employee in the entire company.

12.6 Consider the relations

employee (name, address, salary, plant-number)
machine (machine-number, type, plant-number)

Assume the *employee* relation is fragmented horizontally by *plant-number* and each fragment is stored locally at its corresponding plant site. Assume the *machine* relation is stored in its entirety at the Armonk site. Describe a good strategy for processing each of the following queries.

a. Find all employees at the plant containing machine number 1130.

b. Find all employeed at plants containing machines whose type is "milling machine".

c. Find all machines at the Almaden plant.

d. Find employee ⋈ machine.

12.7 For each of the strategies of Exercise 12.6, state how your choice of a strategy depends upon

• The site at which the query was entered?

• The site at which the result is desired?

12.8 Compute $r \times s$ for the following relations:

r	A	B	C
	1	2	3
	4	5	6
	1	2	4
	5	3	2
	8	9	7

s	C	D	E
	3	4	5
	3	6	8
	2	3	2
	1	4	1
	1	2	3

12.9 Does $r_i \times r_j$ necessarily equal $r_j \times r_i$? Under what conditions does $r_i \times r_j = r_j \times r_i$ hold?

12.10 In order to build a robust distributed system it is important to know what kinds of failures can occur.

    a. List possible types of failure in a distributed system.

    b. Which items in your list are applicable also to a centralized system?

12.11 Consider a failure that occurs during two phase commit for a transaction. For each possible failure listed in Exercise 12.10a, explain how two phase commit ensures transaction atomicity despite the failure.

12.12 Consider a distributed deadlock detection algorithm in which the sites are organized in a hierarchy. Each site checks for deadlocks local to the site and for global deadlocks that involve descendant sites in the hierarchy. Complete a detailed description of this algorithm and argue that it detects all deadlocks. Compare the relative merits of this hierarchical scheme with the centralized scheme and the fully distributed scheme.

12.13 Consider a distributed system with two sites, A and B. Can site A distinguish between the following:

    a. B goes down.

    b. The link between A and B goes down.

    c. B is extremely overloaded and response time is 100 times longer than normal.

What implications does your answer have for recovery in distributed systems?

12.14 Explain the difference between:

    a. fragmentation transparency.

    b. replication transparency.

    c. location transparency.

12.15 If we apply a distributed version of the multiple granularity protocol of Chapter 11 to a distributed database the site responsible for the root of the DAG may be come a bottleneck. Show that the following modifications to that protocol alleviate this problem without allowing any nonserializable schedules

    ● Only intention mode locks are allowed on the root.

    ● All transactions are given all possible intention mode locks on the root automatically.

12.16 Discuss the advantages and disadvantages of the two methods we presented for generating globally unique timestamps.

12.17 Consider the following *hierarchical* deadlock detection algorithm, in which the global wait-for graph is distributed over a number of different *controllers*, which are organized in a tree, Each non-leaf controller maintains a wait-for graph which contains relevant information from the graphs of the controllers in the subtree below it. In particular, let S_A, S_B and S_C be controllers such that S_C is the lowest common ancestor of S_A and S_B (S_C must be unique, since we are dealing with a tree). Suppose that node T_i appears in the local wait-for graph of controllers S_A and S_B. Then T_i must also appear in the local wait-for graph of:

    ● controller S_C

    ● every controller in the path from S_C to S_A

    ● every controller in the path from S_C to S_B.

In addition, if T_i and T_j appear in the wait-for graph of controller S_D and there exists a path from T_i to T_j in the wait-for graph of one of the children of D, then an edge $T_i \rightarrow T_j$ must be in the wait-for graph of S_D.

    Show that if a cycle exists in any of the wait-for graphs, then the system is deadlocked.

12.18 Consider the following deadlock detection algorithm. When transaction T_i, at site S_A, requests a resource from T_j, at site S_B, a request message with timestamp n is sent. The edge (T_i, T_j, n) is inserted in the local wait-for of S_A. The edge (T_i, T_j, n) is inserted in the local wait-for graph of S_B only if T_j has received the request message and it cannot immediately grant the requested resource. A request from T_i to T_j in the same site is handled in the usual manner; no timestamps are associated with the edge (T_i, T_j). The detection algorithm is invoked by a central coordinator by sending an initiating message to each site in the system:

1. Upon receiving this message, a site sends its local wait for graph to the coordinator. Note that each of these wait-for graphs contains all of the local information the site has about the state of the real graph. The graph reflects an instantaneous state of the site, but it is not synchronized with respect to any other site.

2. When the controller has received a reply from each site, it constructs a graph as follows:

   a. The constructed graph contains a vertex for every transaction in the system.

   b. The graph has an edge (T_i, T_j) if and only if:

      i. there is an edge (T_i, T_j) in one of the wait-for graphs.

      ii. an edge (T_i, T_j, n) (for some n) appears in more than one wait-for-graph.

Show that if there is a cycle in the constructed graph, then the system is in a deadlock state, and that if there is no cycle in the constructed graph, then the system was not in a deadlock state when the execution of the algorithm began.

Bibliographic Notes

A survey paper discussing some of the major issues concerning distributed database systems has been written by Rothnie and Goodman [1977]. Several conference proceedings devoted to distributed databases are Delobel and Litwin [1980], and Schneider [1982]. Textbook discussions are offered by Bray [1982], Ullman [1982a], Date [1983], and Ceri and Pelagatti [1984].

Comprehensive discussions concerning computer networks are offered by Davies et al. [1979] and Tanenbaum [1981]. Papers dealing with the problems of implementing the transaction concept in a distributed database are presented by Gray [1981], Traiger et al. [1982], and Spector and Schwarz [1983]. Papers covering distributed concurrency control are offered by Bernstein and Goodman [1980a, 1981a, 1982], Kohler [1981], Garcia-Molina and Wiederhold [1982], Rosenkrantz et al. [1978], and Bernstein et al. [1978, 1980a]. Attar, et al. [1982] discusses the use of transaction in distributed recovery in database systems with replicated data. Hailpern and Korth [1983] describe an experimental database system for a network of personal workstations. Skeen [1981] presents *three-phase commit*, alternative to two-phase commit that alleviates the need for active sites to hold locks held by transactions running at a crashed or inaccessible site.

Performance analysis of various concurrency control schemes are presented by Gelembe and Sevcik [1978], Garcia-Molina [1978], Ries [1979], and Badal [1980, 1981].

Distributed deadlock detections are presented by Gray [1978], Menasce and Muntz [1979], Gligor and Shattuck [1980], Obermark [1982], Chandy et al. [1983], Chandy and Misra [1982], and Rosenkrantz et al. [1978]. Exercise 12.17 is from Menasce and Muntz [1979]. Exercise 12.18 is from Stuart et al. [1984].

Issues in the design of distributed databases are presented by Chen and Akoka [1980], and Ceri et al. [1983]. A paper dealing with horizontal and vertical fragmentation of relations is presented by Chang and Cheng [1980].

Discussions concerning the file and resource allocation in problems are offered by Dowdy and Foster [1982], Chu [1969], Casey [1972], Eswaran [1974], Mahmoud and Riordan [1976], Morgan and Levin [1977], Fischer and Hachbaum [1980], and Trivedi et al. [1980].

Distributed query processing is discussed in Ceri and Pelagatti [1983], Adiba [1980], King [1981], Wong [1977], Hevner and Yao [1979], Cheung [1982], Apers et al. [1983], Epstein et al. [1978], Epstein and Stonebraker [1980], Kershberg et al. [1982], and Chu and Hurley [1982].

Selinger and Adiba [1980] and Daniels et al. [1982]. discuss the approach to distributed query processing taken by the R* system (a distributed version of System R). Theoretical results concerning semi-joins are presented by Bernstein and Chiu [1981], Chiu and Ho [1980], Bernstein and Goodman [1981b], and Kambayaski et al. [1982].

13

Security and Integrity

The data stored in the database needs to be protected from unauthorized access, malicious destruction or alteration, and accidental introduction of inconsistency. In Chapters 10 to 12 we have discussed aspects of preservation of the consistency of data. In this chapter, we examine the ways in which data may become inconsistent or be misused. We then present mechanisms to guard against their occurrence.

13.1 Security and Integrity Violations

Misuse of the database can be categorized as being either intentional (malicious) or accidental. Accidental loss of data consistency may result from:

- Crashes during transaction processing.

- Anomalies due to concurrent access to the database.

- Anomalies due to the distribution of data over several computers.

- A logical error that violates the assumption that transactions preserve the database consistency constraints.

It is easier to protect against accidental loss of data consistency than to protect against malicious access to the database. Among the forms of malicious access are the following:

- Unauthorized reading of data (theft of information).

- Unauthorized modification of data.

- Unauthorized destruction of data.

Absolute protection of the database from malicious abuse is not possible, but the cost to the perpetrator can be made sufficiently high to deter most if not all attempts to access the database without proper authority. The term *database security* usually refers to security from malicious access, while *integrity* refers to the avoidance of accidental loss of consistency. In practice, the dividing line between security and integrity is not always clear. We shall use the term *security* to refer to both *security* and *integrity* in cases where the distinction between these concepts is not essential.

In order to protect the database, security measures must be taken at several levels:

- **Physical**. The site or sites containing the computer systems must be physically secured against armed or surreptitious entry by intruders.

- **Human**. Authorization of users must be done carefully to reduce the chance of an authorized user giving access to an intruder in exchange for a bribe or other favors.

- **Operating system**. No matter how secure the database system is, weakness in operating system security may serve as a means of unauthorized access to the database. Since almost all database systems allow remote access through terminals or networks, software-level security within the operating system is as important as physical security.

- **Database system**. Some authorized database system users may be authorized to access only a limited portion of the database. Other users may be allowed to issue queries, but may be forbidden to modify the data. It is the responsibility of the database system to ensure that these restrictions are not violated.

It is worthwhile in many applications to devote a considerable effort to the preservation of the integrity and security of the database. Large databases containing payroll or other financial data are inviting targets to thieves. Databases that contain data pertaining to corporate operations may be of interest to unscrupulous competitors. Furthermore, loss of such data, whether via accident or fraud, can seriously impair the ability of the corporation to function.

In the remainder of this chapter, we shall address security at the database system level. Despite the importance of physical- and human-level security, these subjects are far beyond the scope of this text. Security within the operating system is implemented at several levels ranging from passwords for access to the system to the isolation of concurrent processes running within the system. The file system also provides some degree of protection. The bibliographic notes reference coverage of these topics in operating system texts. We shall present our discussion of security in terms of the relational data model, although the concepts of this chapter are equally applicable to all data models.

13.2 Authorization and Views

In Chapter 3, we introduced the concept of *views* as a means of providing a user with a "personalized" model of the database. A view can hide data that a user does not need to see. The ability of views to hide data serves both to simplify usage of the system and to enhance security. System usage is simplified since the user is allowed to restrict attention to the data of interest. Security is provided if there is a mechanism to restrict the user to his or her personal view or views. Relational database systems typically provide security at two levels:

- **Relation**. A user may be permitted or denied direct access to a relation.

- **View**. A user may be permitted or denied access to data appearing in a view.

Although a user may be denied direct access to a relation, the user may be able to access part of that relation through a view. Thus, a combination of relational-level security and view-level security can be used to limit a user's access to precisely the data that user needs.

In our bank example, consider a clerk who needs to know the names of the customers of each branch. This clerk is not authorized to see information regarding specific loans and accounts that the customer may have. Thus, the clerk must be denied direct access to the *borrow* and *deposit* relations. In order for the clerk to have access to the information needed, we grant the user access to the view *all-customer* which we defined in Chapter 3 as:

> **create view** *all-customer* **as**
>   (**select** *branch-name, customer-name*
>   **from** *deposit*)
>   **union**
>   (**select** *branch-name, customer-name*
>   **from** *borrow*)

A user may have several forms of authorization on parts of the database. Among these are the following:

- **Read authorization**, which allows reading, but not modification of data.

- **Insert authorization**, which allows insertion of new data, but not the modification of existing data.

- **Update authorization**, which allows modification, but not deletion, of data.

- **Delete authorization**, which allows deletion of data.

In addition to the above forms of authorization for access to data, a user may be granted authorization to modify the database scheme:

- **Index authorization**, which allows creation and deletion of indices.
- **Resource authorization**, which allows the creation of new relations.
- **Alteration authorization**, which allows the addition or deletion of attributes in a relation.
- **Drop authorization**, which allows the deletion of relations.

The **drop** and **delete** authorization differ in that **delete** authorization allows deletion of tuples only. If a user deletes all tuples of a relation, the relation still exists, but it is empty. If a relation is dropped, it no longer exists.

The ultimate form of authority is that given to the database administrator. The database administrator may authorize new users, restructure the database, etc. This form of authorization is analogous to that provided to a "superuser" or operator for an operating system.

A user who has been granted some form of authority may be allowed to pass this authority on to other users. However, we need to be careful about how authorization may be passed among users in order to ensure that we can revoke authorization at some future time.

Let us consider, as an example, the granting of update authorization on the *deposit* relation of the bank database. Assume that, initially, the database administrator (DBA) grants update authorization on *deposit* to users U_1, U_2, and U_3. Users U_1, U_2, and U_3 may in turn pass this authorization on to other users. We represent the passage of authorization from one user to another by an *authorization graph*. The nodes of this graph are the users. An edge (U_i, U_j) is included in the graph if user U_i grants update authorization on *deposit* to U_j. A sample graph appears in Figure 13.1. Observe that user U_5 is granted authorization by both U_1 and U_2.

Suppose that the database administrator decides to revoke the authorization of user U_1. Since U_4 has authorization granted from U_1, that authorization should be revoked as well. However, U_5 was granted authorization by both U_1 and U_2. Since the database administrator did not revoke update authorization on *deposit* from U_2, U_5 retains update authorization on *deposit*. If U_2 eventually revokes authorization from U_5, then U_5 loses the authorization.

A pair of devious users might attempt to defeat the above rules for revocation of authorization by granting authorization to each other as shown in Figure 13.2a. If the database administrator revokes authorization from U_2, U_2 retains authorization through U_3, as shown in Figure 13.2b. If

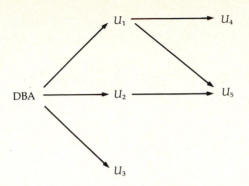

Figure 13.1   An authorization-grant tree.

authorization is revoked subsequently from U_3, U_3 retains authorization through U_2 as shown in Figure 13.2c.

To avoid problems like that above, we require that all edges in an authorization graph be part of some path originating with the database administrator. Under this rule, the authorization graph of Figure 13.2b would still be the result of revocation of authorization from U_2. However, when the database administrator subsequently revokes authorization from U_3, the edges from U_3 to U_2 and from U_2 to U_3 are no longer part of a path starting with the database administrator. Therefore, those edges are deleted and the resulting authorization graph is as shown in Figure 13.3.

Alternative schemes for managing authorization have been used in several database systems. Several of these are discussed in the bibliographic notes and in the exercises.

As an example of how authorization is granted and revoked in an actual database system, we present examples from SQL. To grant authorization, one uses the **grant** statement:

grant <privilege list> **on** <relation name or view name> **to** <user list>

The *privilege list* allows the granting of several privileges in one command. Members of this list may be the privileges **read, insert, drop, delete, index, alteration**, and **resource**, all of which we have discussed earlier. **Update** authorization may be given on all attributes of the relation or only some. If **update** authorization is included in a **grant** statement, the list of attributes on which update authorization is to be granted is listed in parentheses. The following **grant** statement grants three users U_1, U_2, and U_3 update authorization on the *balance* attribute of the *deposit* relation:

grant update (*balance*) **on** *deposit* **to** U_1, U_2, U_3

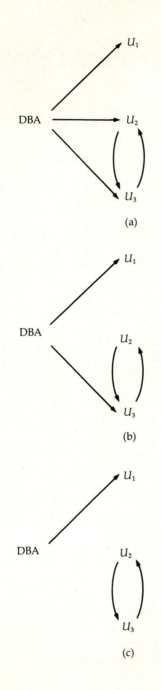

(a)

(b)

(c)

Figure 13.2   Attempt to defeat authorization revocation.

To revoke authorization, the **revoke** statement is used. It takes a form almost identical to that of **grant**:

> **revoke** <privilege list>
> **on** <relation name or view name> **from** <user list>

Thus, to revoke the privilege we granted above, we write:

> **revoke update** (*balance*) **on** *deposit* **from** U_1, U_2, U_3

13.3 Integrity Constraints

The forms of authorization discussed in Section 13.2 are a means by which the database system can be protected against malicious or unauthorized access. Integrity constraints, however, serve a different purpose. They provide a means of ensuring that changes made to the database by authorized users do not result in a loss of data consistency. Thus, integrity constraints guard against accidental damage to the database.

In Chapters 10 and 11, we discussed the notion of a transaction. We required that all transactions preserve the constraints, and using that assumption, showed how to preserve consistency despite system crashes. We saw also how to ensure that no anomalies result from concurrent access to the database. In practice, of course, programs have bugs and interactive users of the database system make mistakes. The integrity control component of the database system is intended to detect as many of these errors as possible.

We have already seen a form of integrity constraint for relational databases in Chapter 6. Data dependencies (functional, multivalued, and join) are statements about the enterprise we are modeling. We wish to

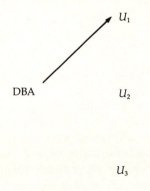

Figure 13.3   Authorization graph.

restrict the database to contain only relations that satisfy these dependencies. In the network model and the E-R model, we saw integrity constraints in the form of:

- **Key declarations**, the stipulation that certain attributes form a candidate key for a given entity set constrains the set of legal insertions and updates.

- **Form of a relationship**, many-to-many, one-to-many, one-to-one. A one-to-one or one-to-many relationship restricts the set of legal relationships among entities of a collection of entity sets.

Another example of an integrity constraint is set retention in the network model.

In general, an integrity constraint can be an arbitrary predicate pertaining to the database. However, arbitrary predicates may be costly to test. Thus, we usually limit ourselves to integrity constraints that can be tested with minimal overhead. This is the purpose behind dependency-preserving decompositions of relation schemes. Recall that in a dependency-preserving decomposition, it is possible to test for satisfaction of the data dependencies without the need to compute any joins. Domain-key normal form (DKNF; see Chapter 6) is an ideal design from the point of view of efficient testing of integrity constraints, since the only forms of constraint that need be tested are key constraints and domain constraints. If the key and domain constraints are satisfied, and the database scheme is in DKNF, then all integrity constraints on the database are satisfied.

Key constraints are one of the most easily tested forms of consistency constraint, especially if an index is maintained on that candidate key. During the process of inserting a record into the database a lookup must be performed using the index and any duplicate key values that may exist are found. Since not all index search keys are candidate keys for the relation (indices may be for secondary keys), we need to declare an index to be either

- **Unique**. Only one record may exist for a key value.

- **Nonunique**. Multiple records are allowed to have the same key value.

Another form of constraint that is easy to test is domain constraints. Testing domain constraints is analogous to runtime-type checking in a programming language. A form of constraint closely related to domain constraints involves the admissibility of null values. We may forbid null values for certain attributes but allow them for others.

Relatively few systems allow the expression of constraints that are more complex than key declarations or domain constraints. The original proposal for the SQL language included a general-purpose construct called the **assert** statement for the expression of integrity constraints.

An assertion pertaining to a single relation takes the form:

assert <assertion-name> **on** <relation-name> <predicate>.

For example, if we wish to define an integrity constraint that no account balance is negative we write:

assert *balance-constraint* **on** *deposit*
  balance ≥ 0

In its most general form, the **assert** statement takes the form:

assert <assertion-name> : <predicate>.

Let us consider a more complicated constraint involving more than one relation scheme. Suppose that we do not allow a customer to open an account unless the customer appears in the *customer* relation. We write the following assertion:

assert *address-constraint*:
  (**select** *customer-name*
   from *customer*)
  contains
  (**select** *customer-name*
   from *deposit*)

When an assertion is made, the system tests it for validity. If the assertion is valid, then any future modification to the database is allowed only if it does not cause an assertion to be violated. This testing may introduce a significant amount of overhead if complex assertions have been made.

Because of the high overhead of assertion testing, an alternative scheme called *triggering* is sometimes used for integrity preservation. A trigger is a statement that is executed automatically by the system as a side effect of a modification to the database.

To design a trigger mechanism, we must:

- Specify the conditions under which the trigger is to be executed.

- Specify the actions to be taken when the trigger executes.

Suppose that instead of allowing negative account balances, the bank deals with overdrafts by setting the account balance to zero and creating a loan in the amount of the overdraft. This loan is given a loan number equal to the account number of the overdrawn account. For the above example, the condition for executing the trigger is an update to the *deposit* relation that results in a negative *balance* value. Let *t* denote the tuple with a negative *balance* value. The actions to be taken are as follows:

- Insert a new tuple *s* in the *borrow* relation with:

$$s[branch\text{-}name] = t[branch\text{-}name]$$
$$s[loan\text{-}number] = t[account\text{-}number]$$
$$s[amount] = -t[balance]$$
$$s[customer\text{-}name] = t[customer\text{-}name]$$

(Note that since *t*[*balance*] is negative, we negate *t*[*balance*] to get the loan amount, a positive number.)

- Set *t*[*balance*] to 0.

13.4 Encryption

The various provisions a database system may make for authorization may not be sufficient protection for highly sensitive data. In such cases, data may be *encrypted*. It is not possible for encrypted data to be read unless the reader knows how to decipher (*decrypt*) the encrypted data.

There are a vast number of techniques for the encryption of data. Simple techniques for encryption may not provide adequate security since it may be easy for an unauthorized user to break the code. As an example of a bad encryption technique, consider the substitution of each character with the next character in the alphabet. Thus:

Perryridge

becomes:

Qfsszsjehf

If an unauthorized user sees only "Qfsszsjehf," there is probably insufficient information to break the code. However, if the intruder sees a large number of encrypted branch names, the intruder could use statistical data regarding the relative frequency of characters (for example, "e" is more common than "x") to guess what substitution is being made.

Good encryption techniques have the following properties:

- It is relatively simple for authorized users to encrypt and decrypt data.

- The encryption scheme depends not on the secrecy of the algorithm but on a parameter of the algorithm called the *encryption key*.

- It is extremely difficult for an intruder to determine the encryption key.

The *Data Encryption Standard* is an approach which does both a substitution of characters and a rearrangement of their order based on an encryption key. In order for this scheme to work, the authorized users must be provided with the encryption key via a secure mechanism. This is a major weakness since the scheme is no more secure than the secureness of the mechanism by which the encryption key is transmitted.

There is an alternative scheme that avoids some of the problems with the Data Encryption Standard. This scheme, called *public-key encryption*, is based on two keys, a *public key* and a *private key*. Each user U_i has his or her own public key E_i and private key D_i. All public keys are published. Each user's private key is known only to the one user to whom the key belongs. If user U_1 wants to store encrypted data, U_1 encrypts it using his or her public key E_1. Decryption requires the private key D_1.

Because the encryption key for each user is public, it is possible to exchange information securely using this scheme. If user U_1 wants to share data with U_2, U_1 encrypts the data using E_2, the public key of U_2. Since only user U_2 knows how to decrypt the data, secure information transfer is accomplished.

For public key encryption to work, there must be a scheme for encryption that can be made public without making it easy to figure out the scheme for decryption. Such a scheme does exist. It is based on the following:

- There is an efficient algorithm for testing whether or not a number is prime.

- No efficient algorithm is known for finding the prime factors of a number.

Data is treated as a collection of integers for purposes of this scheme. A public key is created by computing the product of two large prime numbers P_1 and P_2. The private key consists of the pair (P_1, P_2), and the decryption algorithm cannot be used successfully if only the product $P_1 P_2$ is known. Since all that is published in the product $P_1 P_2$, an unauthorized user would need to be able to factor $P_1 P_2$ in order to steal data. By choosing P_1 and P_2 to be sufficiently large (over 100 digits), we can make the cost of factoring $P_1 P_2$ prohibitively high (on the order of years of computation time even on the fastest computers).

The details of public key encryption and the mathematical justification of its properties are referenced in the bibliographic notes.

13.5 Statistical Databases

Suppose that our bank grants an outsider access to its database under the condition that only statistical studies (averages, medians, etc.) are made on the data and that information about individuals is not divulged. In this section, we examine the difficulty of ensuring the privacy of individuals while allowing use of data for statistical purposes.

One weakness in a statistical database is unusual cases. For example, there may be a city in which only one bank customer lives. Suppose that one asks for the total bank account balances for all customers living in Smalltown. If only one customer happens to live in Smalltown, the system has divulged information about an individual. Of course, a security breach has occurred only if the user knows that only one customer lives in Smalltown. However, that information is easily determined by the statistical query, "Find the number of customers living in Smalltown."

A simple way to deal with potential security breaches like that described above is for the system to reject any query that involves fewer than some predetermined number of individuals. Suppose this predetermined number is n. A malicious user who has an account with our bank can find an individual's balance in two queries. Suppose he wants to find how much money Rollo has on deposit. He chooses n customers and finds:

- x, the total balances for himself and the n customers.

- y, the total balances for Rollo and the n customers.

Rollo's total balance is:

$$y - x + \text{the malicious user's balance}$$

The critical flaw that was exploited in the above example is that the two queries referred to many of the same data items. The number of data items the queries q_1 and q_2 have in common is called the *intersection* of q_1 and q_2.

Thus, in addition to requiring that a query reference data pertaining to at least n individuals, we may require that no two queries have an intersection larger than m. By adjusting n and m, we can increase the difficulty of a user determining data about an individual, but we cannot eliminate it entirely.

These two restrictions do not preclude the possibility of some extremely clever query that divulges individual data. However, if all queries are restricted to computing sums, counts, or averages, and if a malicious user knows only the data value for himself, it can be shown that it will take at least $1 + (n - 2)/m$ queries for the malicious user to determine data about an individual. The proof of this is beyond the scope of this text and is referenced in the bibliographic notes. This fact is only partially reassuring. We can limit a user to less than $1 + (n - 2)/m$ queries, but a conspiracy of two malicious users can result in data being divulged.

Another approach to security is *data pollution*. This involves the random falsification of data provided in response to a query. This falsification must be done in such a way that the statistical significance of the response is not destroyed. A similar technique involves random modification of the query itself. For both of these techniques, the goals involve a trade-off between accuracy and security.

Regardless of the approach taken to security of statistical data, it is possible for a malicious user to determine individual data values. However, good techniques can make the expense in terms of cost and time sufficiently high to be a deterrent.

13.6 Summary

The data stored in the database needs to be protected from unauthorized access, malicious destruction or alteration, and accidental introduction of inconsistency. It is easier to protect against accidental loss of data consistency than to protect against malicious access to the database. Absolute protection of the database from malicious abuse is not possible, but the cost to the perpetrator can be made sufficiently high to deter most if not all attempts to access the database without proper authority.

The concept of *views* provides a means for a user to design a "personalized" model of the database. A view can hide data that a user does not need to see. Security is provided if there is a mechanism to restrict the user to his or her personal view or views. A combination of relational-level security and view-level security can be used to limit a user's access to precisely the data that user needs.

A user may have several forms of authorization on parts of the database. Authorization is a means by which the database system can be protected against malicious or unauthorized access. A user who has been granted some form of authority may be allowed to pass this authority on to other users. However, we need to be careful about how authorization may be passed among users in order to ensure that we can revoke authorization at some future time.

Integrity constraints provide a means of ensuring that changes made to the database by authorized users do not result in a loss of data consistency. Thus, integrity constraints guard against accidental damage to the database. In general, an integrity constraint can be an arbitrary predicate pertaining to the database. However, arbitrary predicates may be costly to test. Thus, we usually limit ourselves to integrity constraints that can be tested with minimal overhead.

Because of the high overhead of assertion testing, an alternative scheme called *triggering* is sometimes used for integrity preservation. A trigger is a statement that is executed automatically by the system as a side effect of a modification to the database.

The various provisions a database system may make for authorization may not be sufficient protection for highly sensitive data. In such cases, data may be *encrypted*. It is not possible for encrypted data to be read unless the reader knows how to decipher (*decrypt*) the encrypted data.

It is difficult to ensure the privacy of individuals while allowing use of data for statistical purposes. A simple way to deal with potential security breaches is for the system to reject any query that involves fewer than some predetermined number of individuals. Another approach to security is *data pollution*. This involves the random falsification of data provided in response to a query. A similar technique involves random modification of the query itself. For both of these techniques, the goals involve a tradeoff between accuracy and security. Regardless of the approach taken to security of statistical data, it is possible for a malicious user to determine individual data values. However, good techniques can make the expense in terms of cost and time sufficiently high to be a deterrent.

Exercises

13.1 Make a list of security concerns for a bank. For each item on your list, state whether this concern relates to physical security, human security, operating-system security, or database security.

13.2 Using the relations of our sample bank database, write an SQL expression to define the following views:

    a. A view containing the account numbers and customer names (but not the balances) for all accounts at the Deer Park branch.

    b. A view containing the name and address of all customers who have an account with the bank, but do not have a loan.

    c. A view containing the name and average account balance of every customer of the Rock Ridge branch.

13.3 For each of the views you defined in Exercise 13.2, explain how updates would be performed (if they should be allowed at all). (Hint: see discussion of views in Chapter 3.)

13.4 In Chapter 3, we described the use of views to simplify use of the database by users who need access to only part of the database. In this chapter, we described the use of views as a security mechanism. Do these two purposes for views ever conflict? Explain.

13.5 What is the purpose of having a special category of authorization for index authorization and resource authorization?

13.6 Database systems that store each relation in a separate operating system file may use the operating system's security and authorization scheme rather than defining a special scheme within the database system. Discuss the advantages and disadvantages of such an approach.

13.7 Construct a set of integrity constraints that apply to our bank database. How easy would it be for the system to enforce these constraints?

13.8 What is the purpose of a "nonunique" key?

13.9 What is a trigger? How can a trigger mechanism assist in the preservation of data integrity?

13.10 What are the advantages of encrypting data stored in the database?

13.11 If data is encrypted, how does this affect the index schemes of Chapter 8? In particular, how might this affect schemes that attempt to store data in sorted order?

13.12 Suppose that the bank of our running example maintains a statistical database containing the average balances of all customers. The scheme for this relation is (*customer-name*, *customer-city*, *avg-balance*). Assume that, for security reasons, the following restrictions are imposed on queries against this data:

- Every query must involve at least 10 customers.
- The intersection of any pair of queries may be at most 5.

Construct a series of queries to find the average balance of a customer. Hint: This can be done in less than 7 queries.

13.13 Perhaps the most important data in any database systems are the passwords that control access to the database. Suggest a scheme for the secure storage of passwords. Be sure that your scheme allows the system to test passwords supplied by users attempting to log into the system.

Bibliographic Notes

The security subsystem of System R is described by Griffiths and Wade [1976] and Fagin [1978]. Their model provided the basis for our discussion of authorization graphs. Zloof [1978] presents the approach taken to security by the QBE database system. Stonebraker and Wong [1974] discuss the Ingres approach to security, which involves the modification of users' queries so as to ensure that they do not access data for which authorization has not been granted.

Several papers provide mathematical analyses of the number of queries required to "break" a database under a variety of assumptions. Among these are Kam and Ullman [1977]. Chin [1978], Demillo, et al. [1978], Dobkin, et al. 1979], and Yao [1979]. Another aspect of security that has been studied from a mathematical standpoint is data encryption. Public-key encryption is discussed by Rivest et al. [1978]. The data encryption standard is presented in [US Dept of Commerce 1977]. Other discussions on cryptography include Lempel [1979], Diffie and Hellman [1979], Simmons [1979], Davies [1980], and Denning [1982], Chin and Ozsoyoglu [1981] discuss the design of statistical databases.

Denning and Denning [1979] survey database security. Textbook discussions of security and integrity include Wiederhold [1983], Ullman [1982a] and Date [1983]. An issue not discussed in this chapter is the legal and social implications of database security. Martin and Norman [1970] and Martin [1973] provides a textbook discussion of some of these issues.

14

New Database Applications

Throughout this book, we have used a bank example to illustrate the concepts we have presented. This example served us well since it illustrates issues that arise in the general area of commercial and academic data processing. In this chapter, we address database applications that do not fit into the traditional data-processing framework.

14.1 Introduction

There are many applications outside the realm of data processing, which may benefit from the use of a database system. Some of these are listed below:

- **Design databases**. In computer-aided design (CAD) systems a large amount of data must be stored to represent the item being designed. The data describing a design are interrelated in a complex manner. Furthermore, there is a need to retain not only the current design, but also a record of previous versions of the design. As a result, the data-processing approach to databases is not adequate.

- **Knowledge bases**. In artificial intelligence and expert systems, information is represented as facts expressed in logic. This collection of facts can be viewed as a database containing knowledge, or as a knowledge base.

- **Multimedia databases**. Data of a graphical nature may be stored in a database. Such data may be accessed based upon the structure of a graphical data item. Database languages designed for data-processing applications are not adequate for such queries. Similar problems arise for audio data, design data, and other types of data with a complex substructure.

- **Environment modeling**. Databases are being used as a component of systems designed to automate software development and to simplify user interaction with a complex computer system. Representation of the components of these environments in a database requires extension of the data models.

These new applications of databases were not considered in the 1970s when most current database systems were being designed. They are being considered now due to the increase in available processing power of computer hardware and its falling cost, and due to the improved understanding of database management that has developed in recent years. It is now economical to consider such applications despite the fact that they were impractical in the 1970s when most current database systems were being designed.

In this chapter, we discuss briefly design databases and knowledge bases in order to illustrate some of the novel ways in which database concepts can be applied to new problems.

14.2 Design Databases

Database systems for computer-aided design (CAD) are used to store and manipulate complete information about a design object. The object could be a computer chip, an automobile, an airplane, etc. In general, an object may be any device or system being designed using a CAD system. We assume that objects are large and have a relatively complex internal structure. The database is accessed by users who are designing components of the object or modifying existing designs. These accesses may be made through query languages (often based on languages like SQL) or accesses may be expressed indirectly through CAD design tools. The designers frequently interact with the database using a graphics terminal through which they move components, insert components, etc. Because of the spatial nature of much of the design process, text-based (that is, nongraphical) languages such as SQL are not sufficient for the design database user. A challenge in the construction of a design database system is to find a data model adequate to represent design data and a language that allows the designer to express queries and modifications of the database in terms of design-objects.

Many current systems are extensions of existing commercial or research database systems. Early CAD systems used special-purpose systems in which a collection of files represent design objects. The primary drawbacks to this approach are the lack of data independence, the complexity of database administration, and the lack of fully general concurrency and recovery systems. These drawbacks are identical to those encountered by data-processing applications before database systems came into widespread use.

Objects have a hierarchical structure (a *design* tree) based upon levels of detail. More generally, objects may have a DAG structure similar to the granularity DAG we saw in Chapter 11. For example, a computer designer may operate at the following levels of detail:

- Boards or cards.

- Chips.

- Internal design of chips: cells, rectangles, etc.

Certain design applications require operation on an entire object. Examples of such applications include testing, cost estimation, simulation, and design-rule checking. Other applications may involve several objects at a lower detail level. Examples include modification of a shared component and design of new cards from a given collection of chips.

14.2.1 Mapping Design Object to a Data Model

Mapping design objects to elements of a relational, network, or hierarchical database leads to several difficulties.

- A design object may be physically too large to fit in a standard record. In Chapter 7, we assumed that records never cross block boundaries; however a design object may be larger than a single block. Another source of long records and fields is text used to describe the design for documentation purposes.

- If a single design object is represented by many records, the user must still be able to manipulate the object as if it were a single unit.

- There are several possible *views* of a design object. There views range from a high-level view in which the design is a "black box" with only the interface specified to a low-level view at which all of the design details are visible. Furthermore, different users may require different representations of the same view. For example, a chip may be represented in logic or in a form that shows its physical layout.

We shall consider only the relational model in this section due to the relatively greater importance of this model and the fact that much of the research in CAD data modeling has involved mapping CAD databases to relations.

The hierarchical nature of design data suggests that the hierarchical model may be useful for design databases. However, a design database includes not only design objects but also descriptive data about the design objects. The combination of general-purpose data with design data has led most researchers in design databases to attempt to embed hierarchical design objects within the relational data model. Figure 14.1 shows a hierarchical scheme for a simplified computer system design database. Each node contains data pertaining to its parent. This data may be simple descriptive data such as an identification number or a name, or it may be data describing the components and the physical relationship of the

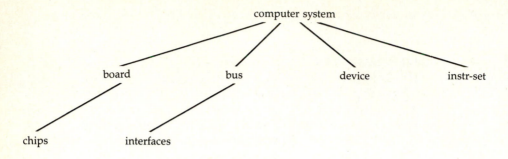

Figure 14.1   Hierarchical scheme for design data.

components. Figure 14.2 shows the scheme of Figure 14.1 expanded so that each node is represented by a relation.

To store the relations of Figure 14.2 in a standard relational database system, we need to create links between relations that represent the hierarchy and to define a storage structure for *long fields* such as *VLSI design* which may be larger than the maximum allowed record size. We address each of these issues in turn.

Each design object at the root level is given a unique identifier (*project-id* in our example). Each tuple of a child relation (*board*, *bus*, etc.) is augmented to include the primary-key value of its parent (*project-id* value, in our example). Thus, the scheme for any relation in the hierarchy must contain a primary key for its parent relation. By using this key value, it is possible to find the parent and children of any tuple. The schemes corresponding to the hierarchy of Figure 14.2 include:

> *computer-system* (*computer-name, project-id, manager, completion-date*)
> *board* (*project-id, board-number, function, size, chip-layout*)
> *chip* (*project-id, board-number, chip-id, chip-name, vendor, VLSI-design*)

The primary key for *computer-system* is *project-id*. Thus, *project-id* is added to the scheme for *board*. Similarly, the primary key of the *board*, that is, *project-id, board-number*, is added to the scheme for *chip*.

We contrast this implementation of hierarchies with the implementation of hierarchical databases we saw earlier in Chapter 7. In the hierarchical model, links (pointers) were used to connect parents and children in the hierarchy. In the design discussed above, primary keys are used in place of links. Primary keys that are used for this purpose may be called *identifiers*.

The above approach allows design data to be represented by relations, but it is no longer possible to access a single design object directly since it is represented by tuples in several relations. In order to permit deletion

computer-system (computer-name, project-id, manager, completion-date)

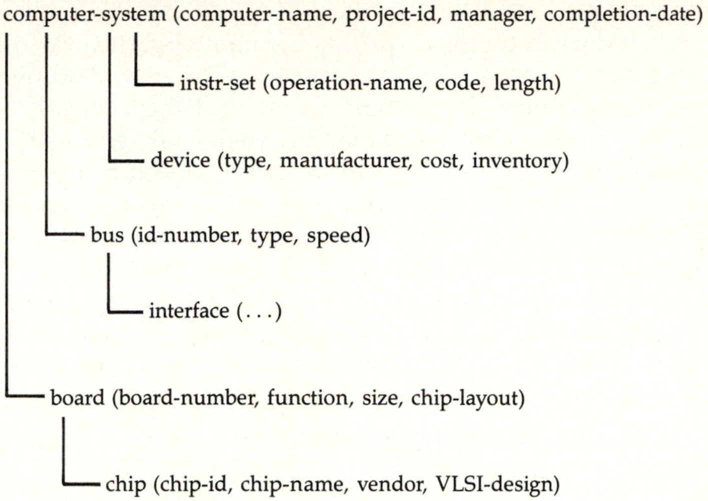

                   └── instr-set (operation-name, code, length)

             └── device (type, manufacturer, cost, inventory)

        └── bus (id-number, type, speed)

             └── interface (. . .)

    └── board (board-number, function, size, chip-layout)

        └── chip (chip-id, chip-name, vendor, VLSI-design)

Figure 14.2   Relation hierarchy.

and movement of design objects, the system must be able to determine which tuples pertain to which objects. This is accomplished by declaring the identifier for each node as part of the DDL specification of the database.

We now consider the physical implementation of long fields. In order to ensure that records remain small (no larger than one block) we store long fields separate from the record itself. All that is placed in the record is a pointer to the long field. The long field itself is stored in a special file (or collection of files) reserved for long field storage. This technique allows us to use the various methods discussed in Chapter 7 to implement relations containing design data.

It is important to emphasize that the above representation of long fields is nothing more than an implementation technique. The user of the database system need not be aware of this technique. To the user, records appear to be a single unit consisting of a collection of fields.

The user interface to a design database must include constructs to allow the extraction of entire design objects without the need to write a complex expression. It is desirable also to include the standard features of relational query languages.

A convenient way to access design objects is by representing the object graphically. The user (designer) can focus on the appropriate level of detail by using either cursor keys or a graphic pointing device like a mouse. An alternative mode of access to design objects is to specify a key value for the root of the object.

If every operation on a design object requires the database system to access the actual data in the database, the resulting overhead is likely to be high since the data corresponding to a design object is spread over several relations. In order to provide efficient access to design objects techniques similar to clustering (see Chapter 7) may be used. This reduces the number of disk block accesses required to read an entire object. Since a designer's operation on a design object is likely to involve several accesses to the object, it is often desirable to copy the entire design object into a data buffer within main memory and keep it there until the designer has completed work on the object. As this copying is being done, pointers reflecting the hierarchical structure of a design object may be inserted into the copy in the buffer to speed access to components of the object.

14.2.2 Versions of Design Objects

In a CAD database it is likely that several designers work on the same object. It is useful to maintain several versions of the object being designed or versions of components of the object. A version may represent:

- A publicly released version of the object.
- A newly created version of the object that has not yet been tested.
- A modified version of the object that is still under development.

A user may need to access a different version of the design object depending on the application. Some examples include:

- Cost estimates for the released version.
- Testing a version.
- Performing a operation on a version under development (as in a case where a designer seeks help from a second designer on a component).

The need to allow users to access versions explicitly has resulted in several models of versions. The most widely used model is the *checkout/checkin* model. In this model, a user "checks out" a copy of an object, operates on this copy, and "checks in" the modified copy, thus creating a new version.

The notion of checkout and checkin corresponds well to a distributed system consisting of:

- A large machine containing design data generally available to designers in their work. This is called the *public* database.

- Several small computers (personal workstations) containing data currently being modified by a design. The data stored on each of these machines is a *private* database.

The actual process of computer-aided design in not as rigidly structured as the above private/public distinction might suggest. If a subgroup of several designers are collaborating closely on a part of a design, a designer in this subgroup may require access to the private database of another designer in this subgroup. This form of interaction is modeled by allowing a semipublic database within each workstation. Data in a designer's semipublic database may be checked out by other designers. The result is a checkout hierarchy. Concurrent checkout and checkin of this form can lead to data inconsistency unless it is managed by an appropriate concurrency control scheme.

14.2.3 Transactions on Design Databases

The techniques we saw in Chapters 10 and 11 for transaction recovery and for the management of concurrent transactions can be applied to design databases. However, direct application of these techniques is not necessarily desirable due to several special characteristics of transactions on such databases. In this section, we consider several of the properties of design transactions that complicate the transaction model.

Due to the hierarchical nature of design data, it is useful to use a multiple-granularity approach to concurrency control. Using our earlier example, a transaction may lock at any of several granularities depending on the level of detail at which the transaction accesses the object. In our example, the granularities may include the entire computer, board granularity, or chip granularity. If objects are represented within a relational database, the object granularities must be combined with the granularities we considered in Chapter 11. A simple form of a multiple-granularity DAG that may result is shown in Figure 14.3.

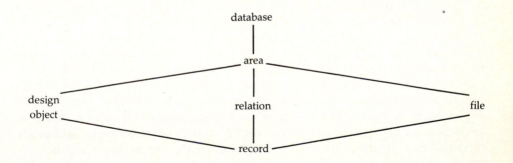

Figure 14.3   Multiple-granularity DAG for design data.

Transactions that involve modification of objects are more complicated and therefore of longer duration than a typical transaction in our bank database. In many cases, a design database transaction is a sequence of steps entered interactively by a designer using various design tools rather than through a single statement in a query language. Human interaction with a transaction results in significantly longer transactions than those that run without any human interaction. Long-duration transactions complicate concurrency control and recovery in several ways:

- Transaction rollback is more costly for a long-duration transaction since more work must be undone.

- The wait time for obtaining a lock held by a long-duration transaction may be quite significant. This results in a lengthy delay for the user who entered the waiting transaction.

- Waits and rollbacks are less acceptable when a user is interacting with a transaction, than when the user enters the entire transaction before expecting a response.

- Committing of transactions is complicated by the need to minimize both waits and rollbacks. It may be necessary to defer committing a transaction that has completed because of the possibility of cascading rollbacks. However, in order to avoid cascading rollback, protocols that increase the probability of waits may have to be used.

Further complication of the transaction model results from the public/private database model. Semi-private databases may contain data written by uncommitted transactions. It is often necessary for designers collaborating on a common project to read such data by means of a checkout operation. The result is a relatively large transaction dependency graph. There is potential for a large number of cascaded rollbacks should the transaction fail.

Several new transaction models are being devised to deal with these problems. Most of these models are beyond the scope of this text and are referenced in the bibliographic notes. In what follows, we discuss several of the concepts providing the foundation for these new transaction models.

In Chapter 11, we presented the concept of a *serializable* schedule. A serializable schedule is equivalent to a serial schedule, that is, one without any concurrency. Serializability is of critical importance in a bank database in which strict accounting procedures must be followed. Although serializability is desirable in a design database, it is not essential. A nonserializable schedule is acceptable provided that the resulting design is correct (in the sense that all consistency constraints are satisfied). By relaxing the requirement of serializability, it is possible to use less restrictive concurrency control techniques, thereby reducing the number of lock waits and deadlocks.

If we follow the techniques of Chapter 10 for recovery, it is necessary to abort all transactions active at the time of a crash. However, an abort of a long-duration design transaction is exceedingly costly, both in terms of the amount of work that must be undone and in terms of the aggravation caused to designers whose decisions are being undone. Therefore, we would like to limit the effects of a rollback by allowing for *partial* rollback of transactions.

There are two primary techniques for allowing partial rollback: *save points* and *transaction nesting*. A save point is a point in the execution of a transaction at which all internal state information is saved. In the event of a crash, the transaction is restarted from the most recent save point.

A *nested* transaction is a transaction containing other transactions. A long-duration transaction may consist of a collection of short-duration transactions. When a short-duration transaction completes, it is committed using the techniques of Chapter 10. In the event of a crash, only those short-duration transactions that are active at the time of the crash need to be aborted.

Nesting of transactions is advantageous for other reasons besides crash recovery. In an interactive design application, designers may wish to undo certain design changes they have made. By grouping changes into nested transactions against the database, two types of undo operations can be performed:

- **Abort**. A designer may abort an active transaction, thereby undoing any changes it has made.

- **Compensating transaction**. A designer may wish to undo a "committed" short-duration transaction. This cannot be accomplished by an abort, since transactions that have been committed cannot be aborted. However, in many applications, it is possible to create a new "compensating" transaction that undoes changes made by another transaction.

The concept of compensating transactions is needed in order to allow an abort of an entire long-duration transaction since transactions nested within the long-duration transaction may have already committed.

14.3 Knowledge Bases

Another direction in which database management is being extended involves the representation of facts expressed in logic.

14.3.1 Knowledge

We have seen (in several data models) how to express simple facts such as "Jones has an account at the Brighton branch." However, we are able only to make limited use of more complex facts or *rules* such as:

- All accounts are either passbook savings accounts, checking accounts or money market accounts.

- Passbook savings accounts pay 5 percent interest.

- Checking accounts have a $5 per month fee.

- Checking accounts pay 5 percent interest if the balance is over $1000; otherwise they pay no interest.

- Money market accounts pay 8 percent interest if the balance is over $2500; otherwise they pay 6 percent interest.

Rules such as these can appear as part of the database consistency constraints that are preserved by transactions (see Chapter 11). They are used only as integrity constraints. In general, they are not used by database systems to speed the processing of queries. In fact, these rules may not even appear explicitly in the database.

Consider the query "Find all money market accounts that pay 15 percent interest." If the system could use the fact that all money market accounts pay 8 percent interest, the system could conclude that the answer to the query is the empty set without ever accessing the database.

Rules can be used to answer queries that cannot be posed in standard database query languages. In database query languages one can obtain information only about data in the database. A knowledge base may be queried to obtain *meta-data*, that is, data about data. A user could ask "What is the best interest rate available on a $2000 deposit?" This query cannot be answered by examining the data, but it can be answered by using the knowledge base. It is possible to determine from the knowledge base that the best available rate is 6 percent. Another example of a fact that can be deduced from the given rules is that passbook savings accounts never pay the highest interest regardless of the balance.

14.3.2 Expert Systems

The additional power of rules is used in *expert systems*. An expert system attempts to emulate the reasoning of a human expert in some knowledge domain. It does this by using both the basic facts stored as data in the database and the rules in the knowledge base. The rules are statements in logic and are expressed typically in the form of an if-then predicate, such as, "If the account is a checking account and the balance is over $1000 then the account pays 5 percent interest."

An expert system is more than a knowledge base query processor. Although the goal of both query processors and expert systems is to answer a query, the queries posed to an expert system may be much more general than those accepted by a database query processor.

A frequent application of expert systems is problem diagnosis. Given a set of symptoms, the rules allow some conclusions to be reached about the nature of the problem. Medicine is an example of the use of expert systems for diagnosis. A collection of symptoms are entered and the system outputs whatever conclusions it can draw.

The response given by an expert system may be a question rather than a fact. Returning to the example of medicine, the system may ask the user for specific additional information about the patient (based on a set of rules for choosing questions) such that the responses are likely to assist it in applying additional rules and thus obtaining a better diagnosis.

Since an expert system finds the answer to a query through logical inference, it can explain how it reached a given conclusion. Consider again the query, "What is the best interest rate available on a $2000 account?" The answer is 6 percent. If the user were to ask "why?" the expert system can retrace its reasoning backwards to explain its answer. The response might be: "Money market accounts pay 6 percent interest if the balance is $2000. Savings accounts always pay 5 percent interest. Checking accounts pay 5 percent interest if the balance is $2000. There are no other types of account." More generally, the explanation is a listing of the rules that were applied in processing the query. The exact form a response takes depends on the individual expert system. Systems vary in the degree to which their interaction with the user approximates natural language.

Explanation of reasoning by an expert system is an important feature since it allows the user to determine if knowledge was overlooked by the system. In those cases where the user has some expertise, the expert system can become a collaborator rather than a query processor. The user may enter the overlooked knowledge and ask the expert system to reexecute the query.

In cases where the user has no expertise, explanation of the expert system's reasoning may enhance user confidence in the system and help to develop some expertise in the user.

Processing a knowledge base query is more complicated than processing a database query. Data in a database is a collection of data values. Data in a knowledge base includes rules that contain variables. Values are assigned to these variables only at query processing time. Thus a knowledge base query processor must be able to maintain and use a list of variable-value bindings. In order for the query processor to locate the applicable rules efficiently in a large knowledge base, indices are needed. These indices are more complex than those we saw in Chapter 8 since rules have a more complex structure than the simple domain values used in the search keys of database indices.

Just as databases change over time as data is inserted, deleted, or updated, so knowledge bases change over time. Thus, it is essential that knowledge bases by modifiable.

Modifying a knowledge base is more complex than modifying a database. When a tuple is added to a database, only a limited amount of testing is required. Usually this involves testing the values for membership in the domain of the respective attribute and testing integrity constraints that are usually a set of functional dependencies. When a rule is added to a knowledge base, it is possible for the rule to contradict information already in the knowledge base. Such updates must be disallowed. It is also possible that the rule being added follows logically from the rules already in the knowledge base. In such cases, the new rule is redundant. The complexity of testing for contradictions and redundancy increases fairly rapidly as the size of the knowledge base grows.

14.3.3 Knowledge Base Implementation

As we have seen, a knowledge base consists of two parts:

- A set of rules.

- A collection of data.

Most early expert systems did not use a database system to manage data. Instead, ad hoc techniques suited to the particular application were used. This was considered an acceptable approach because:

- Knowledge bases were sufficiently small to fit in main memory.

- Performance was not a major concern in initial experimental systems.

The need for more sophisticated knowledge base implementation techniques has arisen in recent years due to:

- The application of expert systems to larger or more complex problems for which larger knowledge bases are needed.

- Commercial interest in obtaining expert systems that run on inexpensive hardware.

These considerations suggest that the reasoning (or rule processing) part of the expert system interact with a standard database system. Such an approach allows much of the efficiency of database storage management and query processing techniques to be applied to knowledge base management.

In its simplest form, the expert system interacts with the database system as a casual user. The expert system submits queries in a database language such as SQL and awaits an answer from the database system. Although this is relatively easy to implement, it is not an optimal design since the rules in the knowledge base are not available for use in processing a database query. Furthermore, in the likely case that the expert system poses a series of related queries, the database system cannot take advantage of the similarity of the queries and must process each one individually.

Because of the inefficiencies of this form of expert system interaction with a database system, several alternatives have been considered, including:

- Loading into the expert system that part of the database that is needed for processing rules. The database itself is stored and maintained separately from the expert system. Periodically, the expert system's copy of the data is updated.

- Implementation of a database system within the expert system.

- Translating into the relational algebra certain logical queries posed to the expert system. The resulting algebra expression is passed to the database system for optimization and execution.

The ultimate solution is probably an integration of database and expert systems into a single system in which the rule processing component has access to low-level internal database system components. Issues involving concurrent access to a knowledge base, distribution of knowledge bases, etc. are only beginning to be addressed.

Current research in the areas of logic databases, expert systems, and artificial intelligence is attempting to address issues in the management of knowledge bases. One interesting approach to this problem is to use expert system techniques to manage the knowledge base itself. A mini knowledge base is maintained that describes conditions under which certain types of reorganization should be performed. The result is a knowledge base that organizes itself based upon the information stored in it and the nature of the queries presented to it.

14.4 Summary

There are many applications outside the realm of data processing, which may benefit from the use of a database system, including: design databases, knowledge bases, multimedia databases, and environment modeling. These new applications of databases have benefited greatly from the increase in available processing power of computer hardware and its falling cost.

Databases for computer-aided design are used to store complete information about a design object. The database is accessed by users who are designing components of the object or modifying existing designs. The designers frequently interact with the database using a graphics terminal through which they move components, insert components, etc. The user interface to a design database must include constructs to allow the extraction of entire design objects without the need to write a complex expression. It is desirable also to include the standard features of relational query languages.

In a CAD database, it is likely that several designers work on the same object. It is useful to maintain several versions of the object being designed or versions of components of the object. A user may need to access a different version of the design object depending on the application. The need to allow users to access versions explicitly has resulted in several models of versions. The most widely used is the checkout/checkin model. Due to the hierarchical nature of design data, it is useful to use a multiple-granularity approach to concurrency control.

Database systems are also being extended to involve the representation of facts (rules) expressed in logic, which can be used to answer queries that cannot be posed in standard database query languages. A knowledge base may be queried to obtain meta-data, that is, data about data. The additional power of rules is used in expert systems, which uses both the basic facts stored as data in the database and the rules in the knowledge base. The rules are statements in logic, and are expressed typically in the form of an if-then predicate. The rule processing part of the expert system interact with a standard database system. Such an approach allows much of the efficiency of database storage management and query processing techniques to be applied to knowledge base management.

Exercises

14.1 Why cannot CAD data be well represented directly using the relational network or hierarchical data models?

14.2 What is a long field and how is it implemented?

14.3 The *two-phase checkout protocol* requires that a transaction not check out data from the public database after data has been checked in. Explain how this protocol ensures database consistency.

14.4 List the primary factors making *knowledge* base management more complex than traditional database management.

14.5 Explain how an expert system might be applied to a university course registration data and knowledge base.

14.6 Would it be desirable to require first normal form (see Section 6.6) in a CAD database or in a knowledge base? Why or why not?

14.7 Consider an airline reservation transaction for a trip from Austin to Fresno. This transaction has 3 nested sub-transactions:

- Reserve a flight from Austin to Dallas.

- Reserve a flight from Dallas to San Francisco.

- Reserve a flight from San Francisco to Fresno.

Explain how compensating transactions may be used if:

a. The San Francisco to Fresno flight is canceled.

b. The passenger decides to cancel his or her entire reservation.

Bibliographic Notes

The structure of databases for CAD applications is discussed in Haskin and Lorie [1982], Lorie et al. [1985], and Katz and Weiss [1984]. Kim et al. [1984] presents the notion of public, semipublic, and private databases. the extension of the transaction model to include nested transactions is discussed in Lynch [1983] and Moss [1981]. Bancilhon et al. [1985a, 1985b] discuss nested transactions, consistency and recovery in CAD databases. They discuss also a notion of database consistency that does not require serializability. Relaxation of the serializability constrain is discussed also by Garcia-Molina [1983].

Vassiliou et al.[1985] presents a survey of knowledge bases and their relation to databases. Hayes-Roth et al. [1983] presents a collection of papers introducing expert systems. A textbook presentation of the fundamentals of artificial intelligence is given by Rich [1983]. Wiederhold et al. [1983a, 1983b] describes the KBMS project in which artificial intelligence techniques are applied to database management. The use of the relational data model as a model for text, user interfaces, and operating systems is discussed by Sciore et al. [1983], Bernstein, et al. [1984], and Henderson, et al. [1983]. Korth and Silberschatz [1985] describe the ROSI project, which is attempting to extend database data models to define an enhanced user interface for operating systems. Kim et al. [1985b] describes a graphics-based query language for this environment. Discussions of extended relational languages incorporating set-valued domains and complex datatypes include Zaniolo [1983], Roth et al. [1985] and Korth [1986].

15

Case Studies

In this chapter, we discuss a few selected database systems that either are commercially available or are experimental systems with significant impact. We do not provide complete details for the selected systems. Rather, we draw attention to some of the more significant features of the systems.

Given the large number of commercial systems available and the large number of systems being released as of this writing, the following discussion of actual systems is far from a complete one. We have chosen particular systems in order to illustrate concepts presented in this book. Thus our selection of a system for this chapter should not be interpreted as an endorsement of the product.

15.1 Relational Systems

The term *relational* has been applied to a large number of systems, including some that, though they use *tables*, do not capture the full spirit of the original definition of the relational data model. In order for us to consider a system to be relational, we require that it meet the following:

- Data is stored in tables.

- No pointers or links are visible to the user.

- The query language is relationally complete.

- Queries may be expressed without the use of iteration or recursion.

Systems that use tables as the basic data structure, but impose restrictions on allowable joins, are not considered relational. We use the term *tabular* for such systems.

15.1.1 System R

The System R research project began at the IBM San Jose Research Laboratory in 1974. The goal of the project was to demonstrate the practicality of the then newly proposed relational data model. This involved both verifying the appropriateness of the relational model as a

user interface and discovering ways of implementing a relational system
for efficient query processing.

The success of this effort is clear both from the commercial products
that are derived from the System R research and from the fact that a
substantial number of fundamental concepts were established by this
research. By 1979, the System R project was completed. Shortly thereafter,
IBM announced the database product *SQL/Data System* (see Section 15.1.2),
and formed the R* distributed database research project to extend the
System R research to distributed databases.

Among the key contributions of the System R effort were:

- The SQL query language.

- Query compilation and optimization.

- Integration of a relational language with a conventional programming
  language.

- Serializability and two-phase locking.

- Multiple granularity locking.

We have discussed SQL in detail in Chapter 3 and presented multiple
granularity locking in Chapter 11.

Overall System Structure

The internal architecture of System R consists of two main components:

- Relational Storage System (RSS), which is responsible for storage
  management (disk storage and main memory), crash recovery, and
  concurrency control.

- Relational Data System (RDS), which is responsible for views,
  authorization, and integrity.

The RSS allows access on a record-by-record basis to relations in the logical
model. Higher-level access is obtained by the RDS interface. This interface
accepts SQL expressions.

On top of the RDS, an arbitrary number of interfaces to the shared
System R database can be built. The most frequently used of these is the
User-Friendly Interface (UFI). UFI is a program that accepts SQL
statements from the user, passes them to the RDS, and displays the
results. Application programs can be written that use the RDS directly.

Query Compilation

Commercial users of database systems have a collection of queries that are
run regularly to generate reports. In order to eliminate the need to choose
a query-processing strategy each time such a query is run, System R allows

for the *precompilation* of queries. Precompilation involves the parsing of the query and the selection of a complete strategy for processing the query. The result of precompilation is called a *plan*. Plans are stored in the System R database and accessed when the query is executed.

Since a plan includes such details as the choice of join strategies and the use of particular indices, it is possible for a plan to become invalid. For example, an index used by a plan might be deleted. In such cases, it is necessary to rerun the query compilation step before the query can be executed.

Host Languages

When we presented the network and hierarchical data models in Chapters 4 and 5, we found it necessary to embed database system access requests within a host programming language. Since the relational model does not require a query language that includes iteration, recursion, or pointers, it is not necessary for us to embed the relational languages we presented in Chapter 3 in a host language. Nevertheless, such a capability is often useful in commercial database applications. For example, a programmer may wish to develop a special-purpose database interface for a particular group of users. To facilitate the development of such applications, System R includes *embedded SQL*, a slightly modified form of SQL that can be used within a host programming language. System R allows two host languages: PL/1 and Cobol. In our discussion, we shall consider PL/1 only.

The primary difficulties in merging the language concepts of SQL into PL/1 have to do with the fact that PL/1 operates on records, while SQL operates on sets of records (relations). Therefore, a mechanism is needed to present the result of an SQL query (that is, a relation) to the PL/1 program one tuple (record) at a time. A *cursor* is defined on relations to be processed by the PL/1 program. A cursor is a pointer to a tuple and serves a function similar to that of currency pointers in the DBTG data manipulation language. The normal method by which a PL/1 program accesses the database is summarized as follows:

- A call is made to a procedure that causes the SQL query to be executed.

- A *cursor* is opened on the relation resulting from execution of the query. This cursor is used to process tuples of the result relation one at a time.

- A *fetch* call is made in order to retrieve the "next" tuple. A fetch retrieves the first tuple of a relation associated with a newly opened cursor. Subsequent fetch calls advance the cursor to the next tuple of the relation and then retrieve the tuple to which the cursor points. The tuple retrieved is placed in a PL/1 record that can be manipulated by the PL/1 program.

- Fetch calls are repeated until all tuples have been processed. A special code returned by the fetch call allows the program to determine when all tuples have been processed.

An actual program is somewhat more complicated than the above indicated since:

- A preprocessor must translate the SQL statements before the program is compiled by the PL/1 compiler. Special commands to the preprocessor are needed.

- A method must be provided to transfer values from a tuple into PL/1 variables.

- The size of tuples returned by a fetch may depend upon input to the program. This occurs, for example, if the user inputs an SQL query to the program as it is executing.

In an actual PL/1 program with embedded SQL, the additional clause, **into**, appears in SQL statements. The **into** clause specifies the PL/1 variables into which the value for each attribute in the **select** clause is to be placed. In order to distinguish PL/1 variables from relation and attribute names, PL/1 variable names have a dollar sign placed in front of them whenever they appear in an SQL statement. PL/1 variables may be used also for comparisons in the **where** clause.

For example, consider the query "Find the name and city of customers with more than x dollars in an account," where x is a variable in our PL/1 program. Assume we use the PL/1 variables a and b to hold a tuple of the result. The query is written as:

> **select** *customer-name, customer-city*
>   **into** $a, $b
>   **from** *deposit, customer*
>   **where** *deposit.customer-name* = *customer.customer-name*
>   and *deposit.balance* > $x

Commands for the System R preprocessor begin with a dollar sign. There are four commands:

- **$declare**. This command is identical to the PL/1 declare command and is used to define PL/1 variables that are used also in SQL queries.

- **$let** <cursor-name> **be** <SQL statement>. This command associates the SQL statement with the cursor name. The processor stores this association for subsequent use. The query is *not* evaluated as a result of a **$let** command.

- **$open** <cursor-name>. This command causes the preprocessor to generate a PL/1 call to a procedure to evaluate the SQL query associated with the cursor. The association between a cursor name and an SQL query must have been defined in a prior **$let** command. A precompiled version of the SQL statement is produced at this time. Note that the **into** statement has no influence on the processing of the SQL query at this point.

- **$fetch** <cursor-name>. This command causes the values of the next tuple of the relation associated with the (open) cursor to be placed in the PL/1 variables listed in the **into** clause.

We illustrate the above commands by showing a program to print the result of our earlier example, "Find the name and city of customers with more than x dollars in an account":

```
$declare a char (20);
$declare b char (20);
$declare x binary fixed (15);
declare rc binary fixed (15);
$let c be select customer-name, customer-city
        into $a, $b
        from deposit, customer
        where deposit.customer-name = customer.customer-name
            and deposit.balance > $x
$open c;
rc = 0;
do while rc = 0;
        $fetch c;
        put skip list (a,b);
end
```

The preprocessor translates the program into a PL/1 program suitable for compilation by the PL/1 compiler. It also precompiles the SQL query and stores the plan for it in the database.

The above example was simplified by the fact that the application programmer knew that the SQL query generated a relation on *customer-name* and *customer-city*. This allowed the variables *a* and *b* to be declared with the correct datatype. Consider the problem faced by a programmer implementing UFI. The programmer does not know in advance what SQL statements will be entered. Indeed, the programmer does not even know what relations will exist when the UFI program is run!

To allow the programs that accept arbitrary SQL queries, System R includes a **describe** command. This command takes a SQL statement as input and returns:

- The arity of the result relation.

- The data type of each attribute of the result relation.

The application programmer must allocate dynamically the variables to accept tuples of the result relation.

Consistency and Concurrency

The concepts of two-phase locking and multiple-granularity locking originated from the System R project. By default, transactions in System R hold all locks until the end of transaction execution in order to ensure serializability and avoid cascading rollback. System R allows for alternative *degrees of consistency* that allow locks to be released early. An application programmer designing a transaction for System R might opt for a weaker degree of consistency since early release of locks should reduce the chances of another transaction having to wait for a lock.

Multiple-granularity locking has worked well in System R. However, a slight modification to the scheme as presented in Chapter 11 was added to deal with the following problem. Often, a transaction accumulates a large number of record-granularity locks on a relation but fails to take a relation-granularity lock. As a result, the lock manager is forced to maintain a large lock table and lock overhead increases. To cope with such a situation, System R automatically performs *lock escalation*. The record-granularity locks are exchanged (if possible) for a lock at the relation or file granularity. This lock escalation procedure is transparent to the application programmer and to the user.

The System R recovery manager uses *both* shadow paging and logging. This combined strategy is a reflection of the evolution of System R from a single-user system (for which shadow paging works well) to a multiuser system. Shadow paging does not generalize well to the case of concurrent accesses to the database. The form of logging used is called *write-ahead logging* and is essentially the same as incremental logging with immediate update as discussed in Chapter 10.

Remarks

System R is well-documented in the open literature due to it being a research project rather than a commercial product. Besides its influence on several commercial products, System R has spawned several subsequent research projects including the R* distributed database project and research into extending System R to support complex objects (see Chapter 14).

15.1.2 SQL/Data System

SQL/Data System (SQL/DS) is a commercial database system available from IBM. It is an intermediate-size system whose scope is between that of mainframe database systems (for example, DB2 and IMS) and personal computer database systems (for example, dBase III). SQL/DS runs under either of two IBM operating systems: DOS/VSE and VM/SP.

There are a large number of similarities between SQL/DS and System R, since the SQL/DS product was influenced strongly by the System R research effort. These similarities include:

- The SQL query language and embedded SQL.

- Precompilation.

- Concurrency control and transaction management.

Most of what was stated in Section 15.1.1 about these subjects is applicable to SQL/DS as well.

An important area in which SQL/DS goes beyond System R is in the ability to extract data from IMS databases using the DL/1 query language of IMS. The DL/1 extract feature allows data from a (hierarchical) IMS database to be copied into part of a (relational) SQL/DS database. Once the data is stored in the SQL/DS system, it can be queried using SQL. It is not possible, however, to modify the IMS database using SQL.

The data definition language of SQL/DS includes the usual SQL statements: **create table**, **create index**, **create view**, etc. In addition, SQL/DS has statements that allow the database administrator control over the physical database structure.

A *database space* (*dbspace* in SQL/DS terminology) is a section of physical disk storage into which relations and their indices are stored. The security mechanism of SQL/DS is used to control the authority to add new relations to a database space. For example, a user may be assigned a personal database space for his own relations. That user is granted resource authority for his personal database space.

When a database space is created, it can be associated with a particular disk. The power to assign database spaces to specific disks in a multi-disk computer system allows the database administrator to distribute the data accesses over several physical devices. This distribution of workload should lead to enhanced performance.

The user interface to SQL/DS includes both a precompiler and an interactive interface similar to System R's UFI. The precompiler syntax is different from that System R, but the basic language constructs and concepts are the same.

The *interactive SQL* interface (ISQL) allows a user to enter SQL queries directly. In addition to SQL statements, ISQL includes statements to control the output format of answers to queries, commands to save and edit queries, and statements to facilitate the generation of reports.

15.1.3 Database 2

Database 2 (DB2) is a commercial database system available from IBM for use on large mainframes running the MVS operating system.

Although DB2 and SQL/DS are distinct systems, there is a high degree of similarity between these two database systems. Both use a nearly identical version of the SQL query language, and nearly identical syntax for embedded SQL. The two systems cannot share data directly, but it is possible to transfer data between SQL/DS and DB2 systems.

The concepts underlying DB2 are similar to those of SQL/DS and, therefore, similar to System R. The primary significance of DB2 is that it has the size and sophistication to handle large databases. Therefore, unlike SQL/DS, DB2 is a competitor of IMS for the management of large databases. The introduction of DB2 in 1983 indicates the increasing importance of the relational data model in the commercial environment and the waning importance of the hierarchical model. The *DXT* features of DB2 allows data to be moved from IMS to DB2 (analogously to the DL/1 extract feature of SQL/DS).

Much of what has been said about System R and SQL/DS is applicable to DB2. Below we note some interesting aspects of DB2 not discussed above.

DB2 interacts with three different subsystems running under MVS each of which provides a form of transaction management. These three subsystems, IMS, TSO (the MVS time-sharing option), and CICS (Customer Information Control System), predate DB2. Thus, the interaction of DB2 with these subsystems was a practical necessity. Nevertheless, it creates an interesting application of the *distributed* database concepts of transaction commit. In Chapter 12, we assumed that a distributed system consists of computers connected by a network. Within DB2, the subsystems all coexist on the same machine. However, as is the case for distributed systems, the subsystems must reach agreement either to commit or abort transactions that use the services of more than one subsystem. This is accomplished in DB2 using the two-phase commit protocol that we saw in Chapter 12.

The DB2 *query management facility* (QMF) is an interface to DB2 that allows interaction with the database using:

- SQL.

- QBE.

- A report writer facility.

The QBE language is discussed in Chapter 3. QBE originally was an entire database system developed at the IBM T. J. Watson Research Center. The most noteworthy feature of the QBE system is its query language. Since QBE and SQL are both relational query languages, it is feasible for a database system to offer its users both languages.

Under QMF, DB2 users may share data even if some users use SQL and others use QBE. The report writer facility is available both to SQL users and QBE users. QMF automatically generates a format for the report. The user may alter this format, if this is desired. The QMF facility has been made available also under SQL/DS.

15.1.4 Oracle

The Oracle database system, available from Oracle Corporation, is a system that, although not developed by IBM, conforms closely to the query language and user interface of the IBM product SQL/DS.

Oracle runs on a wide variety of systems including DEC VAX computers and IBM 370-like computers. Like the IBM systems discussed above, Oracle uses the SQL query language and allows application programs to use embedded SQL. The host languages for which embedded SQL is offered are Cobol, Fortran, and C. In addition to a precompiler approach to embedded SQL, Oracle includes a *call interface* in which SQL statements are interpreted at run time rather than precompiled. There is a close correspondence between calls in the call interface and precompiler statements. Although the call interface eliminates the precompilation step in preparing an application program, the precompilation approach is preferable for programs that will be run several times. Like most commercial systems, Oracle includes a report generation facility. This facility, however, is not patterned after those of the systems discussed above (except for the common use of SQL).

Oracle uses B^+-tree indices with an option for *key compression*. Key compression is a space-saving technique. Rather than storing the entire key in the index, only a part of the key sufficient to identify the correct pointer to follow is stored. This allows for considerable savings for long keys (such as names of people), but has the disadvantage that the full key value can be determined only by reading a database record.

Crash recovery in Oracle is based on *before-image files*. The before-image file holds copies of database blocks that have been modified by uncommitted transactions. These copies are used to roll back aborted transactions. This technique is similar to the shadow-paging technique presented in Chapter 10.

Concurrency control in Oracle uses locking and allows for additional concurrency through the use of the before-image file. This technique is a form of multiversion concurrency control in which only two versions are allowed. Suppose that transaction T_1 is requesting read access to data that

T_2 is modifying. Under the usual form of locking, T_1 must wait for T_2 to release its lock. Oracle, however, allows T_1 to read the data using the values prior to T_2's modification. These values are stored in the before-image file. If before-image data is not desired, T_1 may request a lock that will require it to wait for any concurrent write transactions to unlock the data.

15.1.5 Ingres

At approximately the same time during which the IBM San Jose Research Laboratory was developing the System R prototype, a group at the University of California at Berkeley was developing an experimental database system called Ingres. Although both projects were based on the ideas of the relational data model, the two projects differ substantially in their system design and user interface.

The Ingres research project led to the development of a commercial product with the same name, available through Relational Technology, Inc. In this section, we discuss the academic version of Ingres, though many of our remarks are applicable also to the commercial version.

Overall System Structure

Ingres was developed on a PDP-11 computer running the UNIX operating system. The UNIX operating system influenced the way in which Ingres was structured internally. Several processes are used, each of which is responsible for a specific task:

- Query formulation, user interaction.

- Lexical analysis and parsing, query optimization.

- Execution of queries.

- Index maintenance.

A user request is passed from process to process as necessary.

This multiprocess design allows for concurrency within Ingres itself since, for example, one query can be parsed while another is executing. However, the inter-process communication (via Unix pipes) imposes some overhead. Historically, a major factor motivating the Ingres design was the PDP-11 limitation of 64 kilobyte address spaces for each individual process.

Ingres introduced the query language Quel and an embedding of Quel into the host language C called Equel. Quel was discussed in Chapter 3. Much of the syntax of Equel is of a form similar to that of embedded SQL. The characters "##" are used to indicate a Quel statement appearing within a C program. The "##" characters are used to mark those C declarations that pertain to variables referenced with a Quel statement.

Equel differs from embedded SQL in its analog to SQL's cursors. Recall that in embedded SQL, a cursor is *open*ed for a query and then individual tuples are retrieved by means of a **fetch** call. Equel uses a more structured approach in which a specific body of code is executed once per tuple in the result of a Quel query. Figure 15.1 shows a sample Equel program to print the name and city of customers with more than x dollars in an account. The code delimited by "#{" and "#}" is executed once for each tuple of the result. The values of the tuple on each of the attributes of the result relation are stored in the variables in the **retrieve** clause (a and b in Figure 15.1).

Ingres does not allow precompilation of Quel queries even in cases where the Quel query is embedded in a C (Equel) program. Query optimization is performed as part of query interpretation rather than being done at precompilation time. A particularly useful query optimization technique introduced by Ingres is called *decomposition*. A *query graph* is constructed whose nodes are relations and whose edges represent theta joins or natural joins. If an edge represents a join of a small relation with another relation, the expected result of this join is another small relation. Therefore joins of this sort are processed first. When no such joins remain, decomposition is performed.

Let us illustrate decomposition by considering part of a query graph as shown in Figure 15.2. This graph illustrates a join of three relations, r_1, r_2,

```
## char a[20], b[20];
## float x;
main () {
        .
        .
        .
## range of d is deposit
## range of c is customer
## retrieve a = c.customer-name, b = c.customer-city
## where d.balance > x
    #{ printf ("%5, %7.2f\n", a, b)
    #}
        .
        .
        .
```

Figure 15.1   Sample Equel program.

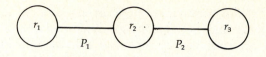

Figure 15.2   Part of an Ingres query graph.

and r_3. Let their schemes be R_1, R_2, and R_3 respectively.   Relation r_2 is decomposed by:

- Building an index on r_1 for $R_1 \cap R_2$ (unless such an index already exists).

- Building an index on r_3 for $R_3 \cap R_2$ (unless such an index already exists).

- Decomposing r_2 into several relations. Each relation is on scheme R_2 and contains exactly one tuple of r_2. A new query graph is produced for each decomposed relation. In each such graph a decomposed relation takes the place of r_2.

- Each query graph is processed and the union of the results is taken.

Since all the query graphs generated by an application of decomposition have the same structure, it is easy to process them.

15.2 Network Systems

The network model forms the foundation of most of the older database systems and some recent systems. In this section, we consider briefly two popular network systems, Total and IDMS.

15.2.1 Total

The Total database system dates from the late 1960s. It runs on a wide variety of machines ranging from minicomputers to mainframes.

Although Total is based on the DBTG model, the query language of Total differs from the one we presented in Chapter 4. The language presented in Chapter 4 is based on the DBTG standard. Total's language, though similar in function, uses a different syntax.

All statements in the Total data manipulation language must be embedded in a host language (Cobol, PL/1, Fortran, or RPG). A call is made to the *database* procedure with parameters that specify the DML statement. These statements are of a nature similar to the **find**, **find owner**, and **find next** commands we saw in Chapter 4, although the terminology used by Total is motivated by some of the concepts of the IMS

DL/1 language. Owner types are called single-entry data sets and member types are called variable-entry data sets.

The internal physical implementation of Total and the access schemes used are unpublished.

15.2.2 IDMS

IDMS is a network database system developed by Cullinane Database Systems, Inc. IDMS adheres closely to the DBTG model as presented in Chapter 4. It includes a detailed data manipulation language allowing the database designer a high degree of control over the physical organization of the database. The data manipulation languages includes features identical (or nearly so) to those of the DBTG DML described in Chapter 4. Additional features are included to allow increased programmer convenience and to allow knowledgeable programmers to write more efficient queries.

An example of a feature in IDMS not covered in Chapter 5 is the **obtain** command, which combines the **find** and **get** commands into one request. An optional **where** clause may be attached to an **obtain** to find and get the next record satisfying the **where** predicate. This feature relieves the programmer of the need to write an explicit test of a record located via the **find** command.

The bibliographic notes reference documents describing in detail the internal file management and index techniques used by IDMS.

15.3 Hierarchical Systems

The hierarchical model is significant primarily because of the importance of IBM's IMS database system. In this section, we discuss both IMS and another widely used hierarchical system, System 2000.

15.3.1 IMS

The IBM Information Management System (IMS) is one of the oldest and most widely used database systems. It runs under the MVS operating system on large IBM 370 and 370-like machines. Since IMS databases have historically been among the largest databases, the IMS developers were among the first to have had to deal with such issues as concurrency, recovery, integrity, and efficient query processing. Through several releases, IMS acquired a large number of features and options. As a result, IMS is a highly complex system. We shall consider only a few features of IMS here.

IMS is based on the hierarchical data model (see Chapter 5). Queries on IMS databases are issued through embedded calls in a host language. The embedded calls are part of the IMS database language DL/1. The language we used in Chapter 5 is a simplified form of DL/1.

Since performance is critically important in large databases, IMS allows the database designer a large number of options in the data definition language. The database designer defines a physical hierarchy as the database scheme. Several subschemes (or views) may be defined by constructing a logical hierarchy from the record types comprising the scheme. There are a variety of options available in the data definition language (block sizes, special pointer fields, etc.) that allow the database administrator to "tune" the system for improved performance.

Several record access schemes are available in IMS:

- HSAM (hierarchical sequential-access method), which is used for physically sequential files (such as tape files). Records are stored physically in preorder.

- HISAM (hierarchical index-sequential access method), which is an index-sequential organization at the root level of the hierarchy.

- HIDAM (hierarchical indexed direct-access method), which is an index organization at the root level with pointers to child records.

- HDAM (hierarchical direct-access method), which is similar to HIDAM but with hashed access at the root level.

The original version of IMS predated the development of concurrency control theory. Early versions of IMS had a simple form of concurrency control. Only one update application program could run at a time. However, any number of read-only applications could run concurrent with an update application. This allowed applications to read uncommitted updates and allowed nonserializable executions. Exclusive access to the database was the only option available to applications that demanded a greater degree of isolation from the anomalies of concurrent processing.

Later versions of IMS included a more sophisticated *program isolation feature* that allowed for both improved concurrency control and more sophisticated transaction recovery techniques (such as logging). These features became of increasing importance as more IMS users began to use online transactions as opposed to the batch transaction that were the norm originally.

The need for high-performance transaction processing led to the introduction of *IMS Fast Path*. Fast Path uses an alternative physical data organization designed to allow the most active parts of the database to reside in main memory. Instead of forcing updates to disk at the end of transaction (as standard IMS does), update is deferred until a checkpoint or synchronization point. In the event of a crash, the recovery subsystem must redo all committed transactions whose updates were not forced to disk. These and other "tricks" allow for extremely high rates of transaction throughput.

IMS database may be queried, though not updated, using SQL. The DXT feature of DB2 and the DL/1 extract feature of SQL/DS allow IMS data to be stored in a relational database on which SQL queries may be issued.

The full details of IMS are beyond the scope of this brief survey. Although IMS is an old system and the hierarchical model is fading in significance, the history and evolution of IMS provide an interesting framework for the study of the development of database system concepts.

15.3.2 System 2000

System 2000 is a hierarchical database system originally developed by MRI Corporation and now available from Intel. System 2000 is available on IBM 370-like computers, Univac 1100 computers, and CDC 6000 and Cyber computers. Although the data model used is the same as IMS, the language features offered by System 2000 differ in several interesting ways from the IMS DL/1 language.

The primary concept in the DL/1 data definition language is the one-to-many parent-child relationship. In our bank example, assume there is a one-to-many relationship between *customer* and *account*. We would design our hierarchical bank database with *account* as a child of *customer*. An alternative manner of viewing this one-to-many relationship is to consider a record that may have repeating fields. Within the *customer* record of a particular customer, we may store the set of accounts belonging to that customer by creating a repeating *account* field. It is this repeating-field approach that motivates the System 2000 data definition language.

In our bank example of Chapter 5, the *customer* record has the fields *customer-name*, *street*, and *customer-city* and the *account* record has the fields *account-number* and *balance*. Below we show the statements for this part of the bank database using System 2000 data definition language.

> 1* *customer-name* (name);
> 2* *street* (name);
> 3* *customer-city* (name);
> 4* *account* (repeating group);
> 5* *account-number* (integer);
> 6* *balance* (money);

The datatypes name, integer, and money are three of the built-in datatypes in System 2000. Each field can be specified as *key* or *nonkey*. A *key* field is one on which System 2000 builds an index.

Consider the query, "Find the name and city of all customers holding an account with a balance greater than $10000." Using the DL/1-like language of Chapter 5, we must loop over all account records for each customer by writing our own **while** loop in a host language. The System

2000 query language, QUEST, allows us to write this query as a single statement:

list *customer-name, customer-city*
while *customer* **has** *balance* > 10000

It is possible also to embed System 2000 queries in a host language. A precompiler processes the program. Parsing of queries is done at the precompilation phase. Like most commercial systems, System 2000 includes facilities to assist in report generation.

15.4 Microcomputer Database Systems

The primary characteristic of microcomputer database systems is simplicity. The limited capability of personal computers limits both the size of the database and the degree of sophistication of the system. Although most database systems are designed with ease of use in mind, this is a critical concern in the personal computer market since users cannot rely on a skilled database administrator for assistance. Each user of a microcomputer database system serves as database administrator.

Let us compare the typical features of microcomputer database systems with those of larger systems:

- **Data model**. Since microcomputer database systems are relatively new, almost all such systems are based on the relational model. Some systems are better described as *tabular* since, though based on tables, they are too primitive to be called relational.

- **Query language**. Even the higher-level languages we have discussed may be too complex for the casual user of a microcomputer database system. Many languages are based on a form interface in which the user interacts with the system by filling in a form.

- **Physical implementation**. The space occupied by the object code of a microcomputer database system is an important issue to system implementors. By reducing the space requirements, it is possible to run the system on machines with less main memory. This can have a major impact on the potential market. As a result, few systems employ sophisticated storage management and indexing techniques. Rather, a single type of index is chosen, and little or no query optimization is performed.

- **Recovery**. Many systems have no recovery subsystem. The user is expected to back up data regularly.

- **Concurrency**. Concurrency control is not needed for single-user personal computers.

The distinction between microcomputer database systems and larger systems is eroding. Early microcomputer database systems were little more than interfaces for accessing a single file of fixed-length records. As the power of personal computers has grown, so has the sophistication and complexity of microcomputer database systems. Indeed, versions of some large-scale database systems are beginning to appear on top-of-the-line personal computers. An example of such a system is SQL/RT on the IBM RT Personal Computer.

In this section, we examine dBase-III, a successful entry in the microcomputer database system market and Lotus 1-2-3, a "spreadsheet database" system.

15.4.1 dBase-III

Ashton-Tate's dBase-III is a revision of the commercially successful dBase-II product. It includes both a data manipulation language and a general-purpose programming language. Although features of these languages are motivated by Cobol, Pascal, and the database languages we have studied, the language of dBase-III is unique. The programming language is necessary for all but the most simple queries since the data manipulation language, by itself, is less powerful than the relational algebra.

Selection and projection can be expressed in dBase-III using the **display** command. For example, let us consider the query, "Find the name of all branches at which Jones has an account." First we enter the statement:

use *deposit*

to indicate that we wish to use the file *deposit* which contains the *deposit* table. The statement:

display all off for *customer* = "Jones", *branch-name*

displays the answer to our query. The **all** keyword forces all records satisfying the query to be displayed rather than just one. The **off** keyword suppresses the printing of record numbers.

Similar syntax is used for the **delete** statement. An interesting feature of deletion in dBase-III is that deleted records are simply *marked* as deleted, but are not actually removed from the database. This allows a user to undo an erroneous delete using the **recall** statement. Only when the user issues the **pack** statement are deleted records removed from the database.

The **append** statement puts dBase-III into insert mode. A form is displayed on the screen with a blank for each field of a record of the table specified by the most recent **use** statement. The user fills in the form.

Computing a join in dBase is more cumbersome than in the query languages we covered in Chapter 3. The user must create a new table containing the join. A **select** command is required to allow the specification of multiple tables in **use** statements. Note that this use of the word **select** does not correspond to either the SQL meaning nor the relational algebra meaning of select. The sequence of statements required to compute:

$$deposit \bowtie customer$$

is:

> **select** 2
> **use** *deposit*
> **select** 1
> **use** *customer*
> **join with** *deposit* **to** *cd* **for** *customer-name = customer − > customer-name;*
>   **fields** *branch-name, account-number,*
>   *customer − > customer-name, balance, street, customer-city*
> **use** *cd*

The two **select** and **use** statements specify the tables being accessed. The *customer* table is joined with *deposit* in the **join** statement. The type of join performed is a theta join, followed by a projection. The **for** clause of the **join** specifies the join predicate. The **fields** clause specifies those attributes onto which the result of the theta join is to be projected. Note that dBase-III uses the notation:

$$table\text{-}name - > attribute\text{-}name$$

rather than the notation

$$relation\text{-}name.attribute\text{-}name$$

that we used in Chapters 3 and 6. The result of the join is a new table *cd* containing the join. The *display* statement can be used to display the result.

If a query involves several joins, a number of large temporary files needs to be created if we follow an approach similar to the one we used above. Unlike large database systems in which we can rely on the query optimizer for efficient computation of joins, dBase forces the user to write a program in order to compute a join of several relations query efficiently.

The dBase programming language includes database access as an integral part of the language, rather than embedding it in an existing language by means of special escape characters (such as the "$" of System R or the "#" of Ingres). We shall not present the full dBase-III programming language here. It has the usual control structures (**if-then-**

else, while, case). In addition, it has a **find** command that allows records with a particular value on a specified field to be located. However, **find** works only on index fields. For other fields, the **locate** command, which performs a linear search, must be used. Once a record has been found (or located), the program may operate on the values of the fields of the record.

It is necessary to use the dBase programming facility more often than one needs to use the embedded SQL facility of System R since the dBase query language is limited in power. The dBase programmer must be aware of the efficiency of the query-processing strategy used while the embedded SQL programmer can rely on the query optimizer to deal with most efficiency considerations.

15.4.2 Spreadsheet/Database Systems

Visicalc, a product of Software Arts, Inc., was the first successful spreadsheet language. Unlike traditional programming languages, a spreadsheet language is two-dimensional in nature. A spreadsheet is a two-dimensional array of cells. Programming with a spreadsheet involves the definition of mathematical relationships among cells. The spreadsheet system maintains these relationships as data is entered. Thus, each cell may have associated with it a *formula* of a *value*.

Figure 15.3 shows the formulae for a simple spreadsheet for gas mileage records for a car. In the spreadsheet, columns are named A, B, ..., and rows 1, 2, ..., . Formulae for computing number of gallons purchased and miles per gallon appear in the spreadsheet. Consider, for example, cell D2 which contains the formula C2/B2. This means the value of D2 is computed by dividing the value in cell C2 by that in B2. Suppose that values are entered into the spreadsheet as shown in Figure 15.4. The spreadsheet, as displayed to the user is shown in Figure 15.5. In place of formulae, the user sees the value of each formula. Special commands are available to display and modify formulae.

Our goal in this section is not to present spreadsheet programming in detail. Instead, we note that it is possible to view a rectangular collection of spreadsheet cells as a table. This suggests a combination of spreadsheet and database languages into a single framework. We illustrate this type of

	A	B	C	D	E
1	miles traveled	price(dollars/gal)	amount paid	gallons	mpg
2				C2/B2	A2/D2
3				C3/B3	A3/D3
4				C4/B4	A4/D4
5				C5/B5	A5/D5

Figure 15.3   Gas mileage spreadsheet––formulae.

	A	B	C	D	E
1	miles traveled	price(dollars/gal)	amount paid	gallons	mpg
2	351	1.099	9.00		
3	292	1.119	8.25		
4	302	1.099	8.70		
5	289	1.079	9.10		

Figure 15.4   Gas mileage spreadsheet: data values entered.

language using the Lotus 1-2-3 product of the Lotus Development Corporation.

A 1-2-3 scheme for a table is defined by entering the field (attribute) name for each column in row 1. Only the first row may be used for this purpose. Relatively little is demanded of the user with regard to data types. All the user must do is decide how many characters are needed to display the values in each column. Thus, in effect, all domains are of type *string* with some user-specified length. Data is entered into the spreadsheet database in the same way as ordinary spreadsheet data.

Lotus 1-2-3 tables differ from simple spreadsheets in that tables may be sorted and searched. The sort command (/DS) requests a contiguous range of rows to sort, and the sort key (the columns on which the rows are to be sorted).

In order to retrieve data from a Lotus 1-2-3 table, one uses the /DQ (for "data query") command. As in the sort command, a contiguous range of rows for the search must be specified. The predicate is specific by creating a template table whose column headers are the names of those fields in which a predicate is to be specific. The predicate is entered into this template in a form reminiscent of QBE. The ith row of the template specifies a predicate P_i. The query is:

$$P_1 \wedge P_2 \wedge \cdots$$

	A	B	C	D	E
1	miles traveled	price(dollars/gal)	amount paid	gallons	mpg
2	351	1.099	9.00	8.19	42.0
3	292	1.119	8.25	7.37	39.6
4	302	1.099	8.70	7.92	38.0
5	289	1.079	9.10	8.43	34.3

Figure 15.5   Gas mileage spreadsheet: result displayed to user.

	A	B	C	D	E
1	miles traveled	price(dollars/gal)	amount paid	gallons	mpg
2	351	1.099	9.00	8.19	42.0
3	292	1.119	8.25	7.37	39.6
4	302	1.099	8.70	7.92	38.0
5	289	1.079	9.10	8.43	34.3
6		price(dollars/gal)			
		1.099			

Figure 15.6   Query to find rows where price is 1.099.

Each P_i is a conjunction of conditions pertaining to individual fields. If a constant C appears in column i in a row, only table rows with the value C in column i will be retrieved. Figure 15.6 shows the query, "Find all records for which the price is \$1.099."

To specify conditions involving comparisons other than equality, ">", "<", etc. may be used. There is no direct analog to QBE's domain variables, but the spreadsheet location of the first row's value on a field can be used as a form of domain variable. Figure 15.7 shows the query, "Find records for all tankfuls for which mpg was between 40 and 50 miles per gallon."

For any 1-2-3 query, the rows that form the result are copied to an output *range*, that is, a section of the spreadsheet specified by the user as a parameter to a /DQ command.

We have not covered all the features of the /DQ command. However, it should be clear that although the most basic queries are not difficult to express, the query language lacks the power and generality of the query languages covered in Chapters 3, 4 and 5.

	A	B	C	D	E
1	miles	price	amount	gallons	mpg
2	351	1.099	9.00	8.19	42.0
3	292	1.119	8.25	7.37	39.6
4	302	1.099	8.70	7.92	38.0
5	289	1.079	9.10	8.43	34.3
6	miles	price	amount	gallons	mpg
					+E2 > 40 *and* E2 < 50

Figure 15.7   Query to find rows where mpg is between 40 and 50.

Bibliographic Notes

The distinction bewteen relational and tabular database systems is based on [Codd 1982].

Various aspects of System R are presented in a large number of published papers. Astrahan et al. [1976], Astrahan et al. [1979], and Blasgen et al. [1981] present an overview of System R. Chamberlin et al. [1976] introduced the SQL language, An analysis of the human factors of SQL is given by Chamberlin [1980], Reisner [1977] and Reisner et al. [1975]. Concurrency control in System R is discussed in [Eswaren et al. 1976], [Gray 1978], [Gray et al. 1975, 1976]. Gray et al. [1981a] discusses the System R approach to crash recovery. Security and authorization in System R is discussed by Griffiths and Wade [1976], Fagin [1978], and Chamberlin et al. [1978]. Lorie and Wade [1979] and Selinger et al. [1979] explain how query compilation is done in System R. Chamberlin et al. [1981] gives an overview of System R written after the completion of the project.

An overview of R*, an experimental distributed version of System R, is presented in Williams et al. [1982]. A more detailed survey of the R* approach to distributed data management is given in [Lindsay et al. 1980]. Recovery is discussed in Traiger et al. [1982]; distributed naming in Linsday [1981]; distributed execution of data definition statements in Wilms et al. [1983]; the transaction model in Lindsay et al. [1984]; and distributed query compilation in Daniels et al. [1982].

SQL/DS is described in [IBM 1982]. Date [1984] gives a detailed description of the Database2 (DB2) product. The Oracle System is described in [Oracle 1983].

The most significant papers arising out of the Ingres research project have been collected in [Stonebraker 1986]. This collection includes a retrospective on Ingres [Stonebraker 1980], a history of the implementation of Ingres [Stonebraker et al. 1976], and a discussion of the relationship between database systems and operating systems [Stonebraker 1981]. The [Stonebraker 1986] collection discusses all aspect of the Ingres project, including the decision to produce a commercial version of Ingres. [RTI 1983] describes the commercial version of Ingres. The decomposition approach to query optimization use by Ingres is discussed in Wong and Youssefi [1976].

The Total database system is described in [Cincom 1974, 1978]. IDMS is described in Cullinet [1983a, 1983b]. System 2000 is described in [MRI 1974, 1979].

IMS is described in [IBM 1978a] and [McGee 1977]. Obermarck [1980] discusses the IMS program isolation feature, and gives a brief history of the concurrency control component of IMS.

There has been a proliferation of books pertaining to the use of microcomputer software. Among the texts that describe dBaseIII are

Prague amd Hammit [1985], and Ross [1986a]. Among the texts that describe Lotus 1-2-3 are Simpson [1985], and Ross [1986b]. The implementation of data management services on a personal workstation is described by Bissell [1986].

Bibliography

[Adiba 1980] M. Adiba, "Derived Relations: A Unified Mechanism for Views, Snapshots and Distributed Data," IBM Research Report RJ2881, (1980).

[Abrial 1974] J. R. Abrial, "Data Semantics," in **[Klimbie and Koffeman 1974]**, pages 1-59.

[ANSI 1975] "Study Group on Data Base Management Systems: Interim Report," *FDT*, Volume 7, Number 2, ACM, New York, New York, (1975).

[Aho and Ullman 1979] A. V. Aho and J. D. Ullman, "Optimal Partial Match Retrieval When Fields Are Independently Specified," *ACM Transactions on Database Systems*, Volume 4, Number 2, (June 1979), pages 168-179.

[Aho and Ullman 1972] A. V. Aho and J. D. Ullman, *The Theory of Parsing, Translation and Compiling, Volume I: Parsing*, Prentice-Hall, Englewood Cliffs, New Jersey, (1972).

[Aho and Ullman 1973] A. V. Aho and J. D. Ullman, *The Theory of Parsing, Translation and Compiling, Volume II: Compiling*, Prentice-Hall, Englewood Cliffs, New Jersey, (1973).

[Aho et al. 1974] A. V. Aho, J. E. Hopcroft, and J. D. Ullman, *The Design and Analysis of Computer Algorithms*, Addison-Wesley, Reading, Massachusetts, (1979).

[Aho et al. 1979] A. V. Aho, Y. Sagiv, and J. D. Ullman, "Equivalences among Relational Expressions," *Siam Journal of Computing*, Volume 8, Number 2, (June 1979), pages 218-246.

[Aho et al. 1979a] A. V. Aho, C. Beeri, and J. D. Ullman, "The Theory of Joins in Relational Databases," *ACM Transactions on Database Systems*, Volume 4, Number 3, (September 1979), pages 297-314.

[Aho et al. 1979b] A. V. Aho, Y. Sagiv, and J. D. Ullman, "Efficient Optimization of a Class of Relational Expressions," *ACM Transactions on Database Systems*, Volume 4, Number 4, (December 1979), pages 435-454.

[Aho et al. 1983] A. V. Aho, J. E. Hopcroft, and J. D. Ullman, *Data Structures and Algorithms*, Addison-Wesley, Reading, Massachusetts, (1983).

[Aho et al. 1986] A. V. Aho, R. Sethi, and J. D. Ullman, *Compilers: Principles, Techniques, and Tools*, Addison-Wesley, Reading, Massachusetts, (1986).

[Apers et al. 1983] P. M. G. Apers, A. R. Hevner, and S. B. Yao, "Optimization Algorithms for Distributed Queries," *IEEE Transactions on Software Engineering*, Volume SE-9, Number 1, (January 1983), pages 57-68.

[Armstrong 1974] W. W. Armstrong, "Dependency Structures of Data Base Relationships," *Proceedings of the 1974 IFIP Congress*, (1974), pages 580-583.

[Astrahan et al. 1976] M. M. Astrahan, M. W. Blasgen, D. D. Chamberlin, K. P. Eswaran, J. N. Gray, P. P. Griffiths, W. F. King, R. A. Lorie, P. R. McJones, J. W. Mehl, G. R. Putzolu, I. L. Traiger, B. W. Wade, and V. Watson, "System R: A Relational Approach to Data Base Management," *ACM Transactions on Database Systems*, Volume 1, Number 2, (June 1976), pages 97-137.

[Ashtrahan et al. 1979] M. M. Ashtrahan, "System R, a Relational Database Management System," *Computer*, Volume 12, Number 5, (May 1979), pages 43-48.

[Attar et al. 1982] R. Attar, P. A. Bernstein, and N. Goodman, "Site Initialization, Recovery, and Backup in a Distributed Database System," *Proceedings Berkeley Workshop on Distributed Data Management and Computer Networks*, (1982), pages 185-202.

[Bachman 1969] C. W. Bachman, "Data Structure Diagrams," *Journal of ACM SIGBDP* Volume 1, Number 2, (March 1969), pages 4-10.

[Bachman and Daya 1977] C. W. Bachman and M. Daya, "The Role Concept in Data Models", *Proceedings of the International Conference on Very Large Data Bases*, (1977), pages 464-476.

[Bachman and Williams 1964] C. W. Bachman and S. S. Williams, "A General Purpose Programming System for Random Access Memories," *Proceedings of the Fall Joint Computer Conference*, Volume 26, AFIPS Press, (1964), pages 411-422.

[Badal 1980] D. S. Badal, "The Analysis of the Effects of Concurrency Control on Distributed Database System Performance," *Proceedings of the International Conference on Very Large Data Bases*, (1980), pages 376-383.

[Badal 1981] D. Z. Badal, "Concurrency Control Overhead or Closer Look at Blocking vs. Nonblocking Concurrency Control Mechanism," *Proceedings of the Berkeley Workshop on Distributed Data Management and Computer Networks*, (1981), pages 85-104.

[Bancilhon et al. 1985a] F. Bancilhon, W. Kim and H. F. Korth, "A Model of CAD Transactions," *Proceedings of the International Conference on Very Large Data Bases*, (1985), pages 25-31.

[Bancilhon et al. 1985b] F. Bancilhon, W. Kim and H. F. Korth, "Transactions and Concurrency Control in CAD Databases," *Proceedings of the IEEE International Conference on Computer Design: VLSI in Computers*, (1985), pages 86-90.

[Batory and Gotlieb 1982] D. S. Batory and C. C. Gotlieb, "A Unifying Model of Physical Databases," *ACM Transactions on Database Systems*, Volume 8, Number 2, (June 1982), pages 509-539.

[Bayer 1972] R. Bayer, "Symmetric Binary B-trees: Data Structure and Maintenance Algorithms," *Acta Informatica*, Volume 1, Number 4 (1972), pages 290-306.

[Bayer and McCreight 1972] R. Bayer and E. M. McCreight, "Organization and Maintenance of Large Ordered Indices," *Acta Informatica*, Volume 1, Number 3, (1972), pages 173-189.

[Bayer and Schkolnick 1977] R. Bayer and M. Schkolnick, "Concurrency of Operating on B-trees," *Acta Informatica*, Volume 9, Number 1, (1977), pages 1-21.

[Bayer et al. 1978] R. Bayer, R. M. Graham, and G. Seegmuller (Editors), *Operating Systems: An Advanced Course*, Springer-Verlag, Berlin, Germany, (1978).

[Beeri et al. 1977] C. Beeri, R. Fagin, and J. H. Howard, "A Complete Axiomatization for Functional and Multivalued Dependencies," *Proceedings of the ACM Sigmod International Conference on Management of Data*, (1977), pages 47-61.

[Beeri et al. 1983] C. Beeri, R. Fagin, D. Maier, and M Yannakakis, "On the Desirability of Acyclic Database Schemes," *Journal of the ACM*, Volume 30, Number 3, (July 1983), pages 479-513.

[Benneworth et al. 1981] R. L. Benneworth, C. D. Bishop, C. J. M. Turnbull, W. D. Holman, and F. M. Monette, "The Implementation of GERM, an Entity-Relationship Data Base Management System," *Proceedings of the International Conference on Very Large Data Bases*, (1981), pages 478-484.

[Bernstein 1976] P. A. Bernstein, "Synthesizing Third Normal Form Relations From Functional Dependencies," *ACM Transactions on Database Systems*, Volume 1, Number 4, (December 1976), pages 277-298.

[Bernstein and Chiu 1981] P. A. Bernstein and D. W. Chiu, "Using Semijoins to Solve Relational Queries," *Journal of the ACM*, Volume 28, Number 1, (January 1981), pages 25-40.

[Bernstein and Goodman 1980a] P. A. Bernstein and N. Goodman, "Timestamp-based Algorithms for Concurrency Control in Distributed Database Systems," *Proceedings of the International Conference on Very Large Data Bases*, (1980), pages 285-300.

[Bernstein and Goodman 1980b] P. A. Bernstein and N. Goodman, "What Does Boyce-Codd Normal Form Do?," *Proceedings of the International Conference of Very Large Data Bases*, (1980), pages 245-259.

[Bernstein and Goodman 1981a] P. A. Bernstein and N. Goodman, "Concurrency Control in Distributed Database Systems," *ACM Computing Surveys*, Volume 13, Number 2, (June 1981), pages 185-221.

[Bernstein and Goodman 1981b] P. A. Bernstein and N. Goodman, "The Power of Natural Semijoins," *Siam Journal of Computing*, Volume 10, Number 4, (December 1981), pages 751-771.

[Bernstein and Goodman 1982] P. A. Bernstein and N. Goodman, "A Sophisticate's Introduction to Distributed Database Concurrency Control," *Proceedings of the International Conference on Very Large Data Bases*, (1982), pages 62-76.

[Bernstein et al. 1978] P. A. Bernstein, N. Goodman, J. B. Rothnie, and C. H. Papadimitriou, "Analysis of Serializability of SDD-1: A System of Distributed Databases (the Fully Redundant Case)," *IEEE Transactions on Software Engineering*, Volume SE-4, Number 3, (May 1978), pages 154-168.

[Bernstein et al. 1980a] P. A. Bernstein, D. W. Shipman, J. B. Rothnie, Jr., "Concurrency Control in a System for Distributed Databases (SDD-1)," *ACM Transactions on Database Systems*, Volume 5, Number 1, (January 1980), pages 13-51.

[Bernstein et al. 1980b] P. A. Bernstein, B. T. Blaustein, and E. M. Clarke, "Fast Maintenance of Semantic Integrity Assertions Using Redundant Aggregate Data," *Proceedings of the International Conference on Very Large Data Bases*, (1980), pages 126-136.

[Bernstein et al. 1980c] P. A. Bernstein, N. Goodman, E. Wong, C. L. Reeve, and J. B. Rothnie, Jr., "Query Processing in a System for Distributed Databases(SDD-1)," *ACM Transactions on Database Systems*, Volume 6, Number 4, (December 1980), pages 52-68.

[Bernstein et al. 1984] A. Bernstein, J. Heller, P. B. Henderson, Z. M. Kedem, E. Sciore, D. S. Warren, L. D. Wittie, and A. Zorat, "A Data Oriented Network System," Technical Report 84/091, Department of Computer Science, State University of New York at Stony Brook, Stony Brook, New York, (1984).

[Biskup et al. 1979] J. Biskup, U. Dayal, and P. A. Bernstein, "Synthesizing Independent Database Schemas," *Proceedings of the ACM Sigmod International Conference on Management of Data*, (1979), pages 143-152.

[Bissell 1986] J. M. Bissell, "Extended File Management for AIX," in **[IBM 1986]**, pages 114-118.

[Bjork 1973] L. A. Bjork, "Recovery Scenario for a DB/DC System," *Proceedings of the ACM Annual Conference*, (1973), pages 142-146.

[Blasgen and Eswaran 1976] M. W. Blasgen and K. P. Eswaran, "On the Evaluation of Queries in a Relational Database System," *IBM Systems Journal*, Volume 16, (1976) pages 363-377.

[Blasgen et al. 1981] M. W. Blasgen, D. D. Chamberlin, J. N. Gray, W. F King, B. G. Lindsay, R. A. Lorie, J. W. Mehl, T. G. Price, G. R. Putzolu, M. Schkolnick, P. G. Selinger, D. R. Slutz, I. L. Traiger, B. W. Wade, and R. A. Yost, "System R: An Architectural Overview," *IBM Systems Journal*, Volume 20, Number 1, (January 1981), pages 41-62.

[Bobrow and Collins 1975] D. G. Bobrow and A. M Collins (Editors), *Representation and Understanding*, Academic Press, New York, New York, (1975).

[Bohl 1981] M. Bohl, *Introduction to IBM Direct Access Storage Devices*, Science Research Associates, Chicago, Illinois, (1981).

[Bolour 1979] A. Bolour, "Optimal Retrieval Algorithms For Small Region Queries," *Journal of the ACM*, Volume 26, Number 2, (April 1979), pages 721-741.

[Bracchi and Nijssen 1979] G. Bracchi and G. M. Nijssen (Editors), *Data Base Architecture*, North-Holland, Amsterdam, the Netherlands, (1979).

[Bracchi et al. 1976] G. Bracchi, P. Paolini, and G. Pelagatti, "Binary Logical Associations in Data Modeling," in **[Nijssen 1976]**, pages 125-148.

[Brachman 1979] R. J. Brachman, "On the Epistemological Status of Semantic Networks," in **[Findler 1979]**, pages 3-50.

[Bray 1982] O. H. Bray, *Distributed Database Management Systems*, Lexington Books, (1982).

[Bubenko et al. 1971] J. A. Bubenko, Jr., B. Langefors, and A. Solvberg (Editors), *Computer-Aided Information Systems Analysis and Design*, Studentlitteratur, Lund, Sweden, (1971).

[Buckley and Silberschatz 1984] G. Buckley and A. Silberschatz, "Concurrency Control in Graph Protocols by Using Edge Locks," *Proceedings of the ACM Sigact-Sigmod Symposium on the Principles of Database Systems*, (1984), pages 45-50.

[Buckley and Silberschatz 1985] G. Buckley and A. Silberschatz, "Beyond Two-Phase Locking," *Journal of the ACM*, Volume 32, Number 2, (April 1985), pages 314-326.

[Burkhard 1976] W. A. Burkhard, "Hashing and Trie Algorithms for Partial Match Retrieval," *ACM Transactions on Database Systems*, Volume 1, Number 2, (June 1976), pages 175-187.

[Burkhard 1979] W. A. Burkhard, "Partial-match Hash Coding: Benefits of Redundancy," *ACM Transactions on Database Systems*, Volume 4, Number 2, (June 1979), pages 228-239.

[Cardenas 1985] A. F. Cardenas, *Data Base Management Systems*, Second edition, Allen and Bacon, Boston, Massachusetts, (1985).

[Carey 1983] M. J. Carey, "Granularity Hierarchies in Concurrency Control," *Proceedings ACM Sigact-Sigmod Symposium on the Principles of Database Systems*, (1983), pages 156-165.

[Casanova 1984] M. A. Casanova, "Mapping Uninterpreted Schemes in Entity-Relationship Diagrams: Two Applications to Conceptual Schema Design," *IBM Journal of Research and Development*, Volume 28, Number 1, (January 1984), pages 82-94.

[Casey 1972] R. G. Casey, "Allocation of Copies of a File in an Information Network," *Proceedings of the Spring Joint Computer Conference*, (1972), pages 617-625.

[Ceri and Pelagatti 1983] S. Ceri and G. Pelagatti, "Correctness of Query Execution Strategies in Distributed Databases," *ACM Transactions on Database Systems*, Volume 8, Number 4, (December 1983), pages 577-607.

[Ceri and Pelagatti 1984] S. Ceri and G. Pelagatti, *Distributed Databases: Principles and Systems*, McGraw-Hill, New York, (1984).

[Ceri et al. 1983] S. Ceri, B. Navathe, and G. Wiederhold, "Distribution Design of Logical Database Schemas," *IEEE Transactions on Software Engineering*, Volume SE-9, Number 4, (July 1983), pages 487-503.

[Chamberlin 1980] D. D. Chamberlin, "A Summary of User Experience with the SQL Data Sublanguage," *Proceedings of the International Conference on Very Large Data Bases*, (July 1980), pages 181-203.

[Chamberlin et al. 1976] D. D. Chamberlin, M. M. Astrahan, K. P. Eswaran, P. P. Griffiths, R. A. Lorie, J. W. Mehl, P. Reisner, and B. W. Wade, "SEQUEL 2: A Unified Approach to Data Definition, Manipulation, and Control," *IBM Journal of Research and Development*, Volume 20, Number 6, (November 1976), pages 560-575.

[Chamberlin et al. 1978] D. D. Chamberlin, et al., "Data Base System Authorization," in **[DeMillo et al. 1978]**.

[Chamberlin et al. 1981] D. D. Chamberlin, M. M. Astrahan, M. W. Blasgen, J. N. Gray, W. F. King, B. G. Lindsay, R. A. Lorie, J. W. Mehl, T. G. Price, P. G. Selinger, M. Schkolnick, D. R. Slutz, I. L. Traiger, B. W. Wade, and R. A. Yost, "A History and Evaluation of System R," *Communications of the ACM*, Volume 24, Number 10, (October 1981), pages 632-646.

[Chandy and Misra 1982] K. M. Chandy and J. Misra, "A Distributed Algorithm for Detecting Resource Deadlocks in Distributed Systems," *Proceedings ACM Sigact-Sigops Symposium on the Principles of Distributed Computing*, (1982), pages 157-164.

[Chandy et al. 1975] K. M. Chandy, J. C. Browne, C. W. Dissley, and W. R. Uhrig, "Analytic Models for Rollback and Recovery Strategies in Database Systems," *IEEE Transactions on Software Engineering*, Volume SE-1, Number 1, (March 1975), pages 100-110.

[Chandy et al. 1983] K. M. Chandy, L. M. Haas, and J. Misra, " Distributed Deadlock Detection," *ACM Transactions on Computer Systems*, Volume 1, Number 2, (May 1983), pages 144-156.

[Chang and Cheng 1980] S. K. Chang and W. H. Cheng, "A Methodology for Structured Database Decomposition," *IEEE Transactions on Software Engineering*, Volume SE-6, Number 2, (March 1980), pages 205-218.

[Chen 1976] P. P. Chen, "The Entity-Relationship Model: Toward a Unified View of Data," *ACM Transactions on Database Systems*, Volume 1, Number 1, (January 1976), pages 9-36.

[Chen 1977] P. P. Chen, *The Entity-Relationship Approach to Logical Data Base Design*, QED Information Sciences, Data Base Monograph Series Number 6, (1977).

[Chen 1979] P. P. Chen, (Editor), *Entity-Relationship Approach to Systems Analysis and Design*, North-Holland, Amsterdam, the Netherlands, (1979).

[Chen 1983] P. P. Chen, (Editor), *Entity-Relationship Approach to Information Modeling and Analysis*, North-Holland, Amsterdam, the Netherlands,(1983).

[Chen and Akoka 1980] P. P. Chen and J. Akoka, "Optimal Design of Distributed Information Systems," *IEEE Transactions on Computers*, Volume C-29, Number 12, (December 1980), pages 1068-1079.

[Cheung 1982] T. Y. Cheung, "A Method for Equijoin Queries in Distributed Relational Databases," *IEEE Transactions on Computers*, Volume C-31, Number 8, (August 1982), pages 746-751.

[Chin 1978] F. Y. Chin, "Security in Statistical Databases for Queries with Small Counts," *ACM Transactions on Database Systems*, Volume 3, Number 1, (January 1978), pages 92-104.

[Chin and Ozsoyoglu 1981] F. Y. Chin and G. Ozsoyoglu, "Statistical Database Design," *ACM Transactions on Database Design*, Volume 6, Number 1, (January 1981), pages 113-139.

[Chiu and Ho 1980] D. M. Chiu and Y. C. Ho, "A Methodology for Interpreting Tree Queries into Optimal Semi-join Expressions," *Proceedings ACM Sigmod International Conference on the Management of Data*, (1980), pages 169-178.

[Chu 1969] W. W. Chu, "Optimal File Allocation in a Multiple Computer System," *IEEE Transactions on Computers*, Volume C-18, Number 10, (October 1969) pages 885-889.

[Chu and Hurley 1982] W. W. Chu and P. Hurley, "Optimal Query Processing for Distributed Database Systems," *IEEE Transactions on Computers*, Volume C-31, Number 9, (September 1982), pages 835-850.

[Cincom 1974] *Total/7* publications: *Application Programming Reference Manual*, PO2-1321-2, *Data Base Administration Reference Manual*, PO2-1322-2. Cincom Systems, Inc., Cincinnati, Ohio.

[Cincom 1978] *OS TOTAL Reference Manual,* Cincom Systems, Cincinnati, Ohio, (1978).

[Clemons 1978] E. K. Clemons, "An External Schema Facility to Support Data Base Update," in **[Shneiderman 1978]**, pages 371-398.

[Clemons 1979] E. K. Clemons, "An External Schema Facility for CODASYL 1978," *Proceedings of the International Conference on Very Large Data Bases*, (1979), pages 119-128.

[CODASYL 1971] "CODASYL Data Base Task Group April 71 Report," ACM, New York, New York, (1971).

[CODASYL 1978] *CODASYL Data Description Language Journal of Development*, Material Data Management Branch, Department of Supply and Services, Ottawa, Ontario, (1978).

[Codd 1970] E. F. Codd, "A Relational Model for Large Shared Data Banks," *Communications of the ACM*, Volume 13, Number 6, (June 1970), pages 377-387.

[Codd 1972a] E. F. Codd, "Further Normalization of the Data Base Relational Model," in **[Rustin 1972]**, pages 33-64.

[Codd 1972b] E. F. Codd, "Relational Completeness of Data Base Sublanguages," in **[Rustin 1972]**, pages 65-98.

[Codd 1982] E. F. Codd, "The 1981 ACM Turing Award Lecture: Relational Database: A Practical Foundation for Productivity," *Communications of the ACM*, Volume 25, Number 2, (February 1982), pages 109-117.

[Cosmadakis and Papadimitriou 1984] S. S. Cosmadakis and C. H. Papadimitriou, "Updates of Relational Views," *Journal of the ACM*, Volume 31, Number 4, (October 1984), pages 742-760.

[Cullinane 1975] Cullinane Corporation, *Integrated Database Management System* (IDMS) Brochure," (1975).

[Cullinet 1983a] Cullinane Database Systems, Inc., *IDMS Sequential Processing Facility,* Order Number TDDB-0801-57P0, Cullinet Software, Cullinane Database Systems, Inc., (1983).

[Cullinet 1983b] Cullinane Database Systems, Inc., *IDMS Programmer's Reference Guide,* Order Number TDDB-0321-5710, Cullinet Software, Cullinane Database Systems, Inc., (1983).

[Daniels et al. 1982] D. Daniels, P. Selinger, L. Haas, B. G. Lindsay, C. Mohan, A. Walker, and P. Wilms, "An Introduction to Distributed Query Compilation in R*," in **[Schneider 1982]**.

[Date 1983] C. J. Date, *An Introduction to Database Systems*, Volume II, Addison-Wesley, Reading, Massachusetts, (1983).

[Date 1984] C. J. Date, *A Guide to DB2*, Addison-Wesley, Reading, Massachusetts, (1984).

[Date 1986] C. J. Date, *An Introduction to Database Systems*, Volume I, Fourth Edition, Addison-Wesley, Reading Massachusetts, (1986).

[Davies 1972] C. T. Davies, Jr., "Recovery Semantics for a DB/DC System," *Proceedings of the ACM Annual Conference*, (1973), pages 136-141.

[Davies 1980] D. W. Davies, "Protection," in *Distributed Systems: An Advanced Course*, Springer-Verlag, Berlin, Germany, (1980), pages 211-245.

[Davies et al. 1979] D. W. Davies, D. L. A. Barber, W. L. Price, and C. M. Solomoides, *Computer Networks and Their Protocols*, John Wiley and Sons, New York, New York, (1979).

[Davis et al. 1983] C. Davis, S. Jajodia, P. A. Ng, and R. Yeh (Editors), *Entity-Relationship Approach to Software Engineering*, North-Holland, Amsterdam, the Netherlands, (1983).

[Dayal and Bernstein 1978] U. Dayal and P. A. Bernstein, "The Updatability of Relational Views," *Proceedings of the International Conference on Very Large Data Bases*, (1978), pages 368-377.

[Dayal and Bernstein 1982] U. Dayal and P. A. Bernstein, "On the Correct Translation of Update Operations on Relational Views," *ACM Transactions on Database Systems*, Volume 3, Number 3, (September 1982), pages 381-416.

[Deheneffe et al. 1974], C. Deheneffe, H. Hennebert, and W. Paulus, "Relational Model for a Data Base," *Proceedings of the IFIP Conference*, (1974), pages 1022-1025.

[Delobel and Litwin 1980] C. Delobel and W. Litwin, (Editors), "Distributed Data Bases," *Proceedings of the International Symposium on Distributed Databases*, North-Holland, Amsterdam, the Netherlands, (1980).

[DeMillo et al. 1978] R. A. DeMillo, D. P. Dobkin, A. K. Jones, and R. J. Lipton, *Foundations of Secure Computation*, Academic Press, New York, New York, (1978).

[Denning 1982] P. J. Denning, *Cryptography and Data Security*, Addison-Wesley, Reading, Massachusetts, (1982).

[Denning and Denning 1979] D. E. Denning and P. J. Denning, "Data Security," *ACM Computing Surveys*, Volume 11, Number 3, (September 1979), pages 227-250.

[Diffie and Hellman 1979] W. Diffie and M. E. Hellman, "Privacy and Authenthication," *Proceedings of the IEEE*, Volume 67, Number 3, (March 1979), pages 397-427.

[Dijkstra 1965] E. W. Dijkstra, "Cooperating Sequential Processes," Technical Report EWD-123, Technological University, Eindhoven, The Netherlands, (1965); *reprinted in* **[Genuys 1968]**, pages 43-112.

[Dobkin et al. 1979] D. Dobkin, A. K. Jones and R. J. Lipton, "Secure Databases: Protection Against User Inference," *ACM Transactions on Database Systems*, Volume 4, Number 1, (March 1979), pages 97-106.

[Dodd 1966] G. G. Dodd, "APL-A Language for Associative Data Handling in PL/I," *Proceedings of the Fall Joint Computer Conference*, (1969), pages 667-684.

[Dowdy and Foster 1982] L. W. Dowdy and D. V. Foster, "Comparative Models of the File Assignment Problem," *ACM Computing Surverys*, Volume 14, Number 2, (June 1982), pages 287-314.

[Draffen and Poole 1980] I. W. Draffen and F. Poole, (Editors), *Distributed Data Bases*, Cambridge University Press, (1980).

[ElMasri and Wiederhold 1983] R. ElMasri and G. Wiederhold, "GORDAS: A Formal High-Level Query Language for the Entity-Relationship Model," in **[Chen 1983]**.

[Ellis 1980a] C. S. Ellis, "Concurrent Search and Insertion in 2-3 Trees," *Acta Informatica*, Volume 14, (1980), pages 63-86.

[Ellis 1980b] C. S. Ellis, "Concurrent Search and Insertion in AVL Trees," *IEEE Transactions on Computers*, Volume C-29, Number 3, (September 1980), pages 811-817.

[Eppinger 1983] J. L. Eppinger, "An Empirical Study of Insertion and Deletion in Binary Search Trees," *Communications of the ACM*, Volume 26, Number 9, (September 1983), pages 663-669.

[Epstein et al. 1978] R. Epstein, M. R. Stonebraker, and E. Wong, "Distributed Query Processing in a Relational Database System," *Proceedings of the ACM Sigmod International Conference on Management of Data*, (1978), pages 169-180.

[Epstein and Stonebraker 1980] R. Epstein and M. Stonebraker, "Analysis of Distributed Database Processing Strategies," *Proceedings of the International Conference on Very Large Data Bases*, (1980), pages 92-110.

[Eswaran 1974] K. P. Eswaran, "Placement of Records in a File and File Allocation in a Computer Network," *Proceedings of the IFIP Congress*, (1974), pages 304-307.

[Eswaran et al. 1976] K. P. Eswaran, J. N. Gray, R. A. Lorie, and I. L. Traiger, "The Notions of Consistency and Predicate Locks in a Database Systems," *Communications of the ACM*, Volume 19, Number 11, (November 1976), pages 624-633.

[Everett et al. 1971] G. D. Everett, C. W. Dissly, and W. T. Hardgrave, *Remote File Management System (RFMS) Users Manual*, TRM-16, Computation Center, University of Texas at Austin, Austin, Texas, (1981).

[Fagin 1978] R. Fagin, "On an Authorization Mechanism," *ACM Transactions on Database Systems*, Volume 3, Number 3, (September 1978), pages 310-319.

[Fagin 1979] R. Fagin, "Normal Forms and Relational Database Operators," *Proceedings of the ACM Sigmod International Conference on Management of Data*, (1979), pages 153-160.

[Fagin 1981] R. Fagin, "A Normal Form for Relational Databases That is Based on Domains and Keys," *ACM Transactions on Database Systems*, Volume 6, Number 3, (September 1981), pages 387-415.

[Fagin 1983] R. Fagin, "Types of Acyclicity of Hypergraphs and Relational Database Schemes," *Journal of the ACM*, Volume 30, Number 3, (July 1983), pages 514-550.

[Fagin et al. 1979] R. Fagin, J. Nievergelt, N. Pippenger, and H. R. Strong, "Extendible Hashing - A Fast Access Method for Dynamic Files," *ACM Transactions on Database Systems*, Volume 4, Number 3, (September 1979), pages 315-344.

[Fagin et al. 1982] R. Fagin, A. O. Mendelzon, and J. D. Ullman, "A Simplified Universal Relation Assumption and its Properties," *ACM Transactions on Database Systems*, Volume 7, Number 3, (September 1982), pages 343-360.

[Findler 1979] N. Findler, (Editor), *Associative Networks*, Academic Press, New York, New York, (1979).

[Finkelstein 1982] S. Finkelstein, "Common Expression Analysis in Database Applications," *Proceedings of the ACM Sigmod International Conference on Management of Data*, (1982), pages 235-245.

[Fischer and Thomas 1983] P. Fischer and S. Thomas, "Operators for Non-First-Normal-Form Relations," *Proceedings of the International Computer Software Applications Conference* (1983), pages 464-475.

[Fisher and Hochbaum 1980] M. L. Fisher and D. S. Hochbaum, "Database Location in Computer Networks," *Journal of the ACM*, Volume 27, Number 4, (October 1980), pages 718-735.

[Ford and Calhoun 1984] R. Ford and J. Calhoun, "Concurrency Control Mechanism and the Serializability of Concurrent Tree Algorithms," *Proceedings of the ACM Sigact-Sigmod Symposium on the Principles of Database Systems*, (1984), pages 51-60.

[Fredkin 1960] E. Fredkin, "Trie Memory," *Communications of the ACM*, Volume 4, Number 2, (September 1960), pages 490-499.

[Fussell et al. 1981] D. S. Fussell, Z. Kedem, and A. Silberschatz, "Deadlock Removal Using Partial Rollback in Database Systems," *Proceedings of the ACM Sigmod International Conference on the Management of Data*, (1981), pages 65-73.

[Garcia-Molina 1978] H. Garcia-Molina, "Performance Comparison of Two Update Algorithms for Distributed Databases," *Proceedings of the Berkeley Workshop on Distributed Data Management and Computer Networks*, (1978), pages 108-119.

[Garcia-Molina 1983] H. Garcia-Molina, "Using Semantic Knowledge for Transaction Processing in a Distributed Database," *ACM Transactions on Database Systems*, Volume 8, Number 2, (June 1983), pages 186-213.

[Garcia-Molina and Wiederhold 1982] H. Garcia-Molina and G. Wiederhold, "Read-only Transactions in a Distributed Database," *ACM Transactions on Database Systems*, Volume 7, Number 2, (June 1982), pages 209-234.

[Garey and Johnson 1979] M. R. Garey and D. S. Johnson, *Computers and Intractability: A Guide to the Theory of NP-Completeness*, Freeman, San Francisco, (1979).

[Gelembe and Sevcik 1978] E. Gelembe and R. Sevcik, "Analysis of Update Synchronization for Multiple Copy Data Bases," *Proceedings of the Berkeley Workshop on Distributed Data Management and Computer Networks*, (1978), pages 69-90..

[Genuys 1968] F. Genuys, (Editor), *Programming Langauges*, Academic Press, London, (1968).

[Gerritsen 1975] R. Gerritsen, "A Preliminary System for the Design of DBTG Data Structures," *Communications of the ACM*, Volume 18, Number 10, (October 1975) pages 551-557.

[Gligor and Shattuck 1980] V. D. Gligor and S. H. Shattuck, "On Deadlock Detection in Distributed Systems," *IEEE Transactions on Software Engineering*, Volume SE-6, Number 5, (September 1980), pages 435-439.

[Gotlieb 1975] L. R. Gotlieb, "Computing Joins of Relations," *Proceedings of the ACM Sigmod International Conference on the Management of Data*, (1975), pages 55-63.

[Gray 1978] J. N. Gray, "Notes on Data Base Operating System," in **[Bayer et al. 1978]**, pages 393-481.

[Gray 1981] J. N. Gray, "The Transaction Concept: Virtues and Limitations," *Proceedings of the International Conference on Very Large Data Bases*, (1981), pages 144-154.

[Gray et al. 1975] J. N. Gray, R. A. Lorie, and G. R. Putzolu, "Granularity of Locks and Degrees of Consistency in a Shared Data Base," *Proceedings of the International Conference on Very Large Data Bases*, (1975), pages 428-451.

[Gray et al. 1976] J. N. Gray, R. A. Lorie, G. R. Putzolu, and I. L. Traiger, "Granularity of Locks and Degrees of Consistency in a Shared Data Base," in **[Nijssen 1976]**, pages 365-395.

[Gray et al. 1981a] J. N. Gray, P. McJones, and M. Blasgen, "The Recovery Manger of the System R Database Manager," *ACM Computing Surveys*, Volume 13, Number 2, (June 1981), pages 223-242.

[Gray et al. 1981b] J. N. Gray, P. Homan, H. F. Korth, and R. Obermarck, "A Straw Man Analysis of the Probability of Waiting and Deadlock," Research Report RJ3066, IBM Research Laboratory, San Jose, California, (1981).

[Griffiths and Wade 1976] P. P. Griffiths and B. W. Wade, "An Authorization Mechanism for a Relational Database System," *ACM Transactions on Database Systems*, Volume 1, Number 3, (September 1976), pages 242-255.

[Hainaut and Lecharlier 1974] J. L. Hainaut and B. Lecharlier, "An Extensible Semantic Model of Data Base and its Data language," *Proceedings of the IFIP Conference*, (1974), pages 1026-1030.

[Haerder and Reuter 1983] T. Haerder and A. Reuter, "Principles of Transaction-Oriented Database Recovery," *ACM Computing Surveys*, Volume 15, Number 4, (December 1983), pages 287-318.

[Hailpern and Korth 1983] B. T. Hailpern and H. F. Korth, "An Experimental Distributed Database System," *Proceedings of the ACM Sigmod-Sigbdp Database Week*, (1983).

[Hall 1976] P. A. V. Hall, "Optimization of a Single Relational Expression in a Relational Database System," *IBM Journal of Research and Development*, Volume 20, Number 3, (1976), pages 244-257.

[Haskin and Lorie 1982] R. Haskin and R. Lorie, "On Extending the Functions of a Relational Database System," *Proceedings of the ACM Sigmod International Conference on the Management of Data*, (1982), pages 207-212.

[Hayes 1977] P. J. Hayes, "On Semantic Nets, Frames and Associations," *Proceedings of the International Joint Conference on Artificial Intelligence*, (1977), pages 99-107.

[Hayes-Roth et al. 1983] F. Hayes-Roth, D. A. Waterman, and D. B. Lenat, (Editors), *Building Expert Systems*, Addison-Wesley, Reading, Massachusetts, (1983).

[Held and Stonebraker 1978] G. Held and M. Stonebraker, "B-trees Reexamined," *Communications of the ACM*, Volume 21, Number 2, (February 1978), pages 139-143.

[Henderson et al. 1983] P. B. Henderson, E. Sciore, and D. S. Warren, "A Relational Model of Operating System Environments," *Proceedings of the DEC Workshop*, (April 1983).

[Hendrix 1977] G. G. Hendrix, "Some General Comments on Semantic Networks," *Proceedings of the International Joint Conference on Artificial Intelligence*, (1977), pages 984-985.

[Hevner and Yao 1979] A. R. Hevner and S. B. Yao, "Query Processing in Distributed Database Systems," *IEEE Transactions on Software Engineering*, Volume SE-5, Number 3, (May 1979), pages 177-187.

[Hinrichs 1985] K. H. Hinrichs, "The Grid File System: Implementation and Case Studies of Applications," Ph.D. Dissertation, Swiss Federal Institute of Technology, Zurich, Switzerland, (1985).

[Holt 1971] R. C. Holt, "Comments on Prevention of System Deadlocks," *Communications of the ACM*, Volume 14, Number 1, (January 1971), pages 36-38.

[Holt 1972] R. C. Holt, "Some Deadlock Properties of Computer Systems," *ACM Computing Surveys*, Volume 4, Number 3, (September 1972), pages 179-196.

[Honeywell 1975] "Integrated Data Store/II: Database Administrator's Guide," Honeywell Information Systems, Waltham, Massachusetts, (1975).

[Horowitz and Sahni 1976] E. Horowitz and S. Sahni, *Fundamentals of Data Structures*, Computer Science Press, Rockville, Maryland, (1976).

[IBM 1978a] IBM Corporation, *Information Management System/Virtual Storage General Information*, IBM Form Number GH20-1260, SH20-9025, SH20-9026, SH20-9027.

[IBM 1978b] IBM Corporation, *Query-by Example Terminal Users Guide*, IBM Form Number SH20-2078-0, (1978).

[IBM 1982] IBM Corporation, *SQL/Data System Terminal Users Guide*, IBM Form Number SH24-5017-1, (1982).

[IBM 1986] IBM Corporation, *hIBM RT Personal Computer Technology*, IBM Form No. SA23-1057, (1986).

[Jaeschke and Schek 1982] Jaeschke and H. Schek, "Remarks on the Algebra of Non First Normal Form Relations," *Proceedings of the ACM Sigact-Sigmod Symposium on Principles of Database Systems*, (March 1982), pages 124-138.

[Jardine 1977] D. A. Jardine (Editor), *The ANSI/SPARC DBMS Model*, North Holland, Amsterdam, the Netherlands, (1977).

[Jarke and Koch 1984] M. Jarke and J. Koch, "Query Optimization in Database Systems," *ACM Computing Surveys*, Volume 16, Number 2, (June 1984), pages 111-152.

[Kam and Ullman 1977] J. B. Kam and J. D. Ullman, "A Model of Statistical Databases and their Security," *ACM Transactions on Database Systems*, Volume 2, Number 1, (January 1977), pages 1-10.

[Kambayashi et al. 1982] Y. Kambayashi, M. Yoshikawa, and S. Yajima, "Query Processing for Distributed Databases Using Generalized Semi-joins," *Proceedings ACM Sigmod International Conference on the Management of Data*, (1982), pages 151-160.

[Katz and Weiss 1984] R. Katz, and S. Weiss, "Design Transaction Management," *Proceedings of the Design Automation Conference*, (1984).

[Kedem and Silberschatz 1979] Z. Kedem and A. Silberschatz, "Controlling Concurrency Using Locking Protocols," *Proceedings of the Annual IEEE Symposium on Foundations of Computer Science*, (1979), pages 275-285.

[Kedem and Silberschatz 1983] Z. M. Kedem and A. Silberschatz, "Locking Protocols: From Exclusive to Shared Locks," *Journal of the ACM*, Volume 30, Number 4, (October 1983), pages 787-804.

[Keller 1982] A. M. Keller, "Updates to Relational Database Through Views Involving Joins," in **[Scheuermann 1982]**, pages 363-384.

[Keller 1985] A. M. Keller, "Updating Relational Databases Through View," Ph.D. Dissertation, Department of Computer Science, Stanford University, Stanford, California, (1985).

[Kerschberg et al. 1976] L. Kerschberg, A. Klug, and D. C. Tsichritzis, "A Taxonomy of Data Models," in **[Lockemann and Neuhold 1976]**, pages 43-64.

[Kerschberg et al. 1982] L. Kerschberg, P. D. Ting, and S. B. Yao, "Query Optimization in Star Computer Networks," *ACM Transactions on Database Systems*, Volume 7, Number 4, (December 1982), pages 678-711.

[Kim 1981] W. Kim "Query Optimization for Relational Database Systems," IBM Research Report RJ3081, IBM Research Laboratory, San Jose, California (1981).

[Kim 1982] W. Kim, "On Optimizing an SQL-like Nested Query" *ACM Transactions on Database Systems*, Volume 3, Number 3, (September 1982), pages 443-469..

[Kim et al. 1984] W. Kim, R. Lorie, D. McNabb, and W. Plouffe, "Transaction Mechanism for Engineering Design Databases," *Proceedings of the International Conference on Very Large Data Bases*, (August 1984), pages 355-362.

[Kim et al. 1985a] W. Kim, D. S. Reiner, and D. S. Batory, (Editors), *Query Processing in Database Systems*, Springer-Verlag, Berlin, Germany (1985).

[Kim et al. 1985b] H. J. Kim, H. F. Korth, and A. Silberschatz, "PICASSO: A Graphical Query Language for Universal Relation Databases," *TR-85-30*, Department of Computer Sciences, The University of Texas at Austin, (1985).

[King 1981] J. J. King, "QUIST: A System for Semantic Query Optimization in Relational Data Bases," *Proceedings of the International Conference on Very Large Data Bases*, (1981), pages 510-517.

[King et al. 1983] R. P. King, H. F. Korth, and B. E. Willner, " Design of a Document Filing and Retrieval Service," *Proceedings of the ACM Sigmod-Sigbdp Database Week*, (1983).

[Klimbie and Koffeman 1974] J. W. Klimbie and K. L. Koffeman (Editors), *Data Base Management*, North Holland, Amsterdam, the Netherlands, (1974).

[Knuth 1973] D. E. Knuth, *The Art of Computer Programming Volume 3: Sorting and Searching*, Addison-Wesley, Reading, Massachusetts, (1973).

[Kohler 1981] W. H. Kohler, "A Survey of Techniques for Synchronization and Recovery in Decentralized Computer Systems," *ACM Computing Surveys*, Volume 13, Number 2, (June 1981), pages 149-183.

[Korth 1981] H. F. Korth, "The Optimal Locking Problem in a Directed Acyclic Graph," *Technical Report STAN-CS-81-847*, Department of Computer Science, Stanford University, Stanford, California, (March 1981).

[Korth 1982] H. F. Korth, " Deadlock Freedom Using Edge Locks," *ACM Transactions on Database Systems*, Volume 7, Number 4, (December 1982), pages 632-652.

[Korth 1983] H. F. Korth, "Locking Primitives in a Database System," *Journal of the ACM*, Volume 30, Number 1, (January 1983), pages 55-79.

[Korth 1986] H. F. Korth, "Extending the Scope of Relational Languages," *IEEE Software*, Volume 3, Number 1, (January 1986), pages 19-28.

[Korth and Silberschatz 1985] H.F. Korth and A. Silberschatz, "ROSI: A User-Friendly Operating System Interface Based on the Relational Data Model," *Proceedings of the International Symposium on New Directions in Computing*, (1985), pages 302-310.

[Korth et al. 1984] H. F. Korth, G. M. Kuper, J. Feigenbaum, A. Van Gelder, and J. D. Ullman, "System/U: A Database System Based on the Universal Relation Assumption," *ACM Transactions on Database Systems*, Volume 9, Number 3, (September 1984), pages 331-347.

[Kroenke 1983] D. Kroenke, *Database Processing*, Second edition, Science Research Associates, Chicago, Illinois, (1983).

[Kung and Lehman 1980] H.-T. Kung and P. L. Lehman, "Concurrent Manipulation of Binary Search Trees," *ACM Transactions on Database Systems*, Volume 5, Number 3 (September 1980), pages 339-353.

[Kung and Robinson 1981] H.-T. Kung and J. T. Robinson, " Optimistic Concurrency Control," *ACM Transactions on Database Systems*, Volume 6, Number 2, (June 1981), pages 312-226.

[Langefors 1963] B. Langefors, "Some Approaches to the Theory of Information Systems," *BIT*, Volume 3, (1963), pages 229-254.

[Langefors 1977] B. Langefors, "Information Systems Theory," *Information Systems*, Volume 2, (1977), pages 207-219.

[Langefors 1980] B. Langefors, "Infological Models and Information User Views," *Information Systems*, Volume 5, (1980), pages 17-32.

[Larson 1982] P. Larson, "Performance Analysis of Linear Hashing with Partial Expansions," *ACM Transactions on Database Systems*, Volume 7, Number 4, (December 1982), pages 566-587.

[Lehman and Yao 1981] P. L. Lehman and S. B. Yao, "Efficient Locking for Concurrent Operations on B-trees," *ACM Transactions on Database Systems*, Volume 6, Number 4, (December 1981), pages 650-670.

[Lempel 1979] A. Lempel, "Cryptography in Transition," *ACM Computing Surveys*, Volume 11, Number 4, (December 1979), pages 286-303.

[Lenzerini and Santucci 1983] M. Lenzerini and C. Santucci, "Cardinality Constraints in the Entity Relationship Model," *Proceedings of the Conference on the Entity-Relationship Approach to Software Engineering*, (1983), pages 529-549.

[Levesque and Mylopoulos 1979] H. J. Levesque and J. Mylopoulos, "A Procedural Semantics for Semantic Networks," in **[Findler 1979]**, pages 93-120.

[Lien and Weinberger 1978] Y. E. Lien and P. J.Weinberger, "Consistency, Concurrency and Crash Recovery," *Proceedings of the ACM Sigmod International Conference on Management of Data*, (1978), pages 9-14.

[Lin et al. 1976] C. S. Lin, D. C. P. Smith, and J. M. Smith, "The Design of a Rotating Associative Memory for a Relational Database Management Application," *ACM Transactions on Database Systems*, Volume 1, Number 1, (March 1976), pages 53-65.

[Lindsay 1981] B. G. Lindsay, "Object Naming and Catalog Management for a Distributed Database Manager," *Proceedings of the International Conference on Distributed Computing Systems*, (1981)

[Lindsay et al. 1980] B. G. Lindsay, P. G. Selinger, C. Galtieri, J. N. Gray, R. A. Lorie, T. G. Price, G. R. Putzolu, I. L. Traiger, and B. W. Wade, "Notes on Distributed Databases," in **[Draffen and Poole 1980]**, pages 247-284.

[Lindsay et al. 1984] B. G. Lindsay, L. M. Haas, C. Mohan, P. F. Wilms, and R. A. Yost, "Computation and Communication in R*: A Distributed Database Manager," *ACM Transactions on Computer Systems*, Volume 2, Number 1, (February 1984), pages 24-38.

[Litwin 1978] W. Litwin, "Virtual Hashing: A Dynamically Changing Hashing," *Proceedings of the 4th International Conference on Very Large Data Bases*, (1978), pages 517-523.

[Litwin 1980] W. Litwin, "Linear Hashing: A New Tool for File and Table Addressing," *Proceedings of the International Conference on Very Large Data Bases*, (1980), pages 212-223.

[Litwin 1981] W. Litwin, "Trie Hashing," *Proceedings of the ACM Sigmod International Conference on Management of Data*, (1981), pages 19-29.

[Lockemann and Neuhold 1976] P. C. Lockemann and E. J. Neuhold, (Editors), *Systems for Large Data Bases*, North-Holland, Amsterdan, the Netherlands, (1976).

[Lomet 1981] D. G. Lomet, "Digital B-trees," *Proceedings of the International Conference on Very Large Data Bases*, (1981), pages 333-344.

[Lorie 1977] R. A. Lorie, "Physical Integrity in a Large Segmented Database," *ACM Transactions on Database Systems*, Volume 2, Number 1, (March 1977), pages 91-104.

[Lorie and Wade 1979] R. A. Lorie and B. W. Wade, "The Compilation of a High Level Data Language," Research Report RJ2598, IBM Research Laboratory, San Jose, California, (1979).

[Lorie et al. 1985] R. Lorie, W. Kim, D. McNabb, W. Plouffe, and A. Meier, "Supporting Complex Objects in a Relational System for Engineering Databases," in **[Kim et al. 1985a]**, pages 145-155.

[Lum 1974] V. Y. Lum, "On the Selection of Secondary Indexes," *Proceedings of the ACM Conference*, (November 1974).

[Lum and Ling 1970] V. Lum and H. Ling, "Multi-Attribute Retrieval With Combined Indices," *Communications of the ACM*, Volume 13, Number 11, (November 1970), pages 660-665.

[Lusk et al. 1980] E. L. Lusk, P. A. Overbeek, and B. Parrello, "A Practical Design Methodology for the Implementation of MS Databases, Using the Entity-Relationship Model," *Proceedings of the ACM Sigmod International Conference on Management of Data*, (May 1980), pages 9-21.

[Lynch 1983] N. A. Lynch, "Multilevel Atomicity--A New Correctness Criterion for Database Concurrency Control," *ACM Transactions on Database Systems*, Volume 8, Number 4, (December 1983), pages 484-502.

[Mahmoud and Riordon 1976] S. Mahmoud and J. S. Riordon, "Optimal Allocation of Resources in Distributed Information Networks," *ACM Transactions on Database Systems*, Volume 1, Number 1, (January 1976), pages 66-78.

[Maier 1983] D. Maier, *The Theory of Relational Databases*, Computer Science Press, Rockville, Maryland, (1983).

[Maier et al. 1981] D. Maier, D. Rozenshtein, S. Salveter, J. Stein, and D. Warren, "Semantic Problems in an Association-Object Query Language," manuscript, Department of Computer Science, State University of New York at Stony Brook, (1981).

[Makinouchi 1977] A. Makinouchi, "A Consideration on Normal Form on Not-necessarily Normalized Relations in the Relational Data Model," *Proceedings of the International Conference on Very Large Data Bases*, (1977), pages 447-453.

[Manber and Ladner 1982] U. Manber and R. Ladner, "Concurrency Control in a Dynamic Search Structure," *Proceedings of the ACM Sigact-Sigmod Symposium on the Principles of Database Systems*, (1982), pages 268-282.

[March et al. 1981] S. T. March, D. G. Severance, and M. Wilens, "Frame Memory: A Storage Architecture to Support Rapid Design and Implementation of Efficient Databases," *ACM Transactions on Database Systems*, Volume 3, Number 3, (September 1981), pages 441-463.

[Martin 1973] J. Martin, *Security, Accuracy, and Privacy in Computer Systems*, Prentice-Hall, Englewood Cliffs, New Jersey, (1973).

[Martin and Norman 1970] J. Martin and A. R. D. Norman, *The Computerized Society*, Prentice-Hall, Englewood Cliffs, New Jersey, (1970).

[McCracken 1980] D. D. McCracken, "A Guide to NOMAD for Applications Development," National CSS, Wilton, Connecticut, (1980).

[McGee 1977] W. McGee, "The Information Management System IMS/VS Part I: General Structure and Operation," *IBM Systems Journal*, Volume 16, Number 2, (June, 1977), pages 84-168.

[Menasce and Muntz 1979] D. A. Menasce and R. R. Muntz, "Locking and Deadlock Detection in Distributed Databases," *IEEE Transactions on Software Engineering*, Volume SE-5, Number 3, (May 1979), pages 195-202.

[Minsky 1968] M. Minsky (Editor), *Semantic Information Processing*, MIT Press, Cambridge, Massachusetts, (1968).

[Morgan and Levin 1977] H. L. Morgan and J. D. Levin, "Optimal Program and Data Locations in Computer Networks," *Communications of the ACM*, Volume 20, Number 5, (May 1977), pages 315-322.

[Moss 1981] J. E. B. Moss, "Nested Transactions: An Approach to Reliable Distributed Computing," Ph.D. Thesis, Department of Electrical Engineering and Computer Science, Massachusetts Institute of Technology, (April 1981).

[MRI 1974] MRI Systems Corporation, "System 2000 Reference Manual," Document UMN-1, (1974).

[MRI 1979] MRI Systems Corporation, "Language Specification Manual: The DEFINE Language," Document LSM-DEF-10, (1979).

[Mylopoulos et al. 1975] J. Mylopoulos, S. A. Schuster, and D. Tsichritzis, "A Multilevel Relational System," *Proceedings of the National Computer Conference*, (1975), pages 403-408.

[Mylopoulos et al. 1976] J. Mylopoulos, A. Borgida, P. Cohen, N. Roussopoulos, J. Tsotsos, and H. K. T. Wong, "TORUS: A Step towards Bridging the Gap between Data Bases and the Casual User," *Information Systems*, Volume 2, (1976), pages 71-77.

[Ng 1981] P. Ng, "Further Analysis of the Entity-Relationship Approach to Database Design," *IEEE Transactions of Software Engineering*, Volume SE-7, Number 1, (January 1981), pages 85-98.

[Nievergelt et al. 1984] J. Nievergelt, H. Hinterberger, and K. C. Sevcik, "The Grid File: An Adaptable Symmetric Multikey File Structure," *ACM Transactions on Database Systems*, Volume 9, Number 1, (March 1984), pages 38-71.

[Nievergelt 1974] J. Nievergelt, "Binary Search Trees and File Organization," *ACM Computing Surveys*, Volume 6, Number 3, (September 1974), pages 195-207.

[Nijssen 1976] G. M. Nijssen, (Editor), *Modeling in Data Base Management Systems*, North Holland, Amsterdam, the Netherlands, (1976).

[Obermarck 1980] R. Obermarck "IMS/VS Program Isolation Feature," Research Report RJ2879, IBM Research Laboratory, San Jose, California, (1980).

[Obermarck 1982] R. Obermarck, "Distributed Deadlock Detection Algorithm," *ACM Transactions on Database Systems*, Volume 7, Number 2, (June 1982), pages 187-208.

[Oracle 1983] Oracle Corporation, *Oracle Users' Guide,* (1983).

[Orestein 1982] J.A. Orestein, "Multidimensional Tries Used for Associative Searching," *Information Processing Letters*, Volume 14, Number 4, (June 1982), pages 150-157.

[Papadimitriou 1979] C. H. Papadimitriou, "The Serializability of Concurrent Database Updates," *Journal of the ACM*, Volume 26, Number 4, (October 1979), pages 631-653.

[Papadimitriou 1982] C. H. Papadimitriou, "A Theorem in Database Concurrency Control," *Journal of the ACM*, Volume 29, Number 5, (October 1982), pages 998-1006.

[Papadimitriou et al. 1977] C. H. Papadimitriou, P. A. Bernstein, and J. B. Rothnie, "Some Computational Problems Related to Database Concurrency Control," *Proceedings of the Conference on Theoretical Computer Science*, (1977), pages 275-282.

[Pecherer 1975] R. M. Pecherer, "Efficient Evaluation of Expressions in a Relational Algebra," *Proceedings of the ACM Pacific Conference*, (1975), pages 17-18.

[Peterson and Silberschatz 1985] J. Peterson and A. Silberschatz, *Operating System Concepts*, Second Edition, Addison Wesley, Reading, Massachusetts, (1985).

[Prague and Hammitt 1985] C. N. Prague and J. E. Hammitt, *Programming with dBase-III*, Tab Books, Blue Ridge Summit, Pennsylvania, (1985).

[Quillian 1968] M. R. Quillian, "Semantic Memory," in **[Minsky 1968]**, pages 227-270.

[Raphael 1968] B. Raphael, "SIR: Semantic Information Retrieval," in **[Minsky 1968]**, pages 33-145.

[Reed 1983] D. Reed, "Implementing Atomic Actions on Decentralized Data," *ACM Transactions on Computer Systems*, Volume 1, Number 1, (February 1983), pages 3-23.

[Reisner 1977] P. Reisner, "Use of Psychological Experimentation as an Aid to Development of a Query Language," *IEEE Transactions on Software Engineering*, Volume SE-3, Number 3, (May 1977), pages 218-229.

[Reisner et al. 1975] P. Reisner, R. F. Boyce, and D. D. Chamberlin, "Human Factors Evaluation of Two Data Base Query Languages: SQUARE and SEQUEL," *Proceedings AFIPS National Computer Conference*, (1975), pages 447-452.

[Reuter 1980] A. Reuter, "A Fast Transaction-Oriented Logging Scheme for UNDO Recovery," *IEEE Transactions on Software Engineering*, Volume SE-6, Number 4, (July 1980), pages 348-356.

[Rich 1983] E. Rich, *Artificial Intelligence*, McGraw-Hill, New York, New York, (1983).

[Ries 1979] D. R. Ries, "The Effect of Concurrency Control on the Performance of a Distributed Database Management System," *Proceedings of the Berkeley Workshop on Distributed Data Management and Computer Networks*, (1979), pages 75-112.

[Ries 1980] D. R. Ries, "Feature Analysis of Relational Concepts, Languages, and Systems for NOMAD and NOMAD2," in **[Schmidt and Brodie 1983]**, pages 257-287.

[Rissanen 1979] J. Rissanen, "Theory of Joins for Relations Databases - A Tutorial Survey," *Proceedings of the Symposium on Mathematical Foundations of Computer Science*, Springer-Verlag, Berlin, Germany, (1979), pages 537-551.

[Rivest 1976] R. L Rivest, "Partial Match Retrieval Via the Method of Superimposed Codes," *Siam Journal of Computing*, Volume 5, Number 1, (1976), pages 19-50.

[Rivest et al. 1978] R. L. Rivest A. Shamir, and L. Adelman, "On Digital Signatures and Public Key Cryptosystems," *Communications of the ACM*, Volume 21, Number 2, (February 1978), pages 120-126.

[Rosenkrantz et al. 1978] D. J. Rosenkrantz, R. E. Stearns, and P. M. Lewis II, "System Level Concurrency Control For Distributed Data Base Systems," *ACM Transactions on Database Systems*, Volume 3, Number 2, (March 1978), pages 178-198.

[Ross 1986a] S. C. Ross, *Understanding and Using dBase-III*, West Publishing, St. Paul, Minnesota, (1986).

[Ross 1986b] S. C. Ross, *Understanding and Using Lotus 1-2-3*, West Publishing, St. Paul, Minnesota, (1986).

[Roth et al. 1984] M. A. Roth, H. F. Korth, and A. Silberschatz, "Extended Algebra and Calculus for ¬1NF Relational Databases,"Technical Report TR-84-36, Department of Computer Sciences University of Texas, Austin, Texas, (1984).

[Roth et al. 1985] M. A. Roth, H. F. Korth, and A. Silberschatz, "SQL/NF: A Query Language for ¬1NF Relational Databases," Technical Report TR-85-19, Department of Computer Sciences University of Texas, Austin, Texas, (1985).

[Rothnie and Goodman 1977] J. B. Rothnie, Jr. and N. Goodman, "A Survey of Research and Development in Distributed Database Management," *Proceedings of the International Conference on Very Large Data Bases*, (1977), pages 48-62.

[Roussopoulos and Mylopoulos 1975] N. Roussopoulos and J. Mylopoulos, "Using Semantic Networks for Data Base Management," *Proceedings of the International Conference on Very Large Data Bases*, (1975), pages 144-172.

[RTI 1983] Relational Technology, "Ingres Reference Manual," Relational Technology, Inc., (1983).

[Rustin 1972] R. Rustin, (Editor), *Data Base Systems*, Prentice-Hall, Englewood Cliffs, New Jersey, (1972).

[Sakai 1980] H. Sakai, "Entity-Relationship Approach to the Conceptual Schema Design," *Proceedings of the ACM Sigmod International Conference on Management of Data*, (1980), pages 1-8.

[Schenk 1974] H. Schenk, "Implementational Aspects of the CODASYL DBTG Proposal," *Proceedings of the IFIP Working Conference on Data Base Management Systems*, (April 1974).

[Scheuermann 1982] P. Scheuermann (Editor), *Improving Database Usability and Responsiveness*, Academic Press, New York, New York, (1982).

[Scheuermann et al. 1979] P. Scheuermann, G. Schiffner, and H. Weber, "Abstraction Capabilities and Invariant Properties Modeling Within the Entity-Relationship Approach," in **[Chen 1979]**, pages 121-140.

[Schiffner and Scheuermann 1979] G. Schiffner and P. Scheuermann, "Multiple View and Abstractions with an Extended Entity-Relationship Model," *Journal of Computer Languages*, Volume 4, (1979), pages 139-154.

[Schmidt and Brodie 1983] J. W. Schmidt and M. L. Brodie, (Editors), *Relational Database Systems: Analysis and Comparison*, Springer-Verlag, Berlin, Germany, (1983).

[Schmidt et al. 1983] J. W. Schmidt, M. Mall, and W. H. Dotzek, "Feature Analysis of the PASCAL/R Relational System," in **[Schmidt and Brodie 1983]**.

[Schneider 1982] H. J. Schneider, "Distributed Data Bases," *Proceedings of the International Symposium on Distributed Databases*, (1982).

[Schneiderman 1976] B. Schneiderman, "Reduced Combined Indexes for Efficient Multiple Attribute Retrieval," *Information Systems*, Volume 2, Number 4, (1976).

[Sciore 1980] E. Sciore, "The Universal Instance and Database Design," Ph.D. thesis, Princeton University, Princeton, New Jersey, (1980).

[Sciore 1982] E. Sciore, "A Complete Axiomatization for Full Join Dependencies," *Journal of the ACM*, Volume 29, Number 2, (April 1982), pages 373-393.

[Sciore et al. 1983] E. Sciore, D. Warren, and P. Henderson, "A Relational Model of Operating System Environments," Technical Report 83/060, Department of Computer Science, State University of New York at Stony Brook, Stony Brook, New York, (1983).

[Selinger and Adiba 1980] P. G. Selinger and M. Adiba, "Access Path Selection in Distributed Database Management Systems," Research Report RJ2338, IBM Research Laboratory, San Jose, California, (1980).

[Selinger et al. 1979] P. G. Selinger, M. M. Astrahan, D. D. Chamberlin, R. A. Lorie, and T. G. Price, "Access Path Selection in a Relational Database System," *Proceedings of the ACM Sigmod International Conference on the Management of Data*, (1979), pages 23-34.

[Senko 1975] M. E. Senko, "Information Systems: Records, Relations, Set, Entities, and Things," *Information Systems*, Volume 1, (1975), pages 3-13.

[Senko 1977] M. E. Senko, "Data Structures and Data Accessing in Database Systems Past, Present and Future," *IBM Systems Journal*, Volume 16, (1977), pages 208-257.

[Shneiderman 1978] B. Shneiderman, (Editor), *Database: Improving Usability and Responsiveness*, Academic Press, New York, New York, (1978).

[Shoshani 1978] A. Shoshani, "CABLE: A Language Based on the Entity-Relationship Model," Technical Paper, Computer Science and Applied Mathematics Department, Lawrence Berkeley Laboratory, Berkeley, California, (1978).

[Silberschatz and Kedem 1980] A. Silberschatz and Z. Kedem, "Consistency in Hierarchical Database Systems," *Journal of the ACM*, Volume 27, Number 1, (January 1980), pages 72-80.

[Simmons 1979] G. J. Simmmons, "Symmetric and Asymmetric Encryption," *ACM Computing Surveys*, Volume 11, Number 4, (December 1979), pages 304-330.

[Simpson 1985] A. Simpson, *The Best Book of Lotus 1-2-3*, Howard W. Sams and Company, Indianapolis, Indiana, (1985).

[Skeen 1981] D. Skeen, "Non-blocking Commit Protocls." *Proceedings of the ACM Sigmod International Conference on the Management of Data*, (1981), pages 133-142.

[Smith and Smith 1977] J. M. Smith and D. C. P. Smith, "Database Abstractions: Aggregation and Generalization," *ACM Transactions on Database Systems*, Volume 2, Number 2, (March 1977), pages 105-133.

[Software AG 1978] "ADABAS *Introduction*," Software AG of North America, Reston, Va., (1978).

[Soisalon-Soininen and Wood 1982] E. Soisalon-Soininen and D. Wood, "An Optimal Algorithm for Testing Safety and Detecting Deadlocks," *Proceedings of the ACM Sigact-Sigmod Symposium on Principles of Database Systems*, (1982), pages 108-116.

[Spector and Schwarz 1983] A. Z. Spector and P. M. Schwarz, "Transactions: A Construct for Reliable Distributed Computing," *ACM Sigops Operating Systems Review*, Volume 17, Number 2, (April 1983), pages 18-35.

[Sperry Univac 1973] *UNIVAC 1100 series, Data Management System (DMS 1100)* publications: *Schema Definition, Data Administrator Reference, American National Standard Cobol (Fielddata), Data Manipulation Language, Programmer Reference*, Sperry Rand Corporation, (1973).

[Stonebraker 1974] M. R. Stonebraker, "A Functional View of Data Independence," *Proceedings of the ACM Sigmod Workshop on Data Description, Access and Control*, (1974) pages 63-81.

[Stonebraker 1980] M. Stonebraker, "Retrospection on a Database System," *ACM Transactions on Database Systems*, Volume 5, Number 2, (March 1980), pages 225-240. Also in **[Stonebraker 1986]**, pages 46-62.

[Stonebraker 1981] M. Stonebraker, "Operating System Support for Database Management," *Communications of the ACM*, Volume 24, Number 7, (July 1981), pages 412-418. Also in **[Stonebraker 1986]**, pages 172-182.

[Stonebraker 1986] M. Stonebraker, (Editor), *The Ingres Papers*, Addison Wesley, Reading, Massachusetts, (1986).

[Stonebraker and Wong 1974] M. Stonebraker and E. Wong, "Access Control in a Relational Database Management System by Query Modification," *Proceedings of the ACM National Conference*, (1974), pages 180-187.

[Stonebraker et al. 1976] M. Stonebraker, E. Wong, P. Kreps, and G. D. Held, "The Design and Implementation of INGRES," *ACM Transactions on Database Systems*, Volume 1, Number 3, (September 1976), pages 189-222. Also in **[Stonebraker 1986]**, pages 1-45.

[Stuart et al. 1984] D. G. Stuart, G. Buckley, and A. Silberschatz, "A Centralized Deadlock Detection Algorithm," Technical Report, Department of Computer Sciences, University of Texas, Austin, Texas, (1984).

[Sundgren 1974] B. Sundgren, "Conceptual Foundation of the Infological Approach to Data Bases," in **[Klimbie and Koffeman 1974]**, pages 61-96.

[Sundgren 1975] B. Sundgren, *Theory of Data Bases*, Mason/Charter, New York, New York, (1975).

[Tanenbaum 1981] A. S. Tanenbaum, *Computer Networks*, Prentice-Hall, Englewood Cliffs, New Jersey, (1981).

[Taylor and Frank 1976] R. W. Taylor and R. L. Frank, "CODASYL Data Base Management Systems," *ACM Computing Surveys*, Volume 8, Number 1, (March 1976), pages 67-103

[Teorey and Fry 1982] T. J. Teorey and J. P. Fry, *Design of Database Structures*, Prentice-Hall, Englewood Cliffs, New Jersey, (1982).

[Todd 1976] S. J. P. Todd, "The Peterlee Relational Test Vehicle - A System Overview," *IBM Systems Journal*, Volume 15, Number 4, (1976), pages 285-308.

[Traiger et al. 1982] I. L. Traiger, J. N. Gray, C. A. Galtieri, and B. G. Lindsay, "Transactions and Consistency in Distributed Database Management Systems," *ACM Transactions on Database Systems*, Volume 7, Number 3, (September 1982), pages 323-342.

[Tremblay and Sorenson 1985] J.-P. Tremblay and P. G. Sorenson, *The Theory and Practice of Compiler Writing*, McGraw-Hill, New York, New York, (1985).

[Trivedi et al. 1980] K. S. Trivedi, R. A. Wagner, and T. M. Sigmon, "Optimal Selection of CPU Speed, Device Capacities and File Assignment," *Journal of the ACM*, Volume 7, Number 3, (July 1980), pages 457-473.

[Tsichritzis and Klug 1978] D. Tsichritzis and A. Klug, (Editors), *The ANSI/X3/SPARC Framework*, AFIPS Press, Montvale, New Jersey, (1978).

[Tsichritzis and Lochovsky 1976] D. C. Tsichritzis and F. H. Lochovsky, "Hierarchical Data-base Management: A Survey," *ACM Computing Surveys*, Volume 8, Number 1, (March 1976), pages 67-103.

[Tsichritzis and Lochovsky 1977] D. C. Tsichritzis and F. H. Lochovsky, *Data Base Management Systems*, Academic Press, New York, New York, (1977).

[Tsichritzis and Lochovsky 1982] D. C. Tsichritzis, F. H. Lochovsky, *Data Models*, Prentice-Hall, Englewood Cliffs, New Jersey, (1982).

[US Dept of Commerce 1977] United States Department of Commerce, *Data Encryption Standard*, National Bureau of Standards Federal Information Processing Standards Publication 46 (January 1977).

[Uhrowczik 1973] P. P. Uhrowczik, "Data Dictionary/Directories," *IBM System Journal*, Volume 12, Number 4, (December 1973), pages 332-350.

[Ullman 1982a] J. D. Ullman, *Principles of Database Systems*, Second edition, Computer Science Press, Rockville, Maryland, (1982).

[Ullman 1982b] J. D. Ullman, "The U. R. Strikes Back," *Proceedings of the Sigact-Sigmod ACM Symposium on Principles of Database Systems*, (1982), pages 10-22.

[Vassiliou et al. 1985] Y. Vassiliou, J. Clifford, and M. Jarke, "Database Access Requirements of Knowledge-Based Systems," in **[Kim et al. 1985b]**, pages 156-170.

[Verhofstad 1978] J. S. M. Verhofstad, "Recovery Techniques for Database Systems," *ACM Computing Surveys*, Volume 10, Number 2, (June 1978), pages 167-195.

[Vorhaus and Mills 1967] A. Vorhaus and R. Mills, *The Time-"Shared Data Management System: A New Approach to Data Management*, Technical Memo. SP-2634, System Development Corporation, Santa Monica, California.

[Wang 1984] S. Wang, "Normal Entity-Relationship Model--A New Method to Design Enterprise Schema," *Proceedings of the IEEE International Conference on Computers and Applications*, (1984).

[Wiederhold 1983] G. Wiederhold, *Database Design*, Second edition, McGraw-Hill, New York New York, (1983).

[Wiederhold et al. 1983a] G. Wiederhold, J. Milton, and D. Sagalowicz, "Applications of Artificial Intelligence in the Knowledge Based Management Systems Project," *IEEE Database Engineering Bulletin*, Volume 6, Number 4, (December 1983), pages 75-82.

[Wiederhold et al. 1983b] G. Wiederhold, J. Milton, and D. Sagalowicz, "Artificial Intelligence in the Knowledge-Based Management Systems Project," *ACM-Sigart Newsletter*, (October 1983), pages 59-63.

[Williams et al. 1982] R. Williams, D. Daniels, L. Haas, G. Lapis, B. Lindsay, P. Ng, R. Obermarck, P. Selinger, A. Walker, P. Wilms, and R. Yost, "R*: An Overview of the Architecture," in **[Scheuermann 1982]**, pages 1-27.

[Wilms et al. 1983] P. F. Wilms, B. G. Lindsay, and P. Selinger, "I Wish I Were Over There: Distributed Execution Protocols for Data Definition in R*," *Proceedings of the ACM Sigmod International Conference on the Management of Data*, (1983), pages 238-242.

[Wong 1977] E. Wong, "Retrieving Dispersed Data from SDD-1: A System for Distributed Databases," *Proceedings of the Berkeley Workshop on Distributed Data Management and Computer Networks*, (1977), pages 217-235.

[Wong and Mylopoulos 1977] H. K. T. Wong and J. Mylopoulos, "Two Views of Data Semantics: A Survey of Data Models in Artificial Intelligence and Database Management," *INFOR*, Volume 15, (1977), pages 344-383.

[Wong and Youssefi 1976] E. Wong and K. Youssefi, "Decomposition-A Strategy for Query Processing," *ACM Transactions on Database Systems*, Volume 1, Number 3, (September 1976), pages 223-241.

[Woods 1975] W. A. Woods, "What's in a Link? Foundations for Semantic Networks," in **[Bobrow and Collins 1975]**, pages 35-82.

[Yannakakis 1981] M. Yannakakis, "Issues of Correctness in Database Concurrency Control by Locking," *Proceedings of the ACM Symposium on the Theory of Computing*, (1981), pages 363-367.

[Yannakakis et al. 1979] M. Yannakakis, C. H. Papadimitriou, and H. T. Kung, "Locking Protocols: Safety and Freedom from Deadlock," *Proceedings of the IEEE Symposium on the Foundations of Computer Science*, (1979), pages 286-297.

[Yao 1979] A. C. Yao, "A Note on a Conjecture of Kam and Ullman Concerning Statistical databases," *Information Processing Letters*, (1979).

[Zaniolo 1979a] C. Zaniolo, "Design of Relational Views over Network Schemas," *Proceedings of the ACM Sigmod International Conference on the Management of Data*, (1979), pages 179-190.

[Zaniolo 1979b] C. Zaniolo, "Multimodel External Schemas for CODASYL Data Base Management Systems," in **[Bracchi and Nijssen 1979]**, pages 157-176.

[Zaniolo 1983] C. Zaniolo, "The Database Language GEM," *Proceedings of the ACM Sigmod International Conference on the Management of Data*, (1983), pages 207-218.

[Zhang and Mendelzon 1983] Z. Q. Zhang and A. O. Mendelzon, "A Graphical Query Language for Entity-Relationship Databases," in **[Davis et al. 1983]**, pages 441-448.

[Zloof 1977] M. M. Zloof, "Query-by-Example: A Data Base Language," *IBM Systems Journal*, Volume 16, Number 4, (1977), pages 324-343.

[Zloof 1978] M. M. Zloof, "Security and Integrity Within the Query-by-Example Data Base Management Language," IBM Research Report RC6982, IBM T. J. Watson Research Center, Yorktown Heights, New York, (1978).

[Zook et al. 1977] W. Zook, K. Youssefi, N. Whyte, P. Rubinstein, P. Kreps, G. Held, J. Ford, R. Berman, and E. Allman, *INGRES Reference Manual*, Department of EECS, University of California, Berkeley, (1977).

Index